Self-Determination

Other Titles in This Series

Westview Special Studies in National and International Terrorism

Self-Determination:
National, Regional, and Global Dimensions
edited by
Yonah Alexander and Robert A. Friedlander

As part of a national and international revolutionary strategy, terrorism has introduced into the struggle for power within and among nations a new mode of violence in terms of technology, victimization, threat, and response. It has also affected our present concepts and perceptions of self-determination. One of the principal questions addressed in this volume is whether self-determination is a necessary precondition for peace, stability, and friendly domestic and international relations based on respect for human rights and fundamental freedoms. The authors also consider the future shape of the political map and focus on the dominant trends and realities of the issue of self-determination, with a view toward identifying consequences for contemporary society and offering explicit recommendations.

Yonah Alexander is professor of international studies and director of the Institute for Studies in International Terrorism at the State University of New York and a research associate at the Center for Strategic and International Studies, Georgetown University.

Robert A. Friedlander is professor of law at the Ohio Northern University College of Law.

Self-Determination: National, Regional, and Global Dimensions

edited by Yonah Alexander
and Robert A. Friedlander

Westview Press / Boulder, Colorado

Westview Special Studies in National and International Terrorism

Copyright© 1980 by Westview Press, Inc.

Published in 1980 in the United States of America by
   Westview Press, Inc.
   5500 Central Avenue
   Boulder, Colorado 80301
   Frederick A. Praeger, Publisher

Library of Congress Catalog Card Number: 80-65075
ISBN: 0-89158-090-5

Printed and bound in the United States of America

To our parents

Contents

Foreword

One of the major concepts in political theory and jurisprudence is self-determination. It advocates the idea that a homogeneous people has the "right" to determine its own destiny as a distinct sovereign nation or the "right" to maintain its own national traditions within a larger political entity. Yet, ever since the establishment of China in 1523 B.C. as the first recorded nation in history, the meaning of the basic concept has been highly controversial. Its validity as an absolute and legitimate "right" to be exercised in the political process within and among nations has been frequently challenged. In the twentieth century, self-determination became a dynamic issue as a consequence of its adoption as the moral foundation of peace by the League of Nations. Contrary to Wilsonian idealism, the reshaping of the map of Europe neither prevented World War II nor saved democracy.

Nevertheless, since the establishment of the United Nations, the principle of self-determination has been espoused with greater vigor. In the past thirty years, the world has seen numerous sovereignty changes: dependent areas that have received their independence; dependent areas that have been incorporated into independent entities; territorial transfers from one country to another; creation of new or changed political entities as a result of dissolution of sovereign governments. Ironically, many of these changes implemented in the name of self-determination have contributed to terrorism, guerrilla warfare, and transnational conflicts.

The question whether this doctrine is a force for stability or international chaos is extremely significant for the balance-of-power assessment in the years ahead. The unique value of this volume is that it analyzes the problem from national, regional, and global perspectives and thereby contributes to a better understanding of the complex issues involved.

Ray S. Cline

Introduction

On October 13, 1975, at the World Peace Through Law Conference held in Washington, D.C., the president of the International Court of Justice proudly referred to the court's reaffirmation of the principle of self-determination as its greatest jurisprudential accomplishment. Self-determination has been a basic doctrine of the United Nations since the very beginnings of that international organization. Definitions vary somewhat, but self-determination is often considered to be the "right" of a "people" to shape their own political, economic, and cultural destinies.

Professor Michla Pomerance terms self-determination "a general prescription for doing justice." Professor Louis Sohn has called it "an idea that revolutionized the world." Yet critics of the self-determination concept declare that it is first and foremost a political weapon, inequitable in its application and unreasonable in its result. Confusion over the nature of the process, and misapplication of its meaning, have distorted self-determination in practice and weakened its potential resolutory role as a legal remedy. There are those who have argued that, through combined misunderstanding and misdirection, the self-determinative principle has been less conflict-resolving than it has been conflict-promoting.

Recent events in Southeast Asia, Southwest Africa, and the Middle East have once again inspired third-party appeals to implement an asserted right of self-determination in these politically volatile areas. Rebellion, civil war, and transnational conflict have been the traditional means by which dissident minorities have sought to end the dominion and control of dominant majorities. The legal-political process has frequently given way to the cult of force, but the claim of right by the repressed minority almost always has been the same—self-determination of peoples.

In December 1978, Dominica, the latest Caribbean island nation to gain its independence from Great Britain, became the 151st member state of the United Nations. Yet, the universality of the world organization is far from complete. Trusteeship territories as well as dependent peoples are continuously claiming the "inalienable right of self-determination" based upon the UN Charter, the two International Covenants on Human Rights, the Declaration on the Granting of Independence to Colonial Countries and Peoples, the twenty-fifth anniversary Declaration on Principles of International Law Concerning Friendly Relations and Cooperation, and countless other General Assembly and Security Council resolutions and declarations.

Much of the civil strife throughout the globe at present is due to so-called national-liberation movements of various sizes and influence seeking to establish independent homelands by means of armed force. No hemisphere and no continent is totally immune. Self-determination has also been used as a rationale for terrorist acts and, by so doing, undermines the very concept of a world public order.

If it is truly to become an international legal right, then self-determination must be exercised within a viable international legal system. The fundamental issue is how to provide a means of legitimizing the revolutionary process within the context of national aspirations and international law. Contemporary international law continues to be a set of practices, but it is only through the exercise of principles that an international operative justice can come into being. Justice in the world arena has many faces, and the rule of law is open to many interpretations.

The purpose of this book is to shed new light on the meaning, process, and effects of the self-determination concept. In this volume, the contributors address three questions. First, is self-determination truly a necessary precondition to international peace and stability? Second, is self-determination a basic international human right and part of the guaranteed fundamental freedoms proclaimed by the world community? And third, what will the effect of self-determination be upon the remaining decades of the twentieth century? Thus, the focus is upon the dominant trends and socio-political realities of the aforementioned issues, emphasizing national, regional, and global perspectives. Another task to which the authors devote themselves is the identification of specific warning signals for contemporary global society. Numerous remedies are also proposed for the uncertain future.

The editors thank the following academic institutions for their cooperation in the preparation of this book: The Institute for Studies of International Terrorism (State University of New York), the Ralph Bunche Institute on the United Nations (City University of New York), the Center for Strategic and International Studies (Georgetown University), and the Ohio Northern University College of Law. These institutions, however, bear no responsibility for the views expressed by the authors.

Yonah Alexander
Robert A. Friedlander

Part 1

The Concept of
Self-Determination

1
Self-Determination:
A Definitional Focus

Jordan J. Paust

"Self-determination" is not a mere phrase. It is an imperative principle of action, which statesmen will henceforth ignore at their peril.

—Woodrow Wilson*

The United Nations Charter states that one of the purposes of the United Nations is to develop friendly relations based upon respect for the principle of equal rights and self-determination of peoples.[1] It is also stated in the Charter that the United Nations shall promote universal respect for and observance of human rights and fundamental freedoms for all so as to assure "the creation of conditions of stability and well-being which are necessary for peaceful and friendly relations among nations based on respect for the principle of equal rights and self-determination."[2]

Obviously these rights and principles are interrelated in the Charter language—equal rights, self-determination, human rights, fundamental freedoms—but how? Indeed, how are preferred conditions of well-being, stability, friendly relations, and peace to be interconnected with United Nations and member-state obligations "to take joint and separate action" in order to achieve, for example, a functionally effective respect for and observance of human rights and fundamental freedoms[3] in a context of "stable" governmental control of a people and serious deprivations of human rights? Is self-determination a human right, a fundamental freedom? Is self-determination a necessary precondition to a workable peace, stability, and friendly relations? Just what is "self-determination,"

3

and are these other rights, principles, and conditions relevant to a proper definitional focus? These are merely some of the questions that necessarily arise in this section, but, as the reader will discover, they are questions that are answered elsewhere in various ways and questions that haunt us at every turn within our own study. The problem is not that these questions are unanswerable but that so many "answers" are possible[4] and that nearly all of the possibilities exist in the printed writings of scholars or rhetorical orchestrations of governmental, intergovernmental, and nongovernmental actors.

Whatever one's definition or claim may be, one must pay attention to the recent politico-legal expressions of the United Nations General Assembly during its attempt to provide greater content to Charter norms. More than a "mere phrase" or "principle of action," the General Assembly had declared unanimously in 1970 that self-determination is a right with correlative duties. As the 1970 Declaration on Principles of International Law concerning Friendly Relations and Co-Operation stated: "all people have the *right* freely to determine, without external interference, their political status and to pursue their political status and to pursue their economic, social and cultural development, and every State has the *duty* to respect this right in accordance with the provisions of the Charter."[5] Moreover, the General Assembly implicitly recognized the interdependence between self-determination, human rights, friendly relations, and peace. For example, the preamble to the Declaration stated that the "effective application" of the principle of equal rights and self-determinaton "is of paramount importance for the promotion of friendly relations among states." The same preamble noted the importance of implementing a peace "founded upon freedom, equality, justice and respect for fundamental human rights" and stated further that "subjection of peoples to alien subjugation, domination and exploitation constitutes a major obstacle to the promotion of international peace and security."

Additionally, one should pay significant attention to the definitional elements highlighted by the General Assembly in its important declaration on Charter principles. Within the right-duty passage quoted above, one can also glean evidence of the significant expectation of the international community that a process of self-determination relates most closely to a free or consensual determination of a given peoples of their own political, economic, social, and cultural development. The declaration seems to emphasize this expectation about authority and self-determination by stating clearly in the first paragraph devoted to the principle of equal rights and self-determination that "by virtue of the principle of equal rights and self-determination . . . all peoples have the right freely to determine."

The expectation of the need for a free or consensual determination is also evident in a subsequent paragraph which provides even more insight into definitional elements. As if to illustrate the process of self-determination and to offer a partial definition through the use of relevant examples, the General Assembly declared that "the establishment of a sovereign and independent State, the free association or integration with an independent State or the emergence into any other political status freely determined by a people constitute modes of implementing the right of self-determination by that people." What is most relevant is the free determination of the political status, not the particular form of that status. Thus, self-determination may result in the formation of a new state, a new bloc of states, or "any other political status" and, thus, implicitly the change of state, regional, and substate territorial boundaries.[6]

It seems incorrect, therefore, to define self-determination as the right of a *state* to maintain its present political status and, thus, its territorial integrity.[7] Nowhere in the Charter or in subsequent United Nations declarations is self-determination posed as the right of states. It has always been considered in connection with a "peoples," who may compose part of the population within a given state or even part or all of the populations of several states.[8] The obvious and critical question does not relate to state territorial boundaries per se; the critical question is: who are the "peoples" that are entitled to self-determination?[9] What is the aggregated "self" among the relatively interdependent and independent groups of people that populate our planet to which this label of right and politico-legal description should properly attach? For example, might Jews of various states, consisting of a minority or majority in various states including Israel, constitute a "peoples"? Might Palestinians who constitute a minority in various states constitute a "peoples"?

Such questions are far different from questions posed with a status quo and territorial referent such as: is the state of Israel entitled to self-determination, is any given Arab state entitled to self-determination, or are the Arab states entitled to self-determination? Further, since the General Assembly did not tie the right of self-determination merely to political status but included the right to freely determine economic, social, and cultural rights, one can begin to imagine all sorts of possible applications of such a right beyond the confines of political institutions and status. For example, might not a given people, say American Indians of the Navajo nation or Soviet Jews, be entitled to pursue their own social and cultural determination whether or not they have a separate political or territorial-based status? The author believes that such a claim would be entirely consistent with the General Assembly declaration as well as with several important human rights.[10] Moreover, the relatively free determination of Indian or Jewish social and cultural processes within the United States, for example, would pose no inconsistency. Within the United States, Indian and Jewish peoples might pursue their own social and cultural norms, mores, and so forth while also freely participating in another process of self-determination as citizens and participants in the political, economic, social, and cultural processes intermeshed under the label United States of America.[11]

These last recognitions also compel awareness of the fact that no social or political process in the present global arena is completely free and "self"-determined.[12] The interpenetrations, the global webs of economic, political, and ideological penetrations and interdeterminations, cause one to realize that a functional "self-determination" is a relative "self-determination." And the reverse is true, interdependence is a dynamic and relative interstimulation and interdetermination. Within such a global process then, one might expect the recognition of various sorts of "self-determination" processes as being compatible with, even promotive of, the basic goals of the United Nations Charter, human rights, and other aspects of international law. Indeed, to paraphrase President Wilson, these are socio-politico facts that scholars will henceforth ignore at their peril. For example, it is ludicrous now to argue that adherence to the principle of self-determination allows a given political elite to do whatever it wishes to its fellow citizens (e.g., by depriving individuals of their human right to freedom from torture or other inhumane, cruel, or degrading treatment).[13]

Expanding upon the last point, it is also ludicrous to argue that adherence to the principle of self-determination allows the same sort of political elite to dominate the people of a given state by violence and other human right deprivations and to exclude all other states from rendering any sort of military or economic assistance to the peoples within the state (whether or not they constitute a majority or minority) or to insist upon a maintenance of present state territorial boundaries as the legally recognized curtain behind which such an oppression can continue. Indeed, the legitimacy of self-determination assistance is recognized in the General Assembly Declaration on Principles of International Law, as demonstrable in the case of Bangladesh.[14] Further, as some are apt to forget, the prohibition of territorial dismemberment or impairment is qualified in the General Assembly declaration. It does not recognize a right of present states to a territorial status quo, to territorial integrity *uber alles;*[15] the prohibition applies *only* where the relevant state itself complies with the principle of equal rights and self-determination and is "thus possessed of a government representing the whole people belonging to the territory without distinction as to race, creed or colour."

This last quote from the General Assembly declaration contains a key definitional element. A state that complies with the principle of equal rights and self-determination is one possessed of a government representing each and every person—the whole people—belonging to its territory and a government that represents each and every person "without distinction as to race, creed or colour." No other state complies; no other political elite maintains its control in accordance with the "right" to self-determination. Indeed, without a free and full participation of a given peoples in the governmental process, it would be incorrect to state that such a people enjoy "the right freely to determine . . . their political status" and it would surely be incorrect to state that the political elite govern in accordance with "the freely expressed will of the peoples concerned."[16] Such a recognition is even more explicit in subsequent General Assembly resolutions—resolutions that not only condemn "the illegal racist minority regime" in Rhodesia but set forth certain "conditions [deemed] necessary to enable the people of

Zimbabwe to exercise freely and fully their right to self-determination."[17]

For example, in 1971 the Assembly stressed the need for majority rule "on the basis of one man one vote,"[18] and in 1974 the Assembly stressed the need for "attainment of independence by a democratic system of government" and the requirement that any form of independence "be endorsed freely and fully by the people."[19] One person one vote, a democratic system of government, and a free and full endorsement by the people—these add up to something far different from the dictatorship of rightists or leftists who feign to represent the will of the people. Nothing less than a free and full participation (or the opportunity for participation) by each person would satisfy such a test. As the 1974 Resolution adds, at least one condition "necessary to enable the people . . . to exercise freely and fully their right to self-determination" involves "removal of all restrictions on political activity and the establishment of full democratic freedom and equality of political rights."[20]

Having recognized this key definitional element, the need for a free or consensual and full participation in the political process, one can see the legal relevance of human rights law to questions of self-determination, and I, for one, affirm that whether or not self-determination is a human right the principle of equal rights and self-determination is legally interrelated with human rights and the overall question of authority.[21] To demonstrate the point further, compare the expectations of a need for a free determination of political status, a government representing the whole people, and a "freely expressed will" of the people with the standard of authority and the concomitant rights of the individual and the people recognized in the 1948 Universal Declaration of Human Rights. In my opinion, Article 21 of the Universal Declaration is a necessary referent for a definitional focus. It declares, in a dispositive fashion:

1. Everyone has the right to take part in the government of his country, directly or through freely chosen representatives.
2. Everyone has the right of equal access to public service in his country.
3. The will of the people shall be the basis of the authority of government; this will shall be expressed in periodic and genuine elections which shall be by universal and equal suffrage

and shall be held by secret vote or by equivalent free voting procedures.

I know of no clearer community definition of authority or of, at least, political self-determination. The right of everyone to participate in the government of one's country, the right of equal access to public service, and the right of universal and equal suffrage are human rights that further define community expectations which are highly relevant to definitions or recognitions of self-determination processes. Where a given process of self-determination results in the creation or continuation of a state government, the test of its authority is clear; the only basis of authority, indeed *the* authority, of a government is the freely expressed "will of the people."[22]

Some time in the future, hopefully not too distant, the common folk of humankind will discover and demand those measures of authority declared in their name. Hardly a government, hardly an ideology—whether democratic, socialist, communist, or some combination thereof—exists now that does not feign to represent the authority of its people—to follow "the will of the people." As scholars and participants, we should not defile the myth of universal law by recognizing any political process other than one based upon the will of the people and a free and full participation of each individual as a legitimate process of political self-determination.

We should not confuse elitist control by totalitarians of the right or left with authority. As Thomas Paine expressed so long ago, the "authority of the people" is "the only authority on which government has a right to exist in any country."[23] The same should apply to "liberation" movements,[24] "anti-colonialist" struggles, declarations of martial law, and so forth. For this reason, we should note that a government or a revolution by terrorism is contrary to the principle of self-determination and the human right of each member of a given community to a free and full participation in the political process, a sharing of power.[25] For similar reasons, the international community refused to recognize the claim of the Smith regime in Rhodesia to "self-determination,"[26] and hardly anyone pretends that blacks in South Africa enjoy self-determination.

During the American "anti-colonialist" struggle in the eighteenth century, these standards were not fully applied,[27] but the American Revolution produced some notable expectations about authority that might well have conditioned subsequent generations of people and even the present meaning of "self-determination."[28] The American Declaration of Independence, for instance, expressly declared that governments are properly constituted in order "to secure" the inalienable rights of man, that governments derive "their just powers from the consent of the governed," and that "it is the right of the people to alter or abolish" any form of government which "becomes destructive of these ends." Nearly one hundred years later, President Lincoln upheld the same fundamental expectations even in the face of civil war: "This country with its institutions, belongs to the people who inhabit it. Whenever they shall grow weary of the existing government, they can exercise their constitutional right of amending, or their revolutionary right to dismember or overthrow it."[29]

Thomas Paine had earlier expressed the current expectation about proper reformation of the U.S. federal government. He declared that "the right of reform is in the nation in its original character, and the constitutional method would be by a general convention elected for the purpose. There is moreover paradox in the idea of vitiated bodies reforming themselves."[30] No man or group of elites was to be above the law. Public interests were to be the measure of public decisions, and authority (just power) was to be derived from and ultimately retained by the people.[31] As Alexander Hamilton expressed so well: "The people surrender nothing."[32] This not only meant that delegated, or representative, authority was subject to the ultimate authority of the people, but that delegated authority was subject to retained "rights," including evolving expectations of rights involving all social interactions, and to a retained "power"—i.e., a competence to act, or an authority of the people to restrict, alter, or abolish governmental institutions.[33]

The authority of "the people"—that's an important referent to remember. Just as the holder of some political office or some other individual or group of elites is not the equivalent of "the people," so it is that the majority of any given population is not the equivalent of "the people." As demonstrated above, a proper definition of political self-determination must reflect the need for a freely expressed will of the people, the "whole people." Further, a proper definition must reflect the right of each member of the society to a free and full participation in the political process. Thus, it is fundamental that "self-determination" does not refer merely to a goal value of majority rule within a group of persons, but rather to a full participation in the political process by all individuals and subgroups in the widest sharing of power and enlightenment.[34] In the context of changing patterns of political association, however, complex questions will emerge concerning identification of the relevant "peoples," prior majorities and minorities, and "residual individuals."[35] As Suzuki warns:

> The complexity of the factors involved . . . makes it impossible to recommend rules which would automatically determine the applicability of the right of self-determination. Nevertheless, the preceding analysis of claims clarifies the general normative standards required for the formulation of more specific policy.[36]

Thus, choice is inevitable, as well as contextual change and complexity.[37]

As a useful approach to such questions and to the relevant factors of context, however, I recommend a thorough reading of the two most brilliant studies of self-determination known to date. These are the lengthy studies prepared by Eisuke Suzuki[38] and Lung-chu Chen.[39] In addition to the import of these studies for analytic, scholarly, and decisional tasks, one can also benefit from attention to the insights of these authors into what one might term definitional foci. It is rather unfair both to the authors and the readers to extract definitional foci out of such important contributions to legal scholarship, but, with the caveat "read their works in full," I proceed to incorporate their insights as best I can into the present study.

Suzuki's published work addresses one type of self-determination process, territorial separation from an extant body politic. Addressing this particular form, he states: " 'Self-determination' is a symbolic manifestation of a group's demand for repudiation of an extant public order system to create a new pattern of value effects which it perceives as desirable."[40] Additionally, he notes that this form of self-determination

> can be defined most comprehensively as community response to a process of consociation, or group formation. Since a process of consociation is commenced by individuals who seek common ends, the preference and choice of individuals to participate jointly in the value pro-

cesses constitute the fundamental basis of association in a given community. The size and domain of the group may vary depending on the range and scope of value demands which individuals pursue. [41]

Adding to the recognitions above that self-determination involves the free and full participation of every member of a given society, Suzuki writes:

> It is fundamental to self-determination that the power demanded by a group must be equally shared; hence elites which demand power must be supported by the claimant group as a whole. Neither the puppet State of Manchuria nor the clientele State of Katanga represented the interest of a significant segment of the population concerned. [42]

Suzuki also adds that the right of self-determination is "increasingly gaining recognition as a fundamental human right, particularly as 'a collective right, appertaining to all people and all nations.' "[43] Chen is even more explicit on this point: the title of his work is "Self-Determination as a Human Right."[44] Chen adds:

> The essence of self-determination is human dignity and human rights. Underlying the concept of human dignity is the insistent demand of the individual to form groups and to identify with groups that can best promote and maximize his pursuit of values both in individual and aggregate terms. The formation and reformation of groups are ongoing processes. [45]

"It is the freedom of participation in different value processes [e.g., power, wealth, well-being, respect, enlightenment] which is fundamentally at stake,"[46] Chen writes; and in consideration of political self-determination the "sharing of power is of paramount importance,"[47] as any dictionary definition would seem to bear out.[48]

A final point deserves attention. Self-determination, broadly understood, does not relate merely to participation in the political process or to the shaping and sharing of power. As references above demonstrate, self-determination relates more broadly to participation in all value processes. McDougal and Lasswell provide the broadened focus in their summarized reference to eight values (i.e., power, well-being, enlightenment, respect, and so forth). "It is for values such as these," McDougal writes, "that men have always framed constitutions, established governments, and sought that delicate balancing of power and formulation and fundamental principle necessary to preserve human rights against all possible aggressors."[49] That is man's long struggle

> for participation in the processes by which he is governed, equality before the law, and that wide sharing of power, both formal and real, which we call democracy;
> for sanctity of person, for freedom from arbitrary restraints and cruel and inhuman punishments, and for positive opportunity to develop latent talents for the enrichment and well-being of personality;
> for the enlightenment by which rational decisions can be made and for freedom of inquiry and opinion;
> for that fundamental respect for human dignity which both precludes discrimination based on race, sex, color, religion, political opinion, or other ground irrelevant to capacity and provides positive recognition of common merit as a human being and special merit as an individual;
> for access to resources to produce goods and services necessary to maintain rising standards of living and comfort;
> for acquisition of the skills necessary to express talent and to achieve individual and community values to the fullest;
> for freedom to explain life, the universe, and values, to fix standards of rectitude, and to worship God or gods as may seem best;
> for affection, fraternity, and congenial personal relationships in groups freely chosen;
> for, in sum, a security which includes not only freedom from violence but also full opportunity to preserve and increase all values by peaceful, noncoercive procedures.[50]

To summarize, the right of self-determination, most broadly understood, is the right of all peoples to participate freely and fully in the sharing of all values (e.g., power, well-being, enlightenment, respect, wealth, skill, rectitude, and affection). The right to political self-determination involves this broader focus but may be summarized as the collective right of a peoples to pursue their own political demands, to share power equally, and as the correlative right of the individual to participate freely and fully in the political process. Whether or not collective and individual self-determination are viewed as human rights as such, there is no question that self-determination and human dignity are intricately interconnected with human rights as well as the only legitimate measure of authority—the "will of the people."

Notes

*President Woodrow Wilson, Feb. 11, 1918; cited in Eisuke Suzuki, "Self-Determination and World Public Order: Community Response to Territorial Separation," *Virginia Journal of International Law* 16, no. 4 (1976):781. For a historical account of Wilson's use of the phrase, see Robert A. Friedlander, "Self-Determination: A Legal-Political Inquiry," *Detroit College of Law Review* 1, no. 1 (1975):71-72 (also reprinted as Chapter 13 in this volume).

1. UN Charter, Art. 1(2).
2. UN Charter, Art. 55.
3. See UN Charter, Arts. 55(c) and 56.
4. See also Rupert Emerson, "Self-Determination," *American Journal of International Law* 65, no. 3 (1971):459.
5. United Nations, General Assembly, Resolution 2625, Suppl. 28 (A/8028), emphasis added. Other relevant "duties" follow this language within the resolution. Similar language also appears in treaty law, e.g., the 1966 Covenant on Civil and Political Rights, Art. 1, ——— U.N.T.S. ———, Res. 220A, Supp. 16 (A/6316). The right to self-determination is also recognized in international cases; see, e.g., Advisory Opinion on Western Sahara [1975] I.C.J. 12, 31-33 (paragraphs 55, 58-59), 36; Legal Consequences for States of the Continued Presence of South Africa in Namibia (South-West Africa) notwithstanding Security Council Resolution 276 [1970] I.C.J. 16, 127; and a separate opinion, J. Ammoun, Barcelona Traction Case [1970] I.C.J. 302-30. For evidence of earlier contrasting views about "right," however, see authorities cited in Lung-chu Chen, "Self-Determination as a Human Right," in *Toward World Order and Human Dignity*, ed. M. Reisman and B. Weston (New York: Free Press, 1976), pp. 224-25. For the history of changed attitudes at the UN, see Robert Rosenstock, "The Declaration of Principles of International Law concerning Friendly Relations: A Survey," *American Journal of International Law* 65, no. 5 (1971):731. See also Friedlander, "Self-Determination," pp. 73-75 and authorities cited on p. 88; M. Cherif Bassiouni, "Self-Determination and the Palestinians," *American Journal of International Law* 65, no. 4 (1971):31-33; Yoram Dinstein, "Terrorism and Wars of Liberation Applied to the Arab-Israeli Conflict: An Israeli Perspective," *Israel Yearbook on Human Rights* 3 (1973):79.
6. See also Suzuki, "Self-Determination and World Public Order."
7. See also ibid., pp. 840-48, noting that *uti possidetis* is antithetical to self-determination; Rosenstock, "Declaration of Principles," p. 732; Dinstein, "Terrorism and Wars of Liberation," pp. 79-80. For contrary and ultimately unrealistic views, see Emerson, "Self-Determination," pp. 462-64; Leslie C. Green, "Self-Determination and Settlement of the Arab-Israeli Con-

flict," *American Journal of International Law* 65, no. 4 (1971):48. For evidence of similarly contrary views, see references cited in Ved P. Nanda, "Self-Determination in International Law: The Tragic Tale of Two Cities—Islamabad (West Pakistan) and Dacca (East Pakistan)," *American Journal of International Law* 66, no. 2 (1972):326-27. (Professor Nanda, however, argued for application of the principle of self-determination "above" that of territorial integrity in the context of the emergence of Bangladesh); and Bassiouni, "Self-Determination and the Palestinians," pp. 34, 36, 38.

8. See, for example, the discussion of the difference between "nation" and "state" in J. L. Brierly, *The Law and Nations*, 5th ed. (Oxford: Clarendon Press, 1955), pp. 118-20. See also Dinstein, "Terrorism and Wars of Liberation," p. 80; and Advisory Opinion on Western Sahara, p. 31 (par. 55).

9. See, e.g., Chen, "Self-Determination as a Human Right," pp. 225-26; Dinstein, "Terrorism and Wars of Liberation," pp. 79-80; Bassiouni, "Self-Determination and the Palestinians," pp. 31-32.

10. For relevant human rights, see, e.g., United Nations, General Assembly, Universal Declaration of Human Rights, Arts. 1-2, 7-8, 18-20, and 22. In direct support of the author's opinion is Dinstein, "Terrorism and Wars of Liberation," p. 80, citing Yoram Dinstein, "The International Human Rights of Soviet Jewry," *Israel Yearbook on Human Rights* 2 (1972). See also Friedlander, "Self-Determination," p. 83. The problem of implementing the right of Palestinians, without a present territorial base, to self-determination poses a similar concern; but see Bassiouni, "Self-Determination and the Palestinians," pp. 38-39 (wrongly suggesting, in my opinion, that self-determination can only be implemented by a control of territory). Professor Bassiouni, however, is implicitly open to some sort of "pluralistic society" solution or shared territorial and political control (see ibid., pp. 39, 63-64, 66-67). Thus, I do not believe that his stated need for people and *territory* is as inflexible as it might appear or suggests self-determination only for states.

11. See also Suzuki, "Self-Determination and World Public Order," pp. 859-60.

12. See also Jordan J. Paust and Albert P. Blaustein, *The Arab Oil Weapon* (Dobbs Ferry, N.Y.: Oceana-Sijthoff, 1977), pp. 141-45; and Suzuki, "Self-Determination and World Public Order," pp. 832-35 and references cited.

13. See also Chen, "Self-Determination as a Human Right"; address by President Carter before the United Nations, extract in *American Journal of International Law* 71, no. 3 (1977):515-17.

14. See also Jordan J. Paust and Albert P. Blaustein, *War Crimes Jurisdiction and Due Process: A Case Study of Bangladesh* (1974), pp. 10-11 no. 25, reprinted in part as "War Crimes Jurisdiction and Due Process: The Bangladesh Experience," *Vanderbilt Journal of Transnational Law* 11, no. 1 (1978):1; cf. Rosenstock, "Declaration of Principles," p. 732. On the right of

self-determination during the emergence of Bangladesh, see also Nanda, "Self-Determination in International Law"; Chen, "Self-Determination as a Human Right"; Suzuki, "Self-Determination and World Public Order"; and Dinstein, "Terrorism and Wars of Liberation," p. 80; Jean-Pierre L. Fonteyne, "The Customary International Law Doctrine of Humanitarian Intervention: Its Current Validity under the U.N. Charter," *California Western International Law Journal* 4, no. 2 (1974):203.

15.   See also Chen, "Self-Determination as a Human Right," pp. 227-28 and 242-43; Suzuki, "Self-Determination and World Public Order"; Friedlander, "Self-Determination," pp. 80 and 82.

16.   The quoted language is from the General Assembly Declaration on Principles of International Law. See also Jordan J. Paust, "International Law and Control of the Media: Terror, Repression, and the Alternatives," *Indiana Law Journal* 53 (1978):621.

17.   See, e.g., United Nations, General Assembly, Resolution 3297 (UN Doc. A/RES/3297); vote: 111-0-18.

18.   United Nations, General Assembly, Resolution 2877 (UN Doc. A/8429); vote: 94-8-22.

19.   United Nations, General Assembly, Resolution 3297.

20.   Ibid.

21.   See also Chen, "Self-Determination as a Human Right"; Suzuki, "Self-Determination and World Public Order"; Rosenstock, "Declaration of Principles," p. 732; Emerson, "Self-Determination," p. 475; Dinstein, "Terrorism and Wars of Liberation," pp. 79-80; Friedlander, "Self-Determination," pp. 73, 89, and 91; H. Lauterpacht, "Some Concepts of Human Rights," *Howard Law Journal* (1965):264; Louis B. Sohn and Thomas Buergenthal, *International Protection of Human Rights* (New York: Bobbs-Merrill, 1973), pp. 520-22, 535-36, passim.

22.   See also Advisory Opinion on Western Sahara, pp. 31, 36. For further discussion of the jurisprudential aspects of such a recognition, see also Jordan J. Paust, "The Concept of Norm: A Consideration of the Jurisprudential Views of Hart, Kelsen, and McDougal-Lasswell," *Temple Law Quarterly* 52, no. 1 (1979):9.

23.   Thomas Paine, *The Rights of Man* (1794), pt. 1, p. 8.

24.   See also Suzuki, "Self-Determination and World Public Order," pp. 850-51 and 858; Dinstein, "Terrorism and Wars of Liberation," p. 81.

25.   For further discussion, see Jordan J. Paust, "A Survey of Possible Legal Responses to International Terrorism: Prevention, Punishment, and Cooperative Action, *Georgia Journal of International and Comparative Law* 5, no. 2 (1975):431; Paust, "International Law and Control of the Media."

26.   See Suzuki, "Self-Determination and World Public Order," pp. 816-17.

27.   See, e.g., Louis Henkin, "Constitutional Fathers—Constitutional Sons,"

Minnesota Law Review 60 (1976):113 (an article with which I disagree concerning "authority" and the import of the Ninth Amendment; see supra note 22 and infra note 33).

28. See also Chen, "Self-Determination as a Human Right," pp. 229-35 (historic use of plebiscites).

29. *Lincoln's Stories and Speeches,* Allen ed. (1900), p. 212.

30. Paine, *Rights of Man,* p. 44.

31. Our constitutional case law on this point is clear: authority and sovereignty exist with the people. See, e.g., Afroyim v. Rusk, 387 U.S. 253, 257 (1957); Reid v. Covert, 354 U.S. 1, 5-6 (1956); United States v. Lee, 106 U.S. 196, 208-9, and 219-21 (1882); Ex parte Curtis, 106 U.S. 371, 372 (1882); M'Culloch v. Maryland, 17 U.S. (4 Wheat) 316, 403-5 (1819); Ware v. Hylton, 3 U.S. (3 Dall.) 198, 199 (1796); Chisholm v. Georgia, 2 U.S. (2 Dall.) 419, 454, and 460-63 (1793).

32. *The Federalist,* no. 84 (J. Cooke ed., 1961):578.

33. For further exposition, see Jordan J. Paust, "Human Rights and the Ninth Amendment: A New Form of Guarantee," *Cornell Law Review* 60, no. 2 (1975):231; c.f. Henkin, "Constitutional Fathers."

34. See authorities cited in Paust, "A Survey of Possible Legal Responses," p. 460 n.115.

35. See Suzuki, "Self-Determination and World Public Order," pp. 794-95, passim.

36. Ibid., p. 861. See also Friedlander, "Self-Determination."

37. See also Suzuki, "Self-Determination and World Public Order," pp. 785 ff.

38. See especially ibid., pp. 794-97 and 848-56.

39. Chen, "Self-Determination as a Human Right."

40. Suzuki, "Self-Determination and World Public Order," p. 790.

41. Ibid., p. 782.

42. Ibid., p. 816; see also Chen, "Self-Determination as a Human Right," pp. 211-12; Dinstein, "Terrorism and Wars of Liberation," p. 81.

43. Suzuki, "Self-Determination and World Public Order," p. 828; see also Dinstein, "Terrorism and Wars of Liberation," p. 79.

44. See also Chen, "Self-Determination as a Human Right," pp. 217-19 (historic development into the human rights instruments of the twentieth century); and Dinstein, "Terrorism and Wars of Liberation," p. 79.

45. Chen, "Self-Determination as a Human Right," p. 242.

46. Ibid., p. 201.

47. Ibid., p. 244; see also ibid., p. 241, "the consent of the governed is essential to human dignity"; Dinstein, "Terrorism and Wars of Liberation," p. 79; John Norton Moore, "The Control of Foreign Intervention in Internal Conflict," *Virginia Journal of International Law* 9 (1969):247.

48. See, e.g., *Webster's New Collegiate Dictionary* (1976), "self-determination," p. 1049; *Webster's New World Dictionary* (1956), "self-determination," p. 1322.

49. Myres S. McDougal, *Studies in World Public Order* (New Haven: Yale University Press, 1960), p. 337. Professors McDougal and Lasswell, of course, developed a policy and value-oriented, configurative jurisprudence that is quite useful for addressing problems of self-determination, authority, human dignity, and related questions. See, e.g., Paust, "The Concept of Norm."

50. Ibid., pp. 336-37.

Part 2

North and South America

2

Self-Determination: Canadian Perspectives

Edgar S. Efrat

Canadians have faced several different aspects of self-determination ever since two major European powers, Great Britain and France, laid claim to the northern part of North America. The conflict over sovereignty was resolved in 1759 on the Plains of Abraham, near Quebec City, when the British General Wolfe defeated the French General Montcalm. However, the presence in Canada of two national groups, the French and English, and the emergence of the United States to the south resulted in creating two basic issues of self-determination: pressure by the Francophones for the preservation of their distinct identity against the ascendancy of the Anglophone majority, and the assertion of a national Canadian identity vis-à-vis increasing cultural, economic, and political pressure exerted by the United States, whether real or imagined.

Colonization in North America differed from analogous phenomena in most other places in that settlers in Canada (and in the thirteen American colonies) aspired for permanence from the time of their arrival on the continent. Since Samuel de Champlain founded Quebec in 1608 in New France, the French there called themselves *habitants*, or *Canadiens*, and ceased to be considered as Europeans temporarily overseas. The transfer of sovereignty mattered little, Canada was home, regardless of whether Louis XV or George III appointed the governor-general. The latter catered to the *habitants*, as the Quebec Act of 1774 proved. The act recognized the French language, the Roman Catholic Church, and substantially enlarged territory as the *habitants'* domain.

The American Revolution—battles fought on their land, the influx of Loyalists, and the British defeat—alarmed the *habitants*, but the Constitutional Act of 1791, which divided the remaining British colony into Upper and Lower Canada and granted them a substantial measure of internal autonomy in Lower Canada, laid their fears to rest, at least temporarily. However, the Anglophones in Lower Canada, who had prospered politically and economically, feared the 1791 division. The *parti canadienne*, led by Louis-Joseph Papineau, resorted to violence which gave the British administration a pretense to revoke the union, thereby diluting what limited self-determination the French speakers possessed with the larger mass of the entire colony.

In his report, prepared in anticipation of increased self-government in Canada, Lord Durham described in 1839 what he considered to be the major challenge: "Two nations warring in the bosom of a single state . . . a struggle not of principles but of races" and "the deadly animosity that now separates the inhabitants . . . into the hostile divisions of French and English."[1]

Canada's great moment in history arrived with the promulgation in London of the British North America Act on July 1, 1867. This act, after extensive negotiations and conferences, first in Charlottetown, Prince Edward Island, and later in Quebec, established Canada as the first quasi-independent dominion within the British Empire. The BNA Act based the Canadian constitutional system on two principles: the Westminster parliamentary system and a new confederative mechanism. The latter was an attempt to avoid what was perceived as a major weakness in the American Constitution: the Tenth Amendment's reserving unspecified powers to the states, which contributed to the American Civil War—of very recent memory in 1867.

British constitutional principles, which operate reasonably well in the United Kingdom, are an out-and-out failure when exported to what are still called the "white dominions" and survive only as an aberration. One may venture to predict in the case of Canada, the first of the "white dominions," that, as British influence wanes, so will the power of the British tradition ensconced in the concept of "responsible government."[2]

The unsuitability of the Westminster system for export is further exacerbated in the case of federations. A basic, though unwritten, principle of the Westminster system is the confrontation of the government and its party in Parliament by the opposition and its "shadow" or alternative government—present, able, and willing to assume power and responsibility at the invitation of the politically neutral head of state after a "defeat" of the government inside or outside the chamber. The assumption is that the major parties are national in scope, and that the opposition is nationally recognized. If, however, the opposition consists of several small parties, at odds with each other as much as with the government party, or of regional parties devoid of a national constituency, then the Westminster system becomes severely encumbered. A federal system, obviously, tends to encourage nonhomogeneous parties. The American system, not saddled either with an executive answerable to the legislature for survival or with rigidly enforced party loyalty, does not need such homogeneity. In a Westminster-type federation, however, as is the case in Canada, the absence of homogeneity is frequently critical.

Another severe flaw in the translation of the British system to Canada may be seen in the lack of provision for true territorial representation in the national legislature. The simple, American constitutional compromise of the large-versus-small-state conflict, the "representation-by-population" and "two senators per state" formula, has not been accepted by Canada. The Senate there, like the House of Lords, is removed from the electoral contest. The senators-for-life (or, for appointees after 1965, to age seventy-five) are nominated by the government of the day to vacancies that are only proforma provincial.

In relation to the constitution of the Senate, Canada is deemed to consist of four divisions: Ontario; Quebec; the Maritime Provinces consisting of Nova Scotia, New Brunswick, and Prince Edward Island; and the western provinces of Manitoba, British Columbia, Saskatchewan, and Alberta.[3] Each region is represented in the Senate by twenty-four senators. Newfoundland, which acceded to the Confederation in 1949, was accorded six senators.[4] This division of Senate seats results in one senator per 29,500 inhabitants in Prince Edward Island and one senator per 365,000 in British Columbia. Since the provincial governments or the electorate have no part in filling Senate seats, and a senator has no obligation whatsoever to the province he "represents," the federal function of the upper house in Canada is well-nigh nonexistent. Its function now, as has been frequently pointed out, especially by the New Democratic party opposition, is to serve as a dignified retreat, whereto the prime minister can retire deserving veterans of political wars. Australia, as is well known, emulated the American system by providing for ten senators per state, elected by the people. Federal representation in the Canadian system is approached by what may be termed a "third level" of government: frequent meetings between federal and provincial ministerial counterparts, at which the provincial interests are presented to the federal executive and vice versa. Such a noninstitutional arrangement, to a considerable degree, is dependent for effectiveness on the personalities involved.

Contributing to the weakening of the federal system in Canada are other factors that are attributable to the Westminster system. Notable among these is the almost absolute power the prime minister can exert, when covered by a party majority in the House of Commons. This awesome authority, ordinarily, cannot be checked by components of the federation—either directly, through representation, or indirectly, through reference to residual powers—as would be the case in the American system. An illustration of the application of this power may be seen in the imposition of the War Measures Act in Canada in October 1970. Briefly, the War Measures Act (Rev. Stat. Can. [1952], c. 288) and the Emergency Powers acts (e.g., Can. Stat. 15 Geo. VI. c 5) authorize the federal cabinet to take the necessary speedy action in time of real or apprehended war, invasion, insurrection, or national emergency and, in doing so, to assume powers that would belong to provincial legislatures under normal conditions.[5]

The fragility of the constitutional order was illustrated by the events in Quebec in October 1970.[6] While bombing and sporadic terrorism had been evident since the emergence of the Front de Libération de Québec in 1963, it had seemed possible that these activities could be kept under control by public action. The kidnapping of the British trade commissioner, James Jasper Cross, and of the Quebec provincial minister of labor, Pierre Laporte, who was subsequently murdered by his abductors, convinced the prime minister and the federal minister of justice that federal intervention was called for. They responded by proclaiming the War Measures Act to deal with an "apprehended insurrection." Federal troops were brought in, the FLQ was declared to be an illegal organization, some censorship was imposed throughout Canada, and persons were detained without warrant and without formal charge.

A curious constitutional situation resulted. While the regulations emanated from the federal authorities, those authorities could not be directly accountable to Parliament for the enforcement of the regulations since under the Constitution this responsibility falls on provincial authorities.[7] Such situations create considerable constitutional-legal problems because the Canadian Bill of Rights (Can. Stat. 8-9, Eliz. II, c. 44) exempts the War Measures Act from its guarantees, and the regulations had the effect of setting aside habeas corpus and the right to bail and, often, access to legal counsel.[8]

Two further weaknesses in the Canadian constitutional structure are apparent in the principle of national supremacy as applied to intraprovincial affairs and in the vestiges of constitutional dependence on Great Britain, as reflected in the amendment process of the Canadian Constitution. K. C. Wheare in his classic work, *Federal Government,* qualified the Canadian Constitution as "quasi-federal" because the national executive has the power to disallow any act passed by a provincial legislature, whether or not the act deals with subjects falling within the legislative field exclusively assigned to the provinces.[9] The position of the lieutenant-governor is provincially analogous to that of the governor-general nationally; both are representatives of the Crown and, therefore, formal heads of government in their jurisdiction. The lieutenant-governor is federally appointed and can be instructed by his appointers to withhold his assent from provincial bills and to reserve them for consideration by the federal executive, which may refuse assent if it deems fit. Also, appointments to all the important judicial positions in the provinces are in the hands of the federal executive. Wheare designates these as "unitary elements" in an otherwise strictly federal form of constitution. They are matters in which the provincial governments are subordinate to the federal government and not coordinate with it. They are substantial modifications of the federal principle. One must add, however, that Wheare considers the law of the Constitution to be distinctive from practice, where convention prevails.

In practice, the power of disallowance is used so seldom, and even then usually only when a provincial act is *ultra vires*, that it seems to have operated as a safeguard for the federal principle in the Constitution. Nevertheless, the letter of the law permits the central government to appoint its man to the highest office in each province and gives him the authority to deny assent to provincial legislation—which unlike the royal assent in Britain is not taken as a routine ceremony—and this power must be construed as a weakness in the Canadian federal system.

The second weakness alluded to earlier, the amendment procedure, has the effect that the Constitution of Canada—apart from the few provisions that are subject to amendment by other specified processes—can only be amended by an act of the Parliament of the United Kingdom.[10] The Colonial Laws Validity Act (1865), which preceded the BNA Act, prevented any legislative organ subordinated to the British Parliament from passing legislation repugnant to the provision of British acts unless specifically exempted. The Statute of Westminster (1931) has not removed Canada from the operation of the Colonial Laws Validity Act insofar as the Constitution is concerned. As a result, the Canadian Constitution can be altered—except as provided—only by a further enactment of the British Parliament granted upon a joint address by both houses in Canada. The necessity for such an enactment is the only feature of the amending process that is determined entirely by law proper and does not in any way result from convention. Any attempt to alter the Constitution or to override it by other means would be repudiated by the courts.[11]

The BNA Act provided that either English or French may be used in Parliament, in the Quebec legislature, and nationally in court proceedings.[12] More recently, the Royal Commission on Bilingualism and Biculturalism recommended "that English and French be formally declared the offical languages of the Parliament of Canada, of the federal courts, of the federal government and of the federal administration."[13] The authority of the Canadian Parliament specifically excludes the power to change the status of the English and French languages as protected in the BNA Act.[14] This power is still reserved to the Parliament of the

United Kingdom, as mentioned earlier.[15]

The instability introduced into a federal system by very large constituent units hardly needs elaboration. The delegations of Ontario and Quebec in the House of Commons consist of 162 members of a total of 265, a majority of 60 percent; in the Senate, the two provinces are represented by 48 senators of a total of 102—almost half the membership.[16] Given the Westminster system of party loyalty, figures denoting total provincial representation in Parliament are less significant than party standings, that is, the division of the House along party lines is more important than the number of senators allocated to each province.

As a result, Canada's attitude toward its federal system is divisive on several levels including the historical Anglo-French division which, in addition to language chauvinism, also polarized majority-minority disaffections that led to the establishment of political action groups such as the FLQ and the Parti Quebecois.

The former is now outlawed, but the latter has governed Quebec since November 1976. The Parti Quebecois is currently in the process of preparing a referendum, a very rare occurrence in Canada, on the future status of Quebec. An outspoken advocate of provincial go-it-aloneism, former Quebec Premier Robert Bourassa, said that he was attacking the federal government less freely than his predecessors because he felt a responsibility to defend federalism "which is more vulnerable than it was, say, five years ago." The traditional approach to federal-provincial relations in Quebec, he said, was to attack the federal government fiercely and often—"Hit Ottawa; it's always popular."

Given this substantial list of disintegrative factors in the Canadian system, one may safely say that the federation is held together by a fear of the alternatives, which could be Balkanization or union with the United States.

Another side to the intra-Canadian conflict is reflected by the unilateral nationalism of the French element which is concerned, perhaps overly so, with identity, cultural differences, and alleged economic exploitation. Their widely recognized craving for self-determination is expressed in the slogan *maîtres chez nous* ("masters in our own home"). It expresses itself in the trappings and symbols of nationhood. The provincial legislature is the Assemblée nationale. Quebec missions abroad fly the Fleur-de-lys instead of the Maple Leaf, and Quebec participates as a "sovereign" member in international conferences of the *Francophonie*. (The 1968 conference in Libreville, Gabon, to which Quebec but not Canada was invited, caused a break in diplomatic relations, though the real culprit was France.[17])

The tug-of-war between the two ethnic components of the Confederation is aggravated by the nebulous character of Canada's constitutional document, the British North America Act. Nevertheless, the loose formulation of the act has its defenders:

> One of the constitutional difficulties in Canada has been the instinctive desire of French-speaking Canadians for the definitive document in the grand civil law manner, as distinguished from the Anglo-Canadian pragmatic tradition in legal and political matters. The average Anglo-Canadian legal theorist usually envisages grave dangers in providing premature legal documents as a method of resolving social ills before a social consensus has emerged. French-speaking Canadians, nurtured on a civilian approach to law, prefer the grand legal design in the form of a constitution, with a maximum elucidation of details. I believe there are grave difficulties in widespread constitutional revision until some form of political consensus has emerged in Canada.[18]

It is generally accepted that the document is inadequate, in the constitutional sense, even in the delineation of basic functions. For example: although the Supreme Court of Canada became the final court of appeal in 1949, superseding the right of Canadians to appeal to the Judicial Committee of the Privy Council in London, a transfer effected by an act of the Canadian Parliament, the Constitution itself makes no provision for a Supreme Court.[19] Other glaring omissions from the Constitution are protection for civil rights, parameters for senior officers, or provisions for amendments. Although in practice amendments agreed to by all affected provinces are ratified by the grantor of the Constitution, the *British* Parliament, the fact that a "foreign" legislature holds, at present, ultimate power over Canada's Constitution is an irritant to many Canadians groping for self-determination. The rationale advanced against the "patriation" of the Constitution is the need to protect the entrenched rights of the Francophones against the majority.

Canada's external self-determination is curtailed by overwhelming dependence on the United States, economically—trade and investments—and militarily—defense. In 1976, Canadian exports to the United States amounted to Can. $25,138,600,000 of a total to all countries of Can. $38,146,300,000 (65.9 percent). Canadian imports from the United States in the same year amounted to Can. $25,695,202,000 of total imports from all countries of Can. $37,468,000,000 (68.5 percent). Canada's next-largest trading partner, Japan, received only 6.26 percent of exports and shipped 4 percent of Canada's imports.[20]

U.S. investments in Canada in 1976 were valued at U.S. $33,927,000,000 as a direct investment position[21] (24.7 percent of total U.S. investments abroad, 33.5 percent of U.S. investments in developed countries). In 1975, the net capital outflow from the United States to Canada amounted to $419 million (reduced to $102 million in 1976). U.S. investments in Canada earned $9,445 million in 1975 and $11,298 million in 1976 (57.5 and 60 percent of total U.S. earnings abroad, respectively). U.S. investments in the Canadian oil industry yielded a net profit (after deducting reinvested earnings) of $110 million in 1975 and 1976.

Canadian investments in the United States were valued at $5,859 million in 1976, earning Canada a total of $373 million. (By comparison, Dutch investments in the United States were valued at $6,184 million, earning $689 million.) The Canadian share of foreign investments in the United States in 1976 was 19.4 percent. On the other hand, the Canadian share of imports into the United States in 1976 was 21.7 percent of total foreign U.S. imports. U.S. exports to Canada amounted to 20.9 percent of total U.S. exports.

Canada's trade dependence is simply that about two-thirds of Canada's export trade goes to the United States, while only one-fifth of American exports go to Canada. Tourism, which makes up about 5 percent of Canada's gross national product, yielded Can. $9.2 billion in 1976 (that year registered a 5.9 percent drop in visitors), derived in large part from 32.2 million visitors from the United States. Although the number of Canadians visiting the United States was higher, the percentage of the Canadian tourist contribution to the U.S. GNP was fractional (0.16 percent).[22]

Canada's military options are circumscribed by the minuscule size of her armed forces and minimal budgetary appropriations for defense. Canada's regular armed forces consist of about 78,000 personnel and expenditures of U.S. $3,231 billion in 1976. In 1975, Canada spent U.S. $2,965 billion, 2.2 percent of total output.[23] By comparison, in 1976, the United States had 2.087 million military personnel and spent about $103 billion on defense, 5.9 percent of total output. Among significant NATO members, none allocates a smaller percentage of GNP for defense than Canada. As a result, hardly requiring elaboration, the military cannot be cited at present as an expression of or enforcer of self-determination. The dependence of Canada on the United States for defense and defensive surveillance is obvious. For practical purposes, the defense forces of both nations are almost integrated through NORAD—the North American Air Defense Command—and the joint utilization of land, naval, and air facilities. The proximity of the Trident submarine base at Bangor, Washington, and the ICBM bases along the prairie borders is ominous to some Canadians and reassuring to others.

The area in which an independent course and a vigorous attitude of self-determination was and is pursued is Canadian foreign policy. Canadian participation in international affairs can be divided chronologically into three periods that demonstrate progressive development from a position of colonial dependence to one of complete autonomy.[24] During the first period, from Confederation in 1867 until 1909, Britain controlled and directed all intercourse between Canada and other nations. Resentment of this domination culminated in the creation in 1909 of a Canadian Department of External Affairs. However, the dominion was still under British control, and the second chronological period, 1909 to 1931, shows how Canada gradually attained self-determination in international relations. The last period, from 1931 on, underscores incidents and policy changes that have characterized Canada's role in world affairs since the Statute of Westminster confirmed Canada's position as an autonomous international entity.

In the period from Confederation until 1909, Canadian interests in international affairs were limited by two factors. First, the new nation was preoccupied with internal problems of growth and development, and, secondly, as a part of the British Empire, Canadian external relations came under the direction of the government of the United Kingdom. From the outset, the British Foreign Office saw to it that diplomatic questions remained within its exclusive control and that colonial agents should not enter into direct negotiations with foreign governments. Under Section 9 of the British North America Act, the governor-general was the official channel of communication between London and Ottawa. Originally, this close imperial safeguard created little cause for complaint, but, as Canadian commercial enterprise increased, particularly with the United States, so did the need for closer diplomatic channels of communication. As it was, any note exchanged between the American and Canadian governments had first to be presented to the British ambassador to the United States. It was then sent to England where the Foreign Office referred it to the Colonial Office. From there, it was sent to the governor-general who would then present it to the Canadian government. Any reply required not only a reversal of the above process but also the concurrence of the British government as to its content. Thus, a diplomatic exchange between Ottawa and Washington crossed the Atlantic four times and underwent the close scrutiny of both the Colonial and Foreign offices of the British government.

After repeated suggestions that this cumbersome system be altered and that Canadian "diplomatic" agents be given greater recognition, the governor-general was informed in 1879 that "the Dominion cannot negotiate independently with foreign powers and at the same time reap the benefit which she desires in negotiations from being a part of the Empire."[25] Thus, for the next twenty years Canada participated in international affairs only as a component of the British Empire.

With the advent of war in South Africa in 1898, Canada attempted to assert her independence from imperial control more forcefully. The issue was largely political. Prime Minister Laurier was well aware of the federal difficulties that would arise with Quebec if Britain requested troops from Canada to help fight the Boers. However, the request duly arrived, and many English Canadians sympathized with the idea of dominion participation in the South African war. Although a satisfactory compromise was effected when Laurier sent a contingent of volunteer soldiers, there was widespread resentment throughout Canada at the fact that Britain could demand imperial participation in what was essentially a non-Canadian conflict. This resentment was intensified in 1903 when the United Kingdom negotiated with the United States on behalf of Canada, awarding the Americans what appeared to be a very favorable settlement of the long-standing Alaska boundary dispute. "While the Canadian government then lived up to the letter and spirit of a treaty of which they had never approved, from the first they had good reason to suspect the good faith of the American government and the diplomatic support of the British."[26] Resentment of imperial control over Canadian foreign relations was now coupled with a justified lack of faith in Britain's capacity to negotiate effectively on behalf of Canada.

In 1907, Prime Minister Laurier and his minister of finance ignored Britain's determination to maintain control over dominion treaty-making powers; they traveled to Paris, negotiated, and signed a commercial treaty with France. The British ambassador in Paris did, however, sign the treaty in order to render it a valid document. Three weeks later, a Canadian was sent to Japan to conclude a "gentleman's agreement" with the Japanese government concerning trade. Although Canada still had no diplomatic status except as a part of the British Empire, her representatives continued to act independently whenever they could do so without giving serious offense to Britain. In 1909, an International Joint Commission was established for the purpose of dealing with disputes between Canada and the United States, thus short-circuiting the old, time-consuming route through England.

For the first time in her short history as a nation, Canada was now in an economic position to play a small but important part in the world as an independent, international entity. This fact was recognized in 1909 when a bill was introduced into the House of Commons designed to create a Department of External Affairs. Correspondence relating to international affairs would still be received first by the governor-general and imperial control was largely retained, but on June first of that year the new department came into existence.

On the eve of the First World War, the attitude of England toward greater dominion independence in international matters appeared to relax. "At the Imperial Conference of 1911, it is significant to find Sir Edward Grey for the first time taking the assembled Prime Ministers into his confidence in matters of foreign policy. Already we have the atmosphere of collaboration between equals which was to be the rule in the Empire during the Great War."[27]

This notable change of attitude within the imperial structure encouraged Laurier's successor, Sir Robert Borden, who took a special interest in Canada's developing independence in foreign relations. He placed the newly created Department of External Affairs within the jurisdiction of the prime minister, thereby adding considerable prestige to it.

When Britain declared war on August 4, 1914, she did so on behalf of her empire: Canada, in other words, was automatically at war without prior parliamentary discussion or decision. Considering that Canada's population in 1914 was only eight million, her contribution to the general war effort caused great sacrifice. By the end of 1918, 595,000 Canadians had enlisted of which 420,000 served overseas. The extensive participation in the war by all the dominions was bound to increase their say in the formulation of imperial policy. "After the Imperial War Conference of 1917 . . . it was recognized unreservedly that the Dominions should henceforth be considered as fully grown nations and that they were justified in possessing, even in the conduct of foreign affairs, their own points of view."[28] In accordance with the resolutions of the Imperial War Conference, Canada and the other dominions demonstrated their sovereignty in international matters by signing the Treaty of Versailles as separate entities rather than allowing Britain to sign on their behalf. Thus, although they had entered the war automatically with the British declaration, they ended it by signing the peace treaty independently. Shortly thereafter, Canada joined the League of Nations as a separate signatory.

Canada still possessed no official diplomatic status, and, at the Imperial Conference of 1921, Great Britain was definitely reluctant to make any further concessions to the dominions. At the Imperial Conference in 1923, Canada argued vociferously against the creation of an Imperial Cabinet to direct policy for the whole of the empire. Such a body would have been centered in London and, in spite of dominion representation, would have discouraged future autonomy by solidifying the old idea of a centralized imperial administration. By now, the feeling of the Canadian government was that Canada had earned the right to conduct her own foreign relations, a sentiment she acted on later in 1923 when a member of the Canadian Department of External Affairs negotiated and signed a treaty concerning halibut fishing with the United States.

In the meantime, Canadian participation in the League of Nations was attracting wide attention. There was a basic difference of opinion between the Canadian and the British delegates regarding Art. 10 of the Covenant, based on Canada's growing awareness of her position as a North American rather than a European nation. Article 10 was the basic expression of collective security, and Canada, like the United States, did not wish to be committed to action in Europe should a conflict there result in League intervention. Thus, as early as 1921 there were clear indications of a shift in Canadian policy from a fundamentally British point of view to a North American attitude.

The trend toward dominion independence in international relations which had gathered impetus as a result of the Great War was recognized tangibly in 1926. At the Imperial Conference that year, the British government extended to the dominions full and complete control over their international affairs. As of July 1, 1927, communications from foreign nations went straight to the Department of External Affairs, not the governor-general. In the same year, Vincent Massey was appointed Canadian minister in Washington, and early in 1928 Britain appointed Sir William Clark high commissioner to Canada. As the Department of External Affairs rapidly expanded to meet Canada's new international responsibilities, a legation was established in Paris and a permanent mission established in Japan. The British Empire had become the British Commonwealth of Nations, and, by the time the Statute of Westminster confirmed all that had been gained by 1931, Canada was functioning in her new role as a recognized member of the international community.

In fact, Canadian foreign policy was largely the product of two influences that have continued to operate ever since, one geographic and the other based on tradition. Thus, because of her physical proximity to the United States on the one hand and her traditional attachment to Great Britain on the other, the general course of Canadian foreign policy was largely predetermined. During the late twenties and early thirties, these two influences often conflicted, and external policy was directed toward finding a compromise that would satisfy both sides and, at the same time, protect Canadian interests. As a member of the League of Nations, Canada had differed with Britain over Art. 10 of the Covenant, suggesting a tendency to embrace the prevailing isolationist attitude in America. However, in 1932 the Ottawa Agreements of Imperial Preference were designed to arrest growing economic dependence on the United States.

As the situation in Europe grew worse during the 1930s, Canada followed the American line more and more. "Canadian opinion was isolationist. . . . French Canada feared another war would mean conscription, English Canada that it would strain national unity and again involve the nation to no purpose in another European bloodbath."[29] Canada sympathized with the League of Nations in its attempts to preserve peace but was not prepared to commit her resources to positive action. By 1933, neither the League nor the Commonwealth received Canada's undivided support on the question of collective security. At the British Commonwealth Relations Conference held in Toronto in 1933, both Australia and New Zealand desired to work out common policies and plans for a centralized control of all the potential military power of the Commonwealth, in the belief that a united effort on the part of the Commonwealth was the best means of effecting the ideals of the League. The Canadian delegate replied, "if collective action breaks down, in all probability that would bring about a situation where Canada's North American position as distinguished from its Commonwealth position would prevail."[30] This isolationist attitude was demonstrated further in 1935 when the Canadian representative at Geneva was promptly repudiated by his government when he moved to strengthen economic sanctions against Italy. Prime Minister Mackenzie King made it clear that Canada would consult her own interests first and those of collective security later.

With the outbreak of war in 1939, however, Canada's attachment to Great Britain proved less tenuous than her relatively recent policy of isolation from Europe. Canada declared war independently one week after the British declaration in spite of the neutrality of the United States. Perhaps Canada's most important contribution to the general war effort during the first two years of the conflict was her role as a convenient liaison between Great Britain and the United States. The Canadian government knew the mind of the Roosevelt administration and obviously shared its confidence in the vital negotiations which gained for Britain the moral and material support of the United States.

During this early period of the war, Canada and the United States grew much closer together. The extent to which they identified their interests under the pressures of war in Europe was shown by the establishment of the Permanent Joint Defense Board in 1940, for the protection of America. "Thus when Pearl Harbour came it was a disaster which, while it fell on the United States, was felt in Canada to be a common disaster. Canada had become what it had never been before, and had become permanently, an ally of the United States."[31]

During the war, Canada supported the establishment of the United Nations as an organization to make and secure peace, in spite of Prime Minister King's reservations about the future of the organization once peace was won. Although Canada had no part in shaping the strategy of the war, she did have a place of unusual importance in matters of supply, which resulted also in extraordinary wartime industrial development. With a population of some twelve million to draw on, Canada enlisted one million men and women into her armed forces without compulsory conscription. Besides financing this military effort and the development of her war industry, she gave some four billion dollars to her allies in the form of war material and a one hundred million dollar interest-free loan to the United Kingdom.[32]

As in 1918, Canada emerged from the Second World War in a radically changed international position. Her large contribution to the war effort was again greatly respected and, more important, was responsible for the fact that, by 1946, Canada had developed her industry to the extent that she was now one of the "middle powers" of the world. Her general policy was one of cooperation with America and Britain in the reconstruction of postwar Europe, and a fervent desire not to fall completely under the ever-present influence of the United States.

The main objectives of Canadian policy after 1945 were therefore to preserve Canadian sovereignty and to avoid being isolated with the United States in America. The historic dependence of Canada upon its European connections was now transmuted into the basic principle of Canadian foreign policy, that independence in America is a function of Canada's ties with the rest of the world.[33]

The formation of the United Nations organization in 1945 afforded Canada an excellent opportunity to broaden her interests and responsibilities. She joined as one of the original members, determined to play an active role with the sincere hope that the the new organization might prove more successful than had the League, and endorsed the new United Nations Charter without reservation. As a member of the UN, Canada sent the third-largest contingent of troops to fight in Korea in 1950-1951; was one of the three nations forming the Truce Commission in Indochina (with Poland and India); and took the initiative in calling for the creation of a United Nations Emergency Force which operated in the Middle East and in the Congo—and later on in Cyprus and southern Lebanon. Canada participated actively on UN committees for disarmament.

Shortly after the war, Canada played a leading role in the formation of the North Atlantic Treaty Organization which was designed to meet the growing Communist threat in Europe and was well suited to the Canadian purpose to coordinate the two poles of her external policy, the United Kingdom and the United States. Another major area of Canadian participation in international affairs is the Commonwealth, within which exists a comprehensive system of protective tariffs. Since 1950, Canada has contributed substantially to the Colombo Plan to assist economic development in South and Southeast Asia, and through the Canadian International Development Agency she contributes in excess of one billion dollars annually to the Third World.

Canadian external policy has often differed from both the American and the British in spite of their essential agreement. In 1956, for example, Canada openly differed with Britain during the Suez crisis, and, more recently, Canada disagreed with Britain's projected entry into the European Economic Community (EEC) because British entry into the Common Market rendered Canada more dependent upon the United States economically. [34]

Differences with the United States have been fairly frequent. In spite of American urging, Canada has not yet joined the Organization of American States (OAS). Canadian trade agreements, both with Communist China and with Cuba, have also been a source of friction underscoring Canada's quest for an independent foreign policy. The shapers of Canadian policy in Ottawa are fully aware that economic dependence on the United States is the major infringement of Canada's self-determination due to vulnerability to American economic policy decisions based on self-interest. Various suggestions have been made over the years to mitigate this one-sided relationship. One of the latest was introduced by the then Secretary of State Mitchell Sharp in an address to the Executive of the Canadian Institute of International Affairs in Toronto, 1972.[35] Sharp argued against the laissez-faire attitude currently in operation between Canada and the United States. He also rejected a closer relationship, such as a North American Common Market, which would be even more detrimental than the status quo to Canadian interests. The third option endorsed a search for economic alternatives in the Far East, Europe, and the developing nations.

While the minister did not propose a practical mechanism, only an abstract search for a viable alternative, he focused, nevertheless, on one of the nation's major weaknesses. Many would disagree and postulate that the proximity and size of the United States are more a blessing than a curse. Frequent reference is made to "children of a common mother, dwelling in peace along the world's longest undefended border"—and to the essentially beneficial effects of the close relationship. A substantial part of Canada's exports to the United States are hardly competitive overseas, such as automobile parts (protected by a special treaty) and lumber. Others are not exportable elsewhere, such as hydroelectric power from water resources—shared with the United States according to the Columbia River Treaty ratified by Canada in 1964. There is no doubt that Canada's high standard of living (Canada has the third-highest, non-OPEC GNP in the world according to a 1978 OECD survey) would not be realized were it not for direct and indirect benefits accruing to Canada because of the close American connection. In the process, however, Canada's self-determinaton is curtailed.

One of the more immediate problems facing Canadian governments on the federal and provincial levels concerns the status of Indians, Eskimos, and Métis who increasingly demand self-determination. The first two groups claim aboriginal rights to vast tracts of land, asserting, inter alia, that treaties entered into with the Crown were signed under duress and, in many instances, were breached by government. Although the validity of some claims has been recognized, the resolution of native peoples' claims is at present uncertain.

Perhaps the most important and most elusive aspect in assessing the attitude of Canadians toward self-determination is the psychological factor. All Canadian ethnic groups claim that a hyphenated but distinct Canadian personality actually does exist. One finds dictionaries of Canadian English. Quebecois, a language spoken mainly in rural Quebec, is easily—some claim irritatingly—distinguishable from Parisian French. The Canadian Radio and Television Commission insists on a high percentage of Canadian content in what is transmitted—and even forces a blackout of American commercials on cablevision. Federal legislation limits foreign ownership of periodicals (e.g., *Time, Reader's Digest*) and banks in Canada, and limitations on foreign ownership of real estate are currently under consideration for enactment by provincial legislatures.

Yet, the Canadian public prefers American entertainment, American literature, French wines, European luxury cars, and Japanese compact cars. Westerners holiday in California and Hawaii, easterners in the Caribbean and Florida. They generally prefer holidays in Europe to holidays in Canada, in spite of the attractions Canada has to offer tourists. Many Canadian labor unions prefer affiliation with an international (i.e., American) union because of the substantially increased clout conveyed by the larger membership for dealing with multinational corporations.

In summation, one could cite a hypothetical average Canadian as saying: I know that my capability to shape my destiny is limited, but I am not willing to pay the price a higher measure of self-determination would command.

Notes

1. Gerald M. Craig, ed., *Lord Durham's Report* (Toronto: McClelland and Stewart, 1963).

2. Edgar S. Efrat, "Federations in Crisis—The Failure of the Old Order," *Western Political Quarterly* 25, no. 4 (1972).

3. The British North America Act (1867), Art. 22, as amended 1915,

1949 (hereafter referred to as BNA Act).

4. The actual division of Senate seats at present is: Quebec and Ontario, twenty-four each; New Brunswick and Nova Scotia, ten each; Saskatchewan, Manitoba, Alberta, British Columbia, and Newfoundland, six each; Prince Edward Island, four seats.

5. R. Mac G. Dawson, *The Government of Canada,* 5th ed., rev. by Norman Ward (Toronto: University of Toronto Press, 1970).

6. J. R. Mallory, *The Structure of the Government of Canada* (Toronto: MacMillan of Canada, 1971), p. 322.

7. Ibid. and BNA Act (1967 as amended), Sec. 91, sub-Sec. 27.

8. The bill has been criticized not only because it is not entrenched in the BNA Act, but also because it offers no protection against invasion of rights by the provinces (Dawson, *Government of Canada,* p. 72).

9. K. C. Wheare, *Federal Government,* 4th ed. (London: Oxford University Press, 1963), p. 18.

10. Paul Gerin-Lajoie, *Constitutional Amendment in Canada* (Toronto: University of Toronto Press, 1950), p. 135.

11. Ibid., p. 136.

12. BNA Act (1867), Art. 133.

13. *Report of the Royal Commission on Bilingualism and Biculturalism,* Book 1 (Ottawa: Queen's Printer, 1967), p. 91. This recommendation was enacted into law with the passing of the Official Languages Act (1969) which created four new branches in the Department of the Secretary of State: a Languages Administration Branch, a Public Service Bilingualism Programs Branch, a Social Action Branch, and a Planning and Research Branch (Dominion Bureau of Statistics: Canada, 1971 [Ottawa: Information Canada, 1971]).

14. Addition to the BNA Act (1949), 13 Geo. VI, c. 81 (U.K.).

15. The percentage of speakers of the official languages is approximately: English only, 67 percent; French only, 19 percent; both, 12 percent (*Canadian Pocket Encyclopedia,* 27th ed. [1971-72]). A bill, C-180, recently passed by Parliament made bilingual labeling of most grocery items mandatory throughout Canada. Currently, the federal government spends approximately $53,300,000 on bilingualism development.

16. The number of members of Parliament has been statutorily raised to 282, to take effect after the next election. This change does not substantially change the provincial prorata.

17. French President General de Gaulle did his best to encourage Quebec separatism. His cry from the balcony of Montreal City Hall, in July of 1967, is well known. Less known is his statement which preceded it: "This evening here, and all the way along my route, I found myself in an atmosphere of the same type as that of the Liberation." He concluded with "Vive Montréal! Vive le Québec! Vive le Québec libre! Vive le Canada français et vive la

France!'' (*La Politique étrangère de la France,* Textes et Documents, 2e semestre 1967 [Paris; General Secretariat of the Government, 1968]).

18. Ronald I. Cheffins, *The Constitutional Process in Canada* (Toronto: McGraw-Hill Co. of Canada, 1969), p. 6.

19. For greater detail, see Pierre Elliott Trudeau, *The Constitution and the People of Canada* (Ottawa: Queen's Printer, 1969).

20. Statistics: Canada.

21. Bureau of Economic Analysis, U.S. Department of Commerce.

22. Statistics concerning tourism diverge largely from source to source. Utilized here are Statistics: Canada and the U.S. Department of Commerce.

23. Institute for Strategic Studies, London.

24. This section is based in part on a research paper submitted to the author by A. R. Ross.

25. F. H. Soward, *The Department of External Affairs and Canadian Autonomy, 1899-1939* (Ottawa: Canadian Historical Association, 1956), p. 3.

26. G. P. Glazebrook, *A History of Canadian External Relations* (Toronto: Oxford University Press, 1950), p. 245.

27. A. Siegfried, *Canada* (London: Jonathan Cape, 1937), p. 216.

28. Ibid., p. 217.

29. W. L. Morton, *The Canadian Identity* (Menasha: University of Wisconsin Press, 1961), p. 74.

30. Violet Anderson, *World Currents and Canada's Course* (Toronto: Thomas Nelson and Co., 1937), p. 143.

31. Morton, *Canadian Identity,* p. 75.

32. Ibid., p. 77.

33. Ibid., p. 78.

34. Canada's independent stance in the Suez crisis and the proposal to dispatch a UN contingent to the Middle East resulted in the award of the Nobel Peace Prize to Prime Minister Lester Pearson.

35. The author was present, and this report is based on his notes. The minister's theme was subsequently published as an article, "Canada-U.S. Relations: Options for the Future," in a special issue of *International Perspectives* (Ottawa: Department of External Affairs, Autumn 1972). For extensive discussion, see Brian W. Tomlin, ed., *Canada's Foreign Policy: Analysis and Trends* (Toronto: Methuen Publications, 1978).

3

Self-Determination:
United States Perspectives

John F. Murphy

The present perspective of the United States on self-determination is an elusive will-o'-the-wisp. From a historical perspective, the United States has been a primary promoter of self-determination. Woodrow Wilson is usually viewed as the creator of the principle of self-determination, "although, in fact, he cannot claim true paternity but only foster-fatherhood."[1] At a minimum, Wilsonian ideals contributed to the creation of the mandates system after World War I, and in the United Nations and other international forums the United States played a pivotal role in the decolonization process after World War II, perhaps the principal manifestation of self-determination in action.

Recently, however, U.S. support of self-determination has been much more restrained. The United States has found itself voting against or abstaining on United Nations resolutions on self-determination; subject to sharp criticism for its actions regarding such cases as Micronesia, Spanish (Western) Sahara, and Portuguese (East) Timor; and refusing to participate in or recognize the jurisdiction of international organs concerned with self-determination.

A major reason the United States has had such problems with "self-determination" is that it is a concept of quintessential ambiguity whose scope is a matter of considerable debate. Although self-determination appears in the United Nations Charter[2] and in the International Covenants on Human Rights,[3] none of these documents defines the term. Moreover, neither the world community nor leading publicists have reached a clear consensus on a host of issues that arise out of attempts to apply self-determination to specific situations.[4]

Even a brief survey of these many issues is beyond the scope of this chapter. Rather, our purpose here will be to examine briefly three problem areas that have proven to be especially troublesome for the United States: (1) conflicts between self-determination and territorial integrity; (2) debates over permissible outcomes of a group's exercise of self-determination, i.e., continuation of the status quo ante, independence, free association or commonwealth status, or integration with an adjoining state; and (3) self-determination and the use of armed force.

For each of these areas, this chapter will first attempt to ascertain the nature of and the reasons for the U.S. perspective. It will then seek to evaluate the U.S. position in terms of law and policy and, where appropriate, advance recommendations for possible alternative courses of action.

Self-Determination and Territorial Integrity

During the Wilsonian period after World War I, the self-determination process focused on ethnic groups—nations or nationalities primarily defined by language and culture. Little attention was paid to the question of territorial integrity. On the contrary, in large part because of President Wilson's influence, wide-ranging territorial changes took place. New states arose from and existing states were augmented by the breakup of former German, Austro-Hungarian, Turkish, and Russian empires.[5]

After World War II, the second period of prime historical importance, the process of self-determination underwent a substantial transformation. The peoples viewed as entitled to exercise self-determination no longer were defined in ethnic or cultural terms. Instead, they were geographically determined by their presence within a colonial territory.

Perhaps the most conspicuous manifestations of this shift away from the ethnic approach to defining peoples, with its disintegrative effects, are provisions in United Nations General Assembly Resolution 1514, the Declaration on the Granting of Independence to Colonial Countries and Peoples (hereinafter, General

Assembly Resolution 1514)[6] and the Assembly's Declaration of Principles of International Law concerning Friendly Relations and Cooperation among States in Accordance with the Charter of the United Nations (hereinafter, Friendly Relations Declaration).[7] The most categorical provision is found in General Assembly Resolution 1514 which states, "Any attempt aimed at the partial or total disruption of the national unity and territorial integrity of a country is incompatible with the purposes and principles of the Charter of the United Nations."[8] The Friendly Relations Declaration, which is generally regarded as an authoritative statement of what members of the United Nations agree to be the law of the Charter on seven principles,[9] is more ambiguous on the subject. While proclaiming that self-determination is a principle of international law, that "all peoples" have the right to determine their own destiny without external interference, and that every state is obliged to refrain from any forcible action that would deprive peoples of this inherent right, the declaration qualifies the right by declaring:

> Nothing in the foregoing paragraphs shall be construed as authorizing or encouraging any action which would dismember or impair, totally or in part, the territorial integrity or political unity of sovereign and independent states conducting themselves in compliance with the principle of equal rights and self-determination as described above and thus possessed of a government representing the whole peoples belonging to the territory without distinction as to race, creed or colour.
>
> Every state shall refrain from any action aimed at the partial or total disruption of the national unity and territorial integrity of any state or country.[10]

Some have interpreted these provisions to mean that only states that conduct themselves in accordance with the principle of self-determination are entitled to territorial integrity.[11] Admittedly, a literal reading of the first paragraph quoted above supports this interpretation. However, it is contradicted by the categorical prohibition in the second paragraph against states engaging in "any action aimed" at disrupting the territorial integrity of "any state or country." This interpretation is also contrary to another statement in the declaration of a basic principle of international law: "The territorial integrity and political independence of the state are inviolable,"[12] which is couched in categorical terms without qualifying language. Moreover, the negotiating history of the declaration reveals a strong sentiment on the part of most member states in favor of interpreting the right of self-determination as a rejection of colonialism and not an acceptance of secession.[13] Further overriding concern for territorial inviolability may be found in a statement by former United Nations Secretary-General U Thant[14] and in the position taken by the Organization of African Unity.[15]

In their common Art. 1, the International Covenants on Human Rights strongly affirm that "all peoples have the right to self-determination." However, nowhere in either covenant, nor in the negotiating history of the covenants, can one find a resolution to the issue whether self-determination includes a right to secession. The debates on common Art. 1 reflect a sharp division of opinion and ultimate lack of agreement among states on this issue.[16] The United States expressed no opinion on the secession issue because it had expressed its intention not to sign the covenants in any case.

Since the time of debates on the covenants, the United States, more by its actions than its words, has supported the shift away from the Wilsonian ethnic approach. In addition to supporting the provisions on territorial integrity in the General Assembly resolutions discussed above, the United States consistently has opposed or at a minimum maintained a strict neutrality toward secessionist attempts ostensibly based on self-determination.

It is not difficult to perceive why the United States has viewed the ethnic approach to self-determination with a jaundiced eye. The United States has recently faced, and to some extent is still facing, demands by separatist movements within its own territory. The cases of black and Indian separatist demands are well known. Less well known but indicative of today's milieus is the movement by a group of prominent legislators in Michigan's Upper Peninsula to secede from Michigan and establish a separate state called Superior.[17]

The United States is also uneasy about strong separatist movements in its neighbor to the north. The election of the Parti Quebecois, dedicated to political independence for French-speaking Quebec, to power in November 1976 and the efforts of that party's leader, René Lévesque, to achieve that goal have caused Washington considerable concern. Equally disquieting to the United States is the contagious effect of the Quebec experience. Several other Canadian provinces are reportedly considering the possibility of secession, and Canadian Eskimo leaders have formally presented to Prime Minister Elliott Trudeau and his cabinet a claim to one-fifth of Canada as their own province.[18]

When the United States turns its attention to its allies in Western Europe, it again finds disturbing fissiparous tendencies. Economic difficulties have considerably strengthened independence movements in Scotland and Wales. The trend toward fragmentation is further evidenced by the claims of Catalans and Basques in Spain, Catholics in Northern Ireland, Bretons in France, and Flemish in Belgium.

From the global perspective, the United States finds the situation little better. A primary diplomatic concern of the United States has been the so-called ministate or microstate problem. Full consideration of this problem is beyond the scope of this chapter; it suffices to note for present purposes that at least half of the world's 156 independent countries have a population of under five million, nearly 35 have less than one million, 17 microstates—such as the Bahamas, Grenada, the Maldives, and Qatar—have fewer than 300,000 people, while one, Nauru, has a population of fewer than 7,000. Projections by the Department of State reportedly raise the possibility of 50 additional microstates—such as Antigua, Ifni, and Tahiti, each under 100,000 people—in the foreseeable future. This would expand the community of nations to more than 200, tripling the number since World War II.[19]

For a time, the United States led an effort in the United Nations to establish procedures to prevent a worsening of the current situation in which the United States pays 25 percent of the organization's budget while eighty member countries—contributing at a rate of 0.02 percent—jointly pay only 1.6 percent but wield eighty times the voting power of the United States.[20] However, this effort now has apparently been discontinued, and no end to inflation in the size of UN membership is in sight.[21] The United States, accordingly, is unlikely to support a concept of self-determination that has the potential to increase substantially the number of ministates or microstates in the world community.

U.S. reluctance to recognize a right to secession should not be interpreted as a lack of concern for the rights of minorities. The

United States has treated the problem of minority rights as an area in the human rights field separate and distinguishable from that of self-determination. This also would appear to be the approach taken by legal instruments and institutions in the international human rights field. For example, Art. 1 of the International Convention on the Elimination of All Forms of Racial Discrimination,[22] which the United States has signed but not yet ratified, prohibits "racial discrimination" on the basis of "race, color, descent, or national or ethnic origin." Similarly, under Art. 1 of the International Covenant on Civil and Political Rights,[23] a state party undertakes "to respect and ensure to all individuals within its territory and subject to its jurisdiction the rights recognized in the present Covenant, without distinction of any kind, such as race, color, sex, language, religion, political or other opinion, national or social origin, property, birth, or other status." More specifically as regards the rights of minorities, Art. 27 of the Civil and Political Rights Covenant provides that, "in those States in which ethnic, religious or linguistic minorities exist, persons belonging to such minorities shall not be denied the right, in community with the other members of their group, to enjoy their own culture, to profess and practice their own religion, or to use their own language." Finally, the United Nations Human Rights Commission is authorized to study or, with the consent of the country concerned, to investigate a complaint and issue a report and recommendations to the Economic and Social Council in cases involving a consistent pattern of gross violations of human rights (which include, of course, violations of minority rights).[24] Applying these standards and the measures established to implement them, the United States and the world community might attempt to ensure that minorities can "freely determine their political status and freely pursue their economic, social and cultural development"[25] through means other than secession and the establishment of a separate state.

To be sure, in some instances, it may not be possible to protect the rights of particular peoples as long as they remain within the territory of the dominant group. In such cases, as a last resort, the creation of a separate state or, at a minimum, an autonomous region for the subordinate group should be considered. However, this writer is dubious that one can approach this issue in terms of a legal right to secession in light of the right of the majority of people in a nation-state to territorial integrity. Assuming, *arguendo*, that the principle of self-determination has become a legal norm in international law,[26] this writer would suggest that the right not be defined so as to include a right of secession. Rather, secession should remain one possible expression of self-determination, but as a matter of principle and not of legal right.

So viewed, the issue of self-determination of subgroups within an established nation-state—whether it be one created out of a former colony or a country with an ancient tradition—would be approached primarily through a process of mediation where two or more "selfs" or "peoples" attempt to resolve their differences through a process of negotiation and compromise. Such a process might be aided by the United Nations or other international organizations or by other countries and, in a situation where the human rights of a subgroup are being violated, these same outside factors might bring pressure to bear against the violators. Some of the economic, strategic, cultural, and social factors that might be considered in this mediative process have been exhaustively explored elsewhere and are beyond the scope of this chapter.[27]

As a concluding note to this section, it is submitted that the world community, including the United States, simply will not recognize any legal right to secession and that the case of Bangladesh is not a precedent to the contrary.[28] The secession of East Pakistan from West Pakistan, and the establishment of the State of Bangladesh, was accomplished by a massive, Indian military intervention of most questionable legality and not because of any internationally recognized right of secession. There was neither authorization nor ratification of such action by the world community.[29] Nor, as has been contended elsewhere, has the "success of Bangladesh" changed the perception of the world community on this issue.[30] On the contrary, it has made member states increasingly aware of the dangers of fragmentation and has increased their resolve to oppose claims of secession.[31]

Outcomes of Self-Determination: Independence, Free Association, or Integration with a Sovereign State

Turning now to self-determination in the context of a trust territory or a non-self-governing territory, we shall consider in this section whether a valid exercise of the right to self-determination requires that independence be chosen, or permits other choices as well—i.e., continuation of the status quo ante, free association or commonwealth status, or integration into another state. In recent years, this issue has been especially troublesome for the United States.

The terms of the United Nations Charter, although somewhat elliptical, support the thesis that independence is only one of several available options. Under Art. 73, which sets forth the obligations of administering authorities with respect to non-self-governing territories, the administering authority is enjoined "to develop self-government . . . according to the particular circumstances of each territory and its peoples and their varying stages of advancement."[32] With respect to trust territories, Art. 76 requires administering authorities to promote "progressive development towards self-government or independence as may be appropriate to the particular circumstances of each territory and its peoples and the freely expressed wishes of the peoples concerned, and as may be provided by the terms of each trusteeship agreement."[33] Although independence is not expressly mentioned as an option for non-self-governing territories under Art. 73, the negotiating history of that article indicates that the drafters did not intend to preclude it, and the United States stated its understanding during the San Francisco Conference that the concept of self-government included independence as one of its forms.[34]

United Nations resolutions on self-determination are inconsistent. General Assembly Resolution 1541[35] lists three alternatives for termination of dependent status for non-self-governing territories: independence, free association, or integration with a sovereign state. However, General Assembly Resolution 1541 equates self-determination with independence, which was one reason the United States abstained in the vote on the declaration.[36]

The United States had more success in the negotiations on the Friendly Relations Declaration, which expressly confirms that "the establishment of a sovereign and independent state, the free association or integration with an independent state or the emergence into any other political status freely determined by a people constitute modes of implementing the right of self-determination by that people.''[37] Most recently, the International Court of Justice (I.C.J.), in its advisory opinion on the Spanish Sahara,[38] also has confirmed this view of the permissible outcomes of the exercise of self-determination.

Nonetheless, neither the adoption of the Friendly Relations Declaration nor the statement by the I.C.J. has ended U.S. problems with the strong preference for independence on the part of many United Nations member states, especially those on the Committee of Twenty-Four, established to implement Resolution 1514. As noted by Professor Emerson, in the view of those states, ''self-determination is an inalienable right to which access must remain available until the ultimate option of independence has been exercised.''[39]

This view has caused the Committee of Twenty-Four to bring pressure on the United States to grant independence to such territories as the Virgin Islands, Guam, and American Samoa[40] and to the Commonwealth of Puerto Rico.[41] In response, the United States has argued strenuously that in each of these cases the people of the territory have freely chosen an option other than independence as their preferred status.[42]

A special case in point for the United States is Micronesia or the Trust Territory of the Pacific Islands, the last remaining trusteeship territory and the only ''strategic trust'' established under Art. 82 of the United Nations Charter. Micronesia, which is made up of the Marshall, the Caroline, and the Mariana islands except for Guam, first came under the control of Spain, then Germany, and then was governed by Japan under a League of Nations mandate until Japan's defeat in World War II.[43] In 1947, the United States became the administering authority over the area under a trusteeship agreement with the United Nations. From 1947 until 1960, the United States largely neglected Micronesia. Then, in response to a strongly critical report of a United Nations visiting mission, the United States began to invest substantial sums of money, primarily in education and social services, and to negotiate with representatives of Micronesia regarding the future status of the islands.

These negotiations led in 1975 to the conclusion between the United States and the Mariana Islands of a Covenant to Establish a Commonwealth of the Northern Mariana Islands in Political Union with the United States of America.[44] The covenant was subject to approval by the Mariana Islands District Legislature, by the people of the Mariana Islands in a plebiscite, and by the U.S. Congress. The District Legislature unanimously adopted a resolution that approved the covenant for submission to the people of the islands in a plebiscite to be called by the United States. The plebiscite was held on June 17, 1975, under the supervision of a personal representative of the president of the United States in the presence of an observer-mission from the United Nations Trusteeship Council. The vote approved the covenant by 78.8 percent, with 95 percent of the registered voters in the islands participating.[45] On March 24, 1976, President Ford signed Public Law 94-241,[46] a joint resolution approving the covenant. Under the covenant, the islands would achieve commonwealth upon termination of the trusteeship agreement.[47] The United States has informed the Trusteeship Council that it intends to terminate the trusteeship agreement simultaneously for all parts of the trust territory and not for one part separately.[48]

In the Trusteeship Council, the Soviet Union has strongly criticized the United States for its actions in Micronesia. Specifically, it has charged that the United States is furthering separatist tendencies in Palau and in the Marshalls after separating the Marianas from the rest of the territory; that the United States has not allowed the people of Micronesia to choose independence, the proper outcome of self-determination; and that the United States has taken insufficient steps to fulfill its obligation to develop the territory.[49]

The Soviet Union's charges have been supported by a substantial amount of opinion within the United States.[50] These critics point out that, in the plebiscite on the Marianas, the people were not given a choice between free association and some other political status such as independence. Rather, they had either to accept the commonwealth arrangement or to face an uncertain future under the status quo. Indeed, these critics contend, the United States commenced separate negotiations with the Marianas because the territory-wide Congress of Micronesia began to consider the possibility of eventual independence.

The fragmentation process which started with the Marianas has continued apace. At the time of writing, the Marshalls and Palau have withdrawn from the Micronesian federation, leaving only the districts of Ponape, Truk, Yap, and Kosrae to constitute the Federated States of Micronesia. Moreover, recent reports indicate that the tiny Mortlock group and Faichuk Atoll, both administered from Truk, are demanding that they, too, be given separate political status. The Congress of Micronesia was formally dissolved in October 1978.[51]

The United States thus has failed to maintain unity in the territory. Moreover, the United States may encounter substantial difficulty in the Security Council when it seeks to terminate the trusteeship agreement. In the event the Council decides to oppose the U.S. proposal for termination, it is not clear whether the United States has the authority under the United Nations Charter and the trusteeship agreement to terminate the trust unilaterally without the Security Council's concurrence.[52]

The United States has also been criticized severely for its actions with respect to Spanish (Western) Sahara and Portuguese (East) Timor.[53] In both instances, the United States has supported, explicitly or tacitly, arrangements that failed to allow the peoples of the territories freely to choose between independence or some form of association or integration with neighboring states.

Most striking is the case of Spanish Sahara. Until 1974, the Spanish Sahara, a non-self-governing territory administered by Spain and bordered by Algeria, Morocco, and Mauritania, was regarded as a valueless stretch of desert.[54] Although both Morocco and Mauritania had indicated some interest in the territory based on historic claims these were not pursued. Perhaps as a result the United Nations treated the territory as it would any other whose independence it was promoting. Starting in 1966, the General Assembly asked Spain "to create a favorable climate for the referendum to be conducted on an entirely free, democratic and impartial basis . . . and to provide all the necessary facilities to a United Nations mission so that it could participate actively in the organization and holding of the referendum."[55]

In 1974, however, with the discovery of vast phosphate deposits and the likely existence of coal and iron, the situation changed dramatically. The Moroccan and Mauritanian governments decided to pursue their claims in the International Court of Justice by inducing the General Assembly to request an advisory opinion from the Court asking whether, before its colonialization by Spain, the Western Sahara had belonged to the Morocco empire or the Mauritanian "entity." The Assembly also called on Spain to postpone, pending the I.C.J.'s opinion, the holding of any referendum on the future status of the territory.

Although these tactics did succeed in blocking the holding of a referendum, they did not result in an I.C.J. opinion supportive of the Moroccan and Mauritanian claims. The Court found that there was no evidence of ties of territorial sovereignty between Western Sahara and Morocco or Mauritania "as might affect the application of Resolution 1514 (XV) in the decolonialization of Western Sahara and, in particular, of the principle of self-determination through the free and genuine expression of the will of the peoples of the Territory."[56]

While the I.C.J. was deliberating, a UN visiting mission was examining the situation in the Western Sahara. From its travels and its survey of opinion in the Sahara and in neighboring countries, "it became evident to the Mission that there was an overwhelming consensus among Sahrawis within the Territory in favour of independence and opposing integration with any neighboring country."[57]

These two adverse developments did not deter Moroccan ambitions. The day after the I.C.J. opinion, King Hassan's government announced a massive march of 350,000 "unarmed civilians" who would enter the Sahara "to gain recognition of its [Morocco's] right to national unity and territorial integrity."[58] Not long thereafter, the Spanish government, weakened by the precarious health of General Franco, yielded to pressure and entered into a tripartite agreement partitioning the territory between Morocco and Mauritania and permitting Spain to keep a 35 percent interest in Fosbucraa, the Saharan phosphate company.[59] Spain agreed to establish an interim regime in which a Spanish governor, assisted by Moroccan and Mauritanian deputy governors, would rule until February 28, 1976, at which time its responsibilities would terminate. Algeria, left out of the negotiations, declared that it would refuse to recognize the agreement and that it intended to arm Polisario, the pro-independence movement in the Sahara.

For its part, the United States joined with France in resisting all efforts to have the Security Council order Morocco to halt its march into the territory. It abstained on a General Assembly resolution that called upon Spain to arrange a free and genuine act of self-determination under UN supervision[60] and voted in favor of another, inconsistent, General Assembly resolution that took note of the agreement among Spain, Morocco, and Mauritania partitioning the territory and called on the secretary-general to "consult" with the three-power interim administration in order to "assist" it in holding a "free consultation" with the "Saharan populations."[61]

The United States similarly failed to support the principle of self-determination in the case of Portuguese (East) Timor. There, it abstained on a General Assembly resolution strongly deploring "the military intervention of the armed forces of Indonesia in Portuguese Timor" and calling upon Indonesia "to withdraw without delay . . . in order to enable the people of the Territory freely to exercise their right to self-determination and independence," while recommending to the Security Council "that it take urgent action to protect the territorial integrity of Portuguese Timor and the inalienable right of its people to self-determination."[62] In the Security Council, the United States abstained on a resolution that called on Indonesia "to withdraw without further delay all its forces from the Territory"[63] and resisted efforts to have the Council adopt more stringent measures under Chapter 7 of the Charter.[64]

In both the Saharan and Timorian cases, U.S. actions appear to have been motivated by realpolitik.[65] Morocco and Spain are regarded as protectors of key U.S. interests in the Mediterranean. Polisario, on the other hand, is viewed as suspect because of its ties to Algeria. The United States also wishes to maintain a government in power in Indonesia that is supportive of Western interests, and remembers past Communist attempts at subversion in that country.

Even from a realpolitik perspective, however, one may question whether U.S. interests have been served. At this writing, Algeria continues to support Polisario, and the ultimate outcome of the battle for Western Sahara remains to be determined. If Polisario emerges victorious, it is unlikely to forget U.S. support for the partition between Morocco and Mauritania and might constitute a serious threat to the viability of the Western-oriented regime of King Hassan. At any rate, U.S. tolerance of the historic claims of Morocco to the Western Sahara and of Indonesia to East Timor may have serious implications for such issues as the legitimacy of

Israel's existence, Spanish claims to Gibraltar, and Argentinian to the Falkland Islands. In the words of Professor Franck, "a realist must appreciate that a policy based on the application of force rather than principle has now 'lost' us both Vietnam and Angola while 'gaining' only the Spanish Sahara. If these are the results of a strategy based on winning, perhaps even political realists might yet be persuaded to try a strategy based on concern for normative reciprocal principles."[66]

Self-Determination and the Use of Armed Force

The invocation of self-determination as a justification for the use of armed force is a common practice in the world community, and the United States has repeatedly stressed the dangers such a practice poses to the maintenance of minimum world order. The United States has recognized a right of rebellion against an oppressive government but has resisted intervention by outside states in internal conflicts, citing provisions of the United Nations Charter[67] as well as express prohibitions in the Friendly Relations Declaration[68] and other applicable General Assembly resolutions.[69] In 1976, for example, the United States was one of only four states voting against a General Assembly resolution on self-determination which, inter alia, gave unqualified approval to the use of armed force in order to assist the peoples of Palestine, Namibia, Rhodesia (Zimbabwe), and South Africa to exercise their right to self-determination.[70]

In the southern Africa context, the United States has viewed military assistance to various groups engaged in "wars of national liberation" as contrary to the United Nations Charter and likely to undermine delicate negotiations in progress in Rhodesia, Namibia, and South Africa toward a peaceful resolution of the disputes in those areas. However, U.S. objections, on legal or other grounds, have had little effect as active military support of liberation groups has been forthcoming from many countries.

Three other situations may be briefly noted for purposes of illustrating the attitude of the United States toward the unilateral use of force in the name of self-determination: those of the Palestinians, Biafra, and Bangladesh. With respect to the Palestinians, the United States has resisted the claim that Israel's forceful denial of the Palstinians' right of self-determination gives them the right to respond with military force and to use the territory of neighboring Arab states as staging grounds for guerrilla attacks into Israel.[71]

In the case of Biafra's war of secession against the central government in Lagos, the United States maintained a strict neutral stance. By adopting this position, despite the protests of some scholars calling for "humanitarian intervention,"[72] the United States acted in accord with the overwhelming majority of member states of the world community. Only four African states (Tanzania, Zambia, Gabon, and Ivory Coast) went so far as to support Biafra by the limited step of diplomatic recognition,[73] and the Organization of African Unity took a firm stand in favor of a united Nigeria.[74]

The United States objected strongly to India's intervention in the conflict between West and East Pakistan, which was justified in part by a claim that West Pakistan was forcefully frustrating East Pakistan's right to self-determination.[75] At the time India intervened, the United States was reportedly engaged in negotiations with West Pakistan's government, attempting to induce it to desist from military actions in East Pakistan and to take steps to meet the legitimate demands of the people of East Pakistan for a greater role in governing their affairs.[76]

A critique of U.S. policy with respect to these three situations is beyond the scope of this chapter, although in none of these cases may it be said that U.S. policy was above reproach. However, this writer does favor U.S. opposition to the unilateral use of armed force undertaken in the name of self-determination. Support for unilateral military force, whether it be done under the rubric of "humanitarian intervention," "self-determination," or some other formula, is a sure prescription for chaos. It also is incompatible with the United Nations Charter, which has as its primary purpose the maintenance of international peace and security. States are already too willing to engage in the use of armed force to resolve disputes. Every effort should be made to discourage this tendency, not to promote it. Other means of protecting and promoting self-determination, such as global, regional, and national human-rights programs, are available and should be utilized more effectively. Utilization of these methods is more likely than armed force to advance and enhance the values the principle of self-determination seeks to protect.

Notes

1. Michla Pomerance, "The United States and Self-Determination: Perspectives on the Wilsonian Conception," *American Journal of International Law* 70, no. 1 (1976):1.

2. UN Charter, Arts. 1(2) and 55.

3. Art. 1 of both covenants.

4. The literature on self-determination is vast. A few of the more noteworthy writings include: U. O. Umozurike, *Self-Determination in International Law* (Hamden, Conn.: Shoe String Press, Archon Books, 1972); Eisuke Suzuki, "Self-Determination and World Public Order: Community Response to Territorial Separation," *Virginia Journal of International Law* 16, no. 4 (1976):781; Robert A. Friedlander, "Self-Determination: A Legal-Political Inquiry," *Detroit College of Law Review* 1, no. 1 (1975):1 (also reprinted as Chap. 13 in this volume); Lung-chu Chen, "Self-Determination as a Human Right," in *Toward World Order and Human Dignity,* ed. M. Reisman and B. Weston (New York: Free Press, 1976), pp. 198-261; Ved. P. Nanda, "Self-Determination in International Law: The Tragic Tale of Two Cities—Islamabad (West Pakistan) and Dacca (East Pakistan)," *American Journal of International Law* 66, no. 2 (1972):321; Rupert Emerson, "Self-Determination," *American Journal of International Law* 65, no. 3 (1971):459.

5. For discussions of this process, see Umozurike, *Self-Determination in International Law,* pp. 1-43; and Friedlander, "Self-Determination," pp. 71-75.

6. 15 UN GAOR Supp. 16, at 66, UN Doc. A/4684 (1960).

7. G.A. Res. 2625 and its annex, 25 UN GAOR Supp. 28, at 121, UN Doc. A/8028 (1970).

8. G.A. Res. 1514, operative paragraph 6.

9. Robert Rosenstock, "The Declaration of Principles of International Law concerning Friendly Relations: A Survey," *American Journal of International Law* 65, no. 5 (1971):713, 714-15.

10. G.A. Res. 2625, annex, pp. 122, 124.

11. See, e.g., Chen, "Self-Determination as a Human Right," pp. 227-39.

12. G.A. Res. 2625 and its annex, pp. 122, 124.

13. See Thomas C. Carey, "Self-Determination in the Post Colonial Era: The Case of Quebec," *ASILS International Law Journal* 1, no. 1 (1977):47, 54-55.

14. *U.N. Monthly Chronicle* 7 (Feb. 1970):36.

15. See Emerson, "Self-Determination," p. 465.

16. Carey, "Self-Determination in the Post Colonial Era," pp. 52-53.

17. *New York Times,* 3 January 1977, p. 7.

18. Ibid., 28 February 1976, p. 1.

19. Ibid., 7 June 1977, p. 35.

20. Ibid.

21. See Michael M. Gunter, "What Happened to the United Nations Ministate Problem?" *American Journal of International Law* 71, no. 1 (1977):110.

22. 660 U.N.T.S. 195. The text of the convention is reproduced in *Human Rights: A Compilation of International Instruments of the United Nations* (UN Public Sales No. V. 73, XIV.2, 1973), p. 23; L. Sohn and T. Buergenthal, *Basic Documents on International Protection of Human Rights* (New York: Bobbs-Merrill, 1973), p. 79.

23. For the text of the covenant, see Sohn and Buergenthal, *International Protection,* p. 44.

24. For a description of these procedures, see Malvina H. Guggenheim, "Key Provisions of the New United Nations Rules Dealing with Human Rights Petitions," *New York University Journal of International Law and Politics* 6, no. 3 (1973):427; see also John F. Murphy, "The United Nations and Human Rights: The Human Rights Commission in 1973-74," *Israel Yearbook on Human Rights* (Tel Aviv: Israel Press Ltd., 1974), pp. 48-59.

25. Publicists are divided on this issue, although there now appears to be a substantial majority in favor of the view that the principle of self-determination does enjoy the status of a legal norm in international law. For contrasting views, see Leslie C. Green, "Self-Determination and Settlement of the Arab-Israeli Conflict," *American Journal of International Law* 65, no. 4 (1971):40 (principle only); R. Higgins, *The Development of International Law through the Political Organs of the United Nations* (London and New York: Oxford University Press, 1963), p. 103 (legal norm).

26. See common Art. 1 of the International Covenants on Human Rights.

27. See especially Chen, "Self-Determination as a Human Right," and Suzuki, "Self-Determination and World Public Order."

28. See Thomas M. Franck and Nigel S. Rodley, "The Law, the United Nations and Bangla Desh," *Israel Yearbook on Human Rights* (Tel Aviv: Israel Press, Ltd., 1972), pp. 142-75.

29. Ibid.

30. Chen, "Self-Determination as a Human Right," p. 243.

31. See the report in *New York Times,* 3 January 1977, p. 7.

32. Subparagraph b.

33. Subparagraph b.

34. R. Russell and J. Muther, *A History of the United Nations Charter* (Washington, D.C.: Brookings Institution, 1958), p. 815.

35. UN Doc. A/Res. /RES/1541 (1960).

36. For statements made by the U.S. representative in the United Nations General Assembly in plenary sessions December 6 and 14, 1960, see 44 *Department of State Bulletin* no. 1123 (Jan. 2, 1961), pp. 21-27.

37. G.A. Res. 2625, including its annex.

38. Advisory Opinion on Western Sahara, [1975] I.C.J. 12.

39. Emerson, "Self-Determination," p. 470.

40. See, e.g., *U.N. Monthly Chronicle* 14 (Dec. 1977):47-51.

41. See *1975 Digest of United States Practice in International Law* (Washington, D.C.: Dept. of State, 1976), pp. 90-92.

42. See, e.g., *U.N. Monthly Chronicle* 14 (Dec. 1977):49.

43. For a more extensive history of Micronesia, see Donald F. McHenry, *Micronesia, Trust Betrayed: Altruism v. Self-Interest in American Foreign Policy* (New York: Carnegie Endowment for International Peace, 1975).

44. For the text of the covenant, see *International Legal Materials* 16, no. 2 (1975):344.

45. *1975 Digest*, p. 97.

46. 90 Stat. 263; 48 U.S.C. §1681 note.

47. Art. 1, sec. 101.

48. See *1976 Digest of United States Practice in International Law* (Washington, D.C.: Dept. of State, 1977), p. 59. The United States has announced that it hopes to terminate the trusteeship agreement by 1981 (*New York Times*, 29 December 1978, p. A3).

49. *U.N. Monthly Chronicle* 14 (July 1977):22, 54.

50. See, e.g., McHenry, *Micronesia, Trust Betrayed*.

51. *New York Times*, 7 February 1979, p. A12.

52. McHenry, *Micronesia, Trust Betrayed*, pp. 45-52.

53. See Thomas M. Franck, "The Stealing of the Sahara," *American Journal of International Law* 70, no. 4 (1976):694; Thomas M. Franck and Paul Hoffman, "The Right of Self-Determination in Very Small Places," *New York University Journal of International Law and Politics* 8, no. 3 (1976):331.

54. This discussion of the background to the Spanish Sahara case is drawn largely from Franck, "Stealing of the Sahara."

55. G.A. Res. 2229, 21 UN GAOR Supp. 16, at 73, UN Doc. A/6316 (1966).

56. Advisory Opinion on Western Sahara, p. 68.

57. *Report of the United Nations Visiting Mission to Spanish Sahara,* in *Report of the Special Committee,* UN Doc. A/10023/Add. 5, Annex (1975), p. 4.

58. Letter from the permanent representative of Morocco to the United Nations to the president of the Security Council, October 18, 1975, UN Doc. S/11852 (1975).

59. Franck and Hoffman, "Right of Self-Determination in Very Small Places," p. 341.

60. G.A. Res. 3458(A), UN Doc. GA/5438 (1975), pp. 254-55.

61. G.A. Res. 3458(B), ibid., p. 256.

62. G.A. Res. 3458, ibid., p. 262.

63. S. C. Res. 389 (1976).

64. Franck and Hoffman, "Right of Self-Determination in Very Small Places," p. 349.

65. Franck, "Stealing of the Sahara," p. 721.

66. Ibid.

67. See, e.g., UN Charter, Arts. 2(3) and (4) and 33(1).

68. G.A. Res. 2625 and its annex provides, under its first principle:

> Every state has the duty to refrain from organizing or encouraging the organization of irregular forces or armed bands, including mercenaries, for incursion into the territory of another state.
>
> Every state has the duty to refrain from organizing, instigating, assisting or participating in acts of civil strife or terrorist acts in another state or acquiescing in organized activities within its territory directed towards the commission of such acts, when the acts referred to in the present paragraph involve a threat or use of force.

69. See, e.g., the General Assembly's Declaration on the Inadmissibility of Intervention, which declares its deep concern at "the increasing threat to universal peace due to armed intervention and other direct or indirect forms of intervention threatening the sovereign personality and political independence of States," holds that "armed intervention is synonymous with aggression" and " a violation of the Charter of the United Nations," and condemns armed intervention "for any reason whatsoever" (G.A. Res. 2131 [20], Dedember 21, 1965, 20 GAOR, Supp. 14, pp. 11-12, UN Doc. A/6014).

70. *1976 Digest*, pp. 12-13.

71. For contending claims on this issue, see M. Cherif Bassiouni, "Self-Determination and the Palestinians," *American Journal of International Law* 65, no. 4 (1971):31; and Green, "Self-Determination and Settlement of the Arab-Israeli Conflict," p. 40.

72. See, e.g., Michael Reisman and Myres S. McDougal, "Humanitarian Intervention to Protect the Ibos," *Humanitarian Intervention and the United Nations*, ed. Lillich (Charlottesville, Va.: University Press of Virginia, 1973), pp. 167-95. Cf. Ian Brownlie, "Thoughts on Kind-Hearted Gunmen," ibid., pp. 139-48, and Jean-Pierre L. Fonteyne, "Forcible Self-Help by States to Protect Human Rights: Recent Views from the United Nations," ibid., pp. 197-221.

73. Franck and Rodley, "The Law, the United Nations, and Bangla Desh," p. 296.

74. Resolution passed by the Organization of African Unity heads of state, Kinshasa, September 1967, *International Legal Materials* 6, no. 6 (1967):1243.

75. Franck and Rodley, "The Law, the United Nations and Bangla Desh," pp. 159-63.

76. Ibid., p. 150.

4

Self-Determination: The Latin American Perspective

Natan Lerner

Self-Determination in Latin America

Self-determination, in its main external implications—as equivalent to the right of a people to *freely determine its political status* or, in other words, to be free from any alien sovereignty or to put an end to a colonial status—is, in global terms, no longer a goal yet to be achieved by the peoples of Latin America or of the Caribbean.

A decade and a half after the beginning of the emancipation process, only Cuba and Puerto Rico were still dependent upon Spain. Haiti gained its freedom in 1804, six years prior to the beginning of the continental struggle that began with military operations launched in 1810 and ceased by 1826. Brazil severed its ties with Portugal in a bloodless movement led by Regent Pedro in 1822. Cuba became independent in 1898. With a few exceptions—in 1838 the Central American Federation originated today's several republics, while the Dominican Republic seceded from Haiti in 1848—by the late 1820s, the map of Spanish-America was almost identical to that of today.

With regard to the non-Spanish Caribbean, the process of decolonization and independence took place much later. But the trend that began in 1958 with the creation of the West Indies Federation —which included the major islands, Jamaica, Trinidad, and Barbados —is today virtually an accomplished political fact with even the small islands enjoying self-government in association with Britain, which retains powers and responsibilities for defense and external affairs. Barbados, Grenada, Guyana, Jamaica, Surinam, and Trinidad and Tobago are sovereign members of the United Nations. The French and Dutch West Indies solved their problem by what one author calls "decolonization by incorporation."[1] In the most recent development, Dominica—a British associate state—became an independent republic and joined the British Commonwealth on 3 November 1978. The associated state of St. Vincent is to achieve full independence early in 1979, as agreed in September 1978 at a meeting between British and St. Vincent representatives.

The only Latin American territories with regard to which self-determination is still invoked today are Puerto Rico, Belize (British Honduras), and the Islas Malvinas (Falkland Islands). In the three cases, an absolute application of the principle of self-determination would involve consequences certainly not to the taste of those who champion that principle. When the war of independence of Spanish America and the nonviolent emancipation of Portuguese America culminated, the traditional colonial society had not suffered any radical transformation. However, the political aspect of self-determination was an accomplished fact for Latin America. And, as Art. 6 of the 1960 Declaration on the Granting of Independence to Colonial Countries and Peoples states,[2] any attempt aimed at the partial or total disruption of the national unity and territorial integrity of a country would be deemed incompatible with the UN Charter, and certainly with the interpretation by the UN majority of the notion of self-determination.

Therefore, any discussion of a Latin American perspective with regard to the subject of self-determination—to the extent that it is possible to refer to an all-embracing continental stand in this respect—does not imply a direct interest of the Latin American nations in their own self-determination, in the political sense, or their own struggle against colonization or foreign rule. The topics that still remain to be considered are mainly:

1. the attitude of the continent vis-à-vis self-determination on theoretical, doctrinal grounds, i.e., Latin America's views on self-determination when others are involved, and the position of Latin American spokesmen vis-à-vis the changing approaches in the concept of self-determination;
2. the few, already mentioned, individual instances in which

the right to self-determination is still considered by some an aim to be pursued in Latin America; and

3. the consequences of political self-determination and its full enjoyment, including internal self-determination.

The last includes the freedom of each people to select its form of government and to determine its degree of constitutional autonomy as well as its economic, social, and cultural systems, particularly the right of all peoples to freely dispose of their natural wealth and resources as proclaimed by two international covenants—one on civil and political rights and the other on economic, social, and cultural rights. Of course, this involves the right of every state to be free of any foreign intervention,[3] a permanent problem of Latin American international relations from the days of the Monroe Doctrine on. In this context, and since this is not the place to examine this matter, one should at least mention the question of the legitimacy of any foreign intervention aimed at terminating a situation that is contrary to the right of self-determination, as well as the relevance of the crisis of democracy and representative government to the whole subject of self-determination.[4] Woodrow Wilson already had this subject in mind when he linked recognition of Latin American governments to constitutionalism and self-government, even if "it is difficult to square some of Wilson's actions in Latin America with his principle of self-determination."[5]

Latin American writers and political leaders connect the concept of self-determination with the drive to eliminate any form of *dependency*, an aspiration that plays a role in Latin America that is equivalent to the quest of other peoples for self-determination.[6] For that reason, Latin American writers and politicians usually present their fight against U.S. economic penetration or domination as a struggle for self-determination.

While the history of self-determination "is bound up with the history of the doctrine of popular sovereignty proclaimed by the French Revolution,"[7] self-determination in its modern conception evolved after World War I—with Europe and the Middle East in the minds of those who proclaimed it—and achieved its present modified meaning much later at a stage when the continent politically was already virtually what it is today, with the exception of the Caribbean. This helps us to understand the silence of the major inter-American instruments on the subject, as well as the limited interest shown in it by Latin American authors or other authors writing on the inter-American system.

Minorities in Latin America

Sociological considerations and the Latin American approach to the question of minorities are also relevant. Since the question of external self-determination is related either to the struggle for liberation from foreign domination or to the subsistence of numerically significant minorities who live in a concentrated area, in certain provinces, or in defined regions within the framework of a large state from which they wish to be segregated, it is easy to understand why such an aim is not a problem directly concerning Latin America at present. In Latin America, there are no minorities seeking separation from the state in which they live. Although there are certainly groups on the continent which are bent on preserving their cultural, linguistic, ethnic, or religious individuality, none of them aspires to secede or pretends to enjoy rights other than those expressly recognized in Art. 27 of the UN Covenant on Civil and Political Rights, namely, to maintain their own culture, to profess and practice their own religion, or to use their own language.[8]

In this context, Latin America's political and legal traditions were always opposed to granting minorities special rights, similar to those recognized in Europe. Neither was there any demand for special rights. The Pan-American conferences of Lima (1938) and Mexico (1945) decided that it is sufficient to defend human rights in general, without according special protection to the collective rights of groups that could be defined as minorities from an ethnic, religious, or linguistic viewpoint. The Declaration of Lima stated specifically that "the system of protection of ethnic, linguistic or religious minorities cannot have any application in America, where conditions characterizing the groups to which that term refers do not exist." Some measures—like special protective laws for the indigenous populations, the recognition of collective rights for Indian communities, as in the Mexican Constitution of 1917 or the Mexican Civil Code of 1928, or the attachment of an official character to some native languages—do not imply a departure from this trend.

Rather, they belong to the category of acts of "inverted" or "favorable" discrimination that are accepted as legitimate in order to compensate handicapped sectors of the population that would otherwise remain at a disadvantage.

Since irredentist minorities do not exist in Latin America, it is quite clear that political self-determination could not be a claim put forward by any group on the continent. The existing minorities do have problems, most of which are related to insufficient recognition on the part of the monolithic majority and to the need to develop and consolidate a pluralistic society similar to that which exists in countries like the United States or Canada. However, self-determination is not one of their problems.

The Inter-American System and Self-Determination

As said, continental legal instruments do not refer by name to the principle of self-determination. In contrast to Art. 1(2) of the UN Charter, there is no mention of the word self-determination in the OAS Charter, which stresses the notions of sovereignty and nonintervention. The preamble refers to the desire of the American people, through their respect for the sovereignty of each one, to provide for the betterment of all, in independence, in equality and under law. Article 1 proclaims that the OAS is established, inter alia, to defend the sovereignty of the American states, their territorial integrity, and their independence. Article 5(b) enunciates, among the principles to which American states adhere, the respect for the personality, sovereignty, and independence of states as a component of international order.

In what is essentially a ratification, in other words, of the right of self-determination, Art. 9 establishes that the political existence of the state is independent of recognition by other states.[9] Even before being recognized, the state has those rights that are inherent in its sovereign existence, among them, the right to defend its integrity and independence, to provide for its preservation and prosperity, and to organize itself as it sees fit, subject to no other limitations than the exercise of the rights of other states in accordance with international law.

Article 13 deals with the free development of each state, while Art. 15 refers to one of the main rules of the inter-American system, nonintervention: No state or group of states has the right to intervene, directly or indirectly, for any reason whatever, in the internal or external affairs of any other state. This prohibition includes not only the use of force but also any other form of interference or attempted threat against the personality of the state or against its political, economic, and cultural elements. In the same direction, Art. 16 forbids the use of coercive measures of an economic or political character in order to force the sovereign will of another state.

There is no mention of the right of self-determination in the American Declaration of the Rights and Duties of Man, adopted in 1948 in Bogotá. The American Convention on Human Rights, in force since 18 July 1978 when Grenada became the eleventh country to ratify it, does not contain any article similar to Art. 1 of both international covenants and does not mention the word self-determination.

There is also no official stand of the Organization of American States on the theoretical problem of self-determination. As stated in a note (dated 3 May 1975) to Héctor Gros Espiell, the special rapporteur appointed by the UN Sub-Commission on Prevention of Discrimination and Protection of Minorities to prepare a study on "implementation of United Nations resolutions relating to the right of peoples under colonial and alien domination to self-determination," the General Secretariat of the OAS refused to give any views on the meaning of the right of self-determination from the point of view of the implementation of UN resolutions on that right, "either on behalf of the Organization or on its own behalf." Moreoever, the OAS would not comment on the meaning of the term "peoples under colonial and alien domination" from the point of view of the implementation of the aforementioned resolutions.[10]

In the same note, the General Secretariat of the OAS mentions a series of resolutions adopted by inter-American bodies connected, in one way or another, with the questions of colonialism and self-determination. They are as follows: Resolution 16 of the First Meeting of Consultation (Panama, 1939), on the Transfer of Sovereignty of Geographic Regions of the Americas Held by Non-American States; Resolution 20 of the Second Meeting of Consultation (Havana, 1940), concerning the Provisional Administration of European Colonies and Possessions in the Americas; the Convention on the Provisional Administration of European Colonies and Possessions in the Americas, also agreed upon at the Second Meeting of Consultation; Resolution 33 of the Ninth Inter-American Conference (Bogotá, 1948), on Colonies and Occupied Territories in America and Creation of the American Committee on Dependent Territories; Resolution 6 of the Fourth Meeting of Consultation (Washington, 1951), on Reaffirmation of Inter-American Principles Regarding European Colonies and Possessions in the Americas; Resolution 96 on Colonies and Occupied Territories in America, Resolution 97 on Colonies in American Territory, and Resolution 98 on the American Committee on Dependent Territories, all of the Tenth Inter-American Conference (Caracas, 1954); AG/RES. 107 (III-0/73) adopted by the General Assembly of the OAS at its third regular session (1973), on a Study of the Provisions of the Charter of the Organization on the Admission of New Members; AG/RES. 155 (IV-0/74) adopted by the Assembly at its fourth regular session (1974), on Information on the Constitutional Evolution of the Nonautonomous Territories in the American Hemisphere and other Territories in the Americas Having Ties with Countries outside the Hemisphere; Resolution adopted in 1974 by the Inter-American Juridical Committee on Territorial Colonialism in America, and the resolution of the same committee adopted in 1976 on the Islas Malvinas.

Latin American Views on Self-Determination

Fenwick stresses that the controversial principle of self-determination remains in America, as in the world at large, a political one, not subject to specific rules of law.[11] Perhaps as a result of this approach, Latin American authors in the field of international law do not devote much consideration to the subject. For instance, a classic Argentinean author, L. A. Podestá Costa, points out that "the principle of self-determination, applied through a plebiscite, can be useful in some cases in order to define the future of a borderline region; but it cannot be accepted in absolute terms and, in some cases, it has to be subordinated to given circumstances of greater economic and political importance."[12]

Another Argentinean author and diplomat, Mario Amadeo, only

mentions the right of self-determination in order to assert that it becomes an illusion when a country is economically subordinated to foreigners or when "a colonial mentality prevails in its leaders."[13] A former foreign minister of Guatemala, Carlos Garcia Bauer, criticizes the inclusion of the right to self-determination—a collective and not individual right—in the covenants.[14]

Different is the approach of Gros Espiell, the aforementioned Uruguayan special *rapporteur* appointed by the Sub-Commission on Prevention of Discrimination and Protection of Minorities. In his study, he describes thoroughly the present line of the UN majority in the interpretation of the concept of self-determination. He deals with the legitimacy of the use of force by "liberation movements" who are "fighting against colonial and alien domination" and considers that such movements "have rights and obligations which contemporary international law has been conferring upon them on an increasing scale," and they "can be regarded as subjects of international law." Gros Espiell reaches the conclusion that "the breach by a State of an obligation deriving from the recognition by international law of the right of peoples to self-determination, especially a violation of the duty to refrain from establishing or maintaining colonial domination by force, is an international crime."[15]

As to the views expressed by Latin American governments in the United Nations and in other international forums, they follow the conventional line of supporting decolonization and expressing full solidarity with the Afro-Asian bloc in the United Nations. Latin America, stated a Latin American spokesman,[16] shares with Africa and with all developing regions "special affinities which were rooted in history" and considers right the denunciation of "the policy of the colonial Powers which obstinately prevented the peoples under their domination from acceding to self-determination and independence." This does not only imply support for the national struggles for political self-determination. "In addition to the struggle against colonialism, constant vigilance was required to guard against new forms of colonialism and exploitation and the attempts of industrial powers to colonize the seas."[17] "The nineteenth century had seen the end of slavery, but with it the emergence of a new form of man's domination by man, colonialism, and while the form of colonialism which had developed parallel with the commercial revolution and European expansion of the sixteenth, seventeenth and eighteenth centuries had come to an end on the American continent with the proclamations of independence first by the United States in the eighteenth century and later by the Spanish and Portuguese possessions in Latin America in the nineteenth, there had arisen a new form of colonialism associated with technological and economic change, and one of the purposes of the United Nations was to eliminate it."[18] Support for Resolution 1514 (15), "the catalyst which mobilized the efforts to promote decolonization," is reputed "one of the General Assembly's greatest achievements."[19]

One could quote other statements that follow this conventional pattern. Those already mentioned seem sufficient, however, to demonstrate that the Latin American governments do not lag in voicing complete theoretical identification with the outcry against all forms of colonization and endorsing the Third World view of the concept of self-determination. It is not presented by the Latin Americans as a problem of their own countries, except in the context of the struggle against dependence and in relation to the few remaining cases which constitute a "remnant of colonial expansion in America."[20] Three such cases are on the international agenda.

The Puerto Rican Case

The best-known case, as well as the most important from a demographic viewpoint, is, of course, that of Puerto Rico, which is still under discussion in the United Nations Decolonization Committee. The Puerto Rican case is an exercise in political philosophy in connection with the notion of self-determination. The controversy—within Puerto Rico as well as among Puerto Ricans residing in the United States—with regard to the alternatives of annexation, independence, autonomy, or associate status, well illustrates the extent to which the idea of self-determination is not equivalent to that of independence.

The discussion will reemerge in connection with the 1980 elections, at which the traditional Partido Popular Democrático (PPD) —led by Luis Muñoz Marín, considered the father of the scheme of the Estado Libre Asociado—the Partido Socialista Popular (PSP), and the Partido Independentista Puertorriqueño (PIP) will campaign against full statehood or annexation, supported by the presently ruling Partido Nuevo Progresista (PNP) led by Carlos Romero Barceló.[21]

At present, the formal situation is still the one prevailing since 1952 when Puerto Rico—ceded by Spain to the United States in 1898—acquired the status of a free associated state,[22] as proposed by Luis Muñoz Marín and his party. In 1967, a referendum took place that reaffirmed the commonwealth tie, by a vote in which about 65 percent of those eligible participated. The fact that only 60 percent of those voting favored continuing the present status is seen by those opposing it as an indication of only a minority support for this scheme.

In 1972, the United Nations Decolonization Committee began the discussion of the issue of Puerto Rico. In 1976, the Tanzanian chairman of the committee issued a statement, after the committee had postponed discussion of the subject, reaffirming "the inalienable right of the people of Puerto Rico to self-determination and independence in accordance with General Assembly Resolution 1514 of December 1960." In his statement, the chairman referred to decisions taken in support of Puerto Rican independence at the conferences of nonaligned countries in Lima (1974) and Colombo (August 1976).

On 12 September 1978, the United Nations Decolonization Committee approved—by a vote of ten in favor, including the Soviet Union and China, and twelve abstentions, including Chile and Trinidad and Tobago—a Cuban proposal placing Puerto Rico on the UN's list of colonies. The resolution, which is interpreted as a serious setback for the United States and Puerto Rico's pro-statehood forces, includes a point stating that before there can be a plebiscite on the question of the island's status, the United States must withdraw. Does this international support of Puerto Rico's right to self-determination as equivalent to independence reflect a similar stand on the part of the majority of the island's population? Was the 1967 referendum a true expression of the people's wishes? The 1980 elections might be able to provide replies to these questions.

In the meantime, the increase in violence on the part of the Fuerzas Armadas de Liberación Nacional (FALN) is adding an ominous dimension to the theoretical discussion, complicated enough by the contradictory influences of nationalist feelings on the one hand, and economic advantages resulting from the association with the United States on the other.[23] Offshore oil and the controversy over the extension of territorial rights also are playing a significant role.[24]

In any case, the question of self-determination is still open in Puerto Rico. As long as there is no clear-cut expression of the collective will of an indisputable majority of Puerto Ricans, one can hardly judge if to the interested people self-determination means precisely what it does to the UN majority.

Belize

The case of Belize (British Honduras)[25] is not a simple case of self-determination versus colonialism or foreign domination. Several states were involved in the problem, giving it a multilateral character. Until 1798, Belize was legally Spanish territory in which the British settlers, there since 1638, enjoyed certain rights. The status of the colony was undefined after the Spanish defeat in 1798. The governments of Britain and Guatemala signed a treaty in 1859, by which Guatemala recognized the British rights to the area while Britain undertook to build a highway to Guatemala City. Because the highway was never implemented, Guatemala kept alive its claims to Belize, virtually since the beginning of Central American independence. In 1862, British Honduras formally became a British colony and, in 1884, an "independent colony."

Mexico has officially stated that it has no claim to Belize after signing a border treaty with Great Britain in 1893.[26] The main protagonists of the problem today are, therefore, the governments of Britain and Guatemala[27] and the racially heterogeneous population (114,255 according to a 1966 estimate). The United Nations and its Special Committee on the Situation with Regard to the Implementation of the Declaration of the Granting of Independence to Colonial Countries and Peoples have dealt with the subject. At its 1977 session, the General Assembly adopted Resolution 32-33 which recalls former and similar resolutions on the subject, reaffirms the inalienable right of the people of Belize to self-determination and independence, and urges all states to respect the right of the people of Belize to self-determination, independence, and territorial integrity. The resolution was adopted by 126 votes—including those of the United Kingdom and Mexico—against 4—the Central American republics of Costa Rica, El Salvador, Honduras, and Nicaragua—with 13 abstentions. Guatemala did not take part in the vote.

The Malvinas

The Islas Malvinas or Falkland Islands are a typical case in which historical titles clash with the principle of self-determination, provided one takes the view that self-determination may be exercised by even a tiny population of small territories. In this case, all the limitations of the "adaptable" character and nuances of self-determination arise from the peculiar situation of those small territories for which the international community is trying to find an appropriate status.[28]

The islands, three hundred miles off the South American continent in the Atlantic Ocean, have been held by Britain since 1832. Argentina has been claiming them since 1828. Living there are about two-thousand people, almost all of whom are of British birth or descent, and their desire to continue as a British colony seems beyond doubt, permitting the British to invoke the principle of self-determination. It is clear that the islands cannot become an independent state. On the other hand, the historical titles of Argentina seem well established, and its government argues that it would be irrelevant to consult the tiny population. Like Puerto Rico, the Islas Malvinas could become an example of cases in which "forcing independence upon an unwilling people may violate the principle of self-determination as much as foisting upon a population an alien sovereignty."[29]

Negotiations between Argentina and Britain are under way, with a view to "achieve a stable, prosperous and politically durable future for the Islands, whose people the Government of the United Kingdom will consult during the course of the negotiations." The agreement to hold the negotiations, and the negotiations themselves, "are without prejudice to the position of either Government with regard to sovereignty over the Islands." The negotiations "will be directed to the working out of a peaceful solution to the existing dispute on sovereignty between the two States, and the establishment of a framework for Anglo-Argentine economic cooperation which will contribute substantially to the development of the Islands and the region as a whole."[30]

The Organization of American States, through its Inter-American Juridical Committee, took, in this case, a clear-cut position, declaring that "the Argentine Republic has an incontrovertible right of sovereignty over the Malvinas, and that accordingly the fundamental question to be decided is the procedure to follow for the reintegration of its territory." The committee recalled that "the authentic ideals of our Republics call for putting an end to all occupation, usurpation, enclaves or any form whatever of the continued existence of colonial rule in the Americas."[31] The subject of the desire of the population is not mentioned.

Repeatedly, the United Nations has declared that Resolution 1514 applies to the Malvinas.[32] Recently, in Resolution 31/49 of 1 December 1976, the General Assembly expressed "its gratitude for the continuous efforts made by the Government of Argentina . . . to facilitate the process of decolonization and to promote the well-being of the population of the islands," and called upon the parties "to refrain from taking decisions that would imply introducing unilaterial modifications in the situation."

Conclusions

Self-determination in its political, external meaning is one of the fundamental human rights that were implemented in most countries of Latin America long ago. With the exception of a few cases in which self-determination is still being discussed within the context of the undecided future of certain territories, Latin Americans have no claims left with regard to emancipation from alien domination. They do aspire to be able to fully exercise some of the rights that are the consequence of political self-determination. This should include the unrestricted enjoyment of their economic resources, the possibility of being free of any foreign intervention in their internal affairs, and full, internal self-determination, as equivalent to the right of peoples to freely elect their governments and enjoy the advantages of democracy.

Thus, Latin America is one of the areas of the Third World where self-determination is not a direct and immediate concern of the peoples. Considering themselves part of the Third World, spokesmen for Latin America went along with the new trends advocated in the international community by Third World representatives. Their theoretical support for decolonization and self-determination is adequately recorded.

Concerning the remaining problems, Puerto Rico is an example of the fact that self-determination and political independence do not always have the same meaning. Time will tell if Puerto Ricans, exercising the right to freely express their will, will opt for independence or less than that. If their democratically expressed wish is in favor of association or of another form of political organization, it will be interesting to observe the reaction of the UN majority.

In the case of Belize, overseas colonization conflicts with territorial interests of bordering states. Self-determination is at stake, but it is not the only consideration. With regard to the Malvinas, self-determination clashes with historical titles. Advocates of decolonization are in no position to support self-determination in the case of the tiny Malvinas population.

It does not seem risky, therefore, to conclude that, to Latin Americans, interest in self-determination is not a major issue in the wide spectrum of troublesome problems affecting the continent.

Notes

1. Colin G. Clarke, "The Quest for Independence in the Caribbean," review article in *Journal of Latin American Studies* 9, part 2 (Nov. 1977), pp. 337-45.

2. Resolution 1514 (15), UN General Assembly, 15th sess., Official Records, Supp. 16 (A/4684), p. 66.

3. See D. W. Bowett's remarks in this respect in his address on "Self-Determination and Political Rights in the Developing Countries," at the Sixtieth Annual Meeting of the American Society of International Law, *Proceedings* (Washington, D.C.: 1966), pp. 132-33.

4. Cf. Rupert Emerson, "Self-Determination," *American Journal of International Law* 65, no. 3 (July 1971), p. 65.

5. Cf. Michla Pomerance, "The United States and Self-Determination: Perspectives on the Wilsonian Conception," *American Journal of International Law* 70, no. 1 (Jan. 1976), pp. 15-16.

6. The indiscriminate use of the "dependency" theory to explain all the

problems of Latin America has already been denounced by some authors (see, for instance, Phillipe Schmitter, "Paths to Political Development in Latin America," in Douglas A. Chalmers, ed., *Changing Latin America, New Interpretations of Its Politics and Society* [New York, 1972], pp. 99-100).

7. A. Rigo Sureda, *The Evolution of the Right of Self-Determination* (Leiden, 1973), p. 17.

8. On minorities in Latin America, see Natan Lerner, "Nationalism and Minorities in Latin America," *Patterns of Prejudice* 11, no. 1 (Jan.-Feb. 1977), pp. 17-22.

9. Cf. Charles G. Fenwick, *The Organization of American States* (Washington, D.C., 1963), p. 295. The author, a former director of the Department of Legal Affairs of the Pan-American Union, points out that this principle, already laid down in the Montevideo Convention of 1933, "appears to represent an attempt by the American States to proclaim the right of their own self-determination, whether or not the mother country or any other state refused to recognize the fact of their independence."

10. UN Doc. E/CN.4/Sub.2/390, 22 June 1977, p. 60. For some of the resolutions mentioned, see also *The Inter-American System* (New York, 1966), pp. xxviii ff.

11. Fenwick, *Organization of American States,* p. 295.

12. *Derecho internacional público,* 3rd ed. (Buenos Aires, 1955), vol. 1, p. 65.

13. *Política internacional* (Buenos Aires, 1970), p. 103.

14. *Los Derechos humanos preocupación universal* (Guatemala, 1960), p. 140.

15. Ibid., pp. 22, 109.

16. Statement by Honduran delegate Lopez Villamil, speaking on behalf of his country, Ecuador, Venezuela, and Argentina, 12 June 1969 (UN Doc. A/AC.109/SR.676, p. 11).

17. Statement by Ecuadoran delegate Sevilla Borja, speaking on behalf of all Latin American countries, 18 May 1972 (UN Doc. A/AC.109/SR.863, p. 5).

18. The same delegate on 23 May 1972 (UN Doc. A/AC.109/SR.869, p. 8).

19. The Argentinean delegate, Mr. Guzzetti, 5 October 1976 (UN Doc. A/31/PV. 18, p. 67).

20. Ibid., pp. 68-70.

21. It was a great disappointment to the supporters of annexation to learn that only 20 percent of U.S. public opinion shared their view. Thirty-two percent favored autonomy, while 29 percent were in favor of total independence. (*Latin American Political Report,* 28 July 1978, p. 227).

22. "Free association" with an independent state is one of the alternatives to independence considered in resolutions 742 (8) and 1541 (15) of the United Nations. Here, we cannot go into the question of the presence in the Puerto

Rican case of all the factors enumerated in UN General Assembly Resolution 742 (8) which indicate the existence of free-association status.

23. Nationalist authors advocating full independence do not accept the view that the present status involves economic advantages for the Puerto Rican people. "Poverty, unemployment, and dependence upon food 'gifts' from the metropolis are still the lot of the majority of Puerto Ricans," writes Manuel Maldonado-Denis, editor of the *Revista de ciencias sociales* ("Puerto Rico: An American Showcase for Latin America," in *Latin American Radicalism*, ed. I. L. Horowitz, Josué de Castro, and John Gerassi [London, 1969], p. 362). For a comprehensive description of the Puerto Rican situation, see Robert A. Crampsey, *Puerto Rico* (Newton Abbot, Eng., 1973).

24. *Latin American Political Report*, 14 July 1978, p. 214; *International Herald Tribune*, 18 July 1978; *Newsweek*, 11 September 1978.

25. On the Belize case, for example, G. Santiso Galves, *El caso de Belice* (Guatemala, 1975). A more recent book is C. H. Grant *The Making of Modern Belize* (New York, 1976).

26. See in UN Doc. E/CN.4/Sub.2/SR.715-31/Add.1 and 736-42, p. 116, statement by the Mexican representative recalling the historical rights of Mexico and its tradition of refraining from invoking those rights as opposed to the right of self-determination by the people of Belize.

27. On recent diplomatic developments affecting Belize, see *Latin American Political Report*, 27 January 1978, p. 25.

28. Denise Mathy, "L'autodétermination de petits territoires revendiqués par des Etats tiers," *Revue belge de droit international* (1974), p. 205. See also Jonathan G. Cohen, "Les Iles Falkland (Malvinas)" *Annuaire française de droit international* 18 (Paris, 1972), pp. 235-62.

29. Pomerance, "United States and Self-Determination," p. 4.

30. Joint United Kingdom–Argentine communiqué of 26 April 1977.

31. Declaration of 18 January 1976, transcribed in Gros Espiell, pp. 102-3.

32. See General Assembly Resolution 2065 (20) of 1965.

Part 3

Europe and the Soviet Union

5

Self-Determination:
Western European Perspectives

Harold S. Johnson

Self-determination has its legal and conceptual roots in Western Europe. Its rise paralleled that of the nation-state, and its meaning evolved from the consciousness of group identity and expectations evident in the rise of nationalism during the eighteenth and nineteenth centuries. Nationalism was itself the belief in the predominance of an identifiable group, a nation, as a social and political unit. Its objective was the sovereign status of the national unit.

The nationalism that evolved in Western Europe maintained a political foundation, characterized by a pluralistic and open society. It conceived of the nation as a union of rational citizens, and its development arose from internal forces with leadership from the middle class and organized labor. It did not evolve in response to opposition but, rather, emerged from the social and political forces internal to each state. Because Western nationalism was pluralistic and open, it has maintained a democratic base. When the state became the people's, it became theirs as a nation. Identity rested on the consent of the people as a nation. The exercise of this right—as it was claimed—depended upon the relationship that was believed to exist between nationalism and democracy, which claims that government should rest on the consent of the governed.

The linkage between nationalism and democracy was the early significance of the French Revolution. In the birth of popular sovereignty, the sovereignty of the monarch was transferred to the people, but the unit in which this sovereignty was to be operative was the nation. It was a nation in that people were to consent to be governed. If people were sovereign as a nation, they had to be free to form their own state, and the state had to be free to establish its own government. Each people had an inherent right not only to choose their own form of government but to determine their status as a state. These choices mark the difference between internal and external self-determination. The first concerns the right of a people to form a national unit. The second concerns the right of the national unit to determine its own destiny, primarily in the form of a state. The concept of nationalism has come to be associated with the latter. Democracy provides the justification and means for the former.

Western Europe's initial perspective regarding self-determination was national. It was a blend of democracy—which suggested that, as a nation, people ought to be sovereign—with nationalism, which placed loyalty in the nation. Democratic theory, as evident in the late eighteenth century and throughout the nineteenth, claimed that since the nation did rest on the consent of the people it was sovereign and could determine its own status as a state. The resulting national state was regarded as the political expression of the democratic will of the people as well as the fulfillment of their national aspirations.

The democratic basis for the Western nation remains a significant characteristic in the Western European perspective on self-determination. This emphasis in the nineteenth century began to remove distinctions between external and internal aspects of the concept. National identity, as a basis for a claim, was increasingly recognized to be valid only when internal processes were considered democratic, an assumption that has become questionable in this century. Internal self-determination became the dominant means for determining the nationality upon which external self-determination could be based. The identity of the national unit was conditioned on a process of choice, defined by democratic means. Self-determination in concept became this process. There would be no right to determination as a national unit unless the process for determining the unit were democratic. In the initial debates in the United Nations Commission on Human Rights and in the Third Committee of the General Assembly concerning the meaning of an alleged right of self-determination, the Western European members, who included the major colonial powers, suggested that *if* there were a universal right, it could not be confined to dependent areas but ought to be extended to all people, regardless of where they lived, who had been denied full participation in the affairs of their government. Emphasis was placed on the need for self-determination within the satellite states of Eastern Europe. The position of the Western powers was articulated by the U.S. delegation which stated that in most cases self-determination, a process for determining the wishes of the majority and involving the freedom of a group to become the majority, preceded the granting of self-government or independence.

In the eighteenth and nineteenth centuries, Western European nationalism had emphasized the right of self-governing peoples to determine their own international status. In the twentieth century, faced by the claims of dependent peoples for independence, the emphasis was shifted to the principles of self-government upon which the right could be based.

I

The debates brought focus on a conceptualization of self-determination as either a status or a process, or both. In regard to status, the focus has been on the independence of a people within the international system. The evolution of the principle of self-determination as it found its place in the Charter of the United Nations focused on "respect for the principle of equal rights and self-determination of peoples."[1] The principle, as stated, was introduced by the Soviet Union during the Big Four consultations at San Francisco. It became a sponsors' amendment, without any discussion or interpretation being noted in the American records. During a press conference, Soviet Foreign Minister Molotov indicated that his government supported the movement for dependent countries to achieve national independence as soon as possible. Soviet usage meant to differentiate "nations" from already independent "states."[2]

Hans Kelsen has stated that Art. 1, para. 2, of the United Nations Charter referred to the relations among states. Therefore, he concluded that the term "peoples," in connection with "equal rights," meant states, since only states have "equal rights" according to general international law. Self-determination of peoples, he concluded, meant the sovereignty of the states. The combined principle of equal rights and the self-determination of peoples meant the sovereign equality of the states.[3]

Initial application of this principle during the first two decades of the United Nations was conditioned by the anti-colonial posture of the majority of the membership. In the discussions that took place in the United Nations Commission on Human Rights and in the Third Committee of the General Assembly, the majority of members suggested that the right of self-determination meant that people, especially those of non-self-governing territories, were to decide their own international status. A right was claimed for a majority within a given territory, not considered to be an integral part of another state, which was under the domination of a foreign power. This right, however, was not to be applied to territories which were an integral part of a national entity, so as not to destroy the unity of a nation. The basic principle within the right was that of national sovereignty. Under anti-colonial influence, self-determination meant the achievement of national independence, a status which given "nations" had a right to claim.

The initial position of the colonial powers, and thus Western Europe, was that the principle of self-determination as stated in the United Nations Charter referred to the recognition of the sovereignty of states and their obligation to respect the sovereignty of other states. A people were sovereign because they had equal status with other people. The international system was structured as a system of equal states, the territorial integrity of which was to be respected.

The colonial powers did not welcome interference in the administration of their overseas territories, some of which were considered to be integral parts of an extended national entity. This was the case with Algeria, the overseas Portuguese territories, and some of the Spanish possessions. The international organization rejected all claims that these territories were not colonial and was less willing to allow any form of self-government short of independence for the nationalist movements of the more important territories.

In effect, all members of the United Nations recognized the status of a sovereign entity as inherent in the concept of self-determination. The colonial powers gave emphasis to the existing status they held as the administering authorities over colonial territories. The anti-colonial powers claimed the status for groups they concluded ought to be independent. The colonial powers, conditioned by their own Western heritage, rooted their own sovereign status on the consent of the governed. In their view, status and process were fused. They saw no inconsistency in recognizing sovereignty to rest on consent, in concluding that people could consent to exercise their sovereignty in forms less than independence, and yet rationalizing that only people who had achieved political maturity should be included in the process by which consent would be registered.

The right as claimed by the anti-colonial powers, which included most African, Asian, and Latin American countries, was a limited right. It was to be applied to the territories they considered to be non-self-governing. The United Nations Declaration on the Granting of Independence to Colonial Countries and Peoples (December 14, 1960) resolved that subjection of peoples to alien governance is contrary to the Charter of the United Nations and recommended that political power in all dependent territories be transferred to the people in accordance with their freely expressed will. The General Assembly Resolution (1514) stated further that "inadequacy of political, economic, social or educational preparedness should never serve as a pretext for delaying independence."[4] The Special Committee of Twenty-Four has repeatedly emphasized that, regardless of size, population, or economic conditions, all non-self-governing territories are entitled to enjoy fully the rights set out in the resolution.

The Western European powers, because of these movements toward independence, were confronted with the erosion of their empires. This issue dominated the agenda at the United Nations. Independence of all non-self-governing territories was the goal. Partly defensive, and partly ideological, the Western European powers suggested the extension of the claim for self-determination to peoples, recognized as sovereign, whose circumstances within a given state questioned their degree of political participation and, as such, their status as self-governing. The emphasis was given to the status of the people rather than the territory. If the political processes were not democratic, a people were not considered to be self-determining. Status shifted from international to national, from external to internal. People could not be independent internationally if not internally. In order to have equal status within a state, people must be fully recognized as participants within the internal political processes. Self-determination of a people became identified with the political processes by which a people continued to determine and express their wishes, not only regarding their status legally, but the meaning and fulfillment thereof.

The Western attack on the Soviet satellite system evolved as an inquiry into the depth as well as the scope of self-determination. It is a claim not only that a group shall be free to exist as an association for the majority to shape the destiny of the group. This is the significance of the Western European perspective regarding self-determination as a concept.

II

Paradoxically, while defending their existing status based on their claimed democratic process, the Western European states provided the rationale for adjustments in that status as the democratic processes came under review. History had placed many groups, especially in Europe, in a minority status. It would be highly explosive to allow an unrestricted claim for any group, minority, population of foreign origin, indigenous race, or irredentist faction which felt that it had a grievance.

No state within the United Nations has supported a right to secession, and few states would extend a right of self-determination to minority secessionist movements. The technical committee responsible for outlining the purposes and principles for the United Nations at the San Francisco Conference indicated that the principles of self-determination conformed to the purposes of the Charter only insofar as it implied the right of self-government and not the right of secession.[5]

The dilemma which persisted during the period of debate over self-government rested in claimed distinctions between external and internal self-determination, a distinction that became increasingly difficult for states with a democratic base to clarify. It is one thing to claim that self-determination of peoples should govern the relations that exist among states and another to suggest that it should also govern the relations within a state between a people and their government. To do so is to suggest the means for disintegration of the present, international state system. A Lebanese delegate to the United Nations considered the question as to whether or not people were allowed by their own governments to exercise internal self-determination.[6] He maintained that the question of when to grant a minority the right of self-determination remained unanswered. For those states that equated the right with independence, once a recognized unit (people or nation) had exercised the right, no further recourse was allowable. Rupert Emerson records that in respect to the definition of a "people" entitled to exercise the right of self-determination under the auspices of the United Nations, "once the newly created or newly independent state is in existence, no resort to further self-determination is tolerable."[7]

Following World War I and during World War II, Western European powers gave limited support to a principle of self-determination. In the Paris Peace Conference in 1919 the concept had an appeal whenever it appeared that, by consulting with a given population through a plebiscite, the territory and power of the defeated states could be reduced. President Wilson's central principle, as stated to the Peace Conference on February 24, 1920, was that no government or group of governments had the right to dispose of the territory of or to determine the political allegiance of a free people.[8] Wilson's principle of self-determinaton was utilized to facilitate the territorial adjustments during the peace negotiations. In no case was his concept of national self-determination recognized to the detriment of the victorious Allies. The principle was not a means to justify what the Allies had taken, but only what they might hope to take. With the exception of the Saar question, the western frontier of Germany was determined by other factors. In the east, the frontiers between Poland and Czechoslovakia were determined by other means. Some eastern areas were of doubtful nationality. Furthermore, because some anticipated changes would have put many Germans under what might have been regarded as a less-advanced culture, it was believed, particularly by the British, that it was advisable to consult those inhabitants directly.

The peacemakers in 1919 did not use direct consultations for national liberation. Rather, they set about to sort out the pieces. The task was to match territories with existing nationalities; that is, groups that were already exerting control over definite areas.

While recognizing certain rights for national minorities, it was only to a recognized national majority that a right to self-determination was extended. The use of the plebiscite determined which nationality was in the majority.

The principle of self-determination became one of the principles for which the Allies in World War II avowedly fought. The Atlantic Charter proclaimed that the signers desired to see no territorial changes not in accord with the freely expressed wishes of the people concerned. Later, Prime Minister Churchill asserted this proclamation to be concerned only with the restoration of the sovereignty, self-government, and national life of the states and nations of Europe under the Nazi yoke. Self-determination was identified with a right of subjugated peoples, as nations, to liberation. The European states were viewed by Churchill to fall within this classification; the colonial areas administered by the European empires were not.

Self-determination following both world wars maintained a national base, the components of which were negotiable during the peace settlements. Only defeated states were credited with having subjugated their peoples. With the collapse of the German, Russian, Austro-Hungarian, and Turkish empires, the claims for self-determination from their subject territories were recognized at the close of World War I. The initial defeat of the Western European colonial powers by the Germans, and particularly the Japanese, during World War II also led to an extended claim for liberalization among the peoples of the remaining overseas empires.

Rupert Emerson distinguishes between the peoples for whom self-determination was justified following World War I and those for whom it was claimed following World War II. The difference exists in the ethnic base recognized in the former. Since World War I, no claim has existed to adjust the "national" boundaries of the decolonized territories to coincide with the ethnic frontiers.[9]

With the acceleration of decolonizaton in the last eighteen years, nationalist movements have begun to seek a different base. Groups within recognized states have begun to sense they are less equal than other groups within the state. Their expectations are aroused, in recognition of which they press for a status that will provide redress.

In an effort to focus on subnational groups, whose self-consciousness may give rise to nationalistic claims, some contemporary authors have focused on ethnic groups, with their ethnic consciousness being referred to as ethnonationalism.[10] Whether these are to be referred to as self-conscious ethnic groups or national minorities, it is the consciousness of a separate-group status which provided the basis for a claim for self-determination. In present nationalist movements, it is a claim that group identity is a basis for determining sovereign status and form of government. Connor observes that in all but fourteen of today's states there is at least one significant minority.[11] Among the states he lists as recently having been troubled by internal discord predicated upon ethnic diversity, those in Western Europe are: Belgium, France, Italy, Spain, and the United Kingdom.

For example, a major ethnocultural cleavage in Belgian society has been a division between the Flemings (of German stock) and the Walloons (of Celtic origin). The division is evident geographically with 56 percent of the population living in the northern 40 percent of the country bordering the Netherlands speaking a Dutch dialect, and 34 percent living in the southern area speaking French. The remainder reside in the capital, Brussels. Before World War II, the French-speaking Walloon areas were politically, economically, and culturally dominant. After the war, a heavy flow of investment into Flanders, combined with a decline in the basic coal and steel industries of Wallonia, reversed the two roles economically. In the early 1960s, a language boundary was drawn across the country. Brussels, while falling north of the boundary, was mainly a French-speaking city. The Dutch speakers had no objection to having French a language in Brussels but fought to keep the language boundaries of the city from spreading out into Dutch-speaking territory.

In response to rising pressures, the Belgian coalition government in the summer of 1978 introduced a devolution bill dividing the country into three regions—Flanders, Wallonia, and Brussels—each of which would have an elected assembly and an executive government empowered to conduct economic and industrial policies under broad guidelines established by the central government. The country would be officially divided into two communities—one French-speaking, the other Dutch—to be run by community councillors who would also serve as members of a new national senate.

These councils would handle all questions connected with language such as education, culture, and "personal issues." The central government would be left with responsibilities for defense and foreign affairs, basic taxation, and the overall economy.

Similarly, autonomist movements in France have grown stronger. Significantly, these have been in regions where the language has been other than French. Corsican and Breton separatist movements since 1974 have focused on linguistic and economic survival. The nationalists in Corsica have claimed that two centuries of French rule have witnessed the complete deterioration of agriculture. They insist that profits in construction, touched off by tourism, have gone to speculators from the mainland. Separatists have demanded the departure of thirty-thousand *pieds noir*, former French Algerians who were resettled in Corsica. These *pieds noir* are accused of taking over the best farmland and extending control on wine trade by questionable methods. In response, in April 1975, the French Senate divided Corsica into two departments, resulting from jealousies between the Ajaccio and Bastia areas where extremists had demanded independence. In August of that year, the government outlawed the Corsican separatist movement.

During the past decade, the more activist leaders among the German-speaking population in the province of Bolzano in Italy continued to agitate for total autonomy of the Trentino–Alto Adige region. South Tyrol (the name since applied to Alto Adige) was annexed to Italy after World War I. In 1946, by agreement with Austria, Italy recognized full equality of the German-speaking population in the area with the Italian population; promised preservation of their German ethnic character and the safeguard of their economic and cultural development; and was committed to an extension of autonomy of the region of Trentino–Alto Adige. In 1957, Austria claimed that Italy had not completely carried out the terms of the treaty, allowing systematic infiltration of Italians into the region. Extremists pressed for secession to Austria, and several years of terrorist activity resulted, leading to Italian accusations regarding the Austrian government's encouragement of the extremists. Among the grievances expressed by the German-speaking population were the lack of equality of the German and Italian languages in police and court proceedings and disproportionate job opportunities for the German-speaking population. An agreement between Italy and Austria in November 1969 accepted increased authority for the Alto Adige, reversed its union with Trentino, and changed its name to South Tyrol.

For two decades in Spain, the ETA (Euzkadita Azkatasuna—Basque Homeland and Liberty Party) has sought a Basque state carved from four Spanish and three French Basque provinces. Its most sensational venture was the 1973 assassination of the Spanish prime minister, Adm. Luis Carrero Blanco. Initially, it found support among the Basques because of General Franco's stern repression of regionalism. By acknowledging regionalist culture, King Juan Carlos's government has made separatism less romantic and less revolutionary. Local languages have become legal. A commission began studying the Basque economic privileges lost after the Spanish Civil War in order to revive them.

The Basques have maintained their own traditions, and their industry has supplied Spain with much of its wealth. They have claimed themselves to be a nation in their own right, residing in France as well as Spain. The privileges they have requested in their move toward autonomy—rights to tax, to maintain law and order, and to administer justice—had been theirs prior to the 1930s.

On December 31, 1977, limited home rule was granted the Basque provinces. Under the decree, the Basques have a local government equipped with limited powers handed over by the central government in Madrid. They achieved home rule three months after the Catalans. Other regions hoping for a similar transfer are Galicia, Andalusia, and the Canary Islands. In the last, separatist movements have pressed for complete independence.

In April 1976, the Portuguese government approved provisional statutes that would have established the Autonomous Region of the Azores and Madeira with Portuguese sovereignty administered by a Lisbon-appointed minister for each island and local governments appointed by the respective ministers. The Azores Regional Junta rejected the statutes, seeking economic and monetary autonomy. In early 1978, the Lisbon government began studying a proposal to extend the islands' autonomy to complete control of their economy, police, and public services but was reluctant to go that far, fearing a play into the hands of separatists who desired independence.

There has been a move toward regional autonomy in Western

Europe as a whole. Evident among the Basques, Corsicans, and Bretons, as well as the Azoreans, the movement has spread to the United Kingdom. In the past decade, nationalists in Scotland and Wales have pressed for forms of self-rule. In Wales, the demand has been expressed more in terms of asserting a distinctive cultural personality. Economically, Wales is poor, and the people depend on substantial aid from London. Scotland, however, has always been distinct from England. It has its own established church, legal system, and schools. While poor for generations, it now has the prospect of oil riches from the North Sea.

In the 1974 election, the Scottish National Party, which wants complete independence for Scotland, took 30 percent of the votes, winning eleven of the region's seventy-one seats in Westminster's House of Commons. The Nationalists came second in thirty-six Labour constituencies. A small voter swing could make them the majority party in the region. Significantly, polls indicate that one in six Scots feel there should be more local control.

In late 1976, the Labour government introduced legislation to set up assemblies in Edinburgh and Cardiff to give the Scots and the Welsh a measure of control over their own affairs. The devolved matters were very closely defined, separately for Wales and Scotland. The Scottish Assembly would be able to pass new laws on devolved matters. The Welsh Assembly would have no primary legislative powers over devolved matters. The provisions, while making changes in the government of Scotland and Wales, did not affect the unity of the United Kingdom or the supreme authority of Westminster to make laws for the United Kingdom as a whole. The Westminster government would retain powers over a wide area of finance, aiming to ensure that assembly activities did not operate to the economic disadvantage of other parts of the United Kingdom. A bill on Scotland passed the House of Commons in February 1978. An amendment stipulated that at least 40 percent of registered Scottish voters must vote positively for devolution in a referendum. The bill was referred to the House of Lords, where it has been under review.

In a particularly troubling dissent, the United Kingdom has been plagued since 1968 with an ethnic conflict in Northern Ireland. The civil strife is partially a continuation of issues unresolved at the time of the partition of Ireland in 1921 when six counties of Ulster were permitted to opt out of an association with the Irish Free State, maintaining for themselves a form of home rule which made them autonomous in all local matters as a part of the United Kingdom. An act of Parliament in 1972 reinstituted direct rule from London.

Northern Ireland is internationally a part of the United Kingdom. The majority of the population, as Protestants, profess to be British. A significant minority, one-third, are Roman Catholic, many of whom desire unification with the Republic of Ireland. To do so would place the Protestants in a minority position. Thus, two national minorities contend for survival within the six counties of modern Ulster—a Protestant group, linked by necessity to the British Crown, and a Catholic minority, often referred to as a minority within a minority, linked by religion and culture to the Republic of Ireland. A basic component within the nationality of both is religion. Thus, in Northern Ireland two antagonistic cultural groups exist side by side, and the situation is made more difficult by economic depression and growing unemployment which effect both groups disproportionately. Of the two groups, the Roman Catholic Irish minority are the most socially and economically disadvantaged.

What is more and more evident is that within Western Europe during the past two decades various regions within nations have begun to assert themselves. West Germany has been a federal state since World War II. Italy has embarked in the direction of giving greater power to its regions. Belgium, strained by rivalries between Flemings and Walloons, has become in effect a federal state. In France, Bretons and Corsicans demand regional autonomy, as have the Basques and Catalans in Spain. Supporters of devolution for Scotland and Wales also advocate forms of regional autonomy within England as well.

Advocates for regional autonomy have maintained there is insufficient participation in the central government, there are discrepancies in economic benefits among the regions, and there are discrepancies between their "style of living" and that of the majority within the country. Pressures have led to political violence by groups making demands, in turn leading to the claims of participants and governments of basic violations of human rights. Corsican and Breton separatist movements have claimed responsibility and have been held responsible for bombing within France over the past four years. Basque separatist activity led to a number of death sentences for those apprehended in Spain. IRA (Irish Republican Army) warfare in Northern Ireland led to British retaliation which resulted in an Irish government charge before the European Court on Human Rights against the British for inhuman treatment of prisoners.

III

Perspectives on the concept of self-determination within Western Europe are influenced by movements toward economic and political integration within the European Community. Groups within Western Europe are frequently in a position to choose whether they direct their demands toward national or supranational institutions. Supranationality involves the existence of a community above, but not replacing, the nation-states. Regardless of its form and scope, the aim of the community is the processing of interests that are recognized as community in nature. Sovereignty, as a legal foundation and resting on the will of the people, may be concurrently as applicable at the supranational level as at the national level. The needs of the people may be functional only at the community level and thus may receive direct authorization to be operative at that level. Nationalism is itself dependent upon the recognition of a common interest which can sustain the loyalty of the individuals who compose the nation. If the nature of the interests change or if loyalty is transferred, the basis of the nation is altered. Nationalism may be as forceful at the community level as it is at the state, with the former itself able to solicit loyalty directly.

The concept of supranationality modifies the status accorded sovereignty. It suggests that sovereignty represents not a characteristic but a relationship among various authorities. The various Länder within West Germany are sovereign in respect to one another; they are not individually sovereign in respect to the Republic itself. No Land has control over another, but the Republic has some control over each. Similarly, the Republic is sovereign relative to other members of the European Community. Certain controls rest at the community level, overriding the authority of the individual states regarding certain issues. The Community stands at par with external jurisdictions over certain governmental functions. It is the Community that has evolved an international status relative to these functions rather than the member states individually. The demands of various subnational or ethnic groups for control over certain governmental functions are, in part, a reverse of this process, yet consistent with aims for a people's autonomy. Groups are identifying the areas in which they demand to be at par, and thus sovereign, with other groups.

The European Community itself has accepted responsibility to provide leadership toward regional development, directing aid toward those regions evaluated as being in need of assistance. Assistance is being directed toward regions in the Republic of Ireland, western Ulster, southern France, and southern Italy. Should Greece, Spain, and Portugal become members of the Community, additional areas will be considered. Assistance is available from a Community Regional Fund, a Social Fund, and a European Investment Bank.

In addition, in November 1976, members of the Council of Europe, which includes the nine members of the European Community plus those in associate status, adopted an antiterrorism convention designed to plug the political motivation loopholes and make aerial hijackers and other terrorists liable for extradition to the country where they committed their acts. The members of the European Community went further, concluding that extradition would be automatic when a suspect is wanted on charges for which the prison sentence in both countries is greater than five years.

The European Convention on Human Rights, in force since 1953 among the members of the Council of Europe, provides a regional standard for dealing with individual citizens, regardless of origin. Austria, Iceland, Norway, Sweden, Switzerland, and the nine members of the European Community accept the compulsory jurisdiction of the convention, providing for the right of an individual citizen to charge violations of human rights against his or another government. These human rights are unique in international law.

Western Europe has maintained a democratic base in its concept of self-determination. Movement there has been toward degrees of sovereignty at a regional level. Groups are demanding and receiving recognition of their claims for greater autonomy within the politics of the existing structure. An evolving emphasis on individual human rights has monitored the status of the individual in relation to governments at all levels. This is the legacy of Western Europe as it finds its place in an understanding of the concept of self-determination.

Notes

1. Art. 1, para. 2.

2. Ruth B. Russell, *A History of the United Nations Charter* (Washington, D.C.: Brookings Institution, 1958), p. 810.

3. Hans Kelsen, *The Law of the United Nations* (London: Stevens and Sons, Ltd., 1950), pp. 51-53.

4. General Assembly Resolution 1514 (15), December 14, 1960.

5. UNCIO, Documents, 6, p. 296.

6. A/C.3/SR649, (1955).

7. Rupert Emerson, "Self-Determination," *American Journal of International Law* 65, no. 3 (July 1971), p. 464.

8. United States, *Congressional Record*, 66, p. 3786.

9. Emerson, "Self-Determination," p. 464.

10. Walker Connor, "The Politics of Ethnonationalism," *Journal of International Affairs* 22, no. 1 (1975), p. 3.

11. Ibid., p. 1.

6

Self-Determination: British Perspectives

Thomas E. Hachey

Modern nationalism, or the quest for political self-determination, emerged as a powerful dynamic in contemporary history well before the twentieth century, but it was the First World War which provided the catalyst for this rapidly developing phenomenon.[1] President Woodrow Wilson became the first world leader to endorse the principle of self-determination as an international objective when he proclaimed it as an American and Allied war aim in 1917. But if the implications of that statement were not immediately apparent to the rulers of ethnically heterogenous empires, the consequences soon were.

Wars of national liberation have become the vehicle of political independence for numerous secessionist movements in this century, and their invariable triumphs have profoundly altered the geopolitical landscape.[2] The British Empire, for example, on the eve of World War I, encompassed nearly a quarter of the globe and almost a third of the world's population. Although nearly all of these peoples would achieve self-determination in the time span of little more than another generation, the path to independence was not an easy one despite London's alleged adherence to President Wilson's Fourteen Points. Irish nationalists discovered at the 1919 Paris Peace Conference, as, subsequently, the Egyptians, Indians, and other peoples subject to the British Crown also discovered, that Prime Minister David Lloyd George did not interpret Wilson's pledge of self-determination to apply to any territories other than those of the defeated Central Powers.[3] Indeed, from the time of the Irish nationalists' efforts at the 1919 Peace Conference to the present-day parliamentary deliberations over the Scottish Home Rule Bill, the London government almost consistently either has equivocated or has resisted demands within its several jurisdictions, both at home and abroad, for political self-determination.[4]

Self-Determination and the
Irish Experience (1916-1922)

A considerable portion of this essay is devoted to the Irish experience since no other country can claim to have exercised so profound an influence upon Britain's perception of and attitudes toward demands for self-determination in the twentieth century. Indeed, Irish nationalism, especially since 1916, affected the changing character of the British Empire far more substantively than did the American Revolution of 1776. The Americans, benefiting from geographical distance and the help of a major ally, substituted local for imperial institutions and then defended them by conventional military means. Britain subsequently sought to avoid future ruptures with her other settler colonies by devising an alternative to rebellion for those sufficiently prepared for self-government: the devolution or gradual transfer of power to newly created dominions. By the twentieth century, this formula had been refined into the Commonwealth strategy, immediately effective in the English-speaking dominions and potentially applicable elsewhere.[5] By then, however, the tactics that would become familiar to this century's wars of national liberation already had developed an appeal for an increasing number of Irish nationalists. Therefore, aside from the importance the twenty-six-county Irish Free State has had as a leader in the achievement of self-determination for Commonwealth members between 1922 and 1949, and apart from the critical constitutional questions the six-county province of Ulster poses for Britain today, the real object lessons for Third World anti-colonial leaders like Egypt's Nasser or India's Gandhi are to be found in the British response to the Irish war for independence fought between 1916 and 1921.[6]

From 1886, when Parnell and British Prime Minister William Gladstone concluded the alliance between Irish nationalism and

British liberalism, the Conservative party in England used Ulster's resistance to Irish home rule as a weapon to maintain power and frustrate liberalism. It used the Union as a symbol of Protestant principles, traditional institutions, aristocratic power, private property, and the permanence of the empire. British Conservatives in the Parliament and in the army endorsed and encouraged Ulster Protestant threats in order to defeat the constitutional inevitability of home rule through civil war. Liberal Prime Minister Herbert Asquith had promised the Irish Parliamentary party that England would grant home rule to Ireland in return for its support of the Liberal party at Westminster. The Irish kept their bargain, but Asquith was threatened by civil war in Ulster and a mutiny among British army officers if he attempted to implement what was demonstrably the will of a majority of the British electorate.[7] Asquith asked, and Irish Nationalist party leader John Redmond agreed, to postpone home rule when war with Germany erupted in August 1914.

In order to win Irish nationalist support for the war effort, home rule was placed on the statute books but, with Redmond's consent, the prime minister sought to appease Unionists with a suspensory bill delaying the operation of home rule until after the war was over. For the moment, Britain had narrowly escaped a constitutional crisis, and possibly civil war. But British politicians had not solved the Irish question; they had only postponed a decision. Neither Asquith nor Redmond realized how the stalemate of August 1914 would alter the character of Irish nationalism. Although most of Ireland responded favorably to Redmond's appeal that the Irish join the British in fighting the common enemy, there were men in Ireland who believed their common enemy was England, and they waited for an opportunity to strike out at her.[8]

Irish nationalists drew two lessons from the events of 1914: that the English could not be trusted to honor promises, and that force rather than peaceful or constitutional methods would bring results. These attitudes were reflected in the declining support given to John Redmond's Irish Nationalist party, and in the corresponding growth of popularity the more aggressive Sinn Fein movement enjoyed after 1914. Originally committed to a policy of passive resistance, Sinn Fein, by this date, was becoming increasingly militant in its demand for independence under a dual monarchy in which England and Ireland would share a common crown.[9] The more radical Irish Republican Brotherhood sought the establishment of an Irish republic by physical force, and it was the I.R.B. whose members controlled the key positions in the Irish Volunteers.[10] The latter were predominantly Catholic and nationalist, and their immediate objective was to check the power of the Ulster Volunteers who were Protestant and unionist. James Connolly's small Citizen Army was another militant force, but with a difference. A dual monarchy or a change of flags did not interest Connolly for he viewed the struggle against Britain as a part of the socialist battle against capitalism.[11] In these circumstances, the I.R.B. provided the strongest link in bringing together such diverse elements as the Volunteers, Sinn Fein, and the Citizen Army into an anti-British effort which reached its climax with the Easter Rising of 1916.

Romantic nationalism in Ireland was given its ultimate expression in the rising of 1916. The sabotage, terrorism, and assassinations which would characterize future Irish rebel activities were not a part of the 1916 insurrection. The rising was led by poets and visionaries who hoped by their example to shake the apathy of the Irish people rather than attempt a real but impossible military victory over the British. The participants were uniformed and followed the conventions of war in acting out what they intended as a "blood sacrifice"; they did not indulge in the guerrilla tactics that typified subsequent liberation efforts in Ireland. Not surprisingly, the rebellion went poorly for the Irish idealists. A German ship containing a cargo of arms, timed to arrive just before the rising, was intercepted by British warships off the coast of County Cork. The German captain scuttled his ship, and the consignment of obsolete Russian rifles went to the bottom of the sea.[12] Plans went further awry when Irish Volunteer chief Eoin Mac Neill called off the rebellion and some Dublin leaders refused to accept that order. What was to have been a national rising became a local insurrection limited to Dublin. On Easter Monday, 1916, rebellion leader Padraic Pearse and 1,500 rebels seized several strategic positions in the center of Dublin and declared the establishment of an Irish republic. British troops suppressed the rebellion in a week of bloody fighting which left the heart of the Irish capital in ruins. Over 100 British soldiers died, and more than 300 were wounded.

Only 52 members of the Volunteers and Citizen Army were killed, but over 450 Dublin civilians lost their lives, and 2,614 were wounded by stray bullets and shells.[13]

Ireland had not responded to the rising as Pearse had expected. During the chaos and turmoil of the battle, many Dubliners took advantage of the breakdown of authority and looted stores and shops. At Westminster, John Redmond condemned the rising as a German plot involving only a fanatical and misguided minority of the Irish population. The majority of Irishmen agreed, and many condemned the Republicans and Sinn Feiners as traitors. It was not an unreasonable sentiment in view of the fact that a quarter of a million Irish men served voluntarily in the British army during World War I and their families supported them if not their cause. When Republican prisoners were led through the Dublin streets to prison, they were cursed by the people who lined the way.[14] Padraic Pearse and his comrades may have won little more than the ridicule and contempt of their countrymen, and they may have been forgotten by both Ireland and history if they had been sentenced to long terms in prison.

Reprisal was the immediate response of the English government to the rising. It was a tactic that would be employed repeatedly over the decades by the British in Ireland, almost always with disastrous results. Over a period of ten days, the leaders of the rebellion were court-martialed and executed. James Connolly was so badly wounded that he was executed while strapped to a stretcher. Thirteen others fell before a firing squad before the volume of public protest spared seventy-five others who also had been condemned to death. More than two-thousand Sinn Feiners and Republicans were imprisoned in Ireland and Britain, many of them without trials. The viciousness of the executions and the imprisonment of so many men made the government appear cruel and arbitrary. The "dirty traitors" of Easter Week became gallant martyrs and national heroes. Their portraits adorned the walls of Irish homes and pubs; their speeches and poems were widely sold, read, and quoted. In the space of a few short weeks, the Irish national mood had changed as the British unwittingly fulfilled Padraic Pearse's wish; a blood sacrifice had shaken Ireland from her apathy.[15]

England's war with Germany and the angry Irish reaction to the Easter vengeance almost certainly prompted the London government to adopt a more conciliatory policy toward the Irish in the hope of pacifying that disruptive internal problem. Sinn Fein and Republican prisoners were gradually released over the next two years so that all had been freed by the end of the war. Eamon de Valera, a mathematics teacher who had commanded a Volunteer unit during the Easter Week rebellion, was among those released from jail. He and his comrades immediately began reorganizing the Volunteer Army and promoting candidates for political office under the Sinn Fein party label. Meanwhile, British Prime Minister Lloyd George summoned an Irish Convention representing all shades of opinion—Sinn Fein, Home Rule, and Unionist—to work out an acceptable plan for home rule. Southern Unionists were prepared to cooperate in establishing an Irish parliament, but Ulster Unionists, encouraged by their sympathizers in Britain, refused. John Redmond's Irish Parliamentary party failed to establish a consensus in the face of a Sinn Fein boycott and Ulster's veto, and the convention, which held its first session in July 1917, ended in failure in April 1918.[16] To London, it may have seemed that neither vengeance nor pardon was very effective in dealing with the Irish; in truth, it was more a matter of too little too late. Radicalism was spreading in Ireland, and the British home rule proposals which enjoyed the support of an overwhelming Irish majority in 1914 had considerably less appeal to Irishmen by 1918.

British manpower resources were seriously depleted by the heavy toll taken in the fighting on the western front in 1917, and, with the Russian withdrawal from the war, the London government was in desperate need for more soldiers. In April 1918, Parliament authorized Lloyd George to extend conscription to Ireland. The immediate reaction of Catholic Ireland produced an uncommon unity as the different factions joined ranks against conscription; the Irish party walked out of the House of Commons, and the Irish trade unions, Sinn Fein, and the Catholic Church joined ranks in opposition to the British.[17] Anti-conscription agitation strengthened the Republican forces in Ireland, and the London government turned again to repressive measures. Scores of Sinn Feiners were deported, and others, like de Valera, were sent to prison on the pretext of their complicity in an alleged "German plot"; the war ended, however, before Britain could initiate the draft in Ireland.[18]

Another act in the drama opened after the armistice on November 11, 1918, when it became evident how completely the nationalist movement had been seized by the extremists. In the British election of December 1918, the Sinn Fein party scored an overwhelming victory by winning every Irish seat outside Ulster except four. Seventy-three Sinn Feiners, thirty-six of whom were in prison, were elected to the Westminister Parliament; the Unionists elected twenty-six; and the now-discredited Home Rulers won a mere six seats. Triumphant Sinn Feiners viewed the election as a plebiscite and hailed the outcome as a mandate from the Irish people for an independent republic.[19] Refusing to take their seats at Westminster, the victors instead gathered at Dublin's stately Mansion House where they formed a self-constituted Irish Parliament known thereafter as Dail Eireann. On January 21, 1919, in proceedings which were partly conducted in the Irish language, the Dail issued a declaration of independence and ratified the establishment of Soarstat Eireann, the Irish Republic, proclaimed at Easter 1916. The Dail proceeded to assume the task of administering the country; there emerged courts to supersede the British legal system, boards to settle industrial disputes, and a land bank to make loans to people wishing to purchase farms. The Dail government even sent delegates to the Versailles Peace Conference to plead the case for an independent Irish republic and issued an appeal to the nations of the world for diplomatic recognition.[20]

Warfare began in January 1919 as the Irish Republican Army (the new name of the Irish Volunteers) adopted guerrilla tactics in their attacks on British authorities in Ireland. Young men in civilian clothing ambushed army motorcades, assassinated "spies" and "informers," and shot soldiers and policemen. As the violence spread, the London government, in March 1920, began recruiting ex-servicemen in England and sent them to Ireland as reinforcements for the Royal Irish Constabulary. These notorious Black and Tans—so named because in the absence of sufficient Royal Irish Constabulary uniforms they were given surplus khaki uniforms with black belts—were joined in June 1920 by the Auxiliary Division of the R.I.C. The "Auxis," as they became known in Ireland, were recruited among ex-officers in England. The I.R.A. guerrillas were hopelessly outnumbered, but they had one telling advantage; their anonymity. Dressed in street clothes, they would appear suddenly and attack Tans and Auxis and, almost as quickly, would merge back into the civilian population which sheltered them and refused to inform on them.[21] British forces met terror with terror and resorted once again to reprisals. They burned, looted, and murdered. But rather than breaking the spirit of Irish radicals, the atrocities only stiffened their determination.

Even as the war raged, London attempted to provide a constitutional solution to the most critical problem in any Irish settlement; a political arrangement that would allow the Catholic and Protestant communities of Ireland hegemony in their respective spheres while proceeding toward an ultimate fulfillment of their common destiny. By the end of 1919, Prime Minister Lloyd George had begun toying with the idea of combining a form of Irish self-government with partition of the country. He devised a plan for the creation of *two* parliaments in Ireland, an idea that was different from any previous British proposal and certainly not in accord with the demands that had been made by either the Nationalist or Unionist camps. Under this scheme, each parliament would have had very limited powers on the understanding that both would subsequently amalgamate into a single parliament and government for the whole of Ireland. The conservative provisions of the plan provided for an eventual national parliament in Dublin with powers substantially less than those that had been accorded Ireland in the Home Rule Bill and placed in the Statute Book in 1914. The proposals were scarcely calculated to appeal to the Nationalist element whose representatives in the Dail had overwhelmingly decided upon the establishment of an independent Irish republic and whose partisan forces were already conducting a guerrilla war against the British authorities for that cause. Unionist reaction in Ulster, however, was cautiously receptive.[22]

Lloyd George introduced a bill in February 1920 that generally embraced the proposals he had offered earlier for consideration. The British strategy in seeking to enact the bill was probably twofold: to shelve temporarily an awkward legislative problem and to persuade the United States that London had some Irish policy besides calculated violence. As such, the bill was a palliative and a subterfuge because the British government was aware that a modified form of home rule would never satisfy republicans, nor the majority of the Irish population. And London was equally convinced that Irish independence would have to be resisted by whatever means necessary. Once again, the British resorted to a carrot-and-stick approach to the Irish problem as the government simultaneously intensified the military effort against Sinn Fein while attempting to mediate differences with that foe through a variety of third parties.[23]

Nationalists viewed with contempt the formal proceedings at Westminster pertaining to the Irish bill proposed by Prime Minister Lloyd George. Ulster Unionists were suspicious of the suggested Council of Ireland which was to be representative of both the northern and southern parliaments. The Council was intended to provide a measure of unity from which stronger bonds might be forged. Although the Council's authority was restricted to railways, fisheries, contagious diseases, and only those additional powers the two parliaments agreed to confer upon it, the Unionists were as hostile as the Nationalists to this arrangement. Northern Protestants were particularly dismayed by the part of the proposal that accorded counties Donegal, Monaghan, and Cavan to the southern parliament since these areas, together with the counties of Armagh, Antrim, Down, Derry, Fermanagh, and Tyrone, were all a part of the historic province of Ulster.

The Ulster Unionist Council met on March 4 in Belfast and reluctantly consented to the planned division. Ulster leader Sir Edward Carson bitterly observed that northern Ireland had little other choice since it was calculated that Nationalists would outnumber Unionists if all of Ulster were to be administered by a northern parliament. With six counties, a Unionist and Protestant majority in parliament could be assured even though a large Nationalist minority was unavoidable. It was also reasoned that the economy and resources of the six-county region were sufficiently varied to render it economically capable of subsisting as a separate political entity. Amidst much soul-searching and deep misgivings, therefore, Ulster Unionists made a pragmatic decision to desert their fellow Unionists in Donegal, Cavan, and Monaghan as they had earlier parted company with the Unionists of southern Ireland.[24]

Prime Minister Lloyd George took the initiative in June 1921 and invited Eamon de Valera to join in a tripartite conference between the British government and representatives of northern and southern Ireland. Absent from his proposal were the terms Sinn

Fein had previously found unacceptable, such as the surrender of arms or the barring of certain individuals from the conference table. After consulting with his chief ministers, de Valera replied that he would agree to negotiations on two conditions: an actual truce would have to be declared *before* the president of the Dail Eireann traveled to London and Northern Ireland Prime Minister Sir James Craig was to be excluded from discussions. Lloyd George agreed, and the long-awaited truce came at noon on July 11, 1921. Eamon de Valera arrived in London on the following day, accompanied by four members of his cabinet. In deference to his wishes, Lloyd George met with de Valera and Sir James Craig in separate meetings held at No. 10 Downing Street.[25]

Although the truce seemed to come quite suddenly, there had been frequent unofficial contacts between the opposing sides. Lord Derby, General J. C. Smuts of South Africa, and Archbishop Clune of Australia were but a few of the mediators who held secret talks on behalf of the British government with Sinn Fein representatives. There were also circumstances that inclined both parties toward a truce, if not a negotiated settlement. The British government found itself besieged by appeals from its own citizenry, and many others in America, Europe, and from all parts of the empire called for a cessation of hostilities in Ireland. Conservatives like Robert Cecil changed their position and joined critics of the war while others like Winston Churchill, Lord Birkenhead, and Austen Chamberlain warned Lloyd George that he would never gain national support for his Irish policies until he granted that country the widest possible measure of self-government. Even General Sir Henry Wilson, chief of the Imperial General Staff and hawkish supporter of the war against Sinn Fein, told the prime minister quite bluntly that the choice was "to go all out or to get out."[26]

For its part, the I.R.A. was facing critical shortages of men and materials. Its arsenals had never contained anything more than machine guns, rifles, and homemade bombs, and with the depletion of these the I.R.A. was scarcely able to engage in anything more than harassment. As Michael Collins would later admit, at the time of the truce, Irish resistance could not have lasted more than a few more weeks.[27] The people of the towns and countryside upon whose support, or at least indifference, the guerrillas depended were growing increasingly weary of the long and costly war of attrition. Their physical and psychological endurance had reached the breaking point. People were becoming more anxious for an end to the violence and a return to normalcy than they were about possible political solutions. Like the British, Sinn Fein thought the moment propitious for an armistice since the conditions required to continue the war effort were growing decidedly worse rather than better.[28]

Initial conversations between Lloyd George and de Valera were unproductive. The pragmatic Welsh politician pointed repeatedly to the restrictions under which he had to labor as prime minister of the United Kingdom; the doctrinaire Irish revolutionary responded by lecturing him on the history of English exploitation in Ireland. Lloyd George did offer Ireland virtual dominion status, which was more than any previous British government had ever offered, but he also attached some rather vital qualifications. England would continue to maintain certain air and naval facilities in Ireland, besides reserving the right to recruit volunteers from that country for the British armed forces. A contribution to the British war debt would be stipulated, and the Irish government in the south would be expected to recognize the legitimacy of the northern Ireland parliament.[29] De Valera judged these terms to be unacceptable but agreed to return to Dublin and submit them for the Dail's consideration. That body's recently elected membership renounced the limited dominion status proferred by London, collectively took an oath to bear allegiance to the Irish Republic, and authorized de Valera as president of that Republic to form a new cabinet with which to administer the country.

Neither side wished a total breakdown of negotiations, however, and de Valera made a conciliatory gesture when he announced that he was not "a doctrinaire Republican." He also declared that he would support a treaty that permitted Ireland to enter in a free association with the British Commonwealth of nations. Lloyd George pursued the opportunity for an agreement, and, after a lengthy exchange of letters which were published by newspapers in both countries, the British prime minister offered to join de Valera in another conference. The purpose of the new meeting would be to ascertain how the association of Ireland with the British Empire could be reconciled with Irish national aspirations. For

reasons which neither de Valera nor his biographers have ever satis-
factorily explained, the president of the Irish Republic excluded
himself from the delegation which went to London to negotiate a
treaty. Some have contended that de Valera did not wish to risk
his political reputation by direct association with what he must
have known would be a less than favorable agreement. Others have
defended the decision claiming, as did de Valera himself, that the
Irish president remained in Dublin to ensure that extreme Republican colleagues like Cathal Brugha and Austen Stack did not torpedo
any British proposal short of an outright republic. De Valera also
felt his remaining in Ireland was the best guarantee for ensuring
that an Anglo-Irish treaty would be given careful consideration in
Dublin before it was accepted.[30]

Arthur Griffith, Michael Collins, E. J. Duggan, George Gavan
Duffy, and Robert Barton composed the five-man Irish delegation.
Their counterparts at meetings held at the prime minister's residence in Downing Street were Lloyd George, Austen Chamberlain,
Lord Birkenhead, and Winston Churchill, all men who were experienced in the skills and nuances of politics and diplomacy. Two
questions dominated the conference sessions which extended from
October 11 to December 6, 1921: would Ireland remain within
the empire as a dominion, or be in "external association" with it
as a republic; and would Ulster be included or not. The Irish delegates were never unanimously agreed on the first question, but
they conceded everything—first the republic, then external association—for the sake of winning the second question, a united Ireland,
unpartitioned.[31]

In the course of the deliberations, the British consented to
allow the Irish to design an oath of allegiance that would put primary allegiance to an Irish dominion or "free state" rather than to
the Crown. But de Valera was pressured by the same extreme Republicans he allegedly remained in Dublin to hold in check, and the
Irish president sent word to his delegates in London that neither
the oath nor dominion status could be considered. Michael Collins
and Arthur Griffith, however, were induced to accept dominion
status in return for Lloyd George's promise that Ulster's boundaries would be so contracted by a Royal Boundary Commission that
it would be forced to join southern Ireland in order to survive.
There was an element of deceit on both sides in this bargain. The

prime minister could not predict the consequences should his or any other British government provoke Ulster by any radical reshaping of its boundaries. Lloyd George knew this, but he was seldom troubled by any sense of obligation to deliver on promises. Michael Collins agreed to dominion status for Ireland so that the British would consent to end partition and to abandon Ulster. He, too, was insincere. Collins had no intention of renouncing forever the claim to a republic. Dominion status and membership in the community of nations known as the British Commonwealth were not desirable in themselves. But Collins saw it as a stepping-stone, a new posture from which Ireland could and would strike out again for the cherished republic. As he later told the Dail when urging that assembly to accept dominion status, it was "not the ultimate freedom that all nations desire and develop to, but the freedom to achieve it."[32]

The Irish delegates were told that each of their signatures would be necessary if orders to resume hostilities were not to be sent to the British military command in Ireland.[33] Lloyd George may have been bluffing, but the Irish could not afford to gamble on that assumption and no one knew that better than Michael Collins. Peace had eroded the tight I.R.A. organization, and its intelligence system had become far less effective during the idle months of the armistice. Collins and other leaders who had previously been unfamiliar to authorities were now widely recognized. The majority of the Irish population was content with the peace and could not be depended upon by the I.R.A. for future assistance if the war were resumed. By contrast, the British forces had been given a respite by the truce. They had not abandoned their entrenched positions at the time of the cease-fire, and they had plenty of reserves to draw upon. The likely outcome of a renewed Anglo-Irish war was painfully apparent to reasonable men like Collins and Griffith. At 2:30 a.m. on December 6, 1921, the Irish delegates affixed their signatures to the agreement that ended 120 years of British rule in all but six counties of Ireland.[34]

De Valera rejected the treaty and also led the opposition when the treaty was subsequently debated in the Dail in January 1922. While it is generally believed that a majority of the population in southern Ireland favored the treaty because it wanted peace, impassioned speeches for and against the treaty by scores of repre-

sentatives in the Dail revealed a substantial division among the
Irish leadership.[35] When the tally was finally taken, the treaty was
ratified by a margin of sixty-four votes to fifty-seven. De Valera
promptly resigned as president of the Dail and Arthur Griffith was
elected to succeed him. Some I.R.A. commanders refused to accept
the verdict of their government, and, with the support and encouragement of de Valera and other irreconcilable Republican politicians, they plunged the country into a bloody civil war which
lasted until May 1923. It was left to the provisional government of
the Irish Free State to suppress such internal insurrection since the
British Parliament, which transferred official powers to the Free
State in March 1922, evacuated all of its forces from southern Ireland by December of that year. Civil wars are nearly always more
vicious than those fought against an alien people, and in this respect the violent internecine struggle between Irishmen was no
exception. Rebels who had once fought the state were now themselves the state, and they fought their former comrades with more
viciousness and brutality than anything witnessed by the Anglo-
Irish war. The Irish Free State executed seventy-seven rebels, as
compared to twenty-four military executions by the British in
1920-1921, and eleven-thousand men were in internment camps
by the end of the civil war. Free State casualties included Arthur
Griffith, who died of a heart attack under the strain of leadership
in those difficult days, and Michael Collins, who was assassinated
in his native County Cork by gunmen from the I.R.A. force he had
once controlled. Memories of this fratricidal conflict have left
scars upon the Irish community which survive to the present day.[36]
  On December 6, 1922, the establishment of a Free State government was proclaimed and the provisional government came to an
end. In accordance with the provisions of the Anglo-Irish treaty,
Northern Ireland was allowed to vote on its own future and it
promptly exercised its option not to join the Free State in a decision announced on December 7. Discussons between representatives of Northern and southern Ireland on the boundary question
proved completely fruitless, and the new British Prime Minister
Andrew Bonar Law, a longtime Unionist and Ulster ally, opposed
any redistricting scheme which threatened the existence of Northern Ireland. Several years of unsuccessful bargaining for the annexation of Ulster's Roman Catholic areas finally led Irish Free State

representatives, in an agreement signed in London in 1925, to recognize the boundary of Northern Ireland.[37] In return, the English government relieved the Irish Free State of its obligation to contribute to the British war debt, a concession which scarcely compensated for the perpetuated partition. There was much reason for disappointment for none of Ireland's dreams had been fulfilled:

> Not the Gaelic League's Irish speaking nation, nor Yeats's literary-conscious people, nor the republic of the I.R.B., nor the worker's republic of Connolly, nor Griffith's economically self-sufficient dual monarchy, nor Redmond's home rule within an empire which the Irish had helped to build, nor Carson's United Kingdom.[38]

The Anglo-Irish treaty provided no solution to Ireland's most critical problem, it merely postponed it once more. The expedient of partition left two Irelands to face an uncertain future.

Historically, Britain's perspective of and response to Irish demands for self-determination have been conditioned by Ireland's unique status in contrast with other Crown subjects seeking independence. Ireland, after all, had been an integral part of the United Kingdom since the 1800 Act of Union. But the London government did recognize that Irish nationalists had never been successfully assimilated, and, hence, it agreed to the 1921 Anglo-Irish settlement as the best possible compromise under the existing circumstances. Yet, the Irish nationalists to whom the British, for security reasons, refused to concede an independent republic had already provided a model for guerrilla warfare which would be imitated by other movements of national liberation throughout the empire. Meanwhile, the restless dominion, the Irish Free State, would pioneer the path of emancipation for other dominions within the Commonwealth.[39] And Ireland's divisive influence would not end there either for the Ulster separatists—unionists and nationalists alike—have inspired contemporary self-determination movements in the non-English regions of the United Kingdom, the Scottish and Welsh regions of Great Britain.

Self-Determination and the Commonwealth Experience

Britain's perception of and toleration for varying attempts at self-determination within the Commonwealth-Empire, however, has differed according to the degree of independence sought and the particular constituency seeking it. London always drew a sharp distinction between Crown colonies or imperial dependencies, such as India, and the settler colonies, such as Canada, South Africa, Australia, and New Zealand. The indigenous populations of Crown colonies, whether in Africa, Asia, or in the Western Hemisphere, were governed by viceroys or lord lieutenants representing the British sovereign in an administrative structure which, even if occasionally enlightened, remained essentially imperialistic. By contrast, the settler colonies, or dominions as they came to be known, achieved a measure of political self-determination through an incremental process which the British more often indulged than encouraged.[40]

During World War I, a growing sense of national identity on the part of the dominions, stimulated by their individual contributions and sacrifices in a common cause, led to the substitution of the term Commonwealth for empire in most official communications between dominion spokesmen and the British government. The dominions were states in the process of becoming nations, as South African leader General J. C. Smuts acknowledged in a speech delivered in England on May 15, 1917, in which he remarked: "the so called dominions [are] a number of nations and states, almost sovereign, almost independent, who govern themselves . . . which I prefer to call the British Commonwealth of Nations."[41] If Smuts appeared uncertain as to the precise status of the dominion governments in their evolutionary progression toward eventual sovereignty, so too were the British.[42] Dominions demanded and received representation at the 1919 Paris Peace Conference and membership in the newly formed League of Nations. But ambiguities in the definition of dominion independence persisted until they were partly resolved at the Imperial Conferences in 1926 and 1930. The most significant outcome of these deliberations was London's recognition of the dominions as self-governing members of the empire, equal to Britain in status, while preserving the constitutional prerogatives of the Crown in the external relations of all Commonwealth nations. That relationship was then embodied in the Statute of Westminster which received royal assent on December 11, 1931.

What Britain conceded to her settler colonies, the dominions, but not to her imperial dependencies, was, therefore, a qualified form of self-determination. It permitted a substantial degree of autonomy for internal affairs, rendering dominion parliaments control over their own territories and citizens for nearly all purposes. But dominion citizens were also British subjects, and certain legal cases could still be appealed beyond the highest court of any dominion to the Privy Council in London. Dominion sovereignty was further circumscribed in principle, if not in practice, by the common agreement among Commonwealth nations that London would remain the architect of their mutual foreign policy. That understanding was not consistently observed, however, and it caused his majesty's government notable concern when the Irish Free State, in 1932, acted unilaterally in refusing to recognize a new government in Chile despite its acceptance by London and the other dominions. Moreover, New Zealand later responded similarly by refusing to join the rest of the Commonwealth in recognizing Italy's claim to Ethiopia.[43]

Britain's presumption to exclusive control over the empire's foreign affairs was challenged most consistently within the Commonwealth by the Irish state whose demand for an independent republic had not been reconciled by the 1921 compromise of dominion status. The Irish Free State became the first dominion to establish diplomatic representation in a non-Commonwealth country when, in 1925, it appointed a minister plenipotentiary to Washington. An acrimonious exchange over nomenclature ensued between London and Dublin in 1939 when Irish Prime Minister Eamon de Valera refused to accept a British envoy because of his title. Dublin insisted that he be called "minister," reflecting Eire's status as an independent nation rather than a dominion. London wanted him to be called a high commissioner, as the king's envoy was called in each of the other dominions. Britain's view was that a "minister" was a diplomatic representative in a foreign country, which Eire was not. Furthermore, the king was titular head of both states and could not be asked to appoint a minister to himself. A compromise was finally reached on October 30, 1939, whereby the king's representative was given the title United Kingdom Representative to Eire.[44] The other dominions would later follow the Irish example by appointing their own ministers to non-Commonwealth countries and also by insisting that the title "high commissioner" be discontinued for British envoys to the dominions.[45]

Dublin can indeed be credited with having set the most demonstrable precedents for dominion self-determination. The London government, together with the dominions, had agreed that Eire's 1936 External Relations Act had preserved the essence of the Commonwealth connection because it recognized the Crown for certain limited purposes in relation to foreign countries. The Dublin government, however, had insisted it was not a dominion member of the Commonwealth, but rather a state outside the Commonwealth, associated externally with it and not owing allegiance to the Crown. Since, in the British view, Eire remained a dominion, an extension of that premise was that it was a dominion which remained neutral in 1939. Irish neutrality hence became a test of dominion neutrality. Any challenge to or invasion of Irish rights was thereby tantamount to an invasion of dominion rights. Paradoxically, it was Eire—the dominion which did not deem itself to be a dominion—that demonstrated for all the world the sovereignty which the dominions enjoyed under the Statute of Westminster.[46] Without question, Eire's decision to remain neutral in World War II was facilitated to a large extent by the London government's insistence that Eire was a member of the Commonwealth, a body defined by British statute as being free and voluntary.

What the recently opened archives at the London Public Record Office clearly reveal, particularly in the case of British Cabinet and Dominions Office papers for the period of World War II and its immediate aftermath, is the gradual but indisputable dominion progression toward self-determination.[47] By 1946, British ministers were privately admitting among themselves that it was no longer possible for London to act without dominion approval in Commonwealth foreign policy matters. The dominions had emerged from the war as full partners in fact, as well as in name, in a "commonwealth of nations" which retained a symbolic link with the British Crown out of a sense of traditon and not obligation. And the right of secession from that association was exercised by Eire in 1948 as a further illustration of dominion self-determination when that nation decided to end its constitutional ambiguity by declaring itself a republic. Britain's Lord Chancellor Lord Jowitt all but admitted under questioning in Parliament that London would have considered reprisals against Dublin except that Canada, Australia, and New Zealand warned against such a recourse.[48] The sun had finally set on a substantial part of the British Empire, and a new day had dawned for its newly sovereign dominions.

Self-Determination and the Empire Experience

In July 1945, a Labour government was voted into power in Britain, thereby displacing empire champion Prime Minister Winston Churchill. But Clement Attlee's premiership, which extended from 1945 to 1951, did not witness the introduction of radical Commonwealth-Empire policies as in the instance of Labour's domestic legislation. Indeed, Labour's policy toward the empire was sufficiently moderate as to attract the support of many Conservatives who had begun to see the futility of attempting to maintain a "hard line" against growing colonial demands for self-determination.[49] Moreover, much of British public opinion was either ignorant of or apathetic toward the empire. In 1948, three-quarters of the respondents in a British national survey did not know the difference between a dominion and a colony, and half could not identify a single British colony.[50] To a very large extent, Labour M.P.'s in Parliament shared this public indifference toward the empire and were content to leave most colonial questions to the government ministers responsible for their resolution. These ministers were progressives, but they were also gradualists. Their policies were guided by two considerations which were unlikely to invite Conservative opposition. The first was the clear and irrefutable reality that the emancipation of India, Ceylon, and Burma could not be prudently avoided. The second consideration, which applied to the remainder of the dependent empire, was the practice of "trusteeship." Conservatives could not reasonably object to this practice since it was essentially their own creation.

The central imperative of the trusteeship arrangement obligated the colonial government to prepare the people under its jurisdiction for eventual self-government. This entailed the promotion of educational, welfare, medical, and administrative services, as well as the fostering of the economic prosperity which would support these endeavors and stabilize the new policy. Labour's Colonial Secretary Arthur Creech Jones warned fellow socialists in 1945 not to allow their distaste for imperialism to mislead them into too hasty a colonial retreat which would betray the peoples of the empire and Britain's trust. Trusteeship thus perceived implied that Britain was in Africa and Asia for the good of the populations of those respective continents, and that her aim was to "develop" them to a stage where they could fend for themselves. It was an attractive policy for anti-imperialists because it foresaw the end of empire, while the appeal for imperialists was that it did not foresee it too soon.[51]

Britain's new commitment to preparing her imperial dependencies for eventual self-determination was seemingly manifest in the 1945 Colonial Development and Welfare Act which allocated £120 million to be spent on colonial needs over a ten-year period. Many colonies were significantly assisted as road, houses, and hospitals were built, university colleges were established, and new economic enterprises were begun. Not all of the latter proved successful, however, as was the case with the Tanganyikan groundnuts (peanuts) scheme of 1948, which wasted £36 million trying to cultivate groundnuts in an unsuitable terrain. Further Colonial Development acts were passed in 1949 and 1950, but not all colonies benefited equally. Little was done to balance colonial economics or to diversify crop production, and those colonies that were not thought to have any resources worth developing ultimately used their share of funds merely to cancel overdrafts.[52] All in all, British aid resulted in a mixed record of achievement.

Some regions of the empire, such as India, contained advanced nationalist movements which neither required nor desired continued British tutelage after World War II. By 1946, it became obvious that Britain did not rule in India in any meaningful way. Communal riots and massacres involving Muslims and Hindus broke out in Calcutta during August of that year and soon spread throughout Bengal and Bihar and elsewhere, very rapidly reducing parts of the country to a state of near anarchy. The instigators of these bloody encounters were more frequently from the Muslim community which feared domination by the Hindus in an independent India.[53] The imperialistic attachment to India was, by this date, largely romantic, and romanticism did not pay dividends. Conservatives, accordingly, were not as adamantly opposed to Indian independence as some of their attacks against the Labour government's plan might suggest. And once the date had been set in February 1947, with the transfer of power scheduled for June 1948, the Muslims knew that they only needed to endure in order to achieve their objective of a separate state of Pakistan. The Hindu-dominated nationalist Congress party recognized that with the situation in the Punjab and Bengal as chaotic as it was, an Indian government would be no more successful than the British in controlling it. Reluctantly, the Congress party agreed to a partition and on August 15, 1947, ten months earlier than originally intended, India and Pakistan became independent nations.[54]

For months following the devolution, massive and bloody adjustments were undertaken. Wholesale exchanges of population east and west between the borders of the new states ensued, involving millions of people. Riots in Delhi and elsewhere left more than half a million dead. Almost immediately, a war broke out between India and Pakistan which the United Nations was compelled to settle. Neither the Conservatives nor the Liberals in Britain challenged the wisdom of granting self-determination to the peoples of the Asian subcontinent.[55] Their differences concerned timing, not method. What flattered them most of all was that India and Pakistan both chose to remain in the Commonwealth, though the Commonwealth had to be somewhat altered to accommodate them.[56]

Less than a year later, in January and February of 1948, Burma and Ceylon joined the ranks of the newly independent nations. The latter decided to continue its membership in the Commonwealth, but Burma, not surprisingly, did not. The Burmese had strongly resented a long-standing British policy that permitted unrestricted Indian immigration resulting in an alien community of more than a million out of a total population of seventeen million. The Burmese economy was essentially an agrarian one, and the average Burman could not compete with Indian coolies or artisans. Worse yet, some Indian moneylenders shrewdly conspired to displace the native peasants from their holdings through foreclosure of mortgages. At the end of World War II, the Burmese had embraced the "Asia for Asians" slogan used by Japanese propagandists, and a native constituent assembly in Rangoon adopted a republican constitution which expressly precluded membership in the Commonwealth.[57] London, embarrassed by its inability to defend Burma against attack and conquest, and mindful of both the Anglophobic tenor and the reasons for it in Burma, accepted the repudiation without protest.

African nationalism sprang very suddenly and rapidly into full growth in the years after the war. Aiding the cause of the African nationalists in the late 1940s and 1950s was the support they received from the British left. African leaders like Kwame Nkrumah and Hastings Bamda took encouragement from the events in India and from the fact that the general tide of world opinion seemed at that time to be with them. Powerful friends like Russia, who was supposed to be against empires, and the United States, whose similar claim was seemingly supported by the emancipation of the Philippines, gave the nationalists added encouragement. There was a six-week general strike in Nigeria in 1945, another one in the Sudan in 1947, and serious riots in Accra in the Gold Coast in 1948. None of these was nationalist inspired, but they were used and exploited by nationalists. By 1950, African nationalism was already a power on the west coast and was advancing quickly in East Africa too.

The British responded by blaming the new nationalists for acting prematurely in trying to achieve at once what the government claimed to be preparing them for in easy stages. An important issue of contention between the two sides was the position the traditional chiefs in Africa were to have in any process of self-determination. The nationalists regarded them as little better than British puppets, about as representative of modern democratic African opinion as dukes and earls were of English. But the Labour government in London insisted that the chiefs were essential to an ordered society and also enjoyed the support of the majority of the people. The first democratic elections held in Ghana and Nigeria in 1951-1952 appeared to vindicate all the nationalists' claims to represent the people. Britain acknowledged this outcome by releasing from jail the Gold Coast's leading "extremist," Kwame Nkrumah, and making him prime minister for the interim period before independence.[58]

By October 1951, when the Labour government left office, nationalist demands throughout the empire were already well in advance of Britain's willingness to concede them. Indeed, the next eight or nine years were the most difficult of all for the postwar empire, as nationalists' demands became bolder and their methods more drastic. A Conservative cabinet of ministers was perhaps temperamentally, if not ideologically, less inclined than its Labourite predecessor to recognize the need to adjust quickly to new realties without concern for the imperial image. Conflict sometimes erupted violently. To the colonial wars which were characteristic of the decade, Britain added its own in Malaya (1948-1958), Kenya (1952-1956), and Cyprus (1954-1959), together with skirmishes elsewhere.[59] In 1956, the London government dispatched troops to the Suez Canal to safeguard British interests there in the grand proprietary style of an earlier time. But the intervention ended with humiliating results. It was, however, all a part of the Conservatives' effort to find some means to halt the fall from imperial eminence which had started in 1947. The attempt failed. Yet it may have been necessary to the Conservative conscience to have made it.

In the 1950s, on the fronts where it had chosen to do combat, the new government fought hard. In some areas, it fought to keep colonies, in others, to be able to give them to the right people. In the latter category, it had two notable successes. In Malaya, a costly and brutal jungle war against communist guerrillas, which had begun in 1948, was effectively won by 1955.[60] Power was handed over two years later to a native government whose point of view on all essential matters, such as Britain's rubber interests there, was entirely satisfactory. In 1954, in British Guiana, the native population used the franchise Britain had recently granted in order to select what looked like a Communist administration. The government declined to accept that choice and suspended the constitution until the colony's radical sentiments diminished. In both these cases, there is considerable doubt as to how much support among the people the Communists really had, and the evidence would seem to suggest that Britain's friends were the more numerous element in each population. Similar successes were not enjoyed elsewhere because Britain falsely assumed that the same situation pertained, that the "extremists" were a minority whom the "people" would help defeat. That notion was a not uncommon Conservative delusion.[61]

London was encouraged by her Malayan experience in confronting the next colonial war in Cyprus. That Mediterranean island country exported nothing to Britain, and imported little from her, but by the 1950s it had become the most vital of Britain's possessions because of what recently had been happening around it. By the 1950s, Britain's interest in Middle East oil was at least as vital to her as the sealanes to India had been in the 1880s. Since 1947 and, for Britain, the disastrous conclusion to the Palestine problem, everything had conspired to undermine the influence London felt was essential to safeguard important interests in the region. Violent demonstrations and riots had even compelled the British garrisons to withdraw from the Suez in 1954. With Palestine and Egypt gone, Cyprus became the last bastion of British influence in the eastern Mediterranean and the focus of all her Middle Eastern strategy. British garrisons moved to Cyprus to find themselves taken up, not with defending British interests in the seas and air around them, but with holding Cyprus itself. A native nationalist group known as Eoka, seeking to unite the country with Greece, challenged the British and plunged the island country into the throes of a full-scale guerrilla war.[62]

Cyprus was a more difficult guerrilla war for the British than the one in Malaya because the Turks, as British allies, represented a small minority within the total population and most of world opinion did not support the London government. When Egyptian President Gamal Abdel Nasser nationalized the Suez Canal in 1956, the British, in secret collusion with France and Israel, invaded Egypt, only to be unceremoniously ejected by political realities.[63] Cyprus fell soon afterward, and, in 1960, Britain formally recognized her independence.[64] The object lesson of the Mediterranean experience for Britain should have been that its imperial perspective of the merits of nationalist demands for self-determination should, in the future, consider the attitude of one or more of the superpowers. But imperialist ambitions often feed illusions, and no less so in Britain's instance where defeat really meant retreat, and London's attention turned from the eastern Mediterranean to eastern Africa.

East-central Africa became Britain's substitute for Cyprus as the pivot from which London could protect her vital Middle Eastern interests. The greatest problem was that in none of the central or eastern African colonies except Southern Rhodesia was there a sufficiently large white settlement through which Britain might exercise effective political control of the area. Accordingly, London began promoting a formula whereby power in the colonies appeared to be shared between Europeans and Africans while, in fact, the Europeans, for a generation at least, remained dominant. This proposed policy was alternately called "partnership" and "multiracialism." But British support for the settler cause in Kenya led to the most ferocious nationalist response in all Africa. During the Mau Mau crisis, ten thousand people were killed, including some seventy Europeans and twenty or more Asians. Particularly tragic was the sect's slaughter of several thousand black tribesmen who refused to cooperate with the terrorists against the British. The defeat of the Mau Mau was accomplished by 1956, but London again assumed support where there was none and turned a deaf ear to African nationalists who demanded an end to Britain's enforced federation of Northern and Southern Rhodesia and Nyasaland. Northern Rhodesia's (Zambia's) lucrative copper belt was seen as London's mercantilistic motive, and nationalist leaders felt further betrayed when the British left the blacks under the jurisdiction of white mercenary colonial administrators in east-central Africa. Demonstrations soon led to riots, followed by mass arrests, deportations, bannings, baton charges, and worse. But, again, it was all so futile in the end. The British government persisted in backing the Federation to save the copper belt from the nationalizers, or the Europeans from the Africans, or the Africans from their own "ineptitude," or the continent from communism —or just themselves from the humiliation of another retreat.[65]

By the late 1950s, imperialism was beginning to lose its large capitalist constituency in Britain for the imperial role was proving to be a costly one to sustain. The men of industry and finance were realists, not romanticists. As the fortunes of the empire began to change, the big capitalists began to make their own arrangements with the successor states and to protect their interests as best they could. They did business with whomever was on top: in South Africa where they still had firm control, it was the white supremacists, but, in tropical Africa, it was the new black nationalists. That same spirit of economic pragmatism also shifted the attention of an increasing number of British investors from the uncertain markets of the empire and toward the new European Economic Community.[66]

What began as a trickle in the 1950s, when the Sudan, the Gold Coast (Ghana), and Malaya had been the only colonies to escape the ties of an imperial dependency, soon became a torrent in the 1960s. Beginning with Somalia, Cyprus, and Nigeria in 1960, more than twenty additional colonies won their independence over the next eight years. And the few remaining territories of the empire have continued the secession into the 1970s, with Fiji gaining independence in October 1970, the Bahamas in July 1973, and Grenada in February 1974. At first, it was thought that the Commonwealth would provide an umbrella under which the black and brown nations, together with the white dominions, might yet pose a force to be reckoned with in the world: a society of free nations, cemented by common bonds of tradition, friendship, and mutual interest, that would retain Britain's global influence.[67] London soon discovered that that was but another illusion, however, as the harsh realities of the new order rudely shattered all such hopes.

Trade preferences, together with a common citizenship which was defined by the British Nationality Act of 1948 and allowed Commonwealth citizens unrestricted entry into the United Kingdom, did not produce even an alliance of interests between Britain and her former dependencies. Even the "white" dominions were too separated geographically to share many common interests, and membership in the Commonwealth by the black and the brown nations was not an expression of filial gratitude and loyalty. Rather, it provided merely a convenient platform on the world stage for those nations to air grievances, especially against Britain, and to share in such British aid as was still obtainable. Moreover, Commonwealth members fought each other and broke off diplomatic relations with one another and with the "mother country." In 1961, the African-Asian members led a successful campaign to expel from the family one of its oldest members, South Africa, much to the indignation of her white sister nations. London gradually came to realize that the Commonwealth was not, and never could be, what had been originally intended, and Britain's first serious overture to the Common Market in 1962 signaled the beginning of a new policy that would give priority to European over Commonwealth involvement. Later that same year, Britain amended her "common citizenship" definition of 1948 and began restricting colored immigration from the Commonwealth.[68] Although the organization has survived to the present day, it is now little more than an international debating society with a dubious attachment to a past tradition.

Britain still retains an overseas empire in the late 1970s, but it is a greatly diminished one. Hong Kong, with its four million inhabitants, is on lease from China until 1997. But aside from that crown colony, the total population of Britain's remaining dependencies numbers fewer than a million. In some instances, London has responded with an almost unseemly haste to the separatist demands of parties proposing independence for colonial communities, no matter how ready or viable the new states might be in political or economic terms. The transition from colonial rule to self-rule has proved unsettling for some peoples. This was especially true where, under the artificial conditions created by colonial rule, the establishment of minority communities had been permitted. Their natural assimilation, however, had been discouraged by the presence of an external authority which sheltered them.[69] In countries like Kenya, Rhodesia, India, and Ireland, the artificial suspension of the indigenous political balance of power resulted in some instances in bloody moments of truth and, in others, in the perpetuation of tense or incendiary conditions. Edwin Samuel Montagu, Britain's enlightened secretary of state for India between 1917 and 1922, believed that representative government required not only representative institutions to thrive, but also conventions, customs, and habits which no act of parliament could teach or impose. Consequently, he felt the Indians deserved the chance to work out their own destiny. "Chaos, revolution and bloodshed," warned Montagu in 1930, "will occur, but the results years afterwards might be a more vigorous, more healthy, more self-created [plant] than the plant we have in view."[70] It took London almost another generation to appreciate fully the wisdom of that statement, but in the 1970s it is a lesson learned, however late.

Self-Determination and the
United Kingdom Experience

Ireland, the pacesetter for dominion self-determination which resulted first in the emancipation of the Commonwealth and later the empire, emerged again in the 1960s as an inspiration to home-rule movements within the Scottish and Welsh territories of the United Kingdom. A 1967 coalition of Catholic moderates and Protestant liberals, the Northern Ireland Civil Rights Association, emerged in Ulster as a protest to the apartheid and oppression

which were endemic to life in that province. Their objectives were
not secession or self-determination but jobs, housing, better education, and greater suffrage for the Catholic minority. Northern Ireland Prime Minister Terence O'Neill, partly at the urging of British
Prime Minister Harold Wilson, made a few modest concessions
which brought an immediate response from the fanatics of the
Orange Society lodges. Orange extremists, the timidity of politicians, and the impatience of Catholic radicals—socialist and republican—combined to destroy the spirit and influence of the 1967 civil
rights movement. They also destroyed the Northern Ireland Parliament at Stormont as London promptly suspended that body and
placed the province under direct rule after sectarian feuding intensified almost to the level of a civil war over the next decade.[71]

During those troubled years, British and Ulster politicans alternately spoke, from time to time, of a federal scheme for government of the United Kingdom and of a completely independent
nation of Northern Ireland. Neither idea was new to British politics, nor did the ideas appear any more feasible than they had a
generation or more earlier. But such conjecture did have its impact upon the latent separatist tendencies of some Scottish and
Welsh organizations, and this time London found the irrepressible
spirit of self-determination rising ominously within the realm itself.

Private members' bills for Scottish and Welsh home rule had
been introduced during the Irish home-rule agitation years earlier,
but not until 1975 did a British government introduce proposals
of its own. The Scots had always regarded themselves as a nation,
with a distinct culture, church, and even a separate legal system.
Furthermore, Scotland always has been recognized as a distinct
administrative unit, with a Scottish administration in Edinburgh
and a Scottish Office in London since 1939. The secretary for
Scotland was raised to a secretary of state in 1926 and has responsibilities in Scotland for agriculture, criminal law, education, housing, legal services, local government, roads, prisons, health, and a
host of other services. Wales also retained a national identity with
a strong language tradition, now recognized in the 1967 Welsh Language Act. The minister for Welsh affairs was raised to a secretary
of state in 1964, and a Welsh Office has existed since 1954, though
with fewer responsibilities than the Scottish Office. In Parliament,
there are Welsh and Scottish Grand Committees, made up of all

the Welsh and Scottish members respectively, which consider the details of any legislation for their areas.[72]

Home-rule organization existed in Scotland and Wales in the nineteenth century, but it has been only in recent years that voters have moved from national sentiment to political nationalism in considerable numbers.[73] The present Scottish National Party (SNP) dates from 1934. It has generally supported a moderate home-rule settlement, but its rhetoric, like that of the home-rule Irish, is ambiguous and the movement includes many avowed separatists. The present Welsh Nationalist party, Plaid Cymru, dates from 1925.

The SNP did elect one member of Parliament in 1945, but this was not repeated until a by-election victory in 1969. In October 1974, however, it won eleven seats and was already recognized as a political power to be contended with. Plaid Cymru poses less of a threat than the SNP to the established parties—Conservative, Labour and Liberal—but it won its first seat in a 1966 by-election and won three seats in the 1974 general election. A swing of just a few percentage points in the nationalists' strength in Scotland and Wales could put any government, particularly a Labour government, at their mercy in Parliament. This prospect so alarmed Labour that its ministers appointed a Royal Commission on the Constitution, the Kilbrandon Commission, which sat from 1969 to 1973. The government subsequently produced three White Papers on devolution to Scotland and Wales in 1974, 1975, and 1976, and introduced legislation in the fall of 1976. They made no proposals for England since the Kilbrandon Commission was unable to achieve any consensus view as to what to offer the U.K.'s forty-six million English who also felt alienated from the government. The best that the commission could devise was that England should make do with regional, coordinating advisory councils, but nothing was said in reference to the popular disaffection with Parliament in England. Accordingly, the government decided to postpone action on England and offered instead reforms tailored for the Scottish and Welsh constituencies.[74]

Under the government's proposal, Scotland would have a unicameral assembly of 150 members serving fixed four-year terms. The Welsh would have a unicameral assembly of 80 members serving fixed four-year terms. The Scottish assembly would nominate a chief executive and would then be asked to vote on his/her choice of a cabinet. Moreover, the Scottish assembly would also have power to legislate in a number of areas including local government, health, social work, the arts, science, public housing, industry, land resources, the legal system, and the criminal code. Most of Scotland's domestic life would be within its own jurisdiction, but the United Kingdom Parliament would retain responsibility for foreign relations, the EEC, defense, and international economic relations. Criminal prosecutions and police would also be reserved to the U.K. Parliament because of its ultimate responsibility to protect the state.[75]

The Welsh assembly would have no legislative powers. Instead, it would assume the powers presently exercised by the secretary of state for Wales and other ministers. In practice, this would simply mean the assembly would administer laws passed by the U.K. Parliament. It would further deal with the subject areas devolved to the Scottish assembly, but it would have fewer powers.[76] Neither Scotland nor Wales would have independent powers to raise revenue. All taxes, with the exception of local authority rates (property taxes) would be set and collected by the U.K. Parliament. Each year, Parliament would negotiate with the two executives a blank grant from which each assembly would pay for its respective services.

What is worth noting in all of this is that both Scotland and Wales are currently overrepresented in Parliament. If one vote one value were the measure, Scotland would have fifty-one members, not seventy-one and Wales thirty-one, not thirty-five. Ulster, on the other hand, is underrepresented by several seats. The commission and White Paper devolution proposals say nothing about changing these proportions for reasons which are not difficult to perceive. The reform proposals are the products of a Labour ministry and Labour traditionally has drawn much of its support to win a majority in the House of Commons in Scotland and Wales, not in heavily Unionist Northern Ireland.[77] Hence, Parliament's ultimate sovereignty and the safeguarding of existing representation ratios have been the twin underpinnings of Labour's alternative proposals to the more-radical Scottish and Welsh self-determination schemes.

Therefore, just as the political map of the empire has been substantively altered by self-determination movements in recent decades, it is not inconceivable, even if it is less probable, that the political configuration of the United Kingdom might yet be notably amended. The quest for self-determination is universal, and, at least in some instances, its denial or delay can lead to serious alienation and to violent consequences. What seems clear, however, is that, although the achievement of political self-determination often has been a precondition to peace, stability, and friendly relations, it is not in and of itself a panacea for all domestic or international ills. Independence or home-rule has not automatically strengthened the observance of human rights and fundamental freedoms. Indeed, in Northern Ireland, in Southern Rhodesia, and in other former colonial territories, self-determination often has meant the substitution of a local ascendancy for an imperialist governing class. Yet, on balance, the secessions, liberations, and devolutions in recent political history have been a positive legacy, and Britain's historical perspective on self-determination might usefully remind us of Shakespeare's famous comment upon mercy:

> It is twice bless'd;
> It blesseth him that gives and him that takes.[78]

Notes

1. Jack J. Roth, ed., *World War I: A Turning Point in Modern History* (New York, 1967), pp. 99-107.

2. For an especially instructive essay on this contemporary phenomenon, see Edward H. Carr, *Nationalism and After* (London, 1968), pp. 38-74.

3. An authoritative account of Lloyd George's position at the conference is Harold Nicolson, *Peacemaking 1919* (London, 1933).

4. The House of Commons was sharply divided over a Scotland bill under discussion as recently as November 14, 1977 (see Order Paper No. 8 of that date, p. 468, and the corresponding account in Hansard's *Parliamentary Debates*).

5. "Revolts Against the Crown: The British Response to Imperial Insurgency," manuscript by J. Bowyer Bell.

6. Paul Power, *Gandhi on World Affairs* (Washington, D.C., 1960), p. 83; the Irish struggle against Britain also influenced Nasser (see Giovanni Costigan, "The Anglo-Irish Conflict, 1919-1922: A War of Independence or Systema-

tized Murder?" *University Review* 5, no. 1 [Spring 1968] , p. 66).

7. Ireland brought the British Isles to the very precipice of civil war in 1914 (see George Dangerfield, *The Strange Death of Liberal England* [London, 1935]).

8. For the actual figures on the schism in the Irish nationalist ranks, see Breandan MacGiolla Choille, ed., *Intelligence Notes, 1913-16* (Dublin, 1966), p. 175.

9. Edgar Hold, *Protest in Arms: The Irish Troubles, 1916-1923* (London, 1960), p. 69.

10. Oliver MacDonagh, *Ireland* (Englewood Cliffs, N.J., 1968), pp. 70-71.

11. C. D. Greaves, *The Life and Times of James Connolly* (London, 1961), pp. 318-19.

12. The captain later published his own account of this mission (see Karl Spindler, *The Mystery of the Casement Ship* [Tralee, Ire., 1965]).

13. Hold, *Protest in Arms*, pp. 116-17.

14. Lawrence J. McCaffrey, *The Irish Question, 1800-1922* (Lexington, Ky., 1968), p. 166.

15. P. S. O'Hegarty, *The Victory of Sinn Fein* (Dublin, 1924), pp. 3-4.

16. The definitive study on the convention is R. B. McDowell, *The Irish Convention, 1917-1918* (London, 1970).

17. Robert Kee, *The Green Flag* (London, 1972), p. 619; see also David Miller, *Church, State, and Nation in Ireland, 1898-1921* (Dublin, 1973), pp. 401-7.

18. Dorothy Macardle, *The Irish Republic* (New York, 1965), pp. 253-54.

19. Donald Akenson, *The United States and Ireland* (Cambridge, Mass., 1973), p. 51; see also O'Hegarty, *Victory of Sinn Fein*, p. 32.

20. *Dail Eireann: Minutes of Proceedings*, 21 January 1919, pp. 15-23.

21. C. L. Mowat, *Britain between the Wars* (London, 1968), pp. 66-67.

22. Thomas E. Hachey, *Britain and Irish Separatism: From the Fenians to the Free State, 1867-1922* (Chicago, 1977), pp. 270-74.

23. Lloyd George's private secretary, Philip Kerr, wrote Chief Secretary for Ireland Sir Homar Greenwood of the need to keep the English people aware of the real situation in Ireland since the London government might undertake "very strong action in the near future" (Kerr to Greenwood, 3 May 1920, Lothian MSS).

24. For a contemporary account of this anguished decision reached by the Ulster Unionist Council in March 1920, see Ronald McNeill (Lord Cushendun), *Ulster's Stand for Union* (London, 1922), p. 279; see also Ian Colvin, *The Life of Lord Carson*, Vol. 3 (London, 1936), pp. 377-83.

25. The Earl of Longford and Thomas P. O'Neill, *Eamon de Valera* (Boston, 1971), pp. 132-38.

26. Sir C. E. Calwell, *Field-Marshall Sir Henry Wilson: His Life and Diaries*, Vol. 2 (London, 1927), pp. 246, 295-96.

27. Lord Beaverbrook, *The Decline and Fall of Lloyd George* (New York, 1963), p. 84.

28. O'Hegarty, *Victory of Sinn Fein,* pp. 52-58; C.J.C. Street, *Ireland in 1921* (London, 1922), pp. 145-55.

29. In reporting on his July 14 meeting with de Valera to the king, Lloyd George emphasized that he had not allowed an Irish republic or a separate Irish nation outside the British Empire to be discussed (Lloyd George to George V, 14 July 1921, Lloyd George MSS, F/29/4/69).

30. De Valera's official biography offers these last two explanations, and others, to explain the Irish president's decision to remain in Dublin. They are credible, if not entirely convincing, reasons (Longford and O'Neill, *Eamon de Valera,* p. 146).

31. Mowat, *Britain between the Wars,* pp. 89-91.

32. *Dail Eireann, Official Report: Debate on the Treaty between Great Britain and Ireland Signed in London on 6 December 1921,* (Dublin, n.d.), p. 32.

33. Viceroy Lord Fitzalan had written the prime minister some months earlier to say that the Irish would make demands but that they were in no position to take the field again, "no matter what they ask for, or what is refused them" (Fitzalan to Lloyd George, 18 August 1921, Lloyd George MSS, F/17/2/8).

34. Rex Taylor, *Michael Collins* (London, 1965), pp. 247-52.

35. *Dail Eireann Official Report: Debate on the Treaty,* pp. 5-410.

36. For an excellent account of this period, see Calton Younger, *Ireland's Civil War* (London, 1970).

37. Denis Gwynn, *The History of Partition, 1912-1925* (Dublin, 1950), pp. 222-36.

38. Donal McCartney, "From Parnell to Pearse," in T. W. Moody and F. X. Martin, eds., *The Course of Irish History* (Cork, 1967), p. 312.

39. For the definitive study on the subject, see D. W. Harkness, *The Restless Dominion* (New York, 1970).

40. There are several good histories of the Empire-Commonwealth. Some of these include: Alfred L. Burt, *The British Empire and Commonwealth* (Boston, 1956); W. P. Hall, R. G. Albion, and J. B. Pope, *A History of England and the Empire-Commonwealth* (Waltham, Mass., 1961); and W. D. Hussey, *The British Empire and Commonwealth, 1500 to 1601* (Cambridge, Eng., 1963).

41. Nicholas Mansergh, *The Commonwealth Experience* (New York, 1969), p. 22.

42. Both prior to and during World War II, British government officials debated among themselves regarding the constitutional status of dominion governments (for representative examples of this dialogue, see the Dominions Office general correspondence in Public Record Office class DO/35).

43. W. C. Hankinson, Dominions Office, to Oliver Harvey, Foreign Office, 7 February 1939 (F.O. 371/24150).

44. Dominions Office memorandum to the Foreign Office, 30 October 1939 (FO 372/3319).

45. John Maffey, Dublin, to Sir John Stephenson, Foreign Office, 29 January 1945 (D.O. 35/1228).

46. Nicholas Mansergh, *Survey of British Commonwealth Affairs* (London, 1968), p. 59.

47. See Cab. 65 and Cab. 66; see also D.O. 35.

48. Nicholas Mansergh, *Documents and Speeches on British Commonwealth Affairs, 1931-1952,* vol. 2 (London, 1954), pp. 811-21.

49. Henry Pelling, *Modern Britain, 1855-1955* (New York, 1960), pp. 167-71.

50. David Goldsworthy, *Colonial Issues in British Politics, 1945-1961* (Oxford, 1971), sec. 20.

51. Rita Hinden, *Empire and After* (London, 1949), p. 164.

52. Bernard Porter, *The Lion's Share* (London, 1975), p. 314.

53. Robert Huttenback, *The British Imperial Experience* (New York, 1966), pp. 193-97.

54. Porter, *Lion's Share*, pp. 315-17; see also Huttenback, *British Imperial Experience*, pp. 197-202.

55. For an excellent account of this complex transition, see Leonard Mosley, *The Last Days of the British Raj* (London, 1961).

56. By the mutual agreement of the Commonwealth prime ministers' meeting in London in April 1949, India was permitted to remain within the organization in spite of her establishment of a republican form of government.

57. H. Tinker, *The Union of Burma* (London, 1967), pp. 22-27.

58. Porter, *Lion's Share*, pp. 322-24; see also Goldsworthy, *Colonial Issues in British Politics*, pp. 17-21.

59. For useful accounts of each of these insurgencies, see Richard Clutterbuck, *The Long, Long War: The Emergency in Malaya, 1948-1960* (Hamden, Conn., 1966); Carl G. Rosverg and John Nottingham, *The Myth of "Mau Mau" Nationalism in Kenya* (New York, 1966); and Charles Foley, *Legacy of Strife: Cyprus from Rebellion to Civil War* (London, 1964).

60. For further background, see Sir Robert Thompson, *Defeating Communist Insurgency* (London, 1966).

61. Porter, *Lion's Share*, p. 326.

62. Ibid., pp. 326-27; see also George Grivas, *Guerrilla Warfare and EOKA's Struggle* (London, 1964).

63. For an informative account of the British strategy during the Suez crisis, see Hugh Thomas, *Suez* (New York, 1966), pp. 127-70; see also Sir Anthony Eden, *Full Circle* (Boston, 1960).

64. For a detailed account of the fall, see R. Stephens, *Cyprus: A Place of Arms* (London, 1966).

65. Porter, *Lion's Share*, pp. 328-30.

66. Kenneth Younger, *Changing Perspectives in British Foreign Policy* (London, 1964), pp. 1-14.

67. For an interesting essay on the future of the Commonwealth, see H. Victor Wiseman, *Britain and the Commonwealth* (London, 1965), pp. 123-53.

68. Mansergh, *Commonwealth Experience*, pp. 340-68.

69. Porter, *Lion's Share*, pp. 347-48; see also Margery Perham, *The Colonial Reckoning* (London, 1963).

70. Edwin S. Montagu, *An Indian Diary* (London, 1930), p. 136.

71. Thomas E. Hachey, *The Problem of Partition: Peril to World Peace* (Chicago, 1972), pp. 39-42.

72. Alan J. Ward, "Home Rule and Devolution: A Study of the British Constitution and Regional Nationalism," (Paper presented at the Irish Studies Conference, Chicago, 1977), p. 30.

73. The Liberal party endorsed Scottish and Welsh home rule as early as 1894.

74. Ward, "Home Rule and Devolution," pp. 31-32; see also Great Britain, *Our Changing Democracy: Devolution to Scotland and Wales*, Cmord. 6348 (London: Her Majesty's Stationary Office, 1975).

75. Ibid.

76. *The Economist,* 29 November 1975, p. 15.

77. Ward, "Home Rule and Devolution," p. 34.

78. William Shakespeare, *The Merchant of Venice*, act. 4, sc. 1.

7

Self-Determination in Soviet Politics

Ilya Levkov

Why should we Great Russians, who have been oppressing more nations than any other people, deny the right to secession for Poland, Ukraine, or Finland?

—Lenin
April 20, 1917

Contemporary Soviet Union constitutes an unusual conglomeration of nationalities and covers one-sixth of the globe. It was calculated that the Russian Empire expanded fifty square miles a day over a period of four-hundred years. However, since the acquired territories constituted one, uninterrupted continuum, the empire lacked the characteristic element of classical empires like Holland, Spain, and Britain, i.e., distant and separated territories under its control. These and other empires have long since disintegrated, and only the Russian Empire survived wars and ideological revolutions. In 1913, the territory of the Russian Empire was 22.3 million square kilometers; in 1978, it was 22.4.[1] This empire's ability to survive is even more puzzling in light of the fact that the idea of self-determination was heralded by Soviet leaders as the cornerstone of the Soviet policy toward over a hundred nationalities. This analysis will trace the Soviet concept of self-determination within the Soviet domestic, regional, and international politics and will shed light on how a potential disintegrative concept became an element of territorial consolidation and expansion.

The concept of national self-determination was introduced into the Bolshevik political agenda by Lenin. Since then, it has occupied a permanent place in Soviet declarations and official statements. The leaders of the October 1917 Revolution, who inherited a multinational empire, were faced with the danger of complete disintegration. As a result of this danger, Bolsheviks gave a high priority to the issue of self-determination.

Self-determination was implemented in two stages by creating a federal system: first, by establishing the Russian Socialist Federative Soviet Republic (RSFSR); and second, in 1922, by establishing the Union of Soviet Socialist Republics (USSR). Although the concept of self-determination has remained a core element of Soviet ideology, the advocacy of true political independence has been unthinkable. Some of the major purge trials of the 1930s involved charges of conspiring to separate some national area from the union.

The Soviet federative system is highly complex. It constitutes the final result of the expansion of the Russian Empire, which involved the incorporation of numerous nationalities. It includes thirty-five states and eighteen lesser political entities. The national states are the fifteen union republics and twenty autonomous republics. The eighteen lesser entities consist of eight autonomous regions and ten national districts.[2] Most of these political entities are within the RSFSR; sixteen autonomous republics, five autonomous regions, and ten national districts.[3]

The national and ethnic structure of the Soviet Union is extremely heterogeneous. The census of 1926 listed 178 ethnic groups, and the census of 1959, 101 ethnic groups. The census of 1970 listed only 91 nationalities of more than ten-thousand people each.[4] The Soviets explain the disappearance of some 80 ethnic entities as a result of ethnic consolidation, which they attribute to the fusion of closely related nationalities and nations.[5] In 1970, the Russians constituted 53.4 percent of the total population. The Soviet forecasters predict, however, that by the year 2000 they will have slid to 44.3 percent of the Soviet population.[6] The issue of Soviet ethnic groups—their development, problems, and frictions—does not constitute a part of this article since it is covered widely by unofficial Soviet publications (Samizdat)[7] and by Western analysts.[8]

The Pattern of Soviet Federalism

National self-determination in the Soviet Union was implemented within the framework of Soviet federalism.[9] In accord with this policy, the larger nations were allocated the status of union republics, and the smaller nationalities were granted their right of self-determination in the form of national-territorial autonomy. This national-territorial autonomy was subdivided into three levels: autonomous republic, autonomous region, and national district. In turn, these entities were divided into political and administrative types, an autonomous republic being a political type and autonomous regions and national districts being administrative types.[10] However, a recent Soviet work questions this division of autonomy into political and administrative types, stating that all of the forms are autonomous and, therefore, are independent political units.[11] That analysis introduces a new element into the Soviet theory of federalism by stating that each nation, regardless of its size and form of autonomy, has the right to express its notion of self-determination by secession.[12]

The structures of the governing bodies of the union and autonomous republics strongly reflect the structure of the central federal authorities. They include a Supreme Soviet and Council of Ministries. The constitution of an autonomous SSR must be ratified by the Supreme Soviet of the union republic in which the autonomous republic is located. Each national-territorial autonomy sends representatives to the Soviet of Nationalities. An autonomous republic sends eleven delegates, an autonomous region sends five, and a national district sends one delegate.

The modes of administering the complex system of Soviet federalism are issue-linear, -functional, and -territorial.[13] Although the three are interrelated, numerous difficulties have remained unsolved, and problems of coordination continue to plague the Soviet system.[14] Realizing the limits of industrial and economic development along ethnic lines, the Soviet authorities have repeatedly shifted various ministries back and forth from the republics to the union. Khrushchev's introduction of economic units, Sovnarkhoz, in place of ministries has been abolished, and the ministries reinstated. A "new" type of governing body, the union-republican ministry, was established—actually, reestablished—by a decree of July 10, 1967.[15] Dual control of these ministries became a symbol of the Soviet federative process.

Numerous scholars consider the concept of change to be at the heart of the Marxist system.[16] However, change in Marxist thought does not always take the form of linear development.[17] Thus, a recent study shifts the analysis from the traditional debate, on the usefulness of a bureaucratic versus the totalitarian model, to a new concept that characterizes the contemporary Soviet system, the mono-organizational society.[18] Accepting the conceptualization of the present Soviet system as authoritarian and mono-organizational, the following analysis will focus on the purposes, functions, and dynamics of self-determination in Soviet domestic and foreign policies.

The Ideological Premises

The founding fathers of modern socialism, Marx and Engels, gave only limited attention to the political aspects of nationhood and the process of self-determination. The concept of nation appeared in Marx's thought as a by-product of a historical economic development. According to him, this fiction was created and promoted by a ruling class in order to preserve and expand its control over the means of production. Marx's emphasis on the direct linear development of human history brought him to oppose the reversibility of large, centralized units of capitalism, even when such structures demanded the incorporation of several nationalities. Therefore, the reemergence of small Slav states in Eastern Europe was perceived by Marx as an anachronistic and selfish demand which would hinder the development of an international socialist movement. According to Marx, the eventual abolition of the ruling class would lead to the demise of nations, and, therefore, the state would wither away as a political unit. Any encouragement of nationalism would endanger the growth of class consciousness, which is the major precondition for the creation of an international socialist system.

Marx's followers, who lived in various multi-ethnic societies, realized the limitation of this prescription for the socialist development since they were confronted with the strength of nationalism as a political force. For example, the Polish Social Democrats, led by Rosa Luxemburg, did not see the need to give up nationhood in order to attain socialism. They demanded national self-determination for themselves and for the Balkan states. Another group, led by Karl Renner and Otto Bauer and consisting mainly of Austrian Social Democrats, questioned the necessity of abolishing the national state. Their conclusion was to support the unlimited right of ethnic groups to exercise their cultural autonomy. The basis for this conclusion was that since nationalism and national differences were on the increase it would be wise to incorporate them into socialist theory. By stressing the function of cultural autonomy in the mobilization of the masses, Renner and Bauer introduced a new concept, extraterritorial, national-cultural autonomy. By separating the idea of "nationality" from "territory," this concept eliminated the pretext for national struggles, clearing the road for class struggle only. This idea of extraterritorial, national-cultural autonomy was introduced to the Russian Social Democrats by the Bund-Jewish Socialist party. At their Second Congress, the Russian Social Democrats rejected the idea as a solution to the nationality problem in Russia. However, because of the mounting demands of the socialist parties of Armenia, Byelorussia, and Georgia, the Second Congress incorporated in its final program the right of national self-determination. However, this was more of a declaration of intent, which symbolized the political and cultural equality of nations, than a policy to be implemented.[19]

Lenin first approached the issue of self-determination in 1903. Replying to the Armenian Social Democrats, he wrote: "The Union should eliminate from its program the demand for a *federative republic*, limiting their demands for a democratic republic. . . . It is not the business of the proletariat to prophesy federalism and national autonomy. . . . Concerning the support of demands for national autonomy, it does not constitute a permanent consented obligation of the proletariat. Such support could become necessary but only in specific, extra-ordinary cases."[20] Ten years later, Lenin repeated his position:

So long and so far as different nations constitute a unified state, Marxists will under no circumstances advocate the federative principle or decentralization. The centralized large state is a mighty historical step forward on the path from medieval fragmentation to the future socialist unity of the entire world, and there is not and cannot be any other way to socialism except through such a state, which is indissolubly linked to capitalism.[21]

Lenin advocated self-determination in the form of political self-determination, state independence, and the formation of a nation state.[22] Lenin gave four major reasons for demanding the right to self-determination of the incorporated nationalities in Russia: (1) 57 percent of Russia's population was not Russian, (2) the oppression of these nationalities was much stronger in Russia than in other states (3) a number of the oppressed nationalities had compatriots across the border who enjoyed greater national independence, and (4) bourgeois revolutions and national movements could spread to some of the kindred nationalities within the borders of Russia. Therefore, he concluded that it was the particular, concrete historical features of the national question in Russia that made the recognition of the right of nations to self-determination in that period urgent.[23]

Lenin's goals, which were to be achieved by promoting the right to self-determination, were the unity of the proletariat and the interests of their class solidarity,[24] since the recognition of the right of all nations to self-determination implied a political agency that contained a maximum of democracy and minimum of nationalism.[25] However, he did not generally advocate freedom of secession because he did not want to encourage separatism. Nations, according to Lenin, would resort to secession only when national oppression and national friction made coexistence intolerable and hindered economic intercourse. In that case, the interests of capitalist development and the freedom of class struggle would be served by secession.[26] It is clear that Lenin's major criterion for supporting national aspirations for self-determination was, first and foremost, the self-determination of the proletariat of a given nation.[27] He stated that "the proletariat is opposed to supporting any national aspirations. While recognizing equality and the equal rights of states, the proletariat *values above all* and *places foremost* the alliance of the proletarians of all nations, and assesses any national demand, any national separation, from the angle of the worker's class struggle."[28] Lenin's hope for the stability of Russia's system hung on the belief that, the closer a democratic system is to granting complete freedom to secede, the less frequent and less ardent will be the desire for separation in practice because big states have indisputable economic and political advantages.[29]

There are three major elements in Lenin's position on self-determination: (1) there should be no division of state and party organizations along national lines, (2) national self-determination in the form of secession is available but not advisable, and (3) full democratic and linguistic rights should be extended to all nationalities and ethnic groups. Thus, the fundamental political choice of nationalities was between secession or remaining within the Soviet state. Once this choice was made, no political variations were permitted to remain in the union. Lenin objected to federation as a principle because the aim of socialism was not only the end of the division of mankind into tiny states but their integration.[30] However, neither the April Theses of 1917 nor the Party's Resolution on the National Question of May 12, 1917, mentioned the future structure of the Soviet state.[31]

The natural consequences of this polarization and the final rejection of "national cultural autonomy" created a political vacuum which, in the formative years of the Soviet state, invited challenges from nationalists, federalists, and Russian centralists. Lenin gave no specific explanation for the absence of a plan for the state's structure. A recent Soviet work suggests a rationale for not considering a federal system prior to the revolution: the existing bureaucratic centralism would have to be replaced by democratic centralism, which in turn would enable the remaining democratic changes to occur.[32] However, the concept of federation was never categorically and unconditionally rejected by Lenin, as long as numerous nations composed a united state.

The events that followed the revolution changed Lenin's opinion on the introduction of a federal system as an expression of self-determination. Since the unity of the Russian state was distorted by the events of 1917, federation became a viable solution for retaining the proletarian unity.[33] Thus, Lenin's relationship to federation was not a matter of principle, but a matter of concrete situation which had to be reconsidered at the moment of the practical building of a multinational state. Had the revolution occurred in 1905, the principle of federalism would have been used in spite of Lenin's extreme criticism of it in 1903. The party had to take into account the specifics of the situation without limiting its scope of actions.[34] The proposed state framework of federation forecast an easier way to organize the development of economies and cultures of other nationalities within the statehood provided by the federative system.[35] Contemporary Soviet historians and analysts are adapting Lenin's prerevolutionary views against the loosely tied federation to the political goals and processes of the Soviet Union in the seventies in order to promote one centralized unit.[36]

The Transitional Period

The October Revolution of 1917 and the civil war that ended in 1922 tested Marxist theories concerning the natural affinity among nations governed by dictatorships of the proletariat. Although the provisional government introduced the concept of national self-rule by transferring administrative power to local leaders, it was not ready to promote a policy of secession. The diffusion of central political power greatly assisted the centrifugal forces of various nationalities which were striving for autonomy and independence. The Bolsheviks supported the claims of these nationalities. However, when Finland, Lithuania, Latvia, Estonia, and the Siberian Republic proclaimed independence in January and February 1918, the Bolsheviks realized the urgent need for reformulating their ideological tenets. In order to halt the avalanche of secession, Lenin instructed the Bolsheviks to seize power in every national republic.

The ideological reformulation was adopted at the Eighth Party Congress in March 1919, after the consideration of differing proposals from Lenin, Stalin, and Bukharin. The congress, recognizing the need for a transition period, supported Lenin's self-determination proposals to create a federative unification of states organized on the Soviet pattern.[37] The congress also adopted the policy of national equality, thus clearing the way for the right of political secession. Finally, the level of historical development of each nation was to determine which social class would lead the independence movement.[38] Thus, Lenin's pre-1917 concept of the right to self-determination was gone; instead, he offered *federalism* which had to be redefined as a centripetal and not as a centrifugal force.

The Modalities of Implementation
of the Principle of Self-Determination

It is important to trace the introduction of the federal system in the Soviet Union because it did not stem from ideological or theoretical concepts but from tactical exigencies. This implementation was carried out in a political system that included only two sovereign institutions: the Soviets and the Russian Communist Party. The Party was not divided along national lines but retained it strong hierarchical order. Thus, administrative controls remained highly centralized.

The first stage of the creation of the Soviet federative state occurred in 1918 with the establishment of the Russian Federative Republic. The Third All-Soviet Congress, which convened in January 1918, proclaimed the establishment of this republic as a federation of national Soviet republics. The congress empowered the All-Union Central Executive Committee to prepare a constitution for the proposed federal union. The need to create a workable solution for a state structure was heightened by fears that the Russian state would disintegrate. Between January and May 1918, the following republics, in addition to those listed above, declared themselves independent: Ukraine, Moldavia, Oirot, Byelorussia, North Caucasia, and Transcaucasia. The crux of the problem, however, was retaining the unitary state without negating the promise of self-determination. At the same time, the right of self-determination was limited to the "working masses" (peasants, nonorganized workers). It was not until March 1919 that the proletariat (organized industrial workers) was given this right.

Meanwhile, the Bolsheviks focused their efforts on establishing people's republics, e.g., North Caucasia, Terek-Kosac, Tataro-Bashkirian, and the Turkestan Soviet Federative Republic, within the Russian republic. Between 1920 and 1923, the government of the RSFSR established seventeen autonomous regions and republics within its territory.[39] The constitution, ratified on July 10, 1918, recognized the right of member-republics to secede, without providing a precise federal framework for exercizing this right.[40]

The Period of the Contractual Federation

The formation of Soviet Russia between July 1918 and December 1922 was an experimental stage of Soviet federalism. The seceded republics declared their independence, which was officially recognized by the Soviet regime,[41] and were given the opportunity to enter into contractual federation with the RSFSR. The basis for a contractual federation was set forth in decrees of May 18 and June 1919 issued by the All-Union Central Executive Committee.[42] The first decree called for a unification of the military forces in order to mount a more effective defense. The second decree, "On the Unification of Soviet Republics," called upon the Soviet republics of Russia, Ukraine, Byelorussia, Latvia, Lithuania, and the Crimea to unite their military commands and their ministries of economic management, railroads, finance, and labor. However, only three republics—Ukraine, Byelorussia, and Caucasia—joined the RSFSR.

The contractual federation with Ukraine was established on December 29, 1920, and with Byelorussia on January 16, 1921. The treaties, identical in their content and formulation, were designed to achieve military and economic union. Consequently, the ministries of military and marine affairs, economics, external trade, finance, labor, roads and transportation, and post and telegraph were united. Since each republic was accepted as a sovereign entity, each retained control over its foreign relations.

The union with the Caucasian republics was more complicated and took a different route. The Russian Republic concluded numerous bilateral treaties with each of these republics before they entered into the Caucasian federation, which was established on May 12, 1922, uniting the republics of Azerbaidzhan, Armenia, and Georgia. The RSFSR entered into two treaties with the Georgian Republic concerning military and economic affairs. With Azerbaidzhan, the RSFSR concluded treaties on a military-economic union, on a unified policy of food production, on unifying the post and telegraph, on financial issues, and on external trade.[43] At the same time, an agreement on mutual financial assistance was signed with Georgia and Armenia.[44] The constitutions of these republics established their full political sovereignty.[45] In spite of the political process which consolidated the three independent Caucasian republics, Moscow continued to promote close inter-relationships with the new federation.[46] An additional dimension of the contractual federation was added between the RSFSR and the three people's republics. The treaty with the People's Republic of Khorezm was signed on September 13, 1920, with the People's Republic of Bukhara on March 4, 1921, and with the Far East Republic on February 17, 1922.

The federative process within the RSFSR developed mostly along the line of autonomy. The origins of the autonomous republics stemmed from the demands of local communes. The first one was the Workers' Commune of the Volga Germans, established on October 19, 1918, which developed later into an autonomous region. The Bashkir Autonomous Republic was established on March 20, 1919,[47] and, with the incorporation of the Autonomous Republic of Turkmenistan into the RSFSR in 1921, the number of autonomous republics within the RSFSR was eight.

Those autonomous republics and regions were subject to the laws and institutions of the RSFSR, and their right to self-determination was spelled out in the RSFSR's constitution of 1925. Although, originally, autonomous regions could only develop into autonomous republics, a later constitutional amendment expanded this right to secession.[48] A later interpretation of Stalin's concept of autonomy stated that autonomy could not lead to secession, nor did it constitute a form of independence. Autonomy, according to Stalin, was a concrete form of unification of periphery with the center.[49]

This contractual federation was unique because it did not establish new federal institutions. Rather, the existing institutions of the RSFSR assumed the role of federal institutions. Thus, the federation was not a union, a confederation, nor a federation in the strict sense.[50] In reality, the transfer of economic and military powers by the republics to the institutions of the RSFSR constituted their political incorporation. At this stage of the contractual federation, the RSFSR strove to be the sole representative in foreign affairs. The process of collective representation in foreign affairs began on an ad hoc basis in 1919, when the Italian government invited Soviet Russia to send one delegation to the Genoa Conference. This precedent prompted the final step toward permanent collective representation in foreign affairs. The final agreement on collective representation, which empowered the RSFSR to sign treaties on the behalf of eight republics, was signed between the RSFSR and the eight republics on February 22, 1922. This agreement was permanent and all encompassing.[51]

The final step toward the establishment of the USSR was a union treaty among the RSFSR and the Ukrainian, Byelorussian, and Transcaucasian republics to create one union state. This treaty centralized diplomatic representation and ratification of international treaties, regulation and changes of borders, control over domestic and foreign trade, and internal budgeting and taxation, and created new central and uniform judicial systems and a unified codification of the law. This treaty was incorporated into the first constitution of the USSR on January 31, 1924.

The Expansion of the Soviet Federation

The structural development of the Soviet federation took place on two levels: one, redrawing of boundaries of the union and autonomous republics and elevating numerous national groups into the rank of autonomous republics; and two, the absorption of additional nationalities and the establishment of new union republics. The major redrawing of republic boundaries took place in central Asia and within the Caucasia Socialist Federative Soviet Republic (CSFSR). The central Asian republics—the Turkestan Autonomous Republic, and the peoples' republics of Khorezm and Bukhara—were populated by six nationalities: Uzbek, Turkmen, Kazakh, Tadzhik, Kirghiz, and Kara-Kalpak. The peoples' republics of Khorezm and Bukhara entered the Soviet federation in October 1923 and September 1924, respectively. Their entrance into the union facilitated the establishment of five republics along nationality lines—two union republics, Uzbek and Turkmen; and three autonomous republics, Tadzhik, Kara-Kirghiz, and Kara-Kalpak. This process of providing contained and controlled self-determination for the nationalities of central Asia coincided with the Soviet efforts to consolidate the southern flank of Russia and to prevent unchecked nationalist development. The newly created republics were thereafter incorporated into the federal system and left with only nominal rights.

On March 3, 1924, the RSFSR and the Byelorussian Republic signed a special decree that transferred territories populated by Byelorussians from the RSFSR to the Byelorussian Republic, which doubled its size.[52] Similarly, in 1954, the RSFSR transferred the Crimea peninsula to the Ukrainian Republic.[53] In 1929, the Tadzhik Autonomous Republic was transformed into a full-fledged union republic and officially accepted as such in March 1931. The Kazakh and Kirghiz republics were accepted into the union on December 5,

1936. The next territorial change took place within the Caucasian Federative Republic. As a result of the growing local centralization of power, the Central Committee decided to grant self-determination to each of the three republics by elevating them into union republics.[54] Thus, the 1936 Constitution of the USSR consolidated eleven union republics.

The 1939 Soviet-German division of Poland was done under the aegis of uniting the Ukrainian and Byelorussian populations of Poland with their brethren in the USSR (Molotov's declaration of September 17, 1939). The acquired territory was called Western Byelorussia and Western Ukraine.[55] As a result of the Soviet-Rumanian treaty of August 2, 1940, part of Bessarabia became part of Ukraine.

In 1940, the Soviet Union established five additional republics: Karelo-Finnish, Moldavian, Latvian, Lithuanian, and Estonian. Of these, only the Karelo-Finnish Republic was established without annexing any territory.[56] The Moldavian Republic was established on August 2, 1940, and consisted of the former Moldavian Autonomous Republic and the annexed territories of Bessarabia.[57] The Baltic republics had no problem of divided population, but, as a result of their strategic location and their amicable relations with Germany, the Soviet government "demanded that those states change their government and invite the Red Army."[58] The newly created puppet governments asked to become members of the Soviet federation and were enthusiastically accepted.[59]

The political expediency inherent in Soviet policy toward self-determination is most visible in the case of the Karelo-Finnish Republic. In 1940, the Karelian Autonomous Republic was changed into the Karelo-Finnish SSR in order to retain leverage over Finland. Then in 1956, just prior to Khrushchev's visit of reconciliation to Finland, the Karelo-Finnish SSR was returned to its former status as the Karelian Autonomous Republic, thus lowering the level of self-determination of its population. This was meant as a friendly gesture to Finland.[60]

The process of redrafting administrative boundaries within the republics by the central authority continues up to this day. Decisions for such intrarepublic reorganizations are made by the Supreme Soviet of the USSR. This is indicative of the extreme centralization of decision making in the Soviet federation. Thus, a

Supreme Soviet abolished the Kutaisi and Tbilisi regions of the Georgian SSR on April 23, 1953, established the Krasnovodsk Region in Turkmenian SSR in April 1952, and on May 28, 1953, abolished the regions of Vilnius, Kaunas, Kleipeda, and Shaulai in the Lithuanian SSR.[61]

At the present time, the territorial aspect of the self-determination of the numerous nationalities is stable. The major area of stress and friction is found within the realm of rights and powers of the various republics. The territorial aspect of the principle of self-determination is only one framework for the numerous political processes that took place within the Soviet federation. Another framework of developments, frictions, and changes is the constitutional dimension of the Soviet federation.

The Constitutional Dimension of Soviet Federalism

The structural relationships among the national units of the Soviet federation have undergone significant constitutional changes. These changes modified the authority of each republic and reflected the changing degrees of self-determination allowed to the various national entities within the Soviet federation. The major constitutional landmarks of the Soviet federation were:

1. the constitution of the RSFSR, July 10, 1918;
2. the treaties between the RSFSR and the three republics, 1922;
3. the first constitution of the USSR, 1924;
4. the second constitution of the USSR, December 5, 1936;
5. the constitutional changes of the USSR constitution, February 1944;
6. the third constitution of the USSR, October 7, 1977.

An analysis of the structural changes will point out the original goals and the direction of these constitutional developments.

The constitution of 1918 only regulated the affairs of the Russian Socialist Federative Soviet Republic (RSFSR). However, since the majority of nationalities and ethnic minorities lived within its territory, the stipulation of their rights in the constitution indicated Soviet attitudes toward self-determination in general. In response to the declarations of independence by several republics, the Bolsheviks embarked on a path of reintegration, during which they promised self-determination. The first constitution centralized the major state apparatus and granted only limited rights in response to ethnic demands. The centralized structure (delineated in Arts. 49-52) was concentrated in Moscow. The concept of federation (mentioned in Arts. 2 and 11) was undeveloped for operational implementation. The representation of various nationalities was indirectly expressed through the All-Russian Congress of the Soviets which consisted of one chamber, and the nationalities thus lacked direct representation of their interests and demands. The members of the executive body, the Council of the People's Commissariat, were appointed by the All-Union Central Executive Committee and, hence, also lacked institutional representation of the various national interests. The channeling of those interests was accomplished through the newly established Commissariat of Nationalities, headed by Stalin. However, numerous studies written about the functioning of this commissariat point out that it served as an instrument for containing national self-determination rather than promoting it.[62]

The 1924 constitution represents the first major example of the new Soviet approach to federalism, which was meant as a substitute for national self-determination. Characteristic of this trend was the introduction of contradictory changes through the constitution. Some of the innovations broadened formal representation, and some increased the centrality of governmental control. Increased national representation was obtained by establishing a second chamber in the legislative body, the All-Union Conference of Soviets. This creation of a permanent structural instrument gave a voice to ethnic claims. On the other hand, the centralization measures introduced into the first USSR constitution compared unfavorably with the provisions of the bilateral treaties of 1922.[63] The centralization of power constituted a clear regression from the previous contractual position that allocated more rights to the republics. The expansion of central authority was resisted by the national Bolsheviks to the degree that the central authorities staged the first political purge, which involved Sultan Galiev, Stalin's assistant at the People's Commissariat for National Affairs. The party conference that accused Sultan Galiev of "national deviation" took place simultaneously with the meeting of the commission that was working on the draft of the constitution (June 8, 1923). This was a clear warning to the drafters of the constitution to refrain from the idea of a decentralized type of Soviet federation.

The period of adaptation and redrafting the republican constitution began with the ratification of the first union constitution. On one hand, those changes attempted to achieve uniformity and, on the other hand, the uniqueness and development of each republic. Although the new constitutions of the republics reflected the major principles of the union constitution, several of them lacked some of the principles characterizing the official formula for self-determination. Thus, the 1925 constitutions of the RSFSR and Turkmenian Republic lacked chapters describing their sovereign rights in general and their rights to secede in particular. Similarly, the constitution of the Caucasian Socialist Federative Soviet Republic (CSFSR), drafted in 1925, did not specify its sovereign rights as a member of the USSR nor its right to secede. This absence is particularly puzzling because such provisions appeared in the constitutions of Georgian, Armenian, and Azerbaidzhan republics, all members of the Caucasian federation, as well as in the constitution of the union.

The new federal union was composed of two republics, the Ukraine and Byelorussia, and two federative republics, the RSFSR and CSFSR. The autonomous republics within the RSFSR developed their own constitutions along the cardinal principles of the RSFSR's constitution.[64] However, none of those six constitutions became operative since VTzIK, the All-Union Central Executive Committee, refused to ratify them. The mere fact that a federal institution was in a position to prevent the ratification of a republican constitution points out the limitations on sovereignty of a republic within the Soviet federation.

The official justification for the constitution of 1936 was that the federal state and Soviet society had progressed to a new stage that eliminated the existence of antagonistic classes. This new stage necessitated changes in the state's functions. At this time, the Soviet federation consisted of seven union republics, nineteen autonomous republics, seventeen autonomous regions, and ten national districts—a total of fifty-three national state units. The operation of such an enlarged state mechanism demanded additional authority for the central government in Moscow. Thus, on February

1, 1935, the Central Committee instructed the Seventh Congress of Councils to change the existing constitution by expanding the democratization of the electoral system—changing it from a not equal to an equal system, from indirect to direct election, and from public to secret voting—and by adapting the constitution to social changes—dispossession of individual landowners, collectivization of agriculture, industrialization, etc.[65] In addition to these changes, the new constitution redefined the relationships between the Central Executive committees of the union and the republics because the authoritative power of the union's Executive Committee had grown beyond the prescribed boundaries of the 1924 constitution. In the 1930s, the functions of the council of the People's Commissariat (Sovnarkom) exceeded its constitutional status as an executive branch and developed into a body that issued decrees having the force of law.[66] Numerous federal decrees actually nullified the rights prescribed in Art. 36 of the Ukrainian constitution, which reserved to the Ukraine the right to initiate legislation in the highest federal institutions as well as the power to control the implementation of federal legislation and executive decrees within the territory of the Ukrainian Republic.

The constitutional committee established in 1935 and headed by Stalin contained twelve specialized subcommittees. One of the forefront issues was self-determination, and it was dealt with by the Subcommittee on Central and Local Governing Institutions.[67] The original draft of the preamble to the constitution stated: "The Soviet state is a federation of Soviets [Councils] which are the institutions of the dictatorship of the proletariat and embody state power in the center and in the periphery."[68] This preamble was not included in the constitution of 1936, which also did not include a direct definition of the Soviet multinational state as a federation. Article 13 of that constitution stated that: "The USSR is a unionized state established on the voluntary unification of the equal Soviet Republics." Yakubovskaya, a contemporary Soviet analyst, explains that the term union-state is synonymous with federal state. The reason given for the rejection of the term "federation of the Soviets" is that it was an erroneous formulation since the Soviet state is a federation of states. No reference was made as to why the formulation of the USSR as a "federation of Soviets" was not simply corrected to "federation of states."

The "contractual element" of the union was considered to be the cornerstone of the Soviet federation. Although the treaty of 1922 as such did not appear in the new constitution, the contractual element was retained in the new constitution (Art. 13). The new constitution dealt with the sovereign rights of the republics in an ambiguous way. Here, as in the constitution of 1924, the changes were of a contradictory character. Several changes allegedly expanded the rights of republics, and others tranferred them to the federal authority. Article 14-D gave to the union authorities control of the implementaton of the constitution to ensure the compatibility of the republican constitutions with the constitution of the USSR. The central authorities were also given the task of regulating borders among the union-republics and regulating and establishing new administrative regions within the union-republics (including the power to establish within their territories new autonomous republics). The legislation of civil and criminal codes was placed solely within the domain of the central authorities. The constitution of 1936 significantly expanded the central authority and moved the Soviet state closer to complete centralization. Article 15 provided that a republic's sovereignty was limited by the framework of Art. 14 which listed twenty-three categories as the sole domain of the central institutions.

No new significant rights were assigned to the republics. The number of the all-union ministries was lowered from twelve to seven, and the number of the union-republican ministries rose from three to ten. At the same time, the number of the republican ministries was lowered from six to four, taking away from republican control the Ministry of Justice and the Ministry of Health, which became now union-republican. All these changes left under sole republican control the following four ministries: education, local industry, collective economy (excluding state farms), and social welfare. The right to secede was expressed in Art. 17, without specifying the procedure for it. The absence of this specification is difficult to defend since the subcommittee preparing this article considered various reasons and means for exercising this sovereign right. Stalin's remarks on the need to retain this article points out its nominal character.[69]

During the debate on the new constitution, Stalin unofficially defined the criteria for transforming autonomous republics into union republics, consequently increasing their degree of self-determination. According to Stalin, autonomous republics must have the following three characteristics: (1) they should not be surrounded by union republics, since such a situation would prevent them from exercising their right of secession; (2) the leading nationality must constitute the majority; and (3) it should have a population of one million at least.[70] These characteristics eliminated for most of the nationalities and ethnic minorities of the USSR the opportunity of achieving the highest level of self-determination.

On February 1, 1944, the central authorities introduced two amendments which expanded the sovereign rights of union republics. The first amendment gave each union republic the right to establish and retain republican military units. Consequently, the Commissariat of Defense, which had been a union commissariat, was changed to a union-republican commissariat.[71] The second amendment was more radical. It allowed each republic the right to enter into contracts, agreements, and treaties. Consequently, each republic was allowed to establish its own Commissariat of Foreign Affairs and exchange ambassadors and consuls. The People's Commissariat of Foreign Affairs was transferred from union to union-republican.[72] The explanation for these amendments lies not in a change of heart by Soviet leaders or in the dynamics of their ideological premises but rather in a tactical move to obtain additional seats in the forthcoming United Nations Organization. In addition, Soviet authorities had to harness the rise of nationalism within the Soviet Union which had been officially encouraged during the war. This was done in order to increase the political cohesiveness of the non-Russian nationalities around Moscow. The two constitutional amendments increased the psychological reality of statehood and thus weakened the position of the separatist forces, especially in the recently acquired republics of Moldavia, Lithuania, Latvia, and Estonia.

During the war, several nationalities and ethnic groups lost their forms of statehood. The forms of autonomous republics and regions were enumerated in Arts. 22-29 of the 1936 constitution. Stalin, in his remarks on the constitution, stated that their detailed listing in the constitution was required in order to prevent bureaucrats from redrawing regions and areas.[73] In spite of the constitutional right of self-determination, the following statehoods were dissolved: the German Autonomous Republic in 1941; the autonomous republics of the Balkars, Chechens, Yingush, and Kalmyk and the Karachaev Autonomous Region at the end of 1943 and beginning of 1944; and the Crimean Autonomous Republic in July 1945.

Several years thereafter this process was reversed. On January 7, 1948, the Oirotskaya Autonomous Region was renamed the Gorno-Altai Autonomous Region. On February 19, 1954, the Crimean region was transferred from the RSFSR to the Ukrainian SSR; and on July 16, 1956, the Supreme Soviet of the USSR, by a simple decree, "demoted" the level of self-determination of the Finnish people living within the USSR by changing the Karelo-Finnish SSR into the Karelian Autonomous Republic. On January 9, 1957, the Presidium of the Supreme Soviet of the USSR restored the autonomy of the Balkar, Chechen, Yingush, Kalmyk, and Karachen nationalities, and in July 1958, the Kalmyk Autonomous Region was elevated into the Kalmyk Autonomous Republic. This arbitrary reshuffling of national self-determination and the forms of statehood is indicative of the principal attributes of the place of self-determination in Soviet politics. First, the higher forms of statehood are handled as a capricious privilege rather than as a prescribed constitutional right which stems from the political development of a given nation. Second, the Supreme Soviet and the Presidium have the right to change, add, or dissolve any ethnic area, region, or autonomous republic within any union republic (Art. 14-F).

On February 11, 1957, the Supreme Soviet abrogated its right to consent to the drawing up of new regions and districts within the union republics but retained its right to establish new autonomous republics and autonomous regions in the territories of the union republics.[74] These aspects of Soviet constitutional order negate the concept of self-determination in its theoretical form and repudiate the designated functioning of self-determination within the framework of Soviet federalism.

The process of writing the third Soviet constitution originated within Khrushchev's politics of de-Stalinization. The public announcement came in January 1959, but the ninety-seven-member Constitutional Commission was not established until three years later in April 1962. In December 1964, Brezhnev replaced Khrushchev as Chairman of the Constitutional Commission, stating, as late as June 1966, that the new constitution would be ready for the fiftieth anniversary of the October Revolution in November 1967. Nevertheless, the draft of the constitution was not delivered to the CPSU Central Committee until the plenary meeting of May 24, 1977.[75] The final draft included several changes which reflected ongoing political developments[76] and was adopted on October 7, 1977.

The changes are few but highly illuminating. First, the title of the chapter dealing with the federal structure was changed from "State Structure of the USSR" to "National and State Structure of the USSR." This change might not include specific meaningful developments, but the mere insertion of it, even for pure phraseological decoration, points out the existing awareness of this issue at the highest level. Second, the article that defined the Soviet state in its previous formulation left the definition of the union more open. The old version (Art. 13) stated: "The Union of Soviet Socialist Republics is a federal state formed on the voluntary union of equal Soviet Socialist Republics." The new formulation (Art. 70) reads: "The USSR is an integral, federal, multinational state formed on the principle of socialist federalism as a result of the free self-determination of nations and the voluntary association of equal Soviet Socialist Republics. The USSR embodies state unity of the Soviet people and draws all its nations and nationalities together for the purpose of jointly building communism." This new formulation adds the following new elements: (1) the state is defined as integral and federal instead of plain federal; (2) the reason given for republics joining the union is expanded from a mere voluntary union to an expression of their self-determination; (3) the USSR's embodiment of statehood of all the nations and nationalities detracts from their sovereignty as proclaimed in Art. 78; and (4) the guiding principle of the state is socialist federalism. This concept did not appear in the official draft of the present constitution.

The new constitution has abolished absolutely the rights of republics to establish and retain national military formation as was provided in the constitutional amendments of February 1944. The rights of republics to enter into diplomatic activities has been rephrased. Art. 18-A of the old constitution stated: "Each union republic has the right to enter directly into diplomatic relations with foreign states, to conclude agreements with them and to exchange diplomatic and consular representatives." The new formulation is more vague and diminishes the previous right of a republic to enter into direct diplomatic relations. Since the previous "liberal" formulation was not implemented, except for the participation of the Ukraine and Byelorussia in the United Nations, there is little reason to expect that the new formulation will expand these rights. This constitutional provision is actually superseded by Art. 73-10 which provides that the central high organ of state power will establish a uniform procedure to coordinate the relations of the union republics with foreign states and international organizations.

This vaguely-formulated right of a republic to conduct independent diplomatic relations, which constitutes a major indicator of the republic's sovereignty, has been further eroded by a "Law concerning the Order of Signature, Implementation, and Withdrawal of International Agreements by the USSR" approved on July 6, 1978. This detailed law of thirty articles eliminates rights and roles of the republics in formulating and executing Soviet foreign policy. The entire process is concentrated in the central organs of the government, and any suggestion of international treaty, agreement, convention, pact, protocol, exchange of letters, or notes or any other form of international agreement must be submitted to the Ministry of Foreign Affairs of the USSR. A separate agreement is permitted to various governmental committees in the sphere of foreign trade and scientific exchange. Article 7 of this law indicates that the representatives of a union republic can suggest an international agreement to the union's Ministry of Foreign Affairs through the republic's representatives. However, any republic that becomes part of an international treaty is responsible to the union's Ministry of Foreign Affairs (Arts. 21 and 22). This absence of a union republic's direct international responsibility casts a shadow on its real sovereignty.

Two interesting changes have been made with regard to the rights of the autonomous Soviet socialist republics: (1) Art. 143 states that the Supreme Soviet of the USSR has the exclusive power to carry out the adoption of the constitution, whereas Art. 60-B of the 1936 constitution allocated the right of approval to the Supreme Court of the USSR, and (2) Art. 84 of the new constitution stipulates that "the territory of the Autonomous Republic shall not be altered without its consent"; the similar article of the 1936 constitution, 60-B, allocated the right of consent to the Supreme Soviet of the USSR.

The foregoing analysis suggests that constitutional change has been a legitimate battleground of the colliding interests of the central authority against the demands of the republics. The present constitution did not grant additional rights to the republics, but pressure from the republics has left visible marks on it. Several changes have been clearly stated, and others, which are more subtle, harbor the possibility of future contention within the Soviet federal system.

The Moving Forces of Self-Determination

The search for the major explanatory variables in the dynamics of the Soviet federation leads inevitably to several factors that have a centripetal effect upon the entire system. The most prominent factors are the Communist party, the all-encompassing Soviet economy and the central government. Analysis of these centralizing factors and forces will not be able to provide us with core explanations for future developments since these factors are dependent ones. Numerous studies have been made of the ethnic structure of the CPSU in various republics.[77] The economic and governmental sectors have been the object of numerous changes which reflect tactical solutions for existing situations rather than general guidelines for federal development. Thus, the shuffling and reshuffling of ministries back and forth is a provisional indicator of long-term changes. A recent thorough study of interaction between law and nationalities points to a potentially useful method for discerning the gradual changes in the Soviet federative system.[78]

The independent ideological concepts that are capable of clarifying the dynamics of the Soviet federal system are the concepts of state, nation, and language and culture.

The Concept of State

The role and function of the state enhance and condition the development of the Soviet federal system. Closely knitted into

Marxian philosophy, the concept of state was at the heart of the Bolshevik Revolution. According to Marx's theory, the state constituted an instrument of the ruling class, whose main function was to consolidate and to promote its interests. Thus, the state is a by-product of productive relations among hostile classes and belongs to the superstructure. It will undergo changes in its role and function depending upon the level of economic and social development of the classes. However, since under Marxism man is destined to develop a classless society, the state, as a political framework that serves the ruling class, will wither away.

The political order in Russia after the October Revolution was called "the dictatorship of the proletariat." The civil war, the domestic situation, and international developments called for a strengthening of the Soviet state rather than its withering away. The nationalization of industry, the forced collectivization of the agricultural sector, and the consolidation of Stalin's dictatorship so promoted the strengthening of the state and its organs. Stalin's theoretical handling of this issue was expressed in 1930 in his famous statement: "In order to prepare the state for withering away it must be strengthened. It sounds contradictory comrades, but this is the essence of our policy."

Although the constitution of 1936 declared the disappearance of the hostile classes, the state remained in the form of the "dictatorship of the proletariat."[79] The functioning dogma of democratic centralism disregarded the necessity for a separation of powers and a system of checks and balances. The principle of democratic centralism introduced a monohierarchical structure of power and responsibilities. The lower level of republican and local administrations were strictly subordinated to the higher agencies and to the centrally drawn plan. Under Stalin, almost 70 percent of the industrial establishment was under federal administration, while slightly over 30 percent of the factories and enterprises was controlled by the republics. No legal instrument could restrain the encroachments of the federal government into spheres that were within republic or local responsibility. Thus, this concept of the state capped the entire political system of the Soviet Union and left only a very limited space for self-determination in its federalistic formulation.

One of Khrushchev's most innovative theoretical shifts was to declare that the dictatorship of the proletariat had fulfilled its historic mission and had ceased to be indispensable in the USSR. This new conceptualization of the state was intended to solidify two other drastic changes that were introduced by Khrushchev: (1) the abolition of the all-union ministries and their replacement by the *Sovnar khozy* (economic districts) and (2) the division of the party into industrial and agricultural sections.

These two changes have moved the Soviet system from a tightly controlled democratic centralism toward the direction of economic pluralism. Such a diversified political system could develop into a system that eventually might accommodate the numerous symbols of a relaxed federalism and self-determination of Soviet nationalities. The all-people's state is distinguished from the dictatorship of the proletariat by four features; (1) a broadening of the basis of socialist society to include all the population; (2) a change in the functions of the state, including the transfer of state administration to public organizations; (3) an extension of democratic methods of rule; and (4) an attempt to attract all the people into the administration of the affairs of the society.[80] This new concept was heralded as a cornerstone of Soviet politics:

> The transformation of the dictatorship of the proletariat into a state of the whole people is not a question of terminology, not a mere change of name. It reflects processes in the development of the Soviet land. At the same time, it substantiates in theory the line of the further development and improvement of socialist democracy. That, indeed, is the point of departure for the CPSU in shaping its policy of state construction.[81]

On the operational level, this concept embraced the fields of economy, culture, and politics. Its major feature was to encourage the initiation and self-government of the working masses. As a direct result of this approach, the Ministry of Sports was abolished, and its functions were transferred to various public organizations.

Upon the dismissal of Khrushchev from leadership, Brezhnev's team proceeded to dismantle the economic and party reforms introduced by Khrushchev. It was just a matter of time until this swing to centralism would demand revision of the all-people's state to a more "orthodox" Marxist-Leninist definition. The return to the class content of the Soviet state put an end to the allocation of functions to public or social organizations in governing the state during the period of transition to communism. This change in ideological conceptualization entails the return of the controlled monohierarchical centralism which leaves space neither for the relaxation of the Soviet federal system nor for any new and challenging demands for national self-determination.

In a recent major speech, Brezhnev stressed the class content of the Soviet state: "The several decades of Soviet state have proven that without the working masses and without the socialistic state system there never was, nor ever will be any road to socialism."[82] The same article states that democratic centralism solidified the further development of the Soviet state, i.e., any future developments in the state system could come only from the top. The political system of the USSR is defined as "a concentrated expression of the democratism of the Soviet state, which is an organic fusion of democracy with the state system."[83] The dominant role of the democratic centralism of the CPSU became the guiding model for it within the state's structure.[84] Consequently, the present ideological constellation does not promise any relaxation of the Soviet federal system or self-determination.

The Concept of Nation

The demand for self-determination is usually proclaimed by socializing masses, which consider themselves as nations, or by smaller ethnic groups. In both cases, the notion of nation constitutes the cornerstone of the process of self-determination.

Classical Marxism considers a nation a product of specific social relations and only secondarily a product of ethnic development. The development of such social relationships within society was delineated by the leading class, i.e., the bourgeoisie.[85] Consequently, the nation is a dependent variable in the equation where the ruling class shapes the content of the nation and formulates its goals. This dialectical presentation of the concept of nation has opened the door for a "new type of nation" whose goals and content are set up by the dictatorship of the proletariat.

The classical definition of a nation was made by Stalin and required from an ethnic group three specific conditions: language, historical experience, and territory. Although Lenin realized the role of the psychological factor in the process of a nation's formation, the dominant factor was that of economics.[86] The present Soviet analysis of the spiritual profile of a nation is more refined and divides it into two clusters of characteristics, ideological and psychological,[87] as shown in the diagram. The interplay of these factors takes place within the framework of an "objective dialectic of a nation's formation which consists of national consolidation and assimilation of ethnic entities."[88]

This formulation of the dynamics of nation-building has opened the door to the promotion of the "Soviet People–*Sovetskii Narod*" which would be achieved as a result of an amalgamation or fusion of Soviet nationalities and ethnic minorities. The classical conceptual chain consists of the following stages in the formation process of a nation; tribe, people, nation, supranation (Communist society). The issue of self-determination is functional up to the supranational stage. Since Soviet society is of the stage of "ripe socialism," this national stage of development is between "nation" and "supranation." The process of maturation takes place on all levels of the national structure: economic, ideological, and psychological. The

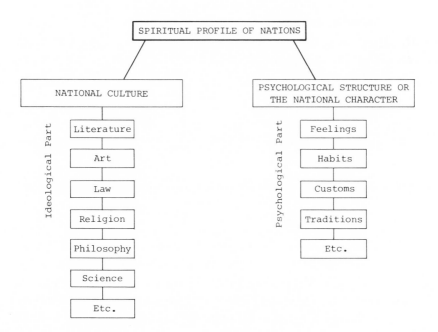

changes within the national culture and language will be analyzed later. This process and/or the degree and speed of national amalgamation is the most decisive factor in the dynamics of Soviet federalism which constitutes the Soviet interpretation of national self-determination.

On the political-formal level, the formation of a new and unique Soviet nation is represented by the following conceptual stages: flourish (*rastzvet*), brotherly cooperation (*Bratskoe sotrudnichestvo*), and rapprochement (*sblizhenie*), which lead finally to fusion (*slianie*). This process of political, ideological, and ethnic amalgamation is supported by an all-encompassing process of forming a new Soviet man.

The unique concept of the Soviet nation is composed of three elements.

1. *Soviet man*—the individual level.[89]
2. *Soviet patriotism*—the group level that gears the loyalty of the Soviet citizen away from the ethnic base and toward the loyalty of the socialist nation.[90] This new loyalty is formulated as "all-national pride of the Soviet man which underscores the inseparable unity and fusion of the whole-Soviet and national elements."[91]
3. *Homogeneity of nations*—the level on which man's national feelings are inseparable from social-class feelings and an individual resides in a national-social environment which consequently leads to the creation of a homogeneic socialist nation.

> The socialist nation is a new social community of people grown out of a nation or nationality of capitalist society in the process of the abolition of capitalism and the victory of socialism. Though on a qualitative new basis, it retains definite ethnic traits of the former national community, its entire mode of political, socio-economic, and cultural life has been transformed in line with socialist, international principles.[92]

Within this process, the territorial aspect of a nation's identity plays only a minor role, and, in spite of Communist awareness of that element, a nation's claim to once-held historical claims are now considered unjustified and untenable.[93] Culture and national consciousness are not immutable and are aligning themselves under the growing influence of the Marxist-Leninist, international ideology.[94] Within the family of Soviet nations, this context of the homogeneous Soviet nation leads to unique types of interrelationships, which scope extends from flourishment to fusion. Since the extreme of this continuum negates the need of self-determination, it will be instrumental to analyze the present stage of those interrelationships.

A voluminous work entitled *The Formation of the Socialist Nations in the USSR* constitutes a vivid example of how Soviet historiography tries to perceive the uniqueness of the new socialist nations. According to this work, the required elements for the formation of a nation are: language, territory, economic life, and its psychological structure.[95] All four elements are required for a process of forming a nation out of an ethnic minority. However, according to this analysis, it is theoretically insolvent and politically harmful to add another element—existence of its own isolated national state. Thus, the dynamics of the nation's content (culture, language, economic relations) and the nonnecessity of a national state constitute the background for the rapprochement and fusion of nations.[96]

The Concept of Language and Culture

The function of language has a paramount importance in the politics of integration. Thus, the diversity in the German language was a deterrent to the unification of a fragmented empire. "Language and political consciousness are elements that go hand in hand and determine the way in which the individual relates to his environment."[97] It has been firmly established that language, as the preeminent manifestation of culture, has historically been no less divisive than religion. The impact of "linguistic turmoil" upon a political system is powerfully demonstrated by the Canadian and Belgian cases.

The Soviet position on the role and function of the Russian language as an official language has undergone numerous changes. Lenin's position on the equality of all languages and against a supremacy of Russian, in particular, was very clear. In his article "Is a Compulsory Official Language Needed?" Lenin rejected the reactionaries who advocated a coercive imposition of the Russian language upon 60 percent of the population of Russia, as well as the "soft pitch" of the liberals who had offered the great and mighty language to the non-Russian nationalities.[98] This demand for equality of languages Lenin incorporated in a declaration, "All nations in the state are absolutely equal, and all privileges enjoyed by any one nation or any one language are held to be inadmissible and anti-constitutional."[99]

Indeed, in the early days of the Soviet republics, each republic codified the equality of the national and Russian languages. The Byelorussian Republic went one step further: Art. 73 of its constitution (1927) states that major laws will be published in the Byelorussian, Yiddish, Russian, and Polish languages.[100] Since then, the Soviet regime has created literacy for forty-eight nationalities and ethnic groups which had only a spoken language.[101]

This growth of artificially created languages does not present the real picture of the issue of the dominant language. In 1959, 10.2 million non-Russians declared Russian as their native tongue. The census of 1970 stated that 13 million non-Russians considered Russian their native tongue, and 48.6 percent of the non-Russian population considered the Russian language as a native tongue or were fluent in it.[102] This statistical trend is a result of a declared policy to promote the Russian language as a second native tongue which would serve as a cultural framework for the development of one socialist culture. Several Soviet historians, who would like to save the national languages from the avalanche of prescriptions concerning the fusion of cultures, try to separate language from culture. To make such separation politically safe, it is done via criticism of Stalin's pamphlet "Marxism and Linguistic Questions" published in 1950.[103]

The causative relationship between the rapprochement of cultures and languages and that of nations is expounded in numerous Soviet statements, scientific conferences, and publications.[104] Moreover, the acceptance of another national language should not be viewed as assimilation, since language does not constitute the only element of national identity.[105] Thus, language, which constituted the necessary element in Lenin's and Stalin's definition of nation, has been declared as "not a must."

In 1978, the issue of language equality reappeared in Soviet politics during the recent redrafting of the new republican constitutions, being done in order to adapt them to the new constitution

of the union. Of the non-Russian republics, only the three Caucasian republics—Georgia, Armenia, and Azerbaidzhan—were granted
a constitutional guarantee that their languages will be codified as
the state language. Thus, the Georgian constitution of 1929 stated:
"The State language of the Georgian SSR is Georgian. National
minorities of the Georgian SSR are assured of the right of free development and use of their native tongue both in their own national cultural institutions as well as in all-state institutions."[106]
This article was carried over into the Georgian constitutions of
1927 and 1937. The Armenian constitution acquired such an article
in 1937, and the Azerbaidzhan constitution only in 1956. Apart
from these three republics, only Turkmenistan had such a clause
in its 1927 constitution, but it was dropped in 1937.

The new draft of the Georgian constitutuion was published in
March 1978, and Art. 75 formulated the language issue as follows:

> The Georgian SSR ensures the use in state and public organs and cul-
> tural and other institutions of the Georgian language and exercises state
> concern for its all-out development. In the Georgian SSR the free use in
> all these organs and institutions of Russian and also of other languages
> of the population used by it is ensured on the basis of equality. Any
> sort of privilege or limitation in the use of one or another language is
> not permitted.[107]

Article 71 of the Armenian draft resembled the Georgian provision
which shifted the status of the republican language away from
being a state language and equalized it with others, including the
Russian language.

A unique phenomenon of spontaneous public protest occurred
in Georgia with the demand for the restoration of the Georgian
language as the state language. In Armenia and Azerbaidzhan, debates took place within their Supreme Soviets. Under these demands and pressure from the intellectual circles, the final versions
of their constitutions restored the previous provisions concerning
the republican languages. Article 75 of the Georgian Republic (72
of the Armenian) states:

> The state language of the Georgian Socialist Republic is Georgian. The
> Georgian SSR exercises public care for the utmost development of the
> Georgian language and guarantees its use in public and social bodies and

in cultural, educational and other institutions. Any sort of privilege or limitation in the use of one or another language is not permitted.[108]

This attempt to challenge the republican language is explainable in the light of the language policies promoting Russian as the language of the new socialist nations.

Rapprochement and the Fusion of Nations

The linguistic element is only one of several elements involved in the rapprochement and fusion of Soviet nations. The other factors are economic and economic-transport,[109] social homogeneity and the growing role of the working class,[110] ideological and national-psychological[111] and, finally, socialist patriotism and international education.[112] All those factors separately and together bring the Soviet leadership to declare time and again that the rapprochement, convergence, and fusion of nations are imminent.

The most authoritative statement on the issue of *sblizhenie*—rapprochement (drawing together)—was issued by the Twenty-second Congress of the CPSU in 1961. "With the victory of communism in the USSR, the nations will draw still closer together, their economic and ideological unity will increase, and Communist traits will develop." This declaration has opened a series of debates, conferences, and consolidation of opposing groups.[113] Numerous regional and all-union conferences discussed openly the prospects of national integration and fusion.[114] A recent content analysis of the code and catchwords of Brezhnev's nationality policy points to a "drawing together" where the national leaders are unanimous on the terms "brotherly" and "the big brother."[115] Thus, the authoritative monthly of the CPSU, *Kommunist*, has stated that quantitative and qualitative changes will have implications not only on social states but also on national structure.[116]

On the one hand, it so happens that numerous small nationalities that have similar origins, language, and culture and that have strong economic and territorial ties consolidate themselves around the much larger and more-developed national community. On the other hand, some national and ethnic groups with these same characteristics either partially or fully merge with another nation of their own free will or the principle of equality.[117]

In the light of these authoritative statements, the concepts and dynamics of culture, language, and nations contribute directly to the limitation of a nation's attempt to assert its claim of self-determination and gradually limit the scope of a nation's demand within the framework of the Soviet federation.

The Problem of the "Fluid" Nationalities

The official Soviet solution for nationalities and ethnic minorities—providing them with a territorial base—has not resolved the issue for several nationalities since they possess no territorial center. Nowadays, these nationalities—Poles, Jews, Tatars, and Germans—have no framework in which to exercise their national identity, and, consequently, their ability to exercise the right of self-determination is very limited. The absence of the territorial element, according to Stalin, denied such groups the right to call themselves a nation.[118] The Soviet leadership dealt with those nationalities only on a tactical level, handled mostly by the People's Commissariat for Nationalities (Narkomnats). Its major function was to propagandize the Bolsheviks' ideas in the language of those fluid nationalities, which at that time also included Latvians, Czechoslovakians, Hungarians, Lithuanians, and the Finns.[119]

The census of 1970 listed eleven nationalities in Russia that did not have national autonomy. Those "fluid" nationalities were Germans, Poles, Koreans, Bulgarians, Greeks, Gypsies, Uighurs, Hungarians, Gagauzis, Romanians, and Kurds. Their total population was listed as 4,877,000. The two present striking examples of "fluid" nationalities within the Soviet federations are the Tatars and the Jews. Although their cases differ drastically from one another, the pattern of Soviet policies toward them contains common elements which are directed to bring about their assimilation.

The Soviet solution for the Jewish Question was divided into two parts, political and territorial. On the political level, a special Jewish Department—*Evsektsiia*—was established within the Party, and it conducted extensive activities among the Jewish masses. The propaganda was conducted in Yiddish and engulfed all sectors of Jewish life: its religion, education, and vocations. The goal was to turn Yiddish-speaking masses into active supporters of the new regime.[120] The territorial solution encompassed the settlement of

Jews in the Crimean peninsula which contained a concentration of Jewish farmers. This project was met with growing anti-Semitic resentment by the local farmers, and the government decided to establish the Jewish National Region (*Bizobidzhan*) which is in the Far East on the border with China.[121] The European Jews refused to migrate from their traditional places; their present migration is one of the results of the absence of national and cultural life for Soviet Jews.[122]

The case of the Crimean Tatars began with the Crimean Autonomous Soviet Socialist Republic which was established on October 18, 1921, as part of the RSFSR. The Tatars numbered 290,000 which constituted 25 percent of the autonomous republic. In May 1944, the entire Tatar population and five other nationalities were uprooted and sent to Siberia and Kazakhstan.[123] This deportation of an entire nation was done under the pretext that the Tatars had collaborated with the Nazi invaders.

The Twentieth Congress of the CPSU in February 1956 exonerated the Tatars from any suspicion of treason. However, on April 28, 1956, just fifty-eight days thereafter, a secret decree (no. 27) stated that the repressed nations would not receive any compensation for their material, nor would they be allowed to return to their previous places of residence.[124] This denial of return has moved the Tatars to write numerous appeals, protests, and proclamations demanding the right to return. The Soviet authorities have replied with several staged trials against the leaders of the Tatars.[125]

These two protracted conflicts point out the difficult dilemma of the Soviet leaders. On the one hand, they would have liked those nationalities to begin to assimilate and to take part in the general drawing together of the Soviet nations. On the other hand, the pressure applied on them is highly chauvinistic and generates animosity which permeates the entire scope of international relationships.

Sovereignty of the Soviet Nations

The present Soviet analysis of national self-determination is that a "nation's right freely to choose the form of its state organization and establish state borders in keeping with the will of the people creates the most democratic prerequisite for the voluntary unification and establishment of a large centralized state."[126] This interpretation is supposed to cover the present structure of Soviet federalism rather than Lenin's definition which stated that "self-determination of nations means the political separation of those nations from alien national bodies and the formation of an independent national state. It is wrong to interpret the right of self-determination as meaning anything but the right to existence as a separate state."[127]

The union republics are considered sovereign states within a state, the USSR, which is also sovereign.[128] Western analysis distinguishes between the following types of Soviet sovereignty: "limited," "potential," and "dormant."[129] The Soviet argument on behalf of a republic's full sovereignty is based on two points. First, the union republics acceded some of their rights to the union, which keeps them in full harmony with its own sovereignty. The fraternal relations between the republics and the union not only do not limit the republic's sovereignty but promote its development and consolidation.[130] Second, sovereignty is defined as a qualitative aspect of the content of state power in all the diversity of its forms. Since the power belongs to the same ruling class, the realization of state sovereignty inevitably assumes a political and legal character.[131]

In spite of these two arguments which are based on a questionable notion of "partial sovereignty," the absence of such characteristic elements of sovereignty as the right to enter into international treaties and agreements leaves a question mark upon the republic's *real* sovereignty. It is sufficient to mention that a union republic cannot have diplomatic relations even with the fraternal states of the socialist camp.

Self-Determination and Soviet Foreign Policy

No discussion of self-determination is complete without mentioning its impact upon international relations. Soviet historians claim that this notion was introduced into the realm of international affairs not by Woodrow Wilson but by Lenin. The following aspects of self-determination have played a role in Soviet foreign policy: (1) irredentism, (2) 1944 constitutional changes, (3) the new notion of nation and the German nations, (4) "socialist camp" growing into "integration," and (5) divided nations.

The western borders of the Ukraine and Byelorussia constituted the borders of the Brest-Litovsk treaty with Germany. This created a situation in which Byelorussian and Ukrainian nationals found themselves in the newly established neighboring states. As a result of this fragmentation, Byelorussia adopted a policy of four official languages—Byelorussian, Polish, Yiddish, and Russian. The absorption of the neighboring territories in September 1939 was called the unification of the western territories. The special decrees of the Supreme Soviet of the USSR which regulated the absorption of those territories into the USSR have also asked the two republics to accept the new territories.[132] Nowadays, Ukrainian historians claim that the unification of these territories was a precondition for the consolidation of the Ukrainian nation.[133] Similar undertakings of irrendentism took place with the Caucasian republics and the republics of central Asia.[134]

The constitutional amendments of February 1944 gave the republics additional representative powers. Since then, the republics have been listed in Soviet textbooks on international law as sovereign subjects of international law. The aim of those amendments according to Aspaturian was

1. to facilitate the legal incorporation of Western Byelorussia and the Western Ukraine by converting an ethically dubious claim based essentially on conquest into the more palatable context of Ukrainian, Byelorussian and Lithuanian self-determination,
2. to provide a fresh basis for legalizing the accession of the Baltic states into the USSR and to make it easier for the United States to retreat from its position of non-recognition,
3. to prepare a juridical foundation for multiple representation in the projected International Organizations,
4. to counter the noxious effects of the renegade troop formations organized by the Nazis with those formed in the Republics.[135]

In the 1978 version of the Law concerning the Order of Signature, Implementation, and Withdrawal of International Agreements by the USSR analyzed earlier, the right of the republics to engage in diplomatic intercourse was diluted and only can be manifested through the union's Foreign Ministry.

A unique aspect of self-determination in Soviet foreign policy appeared when it had to justify the existence of two Germanys on the basis of the classical definition of nation. In this case, the classical definition of nation (language, historical experience, territory) was ignored, and the present formulation declares that the origins and development of a nation are a result of class struggle which is related to the development of capitalistic and socialist social-economic formations.[136] A more precise explanation for the evolution of the GDR's socialist nation is based on the following four factors.

1. The German unification of 1871 obtained with "iron and blood" had crumbled in 1945.
2. At the present time the two German states incorporate diametrically opposed values—labor vs. capital, socialism vs. capitalism.
3. The absolute difference in the economic structure of these two nations.
4. In the situation of the present struggle between socialism and imperialism the mere belonging to the socialist system constitutes an important symptom of socialist nationhood.[137]

Thus, under a specific cluster of political circumstances, the Soviet conceptualization of nation has been radically altered.

The development of the European Economic Community caught the Soviet leadership without instrumental concepts of analysis. The idea of a "United States of Europe" (USE) was actively discussed in the period 1914-1916, and the issue appeared in the program of the Bolshevik RSDRP in September 1914. Lenin's theory of imperialism led him to believe that such a USE would be impossible except in the form of a temporary aggressive alliance. Thus, in 1957-1965, the Soviet Union still perceived the EEC as a form of sharpened contradictions between its members and Britain, the United States, and Japan.[138] The new orientation toward the EEC began with the growing Soviet interest in developing an integrated structure within the Comecon in the mid-sixties. Thus, from 1965, the word *integratsiia* ceased to be placed in quotes although it was still applied only to Western integration and for Comecon the process continued to be *sotrudnichestvo* (cooperation), and only since

1968 has the word *integratsiia* been applied to socialist integration.[139]

However, in spite of detailed familiarity with the EEC and with the literature (Haas Lindberg), the Soviet leadership is unable to perceive this cluster of integrative policies beyond their economic and military implications. This reversible notion of self-determination that occurs in a conflict-free capitalist environment poses the very difficult question, "Who wants the political integration of Western Europe?"[140] Such a political union, according to Soviet scholars, would inevitably lead to a military-political union of Western states. In defense of this conclusion, Shishkov quotes Franz Josef Strauss on the future of a Western federation which would constitute a "balance of power." Although Shishkov recognizes the complexities of political integration, its elements and the degree of its irreversibility, he concludes that the final goal of such political integration is to unite capitalist states against growing world socialism. Among other things, he sees here the loss of independence and sovereignty of the small nations which will be governed by the larger states.[141] Apart from the absence of a coherent comprehensive theory of European integration under capitalism, it is interesting to note that Soviet theorists employ the concept of self-determination to cast a shadow on the political integration of Europe by arguing that it undermines the sovereignty of states, while urging at the same time that the integration of Comecon strengthens the sovereignty of its members.[142]

Self-Determination and Divided States— The Soviet Position

The process of decolonization has opened for the Soviet Union new dimensions for political activity on behalf of the self-determination of evolving states. However, the Soviet political gains of this campaign have been only minimal since the new states have hesitated to accept the Soviet model of socialism and have embarked on their own path to it.[143] During the last decade, several multinational states have experienced the strains of separatism which were advocated by their ethnic and religious minorities.

The cases in which the Soviet Union took a clear position were Nigeria-Biafra, Pakistan-Bangladesh, Northern Ireland–Great Britain, Cyprus, South Africa-Transkei, and Ethiopia-Eritrea. In the case of Canada-Quebec, the Soviet position favored the French separatist movement, but only on a low level. Out of the six listed cases, the Soviet Union supported three—Pakistan, South Africa, Great Britain—for the dissolution of the states in order to implement the right of self-determination of ethnic minorities. In the cases of Nigeria, Cyprus, and Ethiopia, the Soviet Union stood against the demands for self-determination. The explanation for the difference in the Soviet position on self-determination can be seen on two levels: (1) the common aspects of the states involved and (2) the potential tactical goals of the Soviet Union directly related to the given state.

Thus, the cases of self-determination which the Soviets have supported involved neither a federation nor did they include ethnic minorities. The Soviet support of the secession of East Pakistan (Bangladesh) had its roots in the geopolitical situation in Southeast Asia. No Soviet definition of nation, neither the traditional—language, historical, experience—nor the contemporary—socialist nation governed by dictatorship of the proletariat—would support the secession of East Pakistan. The reasoning behind the Soviet position was tactical. The Soviet involvement in Vietnam, the growing tensions with China, and the Soviet desire to retain close and friendly relations with India all moved the Soviet leadership to support the self-determination of Bangladesh. The seceded state received economic, military, and diplomatic support from the Soviet Union, which led to the strengthening of the Soviet position in this area.[144]

The Soviet Union considers Northern Ireland to be, at present, a territory occupied by British troops. The newly convened Assembly of Northern Ireland, the successor of the Ulster Parliament, was dismissed by Soviet analysts as "irrelevant" since the British minister for Northern Ireland, William Whitelaw, could veto any decision of that assembly.[145] The case of Northern Ireland figures prominently in the Soviet press, especially the issue of the case of the *Republic of Ireland* versus *Great Britain* heard before the European Court of Human Rights in Strasbourg.[146] The Soviet position on the self-determination of Northern Ireland is consistent with Russia's traditional approach to the decolonization of nations.

On the African scene, the Soviet Union promoted a policy of consistent support of national-liberation movements. The recent cases of Angola and Mozambique and its present position on Namibia testify vividly to that principle.[147] However, Soviet policy exceeds the mere promotion of self-determination and ventures into the realm of promoting a specific political movement, as was the case in Angola, Rhodesia and Namibia (SWAPO). The existence of a revolutionary element in such movements is a required feature for obtaining Soviet support.[148] Consequently, the evolutionary movements of Rhodesia and those of South Africa are opposed by the Soviet Union, which refused to recognize the self-determination of Transkei—a state established within the Republic of South Africa.

The Soviet position against self-determination in two other cases is more indicative of the essence of Soviet posture on self-determination in general. The Soviet stand in the cases of Nigeria and Cyprus raises several principal questions. The state of Nigeria is a classical example of a new African state. After its independence on October 1, 1960, the state, composed of two-hundred fifty tribes, was divided into four regions which included nineteen states. Each region had its prime minister, ministers, provincial commissioners, and representatives in the House of Chiefs. Formally, this structure resembled the classical model of federalism. On May 24, 1966, the government of Nigeria established a unitary state and changed its name from Federal Republic of Nigeria to Republic of Nigeria. Two months later, August 1, 1966, Lieutenant-Colonel Yakubu Gowon assumed control over the government and declared the new unitary structure invalid, offering to allow his people to decide on the most-desired form of government. The chosen form of federalism lasted nine months, and in May 1967 the eastern region declared independence from the federation and took the name of Biafra. On June 21, 1967, a Nigerian delegation arrived in Moscow and asked for arms. In August, the Soviet delivered fifteen jet transport planes and ten MiG jets and on November 2, 1967, three speedboats and a credit of $56 million.[149] The Soviet analysis of the civil war condemned the regional and tribal trends which were finally stopped by the united working masses.[150]

Two major reasons brought the Soviet Union to take an active role in the struggle to retain the unity of Nigeria. First, prior to these events, the Soviet Union had no foothold in Nigeria, which was closely knitted to the West. By rendering meaningful assistance in retaining unity, the Soviet Union established a base for a long-term influence. "The friendship of Soviet and Nigerian people was born in the struggle for independence, unity and flourishment of Nigeria. The strengthening of this friendship reflects the interests of our people as well as of the entire African continent."[151] Second, the other reason relates to the possible feedback on the Soviet domestic scene had the Soviet Union promoted the independence of Biafra and Benin at the expense of one united state of Nigeria.

The Soviet position on the ethnic conflict in Cyprus was delineated by the perceived maneuvers of NATO to divide the newly born state into Greek and Turkish parts and to retain it as a military outpost.[152] Guided by this perception and promoting a sovereign united Cyprus, the Soviet Union remained sceptical of the idea of the cantonization of Cyprus. This idea was introduced by Turkey and called for the establishment of a federative state composed of two autonomous administrations.[153] The Soviet Union and socialist-fraternal states demanded internationally effective guarantees for independence, sovereignty, and territorial inviolability of the Republic of Cyprus—to be provided by a broad international forum. Thus, the major Soviet motif was to prevent any plan that called for the self-determination of the Greek and Turkish people in Cyprus and, by doing this, to drive a wedge among the NATO parties involved, especially between the United States and Turkey. This Soviet stand, which did not favor the self-determination of the involved parties, indicates that the elements of realpolitik and not the classical concepts of self-determination are dominant within the Politburo.

The Future Prospects of Self-Determination in Soviet Politics

The preceding analysis points out that the concept of self-determination has been used in Soviet politics as a means of preventing the decentralization of the Soviet system and the secession of various nationalities. This radical change of the function of self-determination was achieved largely through redefinition of the concept of "sovereignty," by establishing the concept of double-sovereignty for each republic and thus creating a unique "Soviet federalism." The Soviet approach to sovereignty is that each republic retains its complete sovereignty in spite of its being an integral part of the Union of the Soviet Socialist Republics. Some Soviet scholars are convinced that a Soviet republic can develop itself only within the fraternal family of the Soviet nations.[154]

It should be noted that traditional concepts of sovereignty and federalism have been challenged by Western philosophers and political scientists as well. A contemporary French author finds that national self-determination in alliance with communism is not only objectionable but also is a major obstacle to socialism.[155] Contemporary political science does not endorse a single theory of federalism, but rather allows it to encompass numerous clusters of policies which are both structure and process of government. If directed to the achievement and maintenance of both unity and diversity, federalism is a political and social phenomenon, concerns both ends and means, and is pursued for both limited and comprehensive purposes.[156]

The Soviet system includes various levels of self-determination, i.e., federalism, which are defined in the constitution. In addition to the union republics, there are autonomous (ethnic) republics, autonomous (ethnic) regions, and autonomous (ethnic) districts. This multilevel federalism leaves numerous small ethnic minorities without institutional or political forms of self-determination. The Soviets are well aware of the quality and quantity of the problem of nationalities that they have to cope with and, therefore, try to diffuse the problem by two means: first by expanding ideological propaganda concerning the eliminaton and diffusion of national problems in the USSR and, second, by declaring this kind of conflict as nonlegitimate within the Soviet system. In 1969, the USSR Academy of Sciences established a Scientific Council on Nationality Problems which had the task of providing guidelines for finding practical solutions to this issue.[157] Under the auspices of the council, several regional conferences took place. Those conferences dealt with various aspects of intranational relations, national culture, and national languages.[158] Numerous editorials and articles were devoted to fraternal aspects of intranational relations.[159] The recent case of Armenia is a vivid example of the Soviet policy

of pacifying nationalities with various kinds of irrelevant and sometimes dubious rewards. In October 1978, the Armenian Republic
was awarded the highest Soviet decoration, the Order of Lenin. It
was given to commemorate the 150th anniversary of Armenian
incorporation into the Russian Empire.[160]

It is illuminating to raise here the question of to what extent, if
at all, the development of self-determination in Soviet politics cor-
responds to other political and ideological innovations. The impact
of the dictatorship of the proletariat and that of the all-people's
state have been mentioned. These concepts still delineate the development of the Soviet society within the three traditional stages of
development: (1) building of socialism; (2) socialism, which is a
higher stage of development; and (3) "communism," the classless,
stateless society. However, in 1971, a new stage was officially
launched and added to "developed socialism."[161] According to
Brezhnev, there are four stages of Soviet development: (1) "building socialism," from 1917-1936; (2) "a socialist society," whose
foundations were constructed by 1936; (3) "developed socialism,"
which the Soviet Union reached by the late sixties; and (4) "communism," still the ostensible goal of Soviet society.[162]

The new stage of "developed socialism" is characterized by
interpretation of the economic, social, and political implications
of the contemporary Soviet economy, which can be advanced by
the increase of the centralization of the administration. The fulfillment of this objective is expected to be achieved within the
existing institutions rather than in new ones. The other meaningful
aspect of this new concept is that it was introduced not as an
adaptation of Soviet political structure to changing economic and
social conditions, but was the adaptation of the emerging features
of a modernized society to guidance by established Soviet institutions.[163] In light of this process, no radical change of self-determination in Soviet politics can be expected as a result of this ideological innovation.

The Soviet application of self-determination has been traced on
three levels—national, regional, and international—and therefore
it is important to summarize it and the goals of the three levels.
The most complex problem facing the Soviet leadership is on the
national level. The recently released Soviet archival material shows
the extremity of Stalin's intolerance toward the independent

Ukraine.[164] This chauvinistic approach toward other nationalities was expressed in the post-Stalin period as well.[165] Peculiarly and simultaneously, Soviet policy promoted the concept of social homogeneity (*odnorodnost'*). On the basis of this social homogeneity, Soviet policy also promotes the notion of one socialist nation[166] and one language, Russian, which should function as a bridge among all Soviet nationalities.[167] All these efforts are directed toward achieving one monohierarchical polity void of any national striving for self-assertion and secession.

On the regional level, the Soviet relations with the East European states are of a major concern. After World War II, the Soviet Union resisted establishing a regional federation, in particular, between Bulgaria and Yugoslavia. Of all East European states, only Yugoslavia approached the solution of its nationalities on a federative basis.[168] However, the Yugoslavian model lacked two elements that characterized the Soviet federal system, a theory of dual sovereignty and the right of secession.

The case of Czechoslovakia is very unique. Among the Soviet charges against Dubček's reforms was the charge that the reforms falsified and fabricated the Soviet model of federalism.[169] The application of the Soviet model in Czechoslovakia was resisted because it would have politically paralyzed the small minority of Slovaks. It is interesting to note that Dubček's proposal to federate Czechoslovakia was the only reform that survived the Soviet invasion and the dismantling of his other reforms. In October 1968, a law that federalized Czechoslovakia was passed and became a part of the new constitution in 1969.[170]

The official Soviet position on state sovereignty is contradictory. On the one hand, it denies the existence of absolute sovereignty, and, on the other hand, it supports the national sovereignty in principle.[171] Soviet analysts distinguish between national and state sovereignty. The latter is a political form of the state's absolute independence in domestic and foreign affairs.[172] This Soviet definition of sovereignty, which is widely shared by Western scholars as well, does not prevent a Soviet policy toward the members of the Warsaw Pact of promoting political cohesion of that alliance. The consequence was the invasion of Czechoslovakia under the pretext of defending socialist sovereignty.[173] The final Soviet goal within the military-economic alliance is not spelled out clearly. However, the increased dependence of the East European states upon the Soviet Union could only promote the existing trends of integration with a potential outcome of confederation in the future.

The impact of self-determination on Soviet conduct in international affairs goes back to the Marxist perception of mankind. Marx postulated the absolute unity of mankind as the ideal, and, since international relations presuppose the horizontal division of mankind into nations, the problems relating to horizontal group diversity are directly related to the Marxian doctrine.[174] Within the present world system, nations, regardless of their interdependence, retain the function of property owners and therefore strive to increase their sovereignty. Consequently, as long as separate national identities exist, unity inevitably means hegemony.[175] Developing Kardelj's conceptualization about a nation's trend to dominate national egoism etc., Berki redefines socialism as the highest stage of capitalism. Within this framework, the Soviet Union continues to promote the worldwide self-determination as a means of winning political support in the Third World and weakening Western political and economic alliances.[176]

In 1976, a special symposium in Washington was dedicated to the Soviet dilemma of nationalities and nationalism. A leading scholar of Soviet affairs predicted that it would be embarrassing to Soviet leaders to issue a new constitution which would be virtually indistinguishable from Stalin's and that they would rather contemplate introducing significant modifications in the existing federal system.[177] Nevertheless, it seems that the Soviet leaders did not feel embarrassed when they introduced a more centralized constitution than that of Stalin.

The Soviet determination to prevent any kind of secession or territorial split is powerfully illustrated by the Soviet sacrifice of a Soviet-Japanese treaty. The Soviet leadership refused to pay the Japanese price—the return of Kurile Islands and half of Sakhaline Island—in order to achieve the neutralization of Japan in the Soviet-Sino conflict. This degree of Soviet determination to retain their territorial integrity promises neither new frontiers of self-determination nor new evolution within the Soviet federalism.

Notes

1. The size of the acquired territory, 100,000 square kilometers, is not large, but it is worth noting that the Soviet clashes with China over the Damansky Island involved only several hundreds of square kilometers and the entire Middle East conflict circles around several thousands of square kilometers!

2. "Soviet Federation and Forms of National Statehood of the People of the USSR," *Soviet State and Law* (November 1972):12-13.

3. Presidium of the Supreme Soviet of the RSFSR, *RSFSR—Administrative-Territorial Division, 1972* (Moscow, 1972), p. 5, autonomous republics, pp. 344-420.

4. S. I. Brook, "Ethnographic Process in the USSR," *Soviet Ethnography* 4 (1971):23.

5. Ibid.

6. Roman Szporluk, "Why Some Soviet Sociologists Are Alarmed," *New York Times*, August 27, 1977, Op-Ed. Szporluk reviews the recent Soviet analysis by G. A. Bondarskaya, *Fertility in the USSR: Its Ethnographic Aspect* (Moscow, 1977). For a recent American study concerning the growth of Soviet population and its impact upon the Soviet labor and military forces, see Murray Feshbach and Stephen Rapaway, "Soviet Population and Manpower Trends and Policies," *Soviet Economy in a New Perspective*, a compendium of papers submitted to the Joint Economic Committee, Congress of the United States, October 14, 1976 (Washington, D.C.: U.S. Government Printing Office, 1976), pp. 113-54; see also Warren W. Eason, "Demographic Problems: Fertility," ibid., pp. 155-61. A recent Soviet analysis of manpower in Byelorussia begins with the fact that over 100,000 Jews emigrated from Byelorussia to the United States during the period 1897-1914 (D. I. Valentei et al., eds., *Migration Problems of Population and Manpower* [Moscow, 1970], p. 88).

7. Ivan Dzyuba, *Internationalism or Russification* (New York: Monad Press, 1974); also, *Documents: National Question in the USSR* (1975); *Political Diaries*, 2 vols. (Amsterdam, 1972-1975). For a recent demand to increase the scholarly research about the Ukrainian nation, see the lecture of academician B. A. Rybakov at the Soviet Academy of Sciences, *Herald of the Academy of Sciences of the USSR* 6 (1978):29-30.

8. Teresa Rakovska-Harmstone, "Ethnicity in the Soviet Union," *Annals, AAPSS* 433 (September 1977); Ihor Kamenetsky, ed., *Nationalism and Human Rights: Process of Modernization in the USSR* (Littleton, Colo., 1977); Edward Allworth, ed., *Nationality Group Survival in Multi-Ethnic States: Shifting Support Patterns in the Soviet Baltic Region* (New York: Praeger, 1977); Tõnu Parming and Elmar Järvesoo, *A Case Study of a Soviet*

Republic: The Estonian SSR, Westview Special Studies on the Soviet Union and Eastern Europe (Boulder, Colo.: Westview Press, 1978); and Frantishek Silnicky, *The Nationalities Policy of the CPSU, 1917-1922* (Munich: Suchasnist, 1978).

9. M. O. Reikhel, ed., *Soviet Federalism* (Moscow-Leningrad, 1930), p. 17.

10. Ya. N. Umansky, *Soviet State and Law* (Moscow: Gosyurizdat, 1960), p. 209.

11. V. M. Chkhivadze, ed., *National Relations and State in the Contemporary Period* (Moscow, 1972), pp. 85-97.

12. Ibid., p. 88. The statement goes even further, revealing that many Soviet nations have already done so!

13. M. I. Piskotin et al., eds., *The Governing Apparatus of the Socialist State* (Moscow, 1976), p. 196.

14. Ibid., pp. 252-70.

15. V. V. Kopeichnikov, *The State Mechanism of the Soviet Federation* (Moscow, 1973), pp. 103-4.

16. Chalmers Johnson, ed., *Change in Communist Systems* (Stanford, Calif., 1970), see especially articles by C. Johnson and D. Rustow.

17. Andrew C. Janos, "Systemic Models and the Theory of Change in Comparative Study of Communist Politics," in A. C. Janos, ed., *Authoritarian Politics in Communist Europe* (Berkeley, Calif., 1976), p. 27.

18. T. H. Rigby, "Politics in the Mono-Organizational Society," ibid., pp. 31-80.

19. Richard Pipes, *The Foundation of the Soviet Union*, rev. ed. (New York: Atheneum, 1968), p. 33.

20. V. I. Lenin, "Sochineniia" (Russian), vol. 7, p. 105.

21. V. I. Lenin, *Collected Works*, 4th ed. (Moscow, 1951-1967), vol. 24, p. 144 (henceforth referred to as Lenin).

22. Ibid., "The Right of Nations for Self-Determination," vol. 20, p. 400.

23. Ibid., p. 408. Lenin argued that no nation which oppresses other nations can be free (ibid., p. 413). Lenin expanded this idea to countries of Eastern Europe and to the colonies (see vol. 22, pp. 150-51).

24. Ibid., vol. 20, p. 443.

25. Ibid., p. 434.

26. Ibid., pp. 422-23. The Kadets who argued that such an approach would increase the danger of the disintegration of the state were opposed by the same argument (ibid., pp. 420-21). "If the Ukrainians see that we have a Soviet republic they will not secede, but if we have a Milyukov republic, they will" (ibid., vol. 24, p. 301).

27. Ibid., vol. 20, p. 428.

28. Ibid., p. 411.

29. Ibid., vol. 22, p. 146.

30. Ibid.

31. Ibid., vol. 24, pp. 302-3.

32. Chkhivadze, *National Relations and State*, chap. 3, "National State-hood and National Question," pp. 40-48; see also E. V. Tadevosian, *V. I. Lenin on State-Forms Solution of the National Problem in the USSR* (Moscow: Moscow State University, 1970), pp. 96-108.

33. Chkhivadze, *National Relations and State*, p. 43; Tadevosian, *V. I. Lenin on State-Forms Solution*, p. 96.

34. Chkhivadze, *National Relations and State*, pp. 44-45; Tadevosian, *Lenin on State-Forms Solution*, p. 102.

35. Chkhivadze, *National Relations and State*, pp. 45-46; Tadevosian, *Lenin on State-Forms Solution*, p. 101.

36. Chkhivadze, *National Relations and State*, p. 46; Tadevosian, *Lenin on State-Forms Solution*, pp. 104-5.

37. Tadevosian presents an objective picture of Lenin's hesitations regarding the effectiveness of the federal system (*State-Forms Solution*, p. 104) and criticizes numerous scholars who presented Lenin's policy concerning the federal structure as a consolidated policy in the pre-October period (ibid., pp. 96-100).

38. Pipes, *Foundation of the Soviet Union*, p. 100.

39. Ibid., p. 247.

40. D. L. Zlatopolsky, *The Establishment and Development of the USSR as a Union State* (Moscow: Gosyurizdat, 1954), p. 24. "As a result of the new conditions, created by the October Revolution, the Communist Party, guided by the spirit and not by the letter of Marxism, threw out the outmoded Marxian conclusions about the federalism. The party substituted it with a new conclusion concerning the necessity of federalism within the concrete historical conditions of the Soviet Russia" (ibid., p. 25).

41. See the declarations of independence of Estonia, Lithuania, and Latvia in *History of the Soviet Constitution, 1917-1956* (Moscow: Gosyurizdat, 1957), pp. 176-77 (henceforth referred to as *History*).

42. Ibid., pp. 206-8.

43. Ibid., pp. 259-60, 265-66.

44. Ibid., pp. 299-302.

45. Ibid., pp. 284-99, 321-33, 339-57.

46. See M. S. Kirov's speech at the Plenum of the Trade Unions of Georgia: "When troubles appear over our heads, when this southern sky will get covered by imperialistic clouds, I can assure you that we shall not weep federatively" (ibid., pp. 311-12).

47. V. Lyubimov and B. Yuldashbaev, *Lenin and National Self-Determination: Case Study of Volga and Ural Nations* (Cheboksary, 1967), p. 59.

48. P. G. Semionov, "The Sovereignty of Soviet Nations," *Voprosy Istorii* 12 (December 1965):22-33.

49. Zlatopolsky, *Establishment and Development of the USSR*, p. 71.
50. Jürgen Arnold, *Die nationalen Gebietseinheiten der Sowjetunion* (Cologne: Verlag Wissenschaft und Politik, 1973), p. 29.
51. Zlatopolsky, *Establishment and Development of the USSR*, pp. 107-8.
52. Ibid., pp. 150-51.
53. *History*, pp. 884-85.
54. Zlatopolsky, *Establishment and Development of the USSR*, pp. 164-65.
55. *History*, p. 809.
56. Ibid., p. 810.
57. Ibid., pp. 813-14.
58. Zlatopolsky, *Establishment and Development of the USSR*, pp. 182-83.
59. See the decisions of the Supreme Soviet of August 3, 5, and 6, 1940, in *History*, pp. 814-15. It is interesting to note that within three weeks those republics developed and accepted new constitutions.
60. Ibid., p. 934.
61. Ibid., p. 887.
62. This issue is well defined in Moshe Lewin's *Lenin's Last Struggle* (New York: Pantheon Books, 1968).
63. E. B. Genkina, *The Formation of the USSR* (Moscow, 1947), pp. 142-44.

The 1922 Treaty	The 1924 Constitution
1. Representation of the Union in international relations;	1. Representation of the Union in international relations; conduct of all diplomatic relations; conclusion of political and other treaties with foreign states;
2. Alteration of the external frontiers of the Union;	2. Alteration of the external frontiers of the Union, and also the settlement of questions concerning alteration of the borders between the Union republics;
3. Negotiation of foreign loans;	3. Negotiation of domestic and foreign loans by the USSR and authorization of foreign and domestic loans by the Union republics;
4. Establishment of a foreign and domestic trade system;	4. Control of foreign trade and creation of a domestic trade system;
5. Establishment of the founda-	5. Establishment of the bases and

tions and an overall plan for the entire Union economy, and conclusion of concession agreements;

overall plan for the entire Union economy; allocation of all-Union branches of industry and individual plants; conclusion of concession agreements, both all-Union, and in the name of the Union republics;

6. Regulation of transport, and post and telegraph communications;

6. Administration of transport, and post and telegraph communications;

7. Organization of armed forces for the USSR;

7. Organization and control of the USSR armed forces;

8. Approval of a single USSR state budget; establishment of a monetary, financial and credit system, together with a system of all-Union, republican, and local taxation;

8. Approval of a single USSR state budget to include those of the Union republics; establishment of an all-Union taxation and revenue system, with centralized control over allocations to the Union republican budgets; authorization of additional taxes and levies to supplement the Union republican budgets;

9. All-Union legislation on population resettlement;

9. All-Union legislation on inter-republican population resettlement and the setting up of a resettlement fund;

10. The right of general amnesty.

10. The right of amnesty over all the territory of the Union.

64. The autonomous republics who drafted their own constitutions in the late twenties were: Bashkirian, Tatar, Dagestan, Yakutian, Karelian, and Kirgizian (see S. I. Yakubovskaya, *The Development of the USSR as a Union State, 1922-1936* [Moscow, 1972], pp. 49-50).

65. Ibid., p. 188.

66. Ibid., p. 192.

67. The archival material of ths subcommittee was presented for the first time by Yakubovskaya (ibid., pp. 198-212). In spite of the partial availability of this material, the forthcoming comments are based upon it.

68. Zlatopolsky, *Establishment and Development of the USSR*, pp. 167-68.

69. J. V. Stalin, *On the Project of the Constitution of the USSR*, speech at the Eighth All-Union Congress of Soviets, Nov. 25, 1936 (Moscow: Partizdat, 1936), pp. 34-35.

70. Ibid., pp. 35-36.

71. *History*, p. 823.

72. Ibid., p. 824.

73. Stalin, *On the Project of the Constitution*, p. 37.

74. *Izvestiia*, February 12, 1957.

75. For a detailed analysis of the variants and politics of the new constitution, see George Ginsgurgs, "A Khrushchev Constitution for the Soviet Union: Projects and Prospects," *Ost Europa Recht* 3 (1962); also, Robert Sharlet, "The New Soviet Constitution," *Problems of Communism* (September-October 1977):1-24.

76. It is interesting to note that Brezhnev, in his speech to the Central Committee, May 24, 1977, defended the absence of drastic changes: "Experience has shown that the fundamental elements of the federal structure of the USSR have completely lived up to the expectations. Therefore, there is no need to make any changes of principles and forms of our Soviet socialist federation" (*Pravda*, May 1977).

77. John H. Miller, "Cadres Policy in Nationality Areas; Recruitment of CPSU First and Second Secretaries in Non-Russian Republics of the USSR," *Soviet Studies* 29, no. 1 (1977):3-36.

78. John N. Hazard, "Statutory Recognition of Nationality Differences in the USSR," in Edward Allworth, ed., *Soviet Nationality Problems* (New York: Columbia University Press, 1971).

79. For a detailed Soviet analysis of the dictatorship of the proletariat, see F. Burlatsky, *The State and Communism* (Moscow: Progress Publishers, 1964), pp. 46-52.

80. Roger E. Kanet, "The Rise and Fall of the All-People's State: Recent Changes in the Soviet Theory of State," *Soviet Studies* (July 1968):84, see also Burlatsky, *State and Communism*, pp. 107-18.

81. Burlatsky, *State and Communism*, pp. 119-20.

82. G. Barabashev and K. Sheremet, "The Political Base of the Soviet State," *Pravda*, December 17, 1977.

83. Ibid.

84. N. Petrovichev, "The Democratic Centralism in the Life of the Party and the State," *Pravda*, August 25, 1978. It is interesting to note that an article by A. Kositzyn, "The All-People's State: The Growth of Its Role as an Instrument of Building Communism" (*Izvestiia*, October 8, 1978), states that the central control over the state's economy should be identified with the general state's administration. The author challenges the class divisions and supports several states' functions which were characteristic attributes of the

all-people's state. This article, written by a professor of law, indicates that some factions of Soviet leadership consider the possibility of promoting this concept of decentralization of the state system.

85. P. N. Fedoseev, ed., *Leninism and the National Question in the Contemporary Conditions* (Moscow: Institute of Marxism-Leninism under the Central Committee of the CPSU, 1972), p. 12. This book constitutes the most authoritative thinking on this issue and was also translated into English from the revised edition of 1974 (*Leninism and the National Question* [Moscow: Progress Publishers, 1977] ; henceforth referred to as *Leninism*).

86. Ibid., p. 5.

87. M. N. Rosenko, *The Building of Communism in the USSR and the Natural Development of the Socialist Nations* (Leningrad: Leningrad State University, 1968), p. 130.

88. *Leninism*, p. 24.

89. See *The CPSU on the Formation of the New Man: Collection of Documents and Materials, 1965-1976* (Moscow: Politizdat, 1976), p. 456.

90. Erwin Oberhändler, *Sowjetpatriotismus und Geschichte* (Cologne: Verlag Wissenschaft und Politik, 1967); see also P. M. Rogachev and M. A. Sverdlin, "Patriotism amd Nation," in *Socialism and Nation* (Moscow, 1976), pp. 174-83.

91. Rogachev and Sverdlin, "Patriotism and Nation," p. 177; see also, G. Smirnov, "Soviet People—Patriots and Internationalists," *Pravda*, December 12, 1972; M. P. Kim, *Soviet Nation—A New Historic Entity; Its Origins and Development* (Moscow: Institute of USSR History, Academy of Sciences, USSR, Nauka, 1975), pp. 156-79.

92. *Leninism*, p. 215.

93. Ibid., pp. 215-16.

94. Ibid., p. 219.

95. I. Mayatnikov, ed., *The Formation of the Socialist Nations in the USSR* (Moscow: Gospolitizdat, 1962), p. 9.

96. On the development of the new-shared socialist culture, see *Leninism*, chap. 7, "Socialism and the Mutual Influence and Enrichment of National Cultures," pp. 309-13; see also, Kim, *Soviet Nation*, chap. 6, "The Whole-Soviet Elements in the Cultures of People of the USSR," pp. 180-205; M. N. Rosenko, "Cooperation among the Socialist Nations of the USSR in the Area of Culture and the Formation of a Common Spiritual Make-up of the Soviet People," in Kim, *Soviet Nation*, chap. 5, pp. 148-92; I. M. Muminov, ed., *The Flourishment of Socialist Nations and Their Rapprochement* (Tashkent, 1967), pp. 22-44, 83-93; also *Socialism and Nation*, pp. 51-84, 160-66, 190-95.

97. Claus Mueller, *The Politics of Communication: A Study in the Political Sociology of Languages, Socialization, and Legitimation* (Oxford: Oxford

University Press, 1975), p. 19. Wolfgang Bergsdorf, "Die sanfte Gewalt: Sprache, Denken, Politik" [Sweet Violence: Language, Thinking, Politics], *Aus Politik und Zeitgeschichte* (June 1977):39-47.

98. Lenin, vol. 20, pp. 71-73.

99. Ibid., "Bill on the Equality of Nations and the Safeguarding of the Rights of National Minorities," pp. 281-83. One of the recent explanations given for Lenin's firm position on the equality of all languages points out his father's close relations with ethnic minorities (see Isabelle Kreindler, "A Neglected Source of Lenin's Nationality Policy," *Slavic Review* [March 1977] : 86-100).

100. *History*, p. 593.

101. Mayatnikov, *Formation of the Socialist Nations*, p. 18; Rosenko, "Cooperation among the Socialist Nations," p. 197, presents the following important statistical data: out of the 130 spoken languages in prerevolutionary Russia, only 20 had a developed literacy. At the present time, 50 languages have been formed after the revolution. In 1933, Soviet literature was published in 14 languages; in 1958, 58; in 1965, 67; and in 1966, 89. Between 1956 and 1965 within the RSFSR only, 13 languages have become literary languages.

102. M. I. Kulichenko, ed., *National Relations in a Developed Socialist Society*, chap. 11, "The Development of the Mutual Influence of Languages in a Developed Socialist Society," (Moscow, 1977), p. 208; *Leninism*, p. 319.

103. V. A. Avrorin, "Concerning the Mutual Influence of Language and Culture," in Kim, ed., *Contemporary Problems of the History of National-State-Building in the USSR* (Dushanbe, 1970), pp. 367-68.

104. K. Kh. Hanazarov, "Rapprochement of Nations and National Languages in the Era of Building Communism," in Muminov, *Flourishment of Socialist Nations*, pp. 76-82.

105. Yu. D. Deshirov, "National Languages under the Conditions of the Developed Socialist Society," in *Socialism and Nation*, p. 187.

106. *History*, p. 340.

107. *Zarya Vostoka*, March 24, 1978.

108. Ibid., April 16, 1978.

109. Muminov, *Flourishment of Socialist Nations*, pp. 143-46.

110. Kulichenko, *National Relations in a Developed Socialist Society*, pp. 92-109.

111. *Socialism and Nation*, pp. 190-95.

112. *Leninism*, pp. 325-54.

113. For a detailed historical analysis, see Christian Dueval, "'Accelerated' or 'Gradual' Assimilation?" *Radio Liberty Research*, 15/73 (January 9, 1973).

114. See the summaries of such conferences in "Russification Discussed at Recent Nationality Conference in Estonia," *Radio Liberty Research* 505/76 (December 27, 1976); Elizabeth C. Scheetz, "Recent Discussions of Leninist

Nationality Policy: Domestic and International Implications," *Radio Liberty Research* 473/76 (November 17, 1976); also, Muminov, *Flourishment of Socialist Nations*; M. I. Kulichenko, *Socialism and Nation*, Conference of the Institute of Marxism-Leninism on "The Development and the International Cooperation of Soviet Nations," October 23-24, 1974, published in 1975; Kim, *Contemporary Problems*, Conference in Dushanbe, May 1968.

115. "The Code Words and Catchwords of Brezhnev's Nationality Policy," *Radio Liberty Research* 331/76 (June 29, 1976).

116. N. Tarasenki, "The Drawing Together of Nations—Development in Conformity with the Building of Communism," *Kommunist* 13 (September 1978):65-76.

117. Ibid., p. 66.

118. J. V. Stalin, *Marxism and the National and Colonial Question*, a collection of articles (London 1936; reprinted, 1942), p. 35.

119. For a historical analysis of the fluid nationalities, see Alfred A. Greenbaum, "Soviet Nationalities Policy and the Problem of Fluid Nationalities," in B. Varga and G. L. Mosse, eds., *Jews and Non-Jews in Eastern Europe* (Jerusalem: Israel Universities Press, 1974), pp. 257-69.

120. For an excellent analysis of these processes, see Zvi Gitelman, *Jewish Nationality and Soviet Politics* (Princeton, N.J.: Princeton University Press, 1972), pp. 321-440.

121. Yehoshua Gilboa, *The Black Years of Soviet Jewry* (New York: Little, Brown, and Co., 1971), pp. 226-43.

122. For a detailed presentation of the contemporary situation of Soviet Jewry, see Harry G. Shaffer, *The Soviet Treatment of Jews*, Special Studies in International Politics and Government (New York: Praeger, 1974); William Korey, *The Soviet Cage* (New York: Viking Press, 1973); Eli M. Lederhendler, "Resources of the Ethnically Disenfranchised," in Allworth, ed., *Nationality Group Survival*, pp. 194-227.

123. For a detailed account, see Alexandr Nekrich, *The Punished People* (New York: Norton, 1978).

124. *Archives of Samizdat*, vol. 12, Documents on the Crimean Tatars, AC, No. 379, pp. 1-2.

125. See the compilation of materials in *The Tashkent Trial* (the trial of ten representatives of the Crimean nation, July 1-August 5, 1969), Samizdat Library, no. 7 (Amsterdam: Herzen's Fund, 1976).

126. V. Shevtsov, *National Sovereignty and Soviet State* (Moscow, Progress Publishers, 1974), p. 40.

127. Lenin, vol. 20, p. 397.

128. Umansky, *Soviet State and Law*, pp. 172-90.

129. Arnold, *Die nationale Gebietseinheiten der Sowjetunion*, pp. 53-57.

130. Umansky, *Soviet State and Law*, p. 181.

131. Shevtsov, *National Sovereignty*, pp. 76-77; for a further analysis concerning the compatibility between the sovereignty of the USSR and that of the republics, see pp. 92-99.

132. *History*, pp. 809-10.

133. V. E. Evdokimenko, ed., *International and National in Socialist Society* (Kiev, 1976), p. 165.

134. Detailed analysis of this issue presented by Vernon Aspaturian, *The Union Republics in Soviet Diplomacy* (Geneva, 1960); see also, Z. Avalov, *Georgia's Independence in International Politics, 1918-1921* (Paris, 1924), pp. 188-95; S. Bablumian ("Master of His Destiny," *Izvestiia*, October 17, 1978) states that over 200,000 Armenians from twenty-six countries have returned to the Armenian Republic.

135. Aspaturian, *Union Republics*, pp. 52-53.

136. Heinz Heitzer, "Concerning the Origins of Socialist Nation in the GDR," in Kulichenko, *Socialism and Nation*, p. 213.

137. Hans Müller, "Concerning the Symptoms and the Future Development of Socialist Nation in the GDR," in *Socialism and Nation*, pp. 218-19; V. G. Dolgin, "The Meaning of the Socialist Countries Unity," *Voprosy Filosofii*, no. 5 (1977):3-15. Two recent studies shed additional light on Soviet-German and intra-German affairs in this realm: Christian Meier and Fred Oldenburg, "Der Vertrag DDR/UdSSR als Model für den integrativen Bilateralism in der Sozialistischen Staatengemeinschaft," *Beitrage zur Konfliktforshung* 6, no. 2 (1976):103-44; and Boris Meissner, "Die sowjetische Nationsbegriff und die Frage des Fortbestandes der deutsche Nation" [The Soviet Concept of the Nation and the Question of the Survival of the German Nation], *Europa-Archiv* 32, no. 10 (May 25, 1977):315-24.

138. On the early Soviet perception of the EEC, see Marshall D. Shulman, "The Communist States and Western Integration," *International Organizations* 17, no. 3 (1963):649-62; David F. Forte, "The Response of Soviet Foreign Policy to the Common Market, 1957-63," *Soviet Studies* 1, no. 3 (January 1968):370.

139. Christopher A. P. Binns, "From USE to EEC: The Soviet Analysis of European Integration under Capitalism," *Soviet Studies* 30, no. 2 (April 1978):256-57. By now, *Pravda* and *Izvestiia* have a special column entitled "Paces of Integration."

140. Yu. Shishkov, "Who Wants the Political Integration of Western Europe?" *International Affairs* (Russian ed., Moscow) 7 (1973):76-85. Shishkov was the head of the Group to Study the EEC at the Comecon.

141. Ibid., p. 85.

142. Shevtsov, "Sovereignty and Socialist Economic Integration," chap. 10 in *National Sovereignty and Soviet State*, pp. 155, 175.

143. Alexander Dallin, "The Soviet Union: The Political Activity," in Z.

Brzezinski, *Africa and the Communist World* (Stanford, Calif.: Stanford University Press, 1965), pp. 7-48.

144. The Soviet Union established diplomatic relations with the People's Republic of Bangladesh on January 24, 1972, and voted for its acceptance into the United Nations on August 27, 1972, while the People's Republic of China voted against its acceptance; see also Sidney H. Schauberg, "Campaign by Soviets Wins Bengali Friends," *New York Times*, April 6, 1972.

145. V. Petrov, "Northern Ireland without Change," *International Affairs* (Russian ed., Moscow) 10 (1973):128-29; also, N. Zagorsky, "Northern Ireland—Maneuvering the Modernization of Regime," *International Affairs* (Russian ed.) 2 (1974):127-28.

146. George Usrav, "Soviet Media Coverage of the Case of Northern Ireland versus Great Britain," *Radio Liberty Research* 120/77 (May 20, 1977):1-13.

147. A. Golybin, "Namibia in Its Struggle for Freedom," *International Affairs* (Russian ed.) 11 (1976):65-71; also, Yu. Shvevtsov, "Mosambic," *International Affairs* (Russian ed.) 8 (1975):113-14.

148. The reason given for this approach is that the neo-colonial forces are anti-Communist (see E. Tarabrin, "Ideological Struggle and the National Liberation Movement," *International Affairs* [Russian ed.] 11 [1973]:101-11).

149. *Die Welt* (Hamburg), November 18, 1967.

150. Victor Maevsky, "One State—One Destiny," *Pravda*, November 4, 1970.

151. Ibid.; see also M. Zenovich, "Nation's Hope," *Pravda*, September 30, 1970.

152. V. Kondratiev and S. Vasiliev, "Cyprus—Tragedy and Hopes," *International Affairs* (Russian ed.) 10 (1974):69.

153. Ibid., p. 73.

154. Rosenko, *Building of Communism in the USSR*, p. 188; see also, F. V. Konstantinov et al., eds., *Sociological Problems of International Relations* (Moscow, 1970), pp. 196-202; V. A. Vasilenko, *The Responsibility of State for Violations of International Law* (Kiev, 1976), pp. 95-119; Ivan Bernier, *International Legal Aspects of Federalism* (Hamden, Conn.: Shoe String Press, 1973), pp. 22-24; Ivo Lapenna, "The Soviet Concept of 'Socialist' International Law," in London Institute of World Affairs, *The Year Book of World Affairs, 1975* (New York: Praeger, 1975), pp. 259-62.

155. Jean-François Rever, *The Totalitarian Temptation* (London: Penguin, 1978), pp. 15, 21-22.

156. Dan Elazar, "Federalism: Concept, Structure, and Process" (Lecture delivered at the International Conference on Federalism, Basel, Switzerland, 1975).

157. *Herald of the Academy of Sciences of the USSR* 9 (1969):138.

158. In November 1976, the council organized in Tallin, Estonian Republic,

a conference on the theme, "National Relations and Cooperation of National Cultures in the USSR."

159. "The Creative Power of Fraternal Relations," *Pravda*, October 11, 1978.

160. It was D. F. Ustinov, minister of defense of the USSR, who delivered the major speech and who presented the Order of Lenin to the Armenian Republic by attaching it to the banner of the republic (*Pravda*, October 15, 1978). The sixtieth anniversary of the Estland's Labor Commune, which existed only several months in 1918, was celebrated and officially greeted from the front page of *Izvestiia*, November 21, 1978.

161. Alfred B. Evans, Jr., "Developed Socialism and the Transition to Communism: Problems and Changes in Soviet Communist Ideology," paper delivered at the 1976 annual meeting of the American Political Science Association, Chicago, Ill., September 2-5, 1976, p. 4.

162. Ibid., p. 7.

163. Ibid., p. 1; see also V. E. Guliev and A. I. Shchiglik, "The Party and the State in the System of Socialist Democracy," *Soviet State and Law* 4 (1975):14-15.

164. See a highly revealing letter from D. Manuilsky, secretary of the Central Committee of the Communist Party (Bolsheviks) of Ukraine, to Stalin dated September 4, 1922, in which Manuilsky suggests eliminating the independence of the Ukraine, substituting it with broad autonomy. This letter is presented for the first time by Frantishek Silnicky in his recent book, *Nationalities Policy of the CPSU, 1917-1922*, pp. 268-70. Stalin's famous remark about the independence of the Ukraine was stated in his note to V. P. Zatonsky, chairman of the Central Committee of the Soviets of Ukraine, on April 4, 1918: "You have played already enough on this game of government and republic, it is a prime time to stop it" (ibid., p. 272).

165. "The characteristics of Russian people are: clear mind, firm character and patience. It was the great Russian people who was the decisive power which united the independent Soviet Republics into the USSR" (Zlatopolsky, *Establishment and Development of the USSR*, p. 61). Zlatopolsky is a professor at the Moscow State University!

166. Yu. V. Romley and V. I. Kozlov, "The Analysis of Contemporary Ethnic Processes in the Realm of Spiritual Culture of Nations of the USSR," *Soviet Ethnography* 1 (1975):3-16; I. S. Gurvich, "The Contemporary Ethnic Processes in the USSR," *Soviet Ethnography* 4 (1972):16-33; Yu. V. Arutyunayn, "Social-Cultural Aspects of the Development and Mutual Rapprochement of Nationalities in the USSR," *Soviet Ethnography* 3 (1972):3-18; L. M. Drobizheva, "The Drawing Together of Cultures and Inter-Ethnic Relations in the USSR," *Soviet Ethnography* 6 (1977):3-19; I. S. Gurvich, "Ethno-Cultural Rapprochement of the Peoples of the Soviet Union," *Soviet Ethnog-*

raphy 5 (1977):23-35; see also the recent monograph by M. Kulichenko, *Strengthening the International Unity of the Soviet Society* (Kiev: Politizat of Ukraine, 1976), p. 381.

167. A. Pranda, "The Influence of Bilingualism on Certain Features of Folk Culture," *Soviet Ethnography* 2 (1972):17-25; M. N. Guboglo, "The Social-Ethnic Consequences of Bilingualism," *Soviet Ethnography* 2 (1972):26-36; S. A. Arutyunov, "Bilingualism and Biculturalism," *Soviet Ethnography* 2 (1978):3-14.

168. Peter Jambrek, *Development and Social Change in Yugoslavia* (Lexington, Mass.: Saxon House, 1975), pp. 89-117; see also A. Ross Johnson, *The Transformation of Communist Ideology: The Yugoslav Case, 1945-1953* (Cambridge, Mass.: M.I.T. Press, 1972), pp. 145-56. For a detailed analysis of this issue in each state of Eastern Europe, see Boris Meissner, ed., *Das Selbstbestimmungsrecht der Völker in Osteuropa und China* (Cologne: Verlag Wissenschaft und Politik, 1968), pp. 30-200.

169. *On Events in Czechoslovakia* (Moscow, 1968), p. 60.

170. Ivo Duchacek, "Antagonistic Cooperation: Territorial and Ethnic Communities," *Publius* 7, no. 4 (Fall 1977):16.

171. E. D. Mordzhinskaya, "Sociological Aspects of National Sovereignty," in Konstantinov et al., *Sociological Problems of International Relations*, pp. 196-99.

172. Ibid., pp. 200-201; see also Ivan Bernier, *International Legal Aspects of Federalism*, pp. 23, 32, 64-66.

173. Ole Holsti, Terrence Hopmann, and John Sullivan, *Unity and Disintegration in International Alliances: Comparative Studies* (New York: John Wiley and Sons, 1973), pp. 52-54, 61-64, 113-34.

174. R. N. Berki, "On Marxian Thought and the Problems of International Relations," *World Politics* 1 (1971):80-105. The following remarks are based on Berki's conclusions.

175. Ibid., p. 105.

176. One of the leading slogans of 1978 was, "Let Us Strengthen the Mighty and Unshakable Union of Three Revolutionary Contemporary Powers: World Socialism, International Proletariat, and National Liberation Movements!" *Izvestiia*, October 17, 1978. See also a detailed analysis by Professor M. Senin, "The Socialist Community of Nations: A New Type of International Alliance," *International Affairs* (Russian ed.) 11 (1978):10-18.

177. Jeremy R. Azrael, "Nationality Policy under Brezhnev and Kosygin: Some Introductory Comments," in Carl Linden and Dimitri Simes, eds., *Nationalities and Nationalism in the USSR: A Soviet Dilemma* (Washington, D.C.: Center for Strategic and International Studies, Georgetown University, 1977), p. 42.

Part 4

Asia and Africa

8

Self-Determination Outside the Colonial Context: The Birth of Bangladesh in Retrospect

Ved P. Nanda

In the aftermath of the Indo-Pakistan war in December 1971, the independent nation-state of Bangladesh was born.[1] Within the next four months, more than fifty countries had recognized the new nation.[2] Since India's military intervention was primarily responsible for the success of the secessionist movement in what was formerly known as East Pakistan and for the creation of a new political entity on the international scene,[3] many serious questions stemming from this historic event remain unresolved for the international lawyer. For example: (1) What is the continuing validity of Art. 2(4) of the UN Charter?[4] (2) What is the current status of the doctrine of humanitarian intervention in international law?[5] (3) What action could the United Nations have taken to avert the Bangladesh crisis?[6] (4) What measures are necessary to prevent such tragic occurrences in the future?[7] and (5) What relationship exists between the principle of self-determination in international law and the birth of Bangladesh?

As the debate on all these important issues continues, only the last question, which perhaps has received the least attention by scholars,[8] will be the subject of the present inquiry. The discussion will open with a brief account of the events preceding the Indo-Pakistan war and the socio-economic and political climate in which these events occurred. This description should provide an appropriate framework for investigation of the validity of the claim that the secession of East Pakistan was justified, indeed sanctified, under the principle of self-determination.

Events Preceding the Bangladesh Crisis in a Historical Context[9]

The seeds of the Bangladesh crisis were sown in 1947 when India was partitioned, creating the states of India and Pakistan. The latter consisted of two disparate parts, divided not only by ethnic, linguistic, and cultural differences, but also separated physically by over a thousand miles of Indian territory. The only major bond which initially brought together these seemingly diverse parts, East and West Pakistan, was the common religion of Islam. Within the next two decades, East Pakistan experienced a growing domination of its economic and political life by West Pakistan.[10] Consequently, the religious bond could no longer ensure a lasting unity, and, while East–West Pakistan relations were straining to a breaking point, the initial hostility between East Pakistan and India had eased considerably by the late 1960s.[11]

The general elections in Pakistan in December 1970, the first ever based on the adult franchise, precipitated the crisis. The Awami League party, led by Sheikh Mujibur Rahman, contested the elections on the following six-point platform, which called for a fully autonomous East Pakistan:[12]

1. The Pakistan Constitution shall be federal; a parliamentary form of government shall be elected on the basis of adult franchise and population;
2. The federal government shall be responsible only for defense and foreign affairs, and, subject to the conditions provided in number 3 below, currency;
3. Two separate and freely convertible currencies shall be introduced into East and West Pakistan, or in the alternative, a separate reserve bank will be established in East Pakistan, to prevent the transfer of reserves and flight of capital from East to West Pakistan;
4. Fiscal policy for East Pakistan shall be vested in East Pakistan;
5. There shall be separate foreign exchange earnings for East and West Pakistan; the Constitution shall empower East Pakistan to establish trade and aid links with foreign countries; and

6. East Pakistan shall have a separate militia or para-military force.

On this platform, the Awami League party won 167 seats, a majority in the 313-member National Assembly.[13] A Bengali leader, M. A. Bhashani, called the election results a plebiscite for a sovereign and independent East Pakistan.[14]

The ruling elite in West Pakistan—a military-industrial-landlord-business coalition—was apparently alarmed at the prospect of being ruled by the Awami League party. Also, the ruling coalition considered the East Pakistani demand for political and economic autonomy unacceptable because of the fear that it would deprive the West Pakistani manufactured goods of a captive market and would result in the loss to Pakistan of the bulk of its foreign exchange and valuable raw materials, such as jute and tea.[15]

The West Pakistani military and political leaders exacerbated the volatile situation in East Pakistan when President Yahya Khan postponed the convening of the National Assembly which was due to meet on March 3, 1971, to draft a constitution.[16] Mass demonstrations in East Pakistan followed; the Bengalis greeted Yahya with slogans of *Joi Bangla* ("long live independent Bengal") and brought business to a standstill at Rahman's call for noncooperation with the government.[17] On the eve of the civil war, Rahman said that the East Pakistanis wished only to be "left in peace [and to] live as free people."[18] There ensued serious acts of civil disobedience, including refusal to pay taxes and a total strike in government offices and businesses. These were accompanied by a change in the East Bengali mood which began to reflect a desire for complete independence as opposed to mere autonomy.

Following three weeks of inconclusive negotiations in Dacca betweeen Yahya and Rahman, the Pakistani military struck Dacca without warning on the night of March 25, 1971, and initiated a reign of terror throughout East Pakistan which continued with increasing intensity until December 1971.[19] The general pattern of repression consisted of the destruction and burning of villages on a colossal scale; indiscriminate killing of civilians; sorting out and murdering Hindus, university teachers and students, lawyers, doctors, Awami League leaders and supporters, Bengali military and police officers; and rape on a very wide scale.[20] As a result of these repressive measures, many observers accused the Pakistani armed forces and Razakars—local volunteer militiamen who were collaborators of the Pakistani armed forces in East Bengal—of committing selective genocide, purported to deprive East Pakistan of Bengali leadership.[21]

By December 1971, the continuing wave of terror had forced approximately ten million people to flee East Pakistan and take refuge in India.[22] This, in turn, put a severe strain on India-Pakistan relations, and a full-scale war erupted between the two nations, which ended after thirteen days with the surrender of the Pakistani army.[23] The following account illustrates the nature of the havoc caused by the war: "Thirty million people dislocated by the war. More than 1.5 million homes destroyed. Nine million refugees returning from India to rebuild their lives and homes. War damage drastically reducing rail traffic. Key rail and road bridges destroyed."[24] According to Toni Hagen, the Swiss UN chief in Dacca, destruction suffered by Bangladesh was greater than that suffered by Europe in World War II.[25]

To place these events in a proper socio-economic and political context, it should be noted that the Awami League's call for economic and political autonomy for East Pakistan stemmed from the perceived domination of East Pakistan by the "domineering and alien power" of West Pakistan.[26] The East Pakistani members of the Pakistan National Assembly had constantly charged the central government with discrimination against their unit in not providing them with adequate representation in the army and national civil services and in treating them unfavorably in the allocation of finances and other investments.[27] By the late 1960s, East Pakistan had become the major supplier of West Pakistan's needed raw materials and financial resources and was a major market, and a captive one, for West Pakistan's manufactured goods.[28]

Disparities in Political Processes

The East Pakistanis complained of their treatment in Pakistan as "second-class citizens."[29] They were heavily underrepresented in the civil service and military forces. To illustrate their claim, their representation in central government services of Pakistan after twenty-one years of independence was "barely 15 percent," according to Rahman in his election broadcast of October 28, 1970;[30] East Pakistanis never comprised more than 10 percent of the officer corps;[31] and only one East Pakistani was appointed a cabinet minister in the Pakistani government, holding the finance portfolio for four days.[32] In the Pakistani army, East Pakistani representation was even less than 10 percent, and, of fifty senior army officers who were promoted to the rank of major-general and above since 1947, only one was from East Pakistan.[33]

Regional Economic Disparities

During the first two decades of Pakistan's independence, a net transfer of resources from East to West Pakistan was officially estimated at one billion dollars.[34] The following figures indicate the extent of economic disparity between the two regions,[35] a situation called by Rahman an "appalling record [and] an intolerable structure of injustice."[36] While during the 1950s and 1960s East Pakistan earned 65 to 70 percent of Pakistan's foreign exchange, it received "just a 30 percent return from it,"[37] hardly a fair share by any standard. West Pakistan's regional income in 1970 was 25 percent higher than that of East Pakistan, while in 1947 it was lower;[38] West Pakistan's national income rose by 34.8 percent between 1965 and 1970, while in the East, it rose by 22.1 percent; during that period the annual growth rate of Pakistan was 6 percent as compared with 4 percent by East Pakistan.[39] In April 1970, Professor Anisur Rahman, professor of economics at the University of Islamabad, asserted that the per-capita income of West Pakistan was 100 percent greater than that of East Pakistan.[40] A similar disparity existed in social, educational, and health fields.

In industrial development, the disparity was even more pronounced. At the time of independence in 1947, West Pakistan had very little manufacturing industry. By the end of the decade, almost 70 percent of Pakistan's manufacturing industry was located in the West. The annual increase of agricultural production in the West was 5.5 percent compared with a 3 percent increase in the East. Almost 80 percent of Pakistan's budget and 70 percent of its development fund were spent in West Pakistan.[41]

East Pakistan's economic interests were often at variance with those of West Pakistan. To illustrate, the Indo-Pakistan war in 1965, which resulted in the breaking of trade links between the

two countries, had seriously limited East Pakistan's export of com-
modities such as fish and jute, which were primarily dependent on
Indian markets; additionally, it forced East Pakistan to import its
coal and cement from China and Sweden instead of India, at three
times Indian prices.[42]

The Principle/Right of Self-Determination— Prescriptions and Practice

The debate continues on the nature, content, and scope of the
right of a people to self-determination. While divergence of views
may exist on what constitutes a people who can claim this right
and how the right is to be reconciled with the principle of the
"territorial integrity" of member states of the United Nations,
there seems to be a broad consensus on two points: (1) the right
of a people to self-determination encompasses in legal terms the
right of a people to constitute, either alone or jointly with other
peoples, a sovereign nation and (2) in the colonial context, the
principle of equal rights and self-determination of peoples has become an established rule of customary international law.[43]

Among others, Professors McDougal, Lasswell, and Chen,[44] Bassiouni,[45] Dinstein,[46] Emerson,[47] Friedlander,[48] Green,[49] Moore,[50]
Paust,[51] and Reisman and Suzuki[52] have provided useful guidance
in clarifying many perplexing aspects of self-determination. Also,
the definitional focus has been given special attention in other sections of this book. Therefore, discussion in this section will be limited to a brief recounting of the authoritative prescriptions and
practices of the United Nations on self-determination so as to provide the necessary background for relating self-determination to
the secession of Bangladesh.

Prescriptions

Self-determination as a principle is acknowledged in Arts. 1(2)
and 55 of the United Nations Charter. According to Art. 1(2) of
the Charter, one of the purposes of the United Nations is to "develop friendly relations among nations based on respect for the
principle of equal rights and self-determination of peoples." Article
55 explicitly states the relationship between equal rights and self-
determination of peoples, on the one hand, and respect for human

rights and fundamental freedoms, on the other: "With a view to the creation of conditions of stability and well-being which are necessary for peaceful and friendly relations among nations based on respect for the principle of equal rights and self-determination of peoples, the United Nations shall promote . . . universal respect for, and observance of, human rights and fundamental freedoms for all without distinction as to race, sex, language or religion." Also, Art. 73 of the Charter implicitly proclaims the principle[53] and Arts. 2[54] and 56[55] of the Charter create direct obligations for member states pertaining to the implementation of the provisions of Art. 1 and Art. 55.

The right of self-determination finds a clear expression in the International Covenants on Economic, Social, and Cultural Rights and on Civil and Political Rights, which were adopted by the General Assembly in December 1966[56] and went into force in 1976.[57] Article 1, which is common to both covenants, reads: "1. All peoples have the right of self-determination. By virtue of that right they freely determine their political status and freely pursue their economic, social and cultural deveopment. . . . 3. The States Parties to the present Covenant . . . shall promote the realization of the right of self-determination, and shall respect that right, in conformity with the provisions of the Charter of the United Nations."

Earlier, in 1960, the Declaration on the Granting of Independence to Colonial Countries and Peoples[58] acknowledged the "right" of "all peoples to self-determination, by virtue of which they freely determine their political status and freely pursue their economic, social and cultural development."[59] Subsequently, the General Assembly at its twenty-fifth session unanimously adopted the Declaration on Principles of International Law concerning Friendly Relations (hereafter cited as the Declaration),[60] which acknowledged the right of all peoples to determine their political, economic, social, and cultural destiny without any external interference. The Declaration states in the preamble that

the subjection of peoples to alien subjugation, domination and exploitation constitutes a major obstacle to the promotion of international peace and security, [and] the principle of equal rights and self-determination of peoples constitutes a significant contribution to contemporary international law, and that its effective application is of paramount importance for the promotion of friendly relations among states, based on respect for the principle of sovereign equality.

One of the seven principles proclaimed by the Declaration is the principle of equal rights and self-determination of peoples, by virtue of which "all peoples have the right freely to determine, without external interference, their political status and pursue their economic, social and cultural development, and every state has the duty to respect this right in accordance with the provision of the Charter."

While the modes of implementing the right of self-determination may take any of the following forms—"the establishment of a sovereign and independent state, the free association or integration with an independent state or the emergence into any other political status freely determined by its people"—a state's duty toward a people claiming the right to self-determination is

to refrain from any forcible action which deprives peoples referred to above in the elaboration of the present principle of their right to self-determination and freedom and independence. In their actions against, and resistance to, such forcible action in pursuance of the exercise of their right to self-determination, such peoples are entitled to seek and to receive support in accordance with the purposes and principles of the Charter.

Addressing the issue of the territorial integrity of states, the Declaration reads:

Nothing in the foregoing paragraphs shall be construed as authorizing or encouraging any action which would dismember or impair, totally or in part, the territorial integrity or political unity of sovereign and independent states conducting themselves in compliance with the principle of equal rights and self-determination of peoples as described above and thus possessed of a government representing the whole people belonging to the territory without distinction as to race, creed or colour.

While there are ambiguities in the language stated above on the scope of the right of self-determination of a people—full independence or autonomy within a federal structure—the important message seems to be that only a state that is possessed of a "government representing the whole people belonging to the territory without distinction as to race, creed or colour" satisfies the requirement of conducting itself "in compliance with the principle of equal rights and self-determination of peoples."

This statement is significant, for, in order to be entitled to protection from "any action which would dismember or impair . . . [its] territorial integrity or political unity," a state has to meet the requirement of possessing a "government representing the whole people." Read in this light, the principle of self-determination could, under special circumstances, be accorded priority over the complementary opposing principle of territorial integrity. This interpretation is further supported by the statement in the preamble of the Declaration that "the subjection of peoples to alien subjugation, domination and exploitation constitutes a major obstacle to the promotion of international peace and security." Thus, the important tasks facing the international community are identifying the criteria for determining such special circumstances and establishing appropriate institutional and procedural arrangements to facilitate such determination.

State Practices In and Outside the United Nations

Traditionally, there has been little room for the application of self-determination outside the colonial context.[61] But it is hardly surprising that states are unwilling to accept the principle that subgroups within their own population may secede, and, as a consequence, they have usually ignored or rejected claims for territorial separation in a non-colonial setting. Many examples could be cited, including those of Katanga,[62] Biafra,[63] Kurdistan,[64] Tibet,[65] Eritea,[66] the southern Sudan,[67] Northern Ireland,[68] Quebec,[69] and Formosa.[70]

Commenting on United Nations practice, Professor Rupert Emerson has recently written that "the room left for self-determination in the sense of the attainment of independent statehood is very slight, with the great current exception of decolonization."[71] The rationale is not hard to understand either, for "the United Nations would be in an extremely difficult position if it were to interpret the right of self-determination in such a way as to invite or justify attacks on the territorial integrity of its own members."[72]

To illustrate the United Nations practice in the Nigerian conflict, which lasted for over two and a half years,[73] while only five states recognized an independent Biafra,[74] the Biafran claim for self-determination was acknowledged neither at the United Nations nor the Organization of African Unity (OAU).[75] The response of these two organizations is worth recalling—the United Nations never even considered the question, while the OAU strongly favored a unified Nigeria. Emperor Haile Selassie of Ethiopia, one of six heads of state who were members of an OAU consultative committee on Nigeria, asserted that the national unity of individual African states was preferable because it was believed to be an "essential ingredient for the realization of the larger and greater objective of African unity."[76] Also, the OAU Charter specifically mentions the parties' adherence to the principle of "respect for the sovereignty and territorial integrity of each state."[77]

Earlier, during the Congo crisis, the United Nations had offered an organized opposition to Katanga's claim to secede.[78] Subsequently, U Thant stated that the United Nations "has never accepted and does not accept and I do not believe it will ever accept the principle of secession of a part of its Member State."[79] Similarly, leaders of newly independent states have consistently taken the position that the right of self-determination does not include the right of secession.[80]

Appraisal

The right of self-determination is not an individual right, but a collective right. The claim is for participation not only in power processes but in all value processes—power, wealth and resources, respect and rectitude, enlightenment and skill, and affection and well-being.[81] The focus of attention is on deprivation of human rights as it relates to a group communally.[82]

Thus, one of the major tasks is the identification of "peoples" who are claiming the right of self-determination. The process of identifying such peoples usually involves consideration of objective and subjective factors. On the one hand, an ethnic identity linked by a common history, often accompanied by a shared language or religion, may be present while, on the other hand, the group's sense of identity may stem from an ethos or state of mind. However, both subjective and objective elements are often present when a claim for self-determination is made. If we consider that such a claim is a claim for formal power to decide one's future course based upon one's own values and perceptions, it can be pursuasively argued that the subjective factors of one's own identity and a common destiny should control.[83] Thus, the differentiation of a subgroup from the dominant group should turn more upon a psychological perception rather than tangible characteristics or racial attributes.

An additional problem is the determination of the scope of the separation between the subgroup and the dominant group in a body politic. The major question here relates to the extent to which perceptions and commitments are shared by the members of the subgroup. The inquiry has to be focused on how widely the demands articulated by the elites of the subgroup are shared by the members of the subgroup.[84] This will give rise to two further questions: the first is related to the proper percentage of support required to constitute a following sufficient to warrant serious consideration of the claim of self-determination, while the second is related to the identification and accommodation of those who prefer to remain within the body politic.[85]

Along with identifying the group seeking self-determination, another major task is to inquire into the reason underlying the wish to secede. For, in order to determine the validity of the claim, the reasons ought to be compelling, leaving little hope that any action short of separation would satisfy the subgroup's claim for effective participation in the value processes. Given the nature of the state system that characterizes the international community, self-determination cannot be completely divorced from its effects upon the parent state, the surrounding region, or the international community. The claim has to be studied in a total context; a desired change in the international structure by the acceptance of a claim of territorial separation should meet the test of maximizing values that the community as a whole strives to achieve.[86] Claims by a subgroup for territorial separation may be based upon a combination of the following: differences of political belief, the desire to more effectively control and manage one's own resources, or a strong ehtnic or cultural identification with a neighboring group.

In light of the already mentioned "maximization of community values" test by which the validity of the claim to self-determination is to be measured, and in view of the nature of the international system which tends to revolve around its major actors, nation states, it becomes apparent that the different political beliefs, claims to resources, and ethnic or cultural identification cannot form the main thrust of a claim of self-determination.

First, as the current state system is a system that reflects and accommodates divergent views and beliefs as to political and economic organizational structures, it would be dangerous and unworkable to accord legitimacy to claims rising out of ideological belief. Second, claims to resources and group identifications should not, by themselves, justify the validity of the claim to territorial separation by giving it priority over the principle of territorial integrity. Claims arising out of the desire to control and manage one's natural resources are implicit in any claim of self-determination, whether or not such desire makes up a major part of the claim. And finally, although the desire of a people seeking to become attached to a neighboring state, made up of inhabitants with whom the subgroup seeking territorial separation identifies, is emotionally compelling (especially since the colonial powers drew up boundaries without considering the people who would be affected by them), in the absence of other factors related primarily to the lack of the subgroup's participation in the value processes of the body politic, an international blessing to such desire would undermine the stability of the international order by placing it in a perpetual state of flux.

The only reliable test for determining the reasonableness of self-determination has to be the nature and extent of the deprivation of human rights of the subgroup claiming the right. Dramatic developments in international legal norms and state practices over the past three decades have transformed an individual into a subject of international law, capable of exercising rights as an independent entity in the international arena.[87] Also, human rights issues are no longer considered to lie within the "domestic jurisdiction" of a nation state.[88] Indeed, the need is to "focus on the essential relationship between the principle of self-determination and human rights, and assert the essential nature of the right of self-determination as a right that justifies the remedying of a deprivation by restoring self-government."[89] Thus, it is submitted that the principles of self-determination and territorial integrity as well as other related principles of international law such as "humanitarian intervention,"[90] nonintervention,[91] and prohibition of the use of force[92] must be interpreted in the light of individual rights which form the basis of group rights to a dignified human existence.

Self-Determination and Bangladesh

The pertinent questions are: (1) Did the people in Bangladesh constitute an identifiable people in terms of the UN Charter, the international covenants, the Declaration, and other relevant instruments of international law? and, if the answer is in the affirmative, (2) did those people have a valid claim for territorial separation under the principle of self-determination? A brief discussion of these questions follows.

The People of East Pakistan Constituted a Separate, Identifiable People

Since there are no guidelines in the various UN human rights instruments on what constitutes a people, it will be helpful to apply to the population of East Pakistan the various traits commonly used to identify a people. Such traits include a common race or ethnicity, language, culture, religion, history, geography, economy, and a subjective element of an ethos or state of mind.[93]

Differences between the populations of East Pakistan and West Pakistan are rather striking; their only common bond is the emotive symbol of Islam. The physical separation of over a thousand miles add to the racial, cultural, linguistic, and economic differences. If the term race were used in a nonscientific way, connoting differences of physical appearance, dominant characteristics, and behavior, the East Pakistanis, about 73 million in number and constituting 55 percent of the total population of Pakistan, are racially different from the West Pakistanis. Even President Ayub Khan admitted the racial differences between East and West Pakistan, although his remarks were derogatory, belying racial superiority. He suggested that because of a "forced mixture of races" in West Pakistan, the population had benefited from a "fusion of ideas, outlook and culture," while the East Pakistanis "have all the inhibitions of down-trodden races and have not yet found it possible to adjust psychologically to the requirements of the newborn-freedom."[94]

The East Pakistanis speak the Sanskrit-based Bengali language and are consistently opposed to West Pakistan's imposition of the Persian/Arabic-based Urdu;[95] they identify more with Bengali culture and intellectual thought than the predominant Persian and Arabic influences from West Pakistan.[96] An observer has suggested that there can be "no controversy that in art, literature and philosophy, in music, poetry and prose, the Bengali culture has obtained a status which has hardly been paralleled in West Pakistan."[97] Geographically, West Pakistan is mountainous and arid, while the East is deltaic, traversed by many rivers and streams and full of luxuriant vegetation. These geographical features are reflected in social and temperamental differences and in the staple diet which for East Pakistan is rice and for West Pakistan wheat and corn.

A staff study of the International Commission of Jurists concluded its statement of differences between the then two parts of Pakistan in these words:

> West Pakistan turned naturally for its cultural and commercial exchanges towards the Arab Middle East and Iran, East Pakistan toward India and the Asian Far East. Economically, the two wings hardly comprised a natural unity, and the economic conflict with India resulted in East Pakistan being cut off from their natural economic outlet and trading partners in the neighboring parts of India. Quantitatively, each of the wings was large enough in population and territory to constitute a separate nation state.[98]

The assertion that the East Pakistanis constituted a separate Bengali people is further supported by their state of mind, which was reflected in their demands initially for full autonomy and subsequently, in March 1971, for independence. To highlight some of the significant events since August 1947 when Pakistan became independent, as early as February 1948 a Bengali member of the Pakistan Constituent Assembly observed: "[a] feeling is growing among the Eastern Pakistanis that Eastern Pakistan is being neglected and treated merely as a 'colony' of West Pakistan."[99] Four years later, in February 1952, Bengali students held mass demonstrations in Dacca after a decision was made to adopt Urdu as the only state language. The police dispersed them by opening fire, killing twenty-six people and wounding four-hundred more.[100] In March 1954, the United Front, a coalition of the opposition parties in East Pakistan, fought elections on a plank for autonomy. In the elections, which were considered a referendum on the issue of autonomy, the United Front captured 223 out of 237 seats whereas the ruling Muslim League party won only 10 seats.[101] However, in May 1954, the Legislative Assembly was dissolved, the United Front government was dismissed, and governor's rule was proclaimed in East Pakistan.[102]

Pakistan gradually moved from parliamentary democracy to a bureaucratic-military coalition and, in October 1958, a military dictatorship under General Ayub Khan took over. General Ayub stayed in power until March 1969. During this period, people in East Pakistan were restive. Ayub reacted to this mood by warning his followers in Dacca that "they should be prepared to face even a civil war, if forced upon them, to protect the sovereignty and integrity of the country. . . . Civil war was a dangerous thing. But if a nation faces destruction, it has to be accepted."[103] However, a movement for autonomy of East Bengal on the basis of Rhaman's six-point program gathered so much momentum that Ayub Khan could no longer resist it. In March 1969, General Mohammed Yahya Khan, the army commander-in-chief, took control of the government.[104] The overwhelming victory of the Awami League in the December 1970 elections has already been mentioned.[105] By March 1971, there was a growing feeling in East Pakistan for independence, with demonstrations and slogans of *Joi Bangla* ("long live independent Bengal").[106] In August 1971, the Yahya government issued a White Paper that contained an allegation that Rahman and the Awami League had attempted to secure effective independence for East Bengal by constitutional negotiations and that they had planned to launch an armed rebellion to take independence by force if constitutional negotiations failed.[107]

It should be noted that, while initially East Pakistanis had opted for autonomy for their province with a federation or confederation and the six-point program reflected the desire for autonomy, the breakdown of negotiations in March 1971 for the convening of the National Assembly marked a new era in the East Bengali mood.

There had been demands for an independent Bangladesh even before the postponement of the assembly, but with that postponement the Bengali people's demand was for full independence because they had realized that without it they would have no opportunity to participate in the various value processes including the power process.[108]

The People of East Pakistan Had a Justifiable Claim for Territorial Separation

The East Pakistani claim for territorial separation was justified by a combination of several factors—racial, cultural, geographic, and linguistic differences between East and West Pakistan;[109] the striking economic and political disparities from which the East Pakistanis suffered for a period of over two decades;[110] and the use of brutally repressive measures by the West Pakistani military forces to crush the East Pakistanis.[111]

To apply the UN prescription for self-determination as contained in the Declaration,[112] the state of Pakistan never possessed a "government representing the whole people belonging to the territory without a distinction as to race, creed or colour" and, therefore, never satisfied the Declaration requirement of conducting itself "in compliance with the principle of equal rights and self-determination of peoples." Consequently, Pakistan was not entitled to protection from "any action which would dismember or impair . . . [its] territorial integrity or political unity."[113] Events following the December 1970 elections and the postponement of convening the National Assembly in March 1971—Rahman's call for noncooperation, mass demonstrations, and demand for complete independence for Bangladesh—reflected the East Bengali perception that their basic rights could be secured only after territorial separation.

What followed the March 25 crackdown by the military has been described by Justice A. S. Chowdbury, vice-chancellor of the University of Dacca and the Pakistani member of the UN Human Rights Commission, as "atrocities unparalleled in history."[114] A description of the gross violations of human rights was given by John Salzberg, representative of the International Commission of Jurists, in his statement to the UN Sub-Commission on the Prevention of Discrimination and Protection of Minorities:[115] "killing and torture; mistreatment of women and children; mistreatment of civilians in armed conflict; religious discrimination; arbitrary arrest and detention; arbitrary deprivation of property; suppression of the freedom of speech, the press and assembly; suppression of political rights; and suppression of the right of migration. Other reports have indicated that a 'coldblooded, planned' attempt at systematic and selective killing of the leaders of the Awami League, Bengali military and police officials, and intellectuals (especially university teachers, writers and students), was undertaken purportedly to deprive East Pakistan of any future leadership."[116] These atrocities were described by observers as genocide or selective genocide.[117]

Since the state of Bangladesh was accorded early recognition by other states[118] and admittance into the United Nations,[119] it appears that the international community acknowledged the legitimacy of its claim for self-determination.

Appraisal and Recommendations

It is easy to argue that, even in a non-colonial context, East Pakistan's claim for territorial separation was justified. Special circumstances in East Pakistan warranted placing "the demands of self-determination above those of 'territorial integrity' and of a 'non-interventionist' stand on the part of the United Nations. For where violence is perpetrated by a minority to deprive a *majority* of political, economic, social and cultural rights, the principles of 'territorial integrity' and 'non-intervention' should not be permitted to be used as a ploy to perpetuate the political subjugation of the majority."[120]

Difficult cases, however, lie ahead. As the final chapter of colonialism draws to a close, a number of states, new and old, find themselves challenged by restive elements within their borders. Thus, their international community is likely in the future to be faced with many more claims for territorial separation in non-colonial settings. The absence of guidelines for hearing and evaluating such claims will leave little alternative to violence, but, more important, perhaps, it will reflect a retreat from the emerging expectations that the individual has a right to a dignified human existence; for such individual right finds fruition only when the group to which the individual belongs is accorded by the international community the right of territorial separation. Furthermore, the recognition of such a right is likely to have the effect of deterring abusive state practices. If so, the international community as a whole benefits. The lessening of tensions within states is likely to mean less tension between and among states because intrastate conflicts invariably affect the world community, as the recent conflicts in Angola and Zaire have so forcefully demonstrated.[121]

It is submitted that, if a group demanding self-determination is identified, if severe deprivations of human rights exist to the extent that the group is subjected to "alien subjugation, domination and exploitation," and if the claim for territorial separation meets the test of legitimacy by its evaluation in a contexual setting,[122] the claim should be accorded recognition. It should not matter whether the group in question is separate from the state and is territorially based or is dispersed within the state, for the conditions that qualify the group for the validity of its claim to territorial separation must be the distinctiveness of the group and its subjugation based upon that distinctiveness. Thus, the focus should be on the deprivation of the right to participate in the value processes of the body politic, and, while the effect of the territorial separation on world public order should be taken into account, the effect of such separation on the parent state alone should not be the sole determining factor for measuring the legitimacy of such a claim.

If institutions and procedures exist that will acknowledge and legitimize the demands for territorial separation irrespective of their effect upon the parent state alone, states are likely to be encouraged to take measures to provide all their citizens with basic human rights. Certainly, the international community, through its established norms, institutions, and procedures, should first address strategies short of territorial separation to promote the subgroup's participation in the value processes of the body politic; but, where there is no alternative to territorial separation, then it must respond efficiently and effectively to whatever repercussions may follow such separation.

At the United Nations, the secretary-general should invoke his or her authority under Art. 99[123] to bring the matter before the Security Council, which under the Charter has the primary responsibility of dealing with situations because of their gravity and potential threat to international peace. In the face of inaction by the Security Council, the General Assembly has ample authority to make appropriate recommendations. Of utmost importance, however, is the involvement of the UN human rights machinery in situations where claims for territorial separation are made. Specifically, the Sub-Commission on the Prevention of Discrimination and the Protection of Minorities should take the initiative, for it has been authorized to do so in those situations that reveal a consistent pattern of violations of human rights based upon the information available to the subcommission.[124] Also, the UN Commission on Human Rights might be authorized to meet in emergency sessions to discuss situations that demand urgent and immediate attention because of "the imminent threat or willful destruction of human life on a massive scale," a suggestion made by the International Commission of Jurists during the Bangladesh crisis.[125] Perhaps a high-ranking official of the UN Commission on Human Rights should be authorized to undertake some initial investigation and recommend measures for the commission.[126] Additionally, where applicable, the machinery available under the International Convention on the Elimination of all Forms of Racial Discrimination[127] and other UN instruments should be used.

In sum, a close link exists between human rights and self-determination and between massive violations of human rights and international peace and security. It seems imperative that at this stage the traditional principle of self-determination which was primarily instrumental for the dramatic transformation of former colonies into independent nation-states be extended in scope to include the right for territorial separation of any people "subjugated, dominated and exploited," who, because of their group identification, are deprived of the opportunity to participate in the value processes of a body politic. It is the responsibility of the international community to devise appropriate institutions, procedures, and strategies to implement this right.

Notes

1. See generally, *Bangladesh: Crisis and Consequences* (New Delhi: Deen Dayal Research Institute, 1972); D. Mankekar, *Pakistan Cut to Size* (New

Delhi: Indian Book Co., 1972); *Pakistan Political System in Crisis: Emergence of Bangladesh,* eds. S. P. Varma and V. Narain (Jaipur: University of Rajasthan, 1972).

2. *The Economist* (April 8, 1972):47.

3. For an account of the war between India and Pakistan which began on December 3, 1971, and ended thirteen days later on December 16 with the surrender of the Pakistani army, see Mankekar, *Pakistan Cut to Size*; S. K. Chowdhury, *The Genesis of Bangladesh* (New York: Asia Publishing House, 1972), pp. 168-69.

4. Art. 2, para. 4 of the UN Charter reads: "All members shall refrain in their international relations from the threat or use of force against the territorial integrity or political independence of any State, or in any other manner inconsistent with the Purpose of the United Nations." For two divergent viewpoints on the continuing validity of Art. 2(4), see T. Franck, "Who Killed Article 2(4)?" *American Journal of International Law* 64 (1970):809; L. Henkin, "The Reports of the Death of Article 2(4) Are Greatly Exaggerated," *American Journal of International Law* 65 (1971):544.

5. See, e.g., R. Lillich, ed., *Humanitarian Intervention and the United Nations* (Charlottesville: University Press of Virginia, 1973).

6. See, e.g., V. Nanda, "A Critique of the United Nations Inaction in the Bangladesh Crisis," *Denver Law Journal* 49 (1972):56.

7. Ibid., pp. 64-67.

8. For prior discussion of the subject, see Chowdhury, *Genesis of Bangladesh,* pp. 192-210; East Pakistan Staff Study, "Right of Self-Determination in International Law," *International Commission of Jurists Review* 8 (June 1972): 42-52; V. Nanda, "Self-Determination in International Law: The Tragic Tale of Two Cities—Islamabad (West Pakistan) and Dacca (East Pakistan)," *American Journal of International Law* 66 (1972):321; K. Nayar, "Self-Determination: The Bangladesh Experience," *Revue des droits de l'homme* 7 (1974):231

9. In addition to the sources cited in note 1, see, e.g., M. Ayoob et al., *Bangla Desh—A Struggle for Nationhood* (Delhi: Vikas Publications, 1971); *Bangla Desh Documents* (New Delhi: Ministry of External Affairs, Government of India, 1971); G. Chowdhury, *The Last Days of United Pakistan* (Bloomington: Indiana University Press, 1974); D. Loshak, *Pakistan Crisis* (New York: McGraw Hill, 1971); K. Siddiqui, *Conflict, Crisis, and War in Pakistan* (New York: Praeger, 1972); A. Mascarenhas, *The Rape of Bangladesh* (Delhi: Vikas Publications, 1972); E. Mason, R. Dorfman, and S. Marglin, *Conflict in East Pakistan: Background and Prospects* (London: Bangladesh Action Committee, 1971); R. Payne, *Massacre* (New York: MacMillan, 1973).

10. *Bangla Desh Documents,* p. 5; Chowdhury, *Genesis of Bangladesh,* pp. 9-19; Nanda, "Self-Determination in International Law," pp. 328-30; Naqvi, "West Pakistan's Struggle for Power," *South Asian Review* 4 (April 1971):213.

11. The following account demonstrates the prevailing East Pakistani mood in the late 1960s. The Awami League launched a mass movement for autonomy of East Pakistan in 1966. In January 1968, the Pakistani government announced that it would prosecute 28 people for conspiring to bring about the secession of East Pakistan, with India's help. Between December 1968 and February 1969, in East Pakistan "at least 117 persons were killed, 464 injured and 1,500 persons were arrested for participating in the movement [for autonomy] " (Chowdhury, *Genesis of Bangladesh*, p. 44).

12. The Awami League Manifesto containing the six-point program is published in *Bangla Desh Documents*, p. 66 (reprinted in *New York University Journal of International Law and Politics* 4 [1971] :524).

13. *Bangla Desh Documents*, p. 130.

14. Cited in "Jai Banglar, Jai," *Far Eastern Economic Review* (Jan. 16, 1971):20-21.

15. See Chowdhury, *Genesis of Bangladesh*, pp. 11-19.

16. *The Economist* (March 6, 1971):19-20; *Far Eastern Economic Review* (March 6, 1971):12.

17. *Far Eastern Economic Review* (March 6, 1971):12; ibid., (March 20, 1971):5-6; *New York Times*, March 17, 1971, p. 17, col. 1; ibid., March 19, 1971, p. 10, col. 1; ibid., March 24, 1971, p. 11, col. 1; *New York Times Magazine*, May 2, 1971, pp. 91-94.

18. *Far Eastern Economic Review* (March 20, 1971):6.

19. See generally, U.S., Congress, Senate, *Hearings before the Subcommittee to Investigate Problems Connected with the Refugees and Escapees of the Senate Committee on the Judiciary*, 92d Congress, 1st Session, 1971 (Washington, D.C.: Government Printing Office, 1971), pt. 1, pp. 95-226, pt. 2, pp. 311-53, pt. 3, pp. 431-811 (hereafter cited as Senate Hearings); U.S., Congress, House, *Hearings before the Subcommittee on Asian and Pacific Affairs of the House Committee on Foreign Affairs*, 92d Congress, 1st Session, 1971 (Washington, D.C.: Government Printing Office, 1971), pp. 35-50; Nanda, "Self-Determination in International Law," pp. 331-33.

20. *New York Times Magazine*, Jan. 9, 1972, pp. 46-48; *Manchester Guardian Weekly*, Dec. 20, 1971, p. 4, cols. 1, 3.

21. N. Cousins, "Genocide in East Pakistan," *Saturday Review* (May 22, 1971):20; *New Yorker* (Feb. 12, 1972):40, 65; Senate Hearings, pp. 118, 120; Nanda, "Self-Determination in International Law," p. 332 notes 81-86.

22. *New York Times*, Jan. 24, 1972, p. 1, cols. 5, 7; ibid., Dec. 13, 1971, p. 16, cols. 3, 6 (statement of India's Defense Minister S. Singh); *New Yorker* (Dec. 11, 1971):166.

23. For an account of the Indo-Pakistan war see Mankekar, *Pakistan Cut to Size*.

24. Cited in the *Christian Science Monitor*, April 4, 1972, p. 1, col. 2; see

also V. Nanda, "Bangladesh Economy in Ruin," *Rocky Mountain News* Global Section), Oct. 1, 1971, p. 1, col. 1.

25. *Time* (Feb. 28, 1972):30; see also, *New York Times*, Dec. 22, 1971, p. 14, col. 1; ibid., Dec. 30, 1972, p. 8, col. 3; ibid., Jan. 24, 1972, p. 1, cols. 5, 7; ibid., p. 8, col. 3.

26. East Pakistan Staff Study, "Right of Self-Determination in International Law," p. 49.

27. The point is made in Jha, "Roots of Pakistani Discord," *Indian Journal of Political Science* 32 (Jan.-March 1971):14, 29 notes 95-96, citing National Assembly of Pakistan debates for the years 1962-1965.

28. Chowdhury, *Genesis of Bangladesh*, pp. 11, 15-19.

29. Gourgey, "Bangla Desh's Leader: Sheikh Mujib," *Venture* (London) 23 (July/Aug. 1971):13.

30. The text is contained in *Seminar* (New Delhi) 142 (June 1972):39-40.

31. W. Barnds, "Pakistan's Disintegration," *World Today* 27 (Aug. 1971): 319-20.

32. Plastri, "Behind the Revolt in East Pakistan," *Dissent* 18 (Aug. 1971): 321.

33. Ibid.

34. Quoted in Gourgey, "Bangla Desh's Leader," p. 13; see also Rahman's address before the December 1970 elections, cited in Chowdhury, *Genesis of Bangladesh*, pp. 18-19.

35. See generally, *Far Eastern Economic Review* (April 24, 1971):57-63; *The Economist* (March 6, 1971):19-20; "Bangla Desh," supplement to *Monthly Commentary on Indian Economic Conditions* (New Delhi, April 1971):9; Chowdhury, *Genesis of Bangladesh*, pp. 12-19; Chowdhury, "Economic Policy and Industrial Growth in Pakistan—A Review," *Pakistan Development Review* 10 (1970):264; 267-68, and authorities cited there.

36. Cited in *Seminar* (New Delhi) 142 (June 1972):40.

37. Cited in Gourgey, "Bangla Desh's Leader," p. 13.

38. These figures are based on a survey by a Pakistani economist, quoted in Ray, "Web of Bourgeois Politics," *Economic and Political Weekly* 6 (June 1971):1221, 1222.

39. Ibid.

40. A. Rahman, "East Pakistan: The Roots of Estrangement," *South Asian Review* 3 (London, 1970):235, 236.

41. Ray, "Web of Bourgeois Politics."

42. See generally, *Far Eastern Economic Review* (April 24, 1971):57-63; *The Economist* (March 6, 1971):19-20.

43. Progress report by Special Rapporteur, *The Historical and Current Development of the Right to Self-Determination on the Basis of the Charter of the United Nations and Other Instruments Adopted by United Nations*

Organs, with Particular Reference to the Promotion and Protection of Human Rights and Fundamental Freedoms, UN Commission on Human Rights, Sub-Commission on Prevention of Discrimination and Protection of Minorities, 29th Session, UN Doc. E/CN.4/Sub. 2/L.641 (July 8, 1976), p. 12. For the various UN resolutions on the subject, see ibid., pp. 7-8. For a selective bibliography on self-determination, see UN Doc. E/CN.4/Sub. 2/377/Add.7 (Jan. 12, 1977).

44. See, e.g., M. McDougal, H. Lasswell, and L. Chen, "The Protection of Respect and Human Rights: Freedom of Choice and World Public Order," *American University Law Review* 24 (1975):919; L. Chen, "Self-Determination as a Human Right," in *Toward World Order and Human Dignity*, ed. M. Reisman and B. Weston (New York: Free Press, 1976), p. 198.

45. M. Bassiouni, "Self-Determination and the Palestinians," *Proceedings of the American Society of International Law* 65 (Sept. 1971):31-40.

46. Y. Dinstein, "Collective Human Rights of Peoples and Minorities," *International and Comparative Law Quarterly* 25 (1976):102.

47. R. Emerson, "Self-Determination," *Proceedings of the American Society of International Law* 60 (1966):135-41; "Self-Determination," *American Journal of International Law* 65 (1971):459.

48. R. Friedlander, "Self-Determination: A Legal-Political Inquiry," *Detroit College of Law Review* 1 (1975):71 (also reprinted as chap. 13 in this volume).

49. L. Green, "Self-Determination and Settlement of the Arab-Israeli Conflict," *Proceedings of the American Society of International Law* 65 (1971):40.

50. J. Moore, "Toward an Applied Theory for the Regulation of Intervention," in *Law and Civil War in the Modern World*, ed. J. Moore (Baltimore, Md.: Johns Hopkins, 1974), p. 3.

51. J. Paust, "Self-Determination: A Definitional Focus," chap. 1 in this volume.

52. See generally, M. Reisman and E. Suzuki, "Recognition and Social Change in International Law: A Prologue for Decisionmaking," in *Toward World Order and Human Dignity*, p. 403; E. Suzuki, "Self-Determination and World Public Order: Community Response to Territorial Separation," *Virginia Journal of International Law* 16 (1976):779.

53. Art. 73 of the Charter deals with non-self-governing territories. The declaration specifically refers "to [ensuring] due respect for the culture of the peoples concerned, their political, economic, social, and educational advancement, their just treatment, and their protection against abuses [and] to develop self-government, to take due account of the political aspirations of the peoples, and to assist them in the progressive development of their free political institutions, according to the particular circumstances of each territory and its peoples and their varying stages of advancement."

54. Art. 2(2) reads: "All Members, in order to insure to all of them the rights and benefits resulting from membership, shall fulfill in good faith the obligations assumed by them in accordance with the present Charter."

55. Art. 56 reads: "All Members pledge themselves to take joint and separate action in cooperation with the Organization for the achievement of the purposes set forth in Article 55."

56. The covenants were adopted by Re. 2200 A (21) Dec. 16, 1966, GAOR Supp. 16 (UN Doc. A/6316, 1966).

57. See E. Schwelb, "Entry into Force of the International Covenant on Human Rights and the Optional Protocol to the International Covenant on Civil and Political Rights," *American Journal of International Law* 70 (1976): 511.

58. G.A. Res. 1564, 15 GOAR, Supp. 16 (UN Doc. A/4684, 1960), p. 66.

59. Ibid.

60. G.A. Res. 2625, 25 UN GOAR, Supp. 28 (UN Doc. A/8028, 1970), p. 121. See also Note, "Toward Self-Determination—A Reappraisal as Reflected in the Declaration on Friendly Relations," *Georgia Journal of International and Comparative Law* 3 (1973):145; R. Rosenstock, "The Declaration of Principles of International Law concerning Friendly Relations: A Survey," *American Journal of International Law* 65 (1971):713.

61. See, e.g., Emerson, "Self-Determination," *American Journal of International Law*, p. 459.

62. See generally, L. Miller, *World Order and Local Disorder* (Princeton: University Press, 1967), pp. 66-116; R. Lemarchand, "The Limits of Self-Determination: The Case of the Katanga Secession," *American Political Science Review* 56 (1962):404.

63. See generally, Baker, "The Emergence of Biafra: Balkanization or Nation-Building," *Orbis* (1968):518; S. Panter-Brick, "The Right of Self-Determination: Its Application to Nigeria," *International Affairs* 44 (1968): 26; Nixon, "Self-Determination: The Nigeria/Biafra Case," *World Politics* 24 (1972):473.

64. See, e.g., Edmonds, "The Kurdish National Struggle in Iraq," *Asian Affairs* 58 (June 1971):147, and "Kurdish Nationalism," *Journal of Contemporary History* (London) 6 (1971):87; Woodson, "We Who Face Death," *National Geographic* 147 (1975):364.

65. See generally, Sinha, "How Chinese Was China's Tibet Region?" *Tibetan Review* (Calcutta) 1 (April 1968):9; Takla, "Taiwan and Tibet," ibid., p. 7; *New York Times*, Sept. 5, 1971, Sect. 1, p. 5, col. 1.

66. See generally, Koehn, "Ethiopian Politics: Military Intervention and Prospects for Further Change," *Africa Today* 22 (April-June 1975):7; Y. Gebre-Medhin, "Eritrea: Background to Revolution," *Monthly Review* 28 (Sept. 1976):52-61; D. Martin, "War in Eritrea," *New Statesman* 89 (Feb. 7,

1975):166-67; E. Morgan, "Geographic Evaluation of the Ethiopia-Eritrea Conflict," *Journal of Modern African Studies* 15 (Dec. 1977):667-74; A. Tseggai, "Case for Eritrean National Independence," *Black Scholar* 7 (June 1976):20-27.

67. See generally, Gray, "The Southern Sudan," *Journal of Contemporary History* (London) 6 (1971):108; Al-Rahim, "Arabism, Africanism, and Self-Identification in the Sudan," *Journal of Modern African Studies* 8 (1970):233.

68. See generally, C. O'Brien, *States of Ireland* (New York: Pantheon Books, 1972); *Saturday Review* (March 18, 1972):25.

69. See, e.g., R. Levesque, "For an Independent Quebec," *Foreign Affairs* 54 (July 1976):734-44; W. Morton, "Quebec in Revolt," *Canadian Forum* 56 (Feb. 1977):13; D. Smith, "Preparing for Independence," ibid., pp. 4-5; *The Economist* (Nov. 20, 1976):15-16.

70. See generally, L. Chen and H. Lasswell, *Formosa, China, and the United Nations: Formosa in the World Community* (New York: St. Martin's, 1967); L. Chen and W. Reisman, "Who Owns Taiwan? A Search for International Title," *Yale Law Journal* 81 (1972):599 note 2, and authorities cited there.

71. Emerson, "Self-Determination," *American Journal of International Law*, p. 465.

72. V. Van Dyke, *Human Rights: The United States and the World Community* (New York: Oxford University Press, 1970), p. 102.

73. For a text of the Declaration of Secession of May 30, 1967, see *International Legal Materials* 6 (1967):679. On January 12, 1970, the Biafran surrender was announced.

74. D. Ijalaye, "Was Biafra at Any Time a State in International Law?" *American Journal of International Law* 65 (1971):553-54.

75. See generally, Panter-Brick, "Right of Self-Determination"; Nanda, "Self-Determination in International Law," pp. 326-27.

76. Report of the OAU Consultative Mission to Nigeria, cited in Ijalaye, "Was Biafra at Any Time a State?", p. 556.

77. Cited in Van Dyke, *Human Rights*, pp. 86-87.

78. Miller, *World Order and Local Disorder*, pp. 66-116.

79. *UN Monthly Chronicle* 7 (Feb. 1970):36.

80. Van Dyke, *Human Rights*, p. 87, cites Indian, Indonesian, and Senegalese leaders taking this position.

81. Professor Myres McDougal articulates these value processes in *Studies in World Public Order* (New Haven: Yale University Press, 1960), pp. 336-37. See also McDougal, Lasswell, and Chen, "The Protection of Respect and Human Rights," p. 919.

82. Chen, "Self-Determination as a Human Right."

83. See generally, Dinstein, "Collective Human Rights," pp. 104-5.

84. The point is made by Suzuki, "Self-Determination and World Public Order," p. 816.

85. Ibid.

86. See generally, ibid., pp. 813-20.

87. The most dramatic illustration of this right is the right of the individual to have access to a supranational arena within the purview of the European Convention on Human Rights, (R. Beddard, *Human Rights and Europe—A Study of the Machinery of Human Rights Protection of the Council of Europe* [London: Sweet and Maxwell, 1973]).

88. The large number of UN resolutions dealing with issues of human rights attests to the validity of the statement made (see works cited in note 43).

89. W. Ofuatey-Kodjoe, *The Principle of Self-Determination in International Law* (New York: Nellen Publishing Co., 1977).

90. Lillich, *Humanitarian Intervention*.

91. See generally, E. Martin, "Interdependence and the Principle of Self-Determination and Non-Intervention," *Department of State Bulletin* 48 (1963):710; J. Moore, "The Control of Foreign Intervention in Internal Affairs," *Virginia Journal of International Law* 9 (1969):247.

92. See works cited in note 4.

93. See generally, Dinstein, "Collective Human Rights," pp. 103-5.

94. Cited in Chowdhury, *Genesis of Bangladesh*, p. 40.

95. See generally, ibid, pp. 23-24; Evan, "The Language Problem in Multi-National States: The Case of India and Pakistan," *Asian Affairs* 58 (June 1971):184-85.

96. See generally, *Illustrated Weekly of India* (May 9, 1971):23; Sayeed, "Islam and National Integration in Pakistan," in D. Smith, ed., *Southeastern Politics and Religion* (1966), p. 407.

97. Chowdhury, *Genesis of Bangladesh*, p. 7.

98. East Pakistan Staff Study, "Right of Self-Determination in International Law," p. 48.

99. Cited in Chowdhury, *Genesis of Bangladesh*, p. 24.

100. Ibid.

101. Ibid., p. 26.

102. Ibid., p. 27.

103. Cited in ibid., p. 43.

104. Ibid., p. 45.

105. See note 13, and the accompanying text.

106. *Far Eastern Economic Review* (Jan. 16, 1971):20-21.

107. Cited in Chowdhury, *Genesis of Bangladesh*, pp. 74-75.

108. The Bangladesh Proclamation of Independence is reprinted in *International Legal Materials* 11 (1972):119.

109. See notes 93-107 and the accompanying text.

110. See notes 29-42 and the accompanying text.

111. See notes 19-25 and the accompanying text.

112. See work cited in note 60.

113. Principle e(7) of the Declaration.

114. *New York Times*, May 30, 1971, p. 5, col. 1.

115. Press release of the International Commission of Jurists, Aug. 16, 1971, pp. 3-4.

116. See sources cited in Nanda, "Self-Determination in International Law," p. 332 notes 81-82.

117. See e.g., *Statesmen Weekly* (New Delhi) Aug. 21, 1971, p. 11, col. 1; *New York Times*, Aug. 17, 1971, p. 3. col. 4.

118. *The Economist* (April 8, 1972):47.

119. On November 29, 1972, the General Assembly adopted Resolution 2937 (17) expressing the desire that Bangladesh be admitted to the United Nations at an early date (*1972 UN Yearbook*, pp. 219-20). On the recommendation of the Security Council, made on June 10, 1974, the General Assembly admitted Bangladesh on Sept. 17, 1974 (*1974 UN Yearbook*, pp. 296-97).

120. Nanda, "Self-Determination in International Law," p. 336. On the Katanga situation, Professor Suzuki convincingly argues: "The denial of the Katangese attempt to secede does not necessarily preclude nor contradict the right of self-determination of a subgroup within a body politic. To determine the lawfulness of separation in the future by relying solely upon the Katanga precedent would be to consider only one side of past events. . . . The territorial integrity of the State is *not* a goal to be pursued. It is merely one of the conditions under which the enjoyment of human rights can be secured. The goal is instead the protection and fulfillment of the fundamental basis for a dignified human existence" (Suzuki, "Self-Determination and World Public Order," p. 807 note 123).

121. See, e.g., J. Garrett, "Lessons of Angola: An Eye-Witness Report," *Black Scholar* 7 (June 1976):2-15; J. Saul, "Angola and After," *Monthly Review* 28 (May 1976):4-15; "Three Factions, Three Countries?" *The Economist* (July 26, 1975):40; ibid. (May 21, 1977):72; ibid. (April 16, 1977):10-11; *Newsweek* (May 29, 1978):34-36; "Keeping Out of It," *Nation* (June 3, 1978):650-52; *New Republic* (May 27, 1978):5-6; *Time* (June 5, 1978):32-34; *U.S. News and World Report* (June 5, 1978):41-42.

122. See Professor Suzuki's criteria to determine the legitimacy of a claim: "The critical questions are whether the subgroup's disidentification is real and whether its demands are compatible with basic community policies. In short, to approximate a public order of human dignity, the test of reasonableness is the determining factor in deciding how to respond to the claim of self-determination. The total context of such a claim must be considered: the potential effects of the grant or denial of self-determination upon the sub-

group, the incumbent group, neighboring regions, and the world community" (Suzuki, "Self-Determination and World Public Order," p. 784).

123. Art. 99 reads: "The Secretary-General may bring to the attention of the Security Council any matter which in his opinion may threaten the maintenance of international peace and security."

124. Pursuant to the authority granted under resolution 8 (23) of the UN Commission on Human Rights (see 42 UN ECOSOC Supp. 6 [1967], p. 131).

125. International Commission of Jurists press release, April 5, 1972, p. 3.

126. See generally, Nanda, "A Critique," pp. 64-67.

127. Adopted by the General Assembly Res. 2106 (20) in December 1965. See generally, M. Reisman, "Response to Crimes of Discrimination and Genocide: An Appraisal of the Convention on the Elimination of Racial Discrimination," *Denver Journal of International Law and Policy* 1 (1971):29.

9

Self-Determination:
The African Perspective

Christopher C. Mojekwu

This chapter begins with the assumption that the problems of minorities and the desire to be self-determined in the human society are as old as human society itself. In this chapter, we would survey how these problems were handled in precolonial African societies, through the colonial interlude, and in contemporary times. We will compare the methods, the cost factors, the successes and the failures of each period.

Self-Determination and Human Rights in Precolonial Africa

The dynamics of precolonial African geopolitics operated in an intricate socio-cultural framework which was cultivated to ensure the maintenance of harmony and equilibrium within a social unit. A dominant group within a family, clan, or community would generally persuade a minority within or close to the group to remain with it so that, together, they could form a bigger unit. The minority recognized the primacy of the majority group because the majority also had a duty to protect the interests of the minority. The two acknowledged the need for each other's existence and recognized the role that each would play in the body politic. The majority had no desire to swallow the minority, and the lesser group did not aspire to supplant the greater side. Each respected the role and the ability of the other, and an equilibrium was generally maintained.

In precolonial times, all able-bodied members of a community shared the duties and the responsibilities of its existence and survival. Likewise, all members enjoyed, as of right, all the natural resources within the community. Where, however, for reasons of depletion of resources, for political and acquisitive ambition, or for major social disagreement, a minority group decided to break away and form a new and independent community of its own, the dominant group, rather than oppose, would, for the peace and harmony of the parties concerned, generally recognize this right and invariably respect it. Indeed, the minority would initiate negotiations for good neighborliness, and the majority would always support the move. Cooperation on economic and defense matters were thereafter mutually arranged. This political flexibility, which allowed for fusion and fission, was an important element in the African political culture. Very often, this factor is forgotten or totally ignored in the analysis of African politics.[1]

Precolonial African society was not static as some historians seem to have treated it. There was both continuity and change as dictated by the needs of the time and the changing values of the society. Empires rose and collapsed, communities grew and declined. Each in its own way brought about a new empire or an improved community.[2] The question of human rights was not just a Western European concept based, as it were, only on the eighteenth-century pronouncements of the French and American revolutions. Human rights was a basic concept very much present in precolonial African society even in the eighteenth and nineteenth centuries. The difference was that the concept of human rights in Africa was based fundamentally on ascribed status. It was a person's place of birth, membership or "belonging" to a particular locality and within a particular social unit, that gave content and meaning to his human rights—social, economic, and political. You had to be born into a social unit or somehow belong to it in order to have any rights which the law of the land could protect. One who lost his membership in a social unit or one who did not belong—a stanger or an outcast—lived outside the range of human-rights protection by the social unit.[3] Such strangers to the community had no rights except those which they could negotiate for, through their hosts or protectors. Acquisition of rights in such circumstances implied that rights could be negotiated by reciprocal arrangements.[4] Quite often strangers who sought integration were accommodated. They had the freedom to retain their most cherished customs while identifying with the major group in essential cultural characteristics. However, the loss of rights within the social unit would mean the loss of nationality or national rights and, again, the loss of human rights.[5]

The second basic difference between the concepts of rights in Western countries and that of precolonial Africa is that while eighteenth- and nineteenth-century European liberal attitudes emphasized individual rights, precolonial Africa of the same period emphasized collective or communal rights. Because the nature and the attributes of individual and collective rights are fundamentally different, the approaches to the understanding of these rights must of necessity be different. Furthermore, while European geopolitics of the eighteenth and nineteenth centuries forced it to develop the concept of the nation-state with its ideas of sovereignty and impersonal authority structure, African societies grouped themselves generally into kinship communities or cultural nations based on common culture, language, customs, and religion. While the European impersonal governments were able to accommodate and control peoples from several ethnic, racial, and cultural origins within the nation-state, African cultural nations controlled kinship groups within its cultural boundaries. It governed through familial chiefs and elders who shared authority with the community at large. The stranger was always kept outside the protection of such cultural nations.

The confusion and instability in contemporary African politics in large measure has been due to the impatience and the intolerance of European colonizers for different political and social concepts outside their own.[6] For example, respect for the clan head and elders, loyalty to the community, respect for and protection of communal rights and communal ownership were destroyed only to introduce European concepts of respect for the impersonal government, loyalty to the colonizing power, and respect for and protection of individual rights and individual proprietary rights over land and property. The consequences of these conflicting concepts manifest themselves in contemporary Africa.

Self-Determination and Colonialism

The history of Western European contacts with African societies, more especially from the eighteenth-century onward, has been a continuous attempt by the West to transform the many cultural national communities and autonomous, though loosely organized, societies into replicas of Western nation-states. To be sure, wherever Europeans have been in Africa, they have shown their impatience and indeed their intolerance of other social and political forms of organization. They have devoted their time, energy, and resources to bringing the African societies in line with the standards of Western nation-states. Throughout the mercantile and colonizing periods of Africa, wherever the Europeans set their foot, whether as traders, missionaries, colonial administrators, or even more recently as bearers of monetary or technological "aids," they insisted directly and indirectly that African societies that did not voluntarily adopt Western nation-state patterns must somehow be induced to toe that line. It did not matter if the "inducing" meant open intervention into African society's internal affairs. It was largely through such intervention, which removed the precolonial authority structures and abridged African societal human rights, that modern African nation-states had their beginnings.

To be more exact, the fact that the emergence of modern nation-states in Africa has taken place in the second half of the twentieth century, and not a century or two earlier, has its own problems. The recent civil wars in Nigeria, Sudan, Angola, and Zaire and the continuing problems of Eritrea, Ethiopia, and Somalia have a direct link to their origins as colonial territories and their emergence as independent states in the twentieth century. But foreign intervention and power politics do not seem to provide a solution to the human desire for self-determination. In Africa, the great complication is that the issues of self-determination are inseparable from the problems of nation-building. The African nation-states did not start as nations and still have a long way to go to become real nations.[7] The political and social implications of all the above have far-reaching consequences in contemporary world affairs. A reassessment of meanings and objectives in Africa is therefore imperative.

We must ask, have there been double standards in contemporary applications of the UN-sponsored right of self-determination for European societies and for African societies? For example, is it conceivable that Canada will fight the province of Quebec if it decides to break away and be self-determined? Why did the British government refrain from using force to call a halt to Ian Smith's unilaterial declaration of independence in Rhodesia some thirteen years ago? Why was it that the same Britain was foremost, by furnishing lethal weapons, in persuading Nigeria to fight the secessionist Biafrans until the secession collapsed?

Must self-determination in Africa be dictated and controlled by foreign interests—be they Cuba, the Soviet Union, the United States, or Arab states? How should modern African nation-states change their own indigenous formulas to respond adequately to the peculiar legacy and the anomalies of colonial boundaries? Can modern African leaders argue seriously that, by their own intelligent and voluntary acts, they decided to adopt the Western-inspired formula of "territorial integrity" into their charter of unity? Does this solve the problems of colonial dismemberment of peoples and cultural nations in Africa? What of the basic questions of human rights, individual and collective, of the peoples of Africa? Could the African social framework of "belonging" and the traditional concept of political flexibility be a more rational method of dealing with each case and bring order and stability back to Africa? Would the Swiss cantonal-confederal system have more meaning in finding acceptable solutions to some of the delicate problems created in Africa by colonialism,[8] or will the Western paradigm of military rule really fuse and integrate the tribes and different cultural communities together in order to generate such a national consciousness that ethnicity in African society would be removed? Would such a rule encourage the freedoms of self-expression, speech, and self-improvement necessary in a democratic society? What would be the cost factor of all these?

We have raised these questions not in the hope of answering them all, but in the belief that any realistic analysis of the problems of self-determination in contemporary Africa must of necessity take notice of some of these questions which have their origins in the colonial heritage.

Self-Determination and UN Declarations:
A Double Standard?

International diplomats at the United Nations commented that 1960 was the year of Black Africa. In the course of that year, seventeen new states of Black Africa joined that organization; presently, there are thirty Black African member states in the UN. Within the first decade of their membership in the United Nations, practically all the new African states have been confronted in some degree with the problems of dissident ethnic groups attempting to break away from the newly created nation-states. Congo Kinshasa (now Zaire), Nigeria, Sudan, Kenya, and Ethiopia are the more impressive examples of this phenomenon. In the context of international politics, these dissident groups were merely attempting to exercise their right of self-determination. Why was this phenomenon nonexistent in the precolonial period? Why is it so frequent in postcolonial Africa? After all, was it not the case that the elite of the various ethnic or tribal groups in the colonial territories joined together in the demand for the political withdrawal of the metropolitan powers?

The answer is simple. On the one hand, the colonial governments suppressed the exercise of fundamental human rights. Freedom of expression, but more importantly, freedom to question or to disagree with a colonizing power was regarded as a criminal act. It was punishable under the rubrics of sedition, seditious libel, or treasonable felony. The penalty was jail for several years.[9] On the other hand, the UN declaration of self-determination has been given various interpretations and applications to suit the major world powers. The original intentions of the declarant have been abrogated, and a double standard has evolved—one for members of the European and Baltic communities, the other for the colonial peoples of color. Consequently, minorities in Africa who believed that the UN declaration meant what it said have been disillusioned and disappointed. Let us briefly look at the biography of this declaration.

Although the Allied nations at the Paris Peace Conference in 1919 accepted President Woodrow Wilson's concept of self-determination as a principle of international law, his original ideas had undergone a strange metamorphosis.[10] The principle was employed to dismantle the German, Austro-Hungarian, Turkish, and the former Russian empires of eastern and southeastern Europe.[11] But the same Allied nations, notably Britain and France, failed to apply the principle to their own colonial and dependent peoples of Asia and Africa. Furthermore, by mere rhetoric, the principle of self-determination was transformed into a "universal human right" capable of assertion as a "legal right" only by individuals, singly or as a predetermined group. Because the Allied nations reserved to themselves "the sole authority in all cases of interpretation," self-determination was again transformed from mere principle into a political remedy. Only the new democratic republics of central Europe and the Baltics benefited from this rhetoric.[12]

One of the primary purposes and principles of the United Nations is the development of "friendly relations among nations based on respect for the principle of equal rights and self-determination of peoples." Within the last three decades, the UN General Assembly has adopted more than fifty resolutions dealing generally and specifically with the concept of self-determination and its application to "subject peoples." The United Nations, itself, has given two meanings to the term self-determination:

1. as a *right* of a state to *choose freely* its political, economic, social, and cultural systems; and
2. as a *right* of a people to *constitute itself* in a state or otherwise *freely* to *determine* the form of its association with an existing state. For example, the *right* of the Puerto Ricans in choosing their ultimate relationship with the United States.[13]

Defined as a theoretical concept, Robert Friedlander states that "self-determination implies the *freedom* of a dissident people to establish on *its own initiative* a viable independent national entity and whatever political and social structures it chooses for the preservation of that entity."[14] Rupert Emerson defines it as "the right of peoples to determine the internal structure and functioning of their society without interference."[15] These modern concepts do not differ materially from the precolonial concepts of self-determination in Africa. They involve the *freedom* which a stranger, a community, a subtribe, or a people have to take into their own hands the direct responsibility of *choosing* where to *belong* without interference, rancor, or opposition. This "freedom to choose" was universally accepted in Africa. For this reason, African political culture accepted fusion, fission, and political flexibility as the necessary means of solving demands for self-determination. It is this freedom to choose that the United Nations has constituted into a right. Self-determination anywhere in the world would involve the right of a people to take into their own hands the full responsibility of determining, without coercion, their own political, economic, and cultural destinies.

In practice, however, self-determination under the United Nations seems to be an unsteady principle, a chameleonic right, and an elusive remedy. To create more confusion, self-determination has been linked with universal human rights, discrimination, racism, etc. It has been paraded by the rhetoricians of the world body as "an inalienable and unchallengeable right" for the multitude of excolonial peoples.[16] In practical terms, however, self-determination for excolonial territories in contemporary Africa has proved to be the UN-sanctioned right of colonial peoples (constituted as a single and indivisible unit, e.g., Nigeria) to achieve independence as speedily and completely as possible, either by agreement with the metropolitan power or, if necessary, by the use of force.[17]

In the latter situation, military aid may be obtained from other states and international agencies.[18] While the "Wilsonian self-determination" assisted the peoples and nations of eastern and southeastern Europe to gain the opportunity of taking the responsibility for shaping their own political, economic, and cultural destinies, "UN-sponsored self-determination" for the colonial peoples of Africa lumped diverse tribal peoples together against their wishes and best interests. In point of fact, the United Nations denied the African peoples that "freedom to choose" and the "right" to take into their own hands the responsibility of shaping their own political, economic, and cultural destinies.

It is not enough that the United Nations should just make the declaration. It is imperative that, for such a declaration to have any meaning, the world body should evoke the democratic principle of "due process"; keep the doors open for a reasonable length of time and make the opportunity readily available, within such reasonable length of time, for colonial peoples to reflect and to be able to exercise their right of self-determination. For otherwise, the early foreclosure of the right after a colonial territory has been granted independence as a unit does not, in democratic terms, give the different peoples within the colonial territory sufficient time to exercise this inalienable right. The damage already done in Africa is great. The foreclosure has made it necessary for the peoples who seek to exercise their inalienable right of self-determination to be crushed. We repeat that this is due in great part to the intolerance and impatience of Westerners to see any good in political or social arrangements other than their own. As was stated earlier, colonial peoples who do not toe the colonialists' line must be made to conform to the nation-state concepts of Western Europe.

Thus, the UN-sponsored self-determination confirmed as nation-states the purely administrative units created by the colonizing powers in Africa. Although the United Nations sponsored "decolonization" and "independence" by its December 1960 resolution, only the top veneer of colonialism has been removed. For, as became evident, virtually all the vestiges of colonial administrative structures, colonial laws, colonial languages, and, indeed, colonial economic structures have been retained in postcolonial Africa. Any hasty attempt by the Africans to dismantle these colonial structures would enrage the metropolitan powers since they have reasoned that their economic interests may no longer be adequately protected if the colonial infrastructure is removed. This would generally lead to the "destabilization" of the new states by the metropolitan powers. Thus, the various ethnic peoples in the excolonial territories have been prevented by the UN interpretation and application of self-determination from ever having the opportunity to take direct responsibility in shaping their own political, economic, and cultural destinies.

Self-Determination and Foreign Intervention

Given the double standard exhibited by the United Nations in the application of its declaration and the fate of African people who have been crushed under the UN duplicity and ambivalence, contemporary events point to the "wisdom" of a carefully planned use of terrorist violence and strong outside military support as the only roads open to dissidents to achieve self-determination. Guinea-Bissau, Mozambique, and the MPLA in Angola are a few examples that, in contemporary Africa, freedom fighters must employ violence in order to get what the world body promised but could not deliver. Given the reasons for failure of the Igbos in Nigeria, the Ovambos in Angola, and the Anya Nya in southern Sudan to secure self-determination, African moderates like presidents Nyerere and Kaunda have openly supported dissidents or freedom fighters in Africa who can muster large followings of guerrillas and who can secure massive military intervention. Since the world body is unable to live up to its declaration, self-determination in Africa can only be achieved through terror-violence and outside intervention. It seems the only way to make the UN-declared myth an African reality.

Self-Determination and the Fallacy of "Territorial Integrity"

During his public statement recognizing the right of the Igbos in Biafra to separate existence, President Nyerere, inter alia, commented that "it is foolish for Africans to stand by idly while millions of Africans are being killed by other Africans in the name of 'territorial integrity'. . . . You cannot kill thousands of people and keep on killing more in the name of 'unity'. There is no unity between the dead and those who killed them, and there is no unity in slavery and those who dominate them." President Nyerere spoke for all African cultural nations or ethnics who are oppressed in Africa. The fallacy of the OAU "territorial integrity" declaration is that by this act the OAU perpetuated the colonial boundaries which all African nationalists regard as atrocious and therefore invalid.[19] Either the Africans are serious in their condemnation of European atrocity in the division of the African continent at the Berlin Conference of 1885, without the presence of one African representative, or they should cease their objections and thank the colonizers for a job well done. Either the colonial boundaries were arbitrarily drawn and did, in fact, cut across traditional boundaries and ethnic societies and divided families, in which case they should be redrawn and adjusted, or the African leaders must admit that they approved the OAU Charter along with territorial integrity because they were compelled to do so by their colonial advisers. Either there is substance in our assertion that colonialism was bad and disruptive of African society, or we must admit our folly in condemning it in the first place.

If the above were true, then African leaders might as well ask the European powers to repossess their territories and run them the way they choose. To be exact, the OAU lifted the hackneyed phrase from the 1960 declaration of the United Nations—"non-interference with the national unity and territorial integrity of member states"—and incorporated it unintelligently into its charter.[20] Through this fallacy of territorial integrity, both the OAU and the African leaders have preserved the greatest monument of colonialism—the irrational division of the African continent based on foreign commercial interests. To be sure, the retention of those boundaries "at all costs" exposes the weakness of African leadership and enables the excolonialists to keep their commerical interests intact, indeed, to control the economic resources of Africa as in the old days. It is very doubtful if this really is what the OAU and the African leadership intend.

It is my view that contemporary African leaders are still mesmerized by the colonial powers, and they are not able to speak their minds. The irony of it all is that, until African leaders dismantle the colonial boundaries, they will continue to live under the spell of colonialism. The colonial boundaries remain undisputably the white man's juju for continued, indirect control of Africa. Break it, and the power of his juju will be gone. The prospects are not healthy for a people who want to be free and self-determined.

Self-Determination and Communal Rights

As can be inferred from what was said earlier, African concepts of rights are very different from that of Western Europe. Communalism and communal-right concepts are fundamental to understanding African society. Do not make the mistake of thinking that the colonial interlude washed away these fundamental cultures in the society. It should be remembered that a handful of Europeans could not have governed Africa if the traditional rulers of Africa had not used traditional structures to rule their people on behalf of the colonizers. As Lucian Pye stated, "Habit, custom, and village relationships gave discipline and order to the lives of most of the people and colonial rulers had to treat only with elite relationship at the top of the society."[21] The conflict in Africa has always stemmed from attempts to force Western concepts and systems on the Africans. Insofar as they have not openly rebelled against the attempts, the erroneous impression is created that they "love" the new system. But concepts like communalism and communal rights are still very much a part of the African life and culture. We might as well recognize that they may not be so easily destroyed.

When, therefore, the UN principle of self-determination was transformed into universal human rights for the individual, it went against the African concept of human rights, which is communal. For how could the human rights of a kinship group, a community, or, indeed, a people be individualized?

Communal rights are based on an ascriptive status. To reject communal rights and introduce individual rights is to destroy the base of African familyhood and African culture. It is as Professor Mildred A. Schwartz said, a most severe punishment which involves the forcible break with both kin and culture, without even the opportunity to acquire new ties.[22] To reject African communal-right concepts and force on Africans Western-based individual rights and nation-state and sovereignty concepts, all in the name of self-determination, is to destroy the very being of the African nationhood. What we are creating in Africa are monsters that Abramson calls "social eunuchs."[23] Such conditions are never sought after voluntarily. It seems that the Africans are somehow coerced into accepting self-determination along with individual human rights. The great American dream was the creation of a free new society in which the commonness of man should transcend all ethnic barriers to create a new America under the theory of the "melting pot." Even with the formidable achievement of the American melting pot, the ethnic revival of the last ten years has proved to be a more powerful and beneficial force in strengthening America rather than weakening it.[24]

Take another example from Africa: What kind of society do we hope to create in Nigeria if we destroy the culture and the social structure of the Hausa, Yoruba, the Igbo, and other ethnics of cultural nations in that territory—a new melting pot of Nigeria or social eunuchs of Nigeria? The melting-pot theory can hardly be true because the historical and the anthropological bases of Nigeria are not the same as those of the United States. The cultural nations, the ethnics, are already well-established foundations of the Nigerian society. Furthermore, you do not destroy a nation in the hope of building a better one out of the ashes of an already dead society. Preserve the cultures of the ethnics in Nigeria by recognizing their existence and the communal rights of the various peoples in Nigeria and we shall have the new Nigerian society based on mutual respect for each other, each ethnic contributing to the greater society—Nigeria.

For example, no Yoruba, even in his wildest dreams, would aspire or even want to be the *obi* of Nnewi in Igbo society. No Igbo would dream of aspiring to be the *oni* of Ife in Yoruba society. In like manner, no Hausa would aspire to be the *olu* of Warri in Itchekiri society.[25] Not only would the ethnics not agree, the individual knows that he does not belong to that cultural group. Yet the Yoruba, the Igbo, and the Hausa would work in mutual respect for the new Nigeria being created under the new constitution.

The general theme in many African countries is to reject multiparty rule for a one-party system. Tanzania is a classic example not only of the one-party state but of an African society developing under African culture—Ujama—familyhood. Ujama is not based on Western socialism but on communalism that is Africa. It seems to me that what Nyerere is doing is going back to the grass roots—reenforcing human rights on a communal foundation, modernizing African society on the solid foundations of African culture, and, finally, absorbing the strangers into the African familyhood after the stranger has served his apprenticeship in cultural orientation.

It seems as if, by default, we have left lawyers and political scientists alone to discuss self-determination and human rights. They have come up with ideas rooted in legalism and constitutionalism. They have framed impressive statements and legislative restraints which have resulted in mere political symbolism. The limited success of self-determination and the human-rights movement in Africa supports the need for another perspective. The time has come when the tools of sociology and anthropology should be used to reevalute our definitions of self-determination as a principle and of human rights as an inalienable right either of the individual or of a community of people.[26]

There is room for further examination of self-determination and collective rights in Africa. It is necessary to conceive of human rights as including conditions of membership to a political community in which the place of ethnic communities will be protected.

The Western view, which operated only in relation to the individual and the state, can no longer be the only view. We must look at the claim of ethnic communities and interpret human rights in terms of communal rights. No matter what we do in Africa, we cannot totally wipe out ethnic and communal considerations. It is unrealistic and unhealthy to do so. For a long time, the Soviet Union has challenged the Western viewpoint on human rights, perhaps only recently with some success. This is now the time for Africa to reassess its stand and state its own viewpoint on communal rights and self-determination.

Conclusion: The Myth and the Reality

The myth of Africa is Africans thinking that at the granting of independence by the metropolitan powers they were finally self-determined and that the nation was born. The reality is that, although they may have won the battle of words or the battle of guns, true self-determination has not been achieved and the nation has only been conceived.

It is a simple matter for a given colonial territory to be independent. It is a much more involved affair for the same territory to be self-determined. In Africa, there were many "selves" within the colonial territory, and they have never had the time nor the opportunity to integrate into one "self" which should become the nation. Self-determination is far wider and more involved than independence. Self-determination applies to a people—a cultural nation—a self that is a social unit. Self-determination in Africa would include the realization of one's innate strengths and weaknesses, a realization of the internal problems of building the nation, and the ability to fashion workable solutions to the nation's problems. Finally, there is the development of a capacity to cope with such problems and resolve them successfully, and with credit, by one's self. Self-determination involves national self-reliance. It involves a psychological change from colonialism to a self-reliant "self" that is able to resolve its problems in its own ways. A modern African state cannot be self-determined until it has built the nation and developed the capacity to resolve its own problems by its own intelligent and independent devices, compatible with its culture and environment.

An example of this difference is seen in the agreement and unity with which all the elite from all ethnic groups in the colonial territories pursued the question of independence against the metropoles. The same elite are no longer agreed or united in the processes of building the nation or in the manner in which the issues of human rights and self-determination are executed. This is the major reason for the presence of dissidents and threats of secession.

It is a myth to accept as an article of faith the immutability of the colonial boundaries and the pious hope that a wholesale transplant of Western structures and paradigms will solve the problems of nationhood in Africa. The reality is that survival and growth can only come from developing the internal strengths of Africa and by resolving its weaknesses through these strengths. To be sure, Africa needs infusion of some ideas from outside to build its strengths.

President Nyerere of Tanzania seems to have discovered this secret of internal strength long ago and has kept close to the path of Ujama or African familyhood. The present military administration in Nigeria, under the leadership of the late Murtala Mohammed and presently under the leadership of General Obasanjo, has learned, after three years of unnecessary civil war and five years of misrule by General Gowon,[27] that the new Nigerian nation will be developed, after all, through the negotiation of a homegrown constitution.[28] In it, all ethnics have free and ample opportunity to deliberate, negotiate, and finally resolve how they should be governed. They will determine what limits they desire to put on their government. It is noteworthy that the division of Nigeria into nineteen states approximates very closely provision of a forum for each of the major ethnics to be self-governing.

The Swiss confederal system which recognizes both a full and a half canton seems to be a pointer for many African states, large or small. What Africa needs is time—time to age in the wood. It needs time to sort out its problems and solve them; time to build the nation. But, as was stated earlier, independence and nation-building in the latter part of the twentieth century are problems by themselves. The understanding of the West is desired on these two factors. Foreign intervention and military build-up are hardly what Africa needs from the West. Perhaps Africa needs to be left alone or its doors closed to arms merchants for some decades.

Realizing that nothing is settled until it is settled right, Africa cannot continue to kill Africans in the name of self-determination, territorial integrity, or unity. There is, in the words of Nyerere, no unity between dead Africans and those Africans who killed them. The African concept of nationhood or nationality should be modernized, expanded, and used in resolving the problems of self-determination and human rights. Political flexibility; the willingness by the majority and the minority to live side-by-side or to be married together; the willingness to negotiate relationships, political, social, and economic; and the readiness to respect each other's views and interests would appear to be more in line with African concepts and culture. These should be edifying guidelines in solving the problems of nation-building and self-determination in Africa.

Notes

1. Much of this analysis is taken from the author's study of African societies, contained in Mojekwu, "The Nature of Law and Justice in an African Tribe" (LL.M. diss., Northwestern University School of Law, 1972), and from "Traditional Law and Justice in Nnewi Community," in Laz Ekwueme, ed., *Perspectives on Igbo Culture*, forthcoming. But see also Elias, *Africa and the Development of International Law* (Dobbs Ferry, N.Y.: Oceana, 1972), chap. 2. Lucian Pye makes a point about the more fundamental level of nation-building process in *Aspects of Political Development* (Boston: Little, Brown, 1966).

2. African historians are unanimous in this statement. See the author's study, "The Nature of Law and Justice"; also Robert July, *Pre-Colonial Africa* (New York: Charles Scribner's Sons, 1975); E. W. Bovill, *The Golden Trade of the Moors* (Oxford, 1968); Robert L. Rotbert, *A Political History of Tropical Africa* (New York: Harcourt, Brace and World, 1965).

3. This difference needs to be emphasized. This is the departure point between the African conception and the Western conception of human rights. Professor Mildred A. Schwartz makes similar comments in "Human Rights in War and Peace: The Case of the Japanese in Canada and the U.S." (Paper delivered at the Nineteenth Annual Conference of the I.S.A., Washington, D.C., February 1978).

4. Reciprocity is an important system that runs through most of the social and economic relationships among Africans. For more information regarding reciprocity in various African societies, consult Hodder and Ukwu, *Markets in West Africa* (Ibadan, Nigeria: Ibadan University Press, 1969); Green, *Igbo*

Village Affairs (New York: Longmans, 1965); Bohannan, *Africa and the Africans* (Evanston, Ill.: Northwestern University Press, 1964); Bohannan and Dalton, *Markets in Africa* (Evanston, Ill.: Northwestern University Press, 1962); July, *Pre-Colonial Africa*.

5. See Schwartz's paper referred to in note 3. She emphasizes this loss of nationality and human rights in the Japanese-American case.

6. See also similar comments by Pye, *Aspects of Political Development*.

7. For a fuller discussion of this subject, see the author's contribution in Mojekwu and Lors, eds., *African Society, Culture, and Politics* (Washington, D.C.: University Press of America, 1977), chap. 10, pp. 191-200.

8. For more detail on the author's views on the Swiss model, see Mojekwu, *Handbook of Selected Constitutions* (Port Harcourt, Nigeria: C.M.S. Press, 1966).

9. Most of the leaders of Africa were at one time or another arrested and tried on such charges: Wallace Johnson of Sierra Leone and Nigeria, Nkrumah of Ghana, Macaully of Nigeria, Azikiwe of Nigeria, Kaunda of Zambia, and Jomo Kenyata for the Mau Mau uprising in Kenya.

10. Although Wilson had embraced the concept of self-determination as a principle of the "consent of the governed," this expression does not appear anywhere in his Fourteen Point program. Although he has now inherited the principle as of his making, many commentators are critical that Wilson himself was ambivalent in what he meant and more so in the application of the principle. This led to confusion, misunderstanding, and the misapplication of the principle soon after its inception. But see the very illuminating articles of Robert A. Friedlander, "Self-Detemination: A Legal-Political Inquiry," *Detroit College of Law Review* 1, no. 1 (1975), reprinted as chap. 13 in this volume, and Michla Pomerance, "The United States and Self-Determination: Perspectives on the Wilsonian Conception," *American Journal of International Law* 70, no. 1 (1976).

11. Wilson's failure to make this principle apply uniformly—to, say, Ireland or the dependent territories of the Allied powers—has been severely criticized (see Pomerance, "The United States and Self-Detemination," pp. 8-9). Friedlander notes that, since the Bolshevik Revolution of November 1917, Russia was technically no longer an enemy, but was "definitely a source of great concern to the Allies" (Friedlander, "Self-Determination," p. 71, note 4).

12. A point Friedlander emphasizes in his "Self-Determination." This was so because of the double standard and the ambivalence of Wilson and the Allied nations. But see Wilson's address at Indianapolis on September 4, 1919, where he claimed that the Allied powers were "sitting there with pieces of the Austro-Hungarian empire in their hands. . . . We are sitting there with various dispersed assets of the German Empire in our hands . . . but we did not have our own dispersed assets in our hands" (see Ray S. Baker and William E.

Dodd, eds., *The Public Papers of Woodrow Wilson: War and Peace*, 2 vols. (New York: Harper and Brothers, 1927), pp. 616-17; see Pomerance, "The United States and Self-Determination," p. 9).

13. Muhammad Aziz Shukri, *The Concept of Self-Determination in the United Nations* (Damascus: Al Jadidah Press, 1965).

14. Friedlander, "Proposed Criteria for Testing the Validity of Self-Determination as It Applies to Disaffected Minorities," *Chitty's Law Journal* 25, no. 10 (Dec. 1977):1 (emphases added). See also Friedlander, "Self-Determination."

15. Rupert Emerson, "The Fate of Human Rights in the Third World," *World Politics* (January 1975):205.

16. By Resolution 1514 (15) in 1960, the UN made the important "Declaration on the Granting of Independence to Colonial Countries and People." This resolution of the General Assembly on December 14, 1960, was adopted by eighty-nine votes for and none against, with nine abstentions; namely, the United States, United Kingdom, France, Portugal, Australia, Belgium, Dominican Republic, Spain, and South Africa. Thirty-seven of the yes votes were from African states.

17. The UN resolution of November 1968 called on Portugal to hand over power to her colonial peoples. It seems that the UN resolution supports the use of force so long as the territory is still under colonial rule. Whether the UN will use force to make practical its claim of Namibia is a matter for speculation.

18. The OAU, through its Decolonization Committee, has aided freedom fighters in securing their freedom. Guinea-Bissau, Angola, and Mozambique were aided by foreign and African nations. Nkomo's faction in Zimbabwe is supported by the OAU committee.

19. The 1960 declaration of the UN had limiting factors on the "self" that are to be determined. It declared that "Any attempt aimed at the partial or total disruption of the national unity and territorial integrity of a country is incompatible with the purpose and principles of the Charter of the United Nations." The OAU has applied this principle in African cases. It would appear that the principle is misapplied. The position of a "settled country" and a "colonial creation" are different. There was no "national unity" or settled territorial claim in a colonial state. The tribal nations were not given the opportunity to state their claims or to challenge the creation of a new nation-state. There could be no assurance of national unity and territorial acceptance of boundaries in a colonial territory as such.

20. See the remarks already made in note 19.

21. Pye, *Aspects of Political Development*, p. 10.

22. Schwartz, "Human Rights in War and Peace," p. 25.

23. Ibid.

24. See editorial opinion by Ward W. Smith, "Is the Melting Pot Curdling?" *Christian Science Monitor*, April 21, 1978.

25. The position of a ruler of an ethnic group cannot be aspired to by an outsider to that group. The members of the group would not accept such a ruler. He would have no legitimacy to rule.

26. Schwartz has emphasized these same points in her paper, "Human Rights in War and Peace."

27. The opinion of the author, who was a senior cabinet member of the Biafran leadership, was that the civil war was fought because of the ineptitude of Gowon to handle political negotiations and affairs. Furthermore, Harold Wilson, the British prime minister at the time, was a most unreliable political character to occupy No. 10 Downing Street as the prime minister of England. Because the Nigerian prime minister—his host—was assassinated in January 1966 during the first coup, Wilson felt personally obliged to revenge his death by inducing Gowon to attach Biafra. Biafran secession was the only way left for Biafra to call the attention of the world to the killing of the Igbos and the continued oppression of Igbo federal civil servants. With the encouragement of Harold Wilson's accredited agent and personal solicitor, Lord Goodman, the author was authorized by the Biafran government to pursue a secret mission for peace and settlement. The author had reached an agreement with Lord Goodman for a workable settlement that could have stopped the war. But Harold Wilson reneged at the last moment without warning to the author and presumably without explanation to his accredited agent. Gowon's misrule of Nigeria after the civil war and his subsequent ouster along with his alleged involvement in the assassination of Murtala Mohammed seem to confirm the opinion of the author about Gowon's incompetence and the futility of the war he started. Gowon could have negotiated successfully with Biafra or he could have held onto his blockade. The Igbo businessmen would have sought other avenues to negotiate with Nigeria in order to get the blockade lifted. By Gowon's attack of the Biafrans, he rallied the elite and the common people against Nigeria to a point that any discussion on surrender or settlement outside full self-determination was opposed by the Biafrans.

28. For more on the Nigerian Constitution, its strengths and its weaknesses, see the author's "Nigerian Constitutionalism," in *NOMOS XX Yearbook on Constitutionalism*, New York University Press, forthcoming.

Part 5

The Middle East

10

Self-Determination and the Middle East Conflict

Yoram Dinstein

Self-Determination as a Collective Human Right

Self-determination must be perceived as an international human right. This is frequently hard to grasp inasmuch as self-determination can be exercised only by a people—namely, a group or a community—as distinct from an individual human being. However, international human rights are not monolithic, and a cardinal line of division has to be drawn between individual and collective human rights.

Individual human rights (for instance, freedom of expression) are bestowed upon every single human being personally. Collective human rights are granted to human beings communally, that is to say, in conjunction with one another, within the ambit of a group: a people or a minority.[1] Self-determination is just one among several collective human rights which are recognized nowadays under international law.

The reason why collective human rights in general, and self-determination in particular, are still human rights even though conferred on a group (a people in the case of self-determination) is that the group in question is not a corporate entity and does not possess a legal personality. Like all other human rights, collective human rights are accorded to human beings directly, without the interposition of the legal personality of a corporate entity, especially that of the state. The nature of these rights requires, however, that they shall be exercised jointly rather than severally.

Self-Determination as a Right Under
Existing International Law

The right of self-determination is proclaimed in the two 1966 International Covenants on Human Rights: the one on Civil and Political Rights and the other on Economic, Social, and Cultural Rights. Article 1(1), which is common to both covenants, states: "All people have the right of self-determination. By virtue of that right they freely determine their political status and freely pursue their economic, social and cultural development."[2]

The covenants came into force only in 1976 and, as yet, are legally binding on less than one-third of the international community. Consequently, it is important to establish whether the right of self-determination has an independent existence, beyond the scope of the covenants, as an integral part of customary international law. There is, indeed, an influential school of thought that denies that self-determination is a legal right, with a corresponding duty, insofar as states not bound by the covenants are concerned.[3] For noncontracting parties, it is contended, self-determination is merely a political clarion call that they are under no obligation to heed. But the better view is that the right of self-determination has acquired, over the last decade or two, the lineaments of *lex lata*.

The political conception of self-determination for peoples has been gaining support since the days of the French Revolution, but particularly so from the end of the First World War. Although the Covenant of the League of Nations did not confirm it directly, one can detect. the first burgeoning of the right within positive international law in the mandates system of the League. In the words of the International Court of Justice, in its judgment of 1962 in the South-West Africa cases: "The essential principles of the Mandates System consist chiefly in the recognition of certain rights of the peoples of the underdeveloped territories."[4]

Clearly, in the era of the League of Nations it was impossible to talk of a right of self-determination in the full sense of the term—not even within the confines of the mandates system—inasmuch as the authority to decide when a people was ripe for independence was given not to itself, but to external powers (the League and the mandatory state). Nevertheless, as was pointed out by the Hague

Court in 1971, in its Advisory Opinion on the Namibia case: "It is self-evident that the 'trust' had to be exercised for the benefit of the peoples concerned, who were admitted to have interests of their own and to possess a potentiality for independent existence on the attainment of a certain stage of development."[5] The Court went on to say that "the ultimate objective of the sacred trust was the self-determination and independence of the peoples concerned,"[6] and it added: "Furthermore, the subsequent development of international law in regard to non-self-governing territories, as enshrined in the Carter of the United Nations, made the principle of self-determination applicable to all of them."[7] More recently, in 1975 in the Western Sahara case, the Court took for granted the "principle of self-determination as a right of peoples."[8]

The right of self-determination of peoples is mentioned in the Charter of the United Nations in two places: in the list of the general purposes of the organization (Art. 1[2]) and in the provision relating to the specific purposes of the United Nations in the promotion of economic and social cooperation (Art. 55).[9] Yet we must distinguish between a purpose that states merely have to strive to attain and a plain legal duty which must be discharged as such. It is preferable to regard the right of self-determination as derived not from the phraseology of the Charter, but from the practice of states after the establishment of the organization. This practice verifies the existence of the right of self-determination, and the "population explosion" that has occurred in the international community since the early 1960s eloquently testifies to it.

Sometimes the right of self-determination of a given people gains special confirmation by treaty. Thus, in the 1973 Paris Agreement on Ending the War and Restoring Peace in Vietnam, the United States and North Vietnam recognized the right to self-determination of the South Vietnamese people.[10] In view of the general application of the right of self-determination under customary international law, such reassertion of the right in a specific instance is redundant, unless, of course, it is contested that a certain group (e.g., the South Vietnamese) may be regarded as a separate people entitled per se to self-determination.

Considering that customary international law in this area is fairly new and not very precise, the contours of the right of self-determination are somewhat blurred. Conventional international law, too, is not particularly helpful in removing doubts pertaining to the definition of self-determination, since the formula used in Art. 1(1) of the human rights covenants is quite laconic. If we take the statement "All peoples have the right of self-determination" as our guide, three expressions seem to require elaboration, i.e., "all," "peoples," and "self-determination." Let us proceed to ask (1) what is a "people"? (2) how comprehensive is the term "all"? and (3) what is the exact meaning of the phrase "self-determination"?

What Is a "People"?

It is necessary to differentiate between a people and a nation. A nation is easy to define as it consists of the entire citizen body of a state. All the nationals of the state form the nation. In each state there is one nation, and this is why the terms state and nation have become practically interchangeable. But within the compass of one state and one nation there can exist several peoples, large and small. Such a state is usually called "multinational," but what is actually meant is that the (one) nation comprises several peoples.

It is exceedingly difficult to define the term "people." There is no acid technical test which would enable us to determine whether a cluster of human beings constitutes a people. Even the number of the members of a group does not settle the issue: a people may consist of vast millions or of several scores of families (though, clearly, a single family or clan may not seriously claim to be a people).

Peoplehood must be seen as contingent on two separate elements, one objective and the other subjective. The objective element is that there has to exist an ethnic group linked by common history. The strength of the ethnic-historical link is admittedly a matter of contention. Frequently, it is suggested that the link must express itself, inter alia, in a common territory, religion, or language, but these requirements are unduly harsh. The vicissitudes of history are such that an ethnic group may lose its territory, split up into various religious factions, and speak in many different tongues. A period of trial and error serves as a crucible for the ethnic identity. If it does not disappear in time and space, its diverse mutations must be viewed with tolerance. In fact, as was indicated by Renan, peoplehood is cemented by shared memories of common suffering.[11] On the other hand, a random group of persons, lacking any common tradition, cannot be categorized as a people. When tens of thousands of men and women assemble temporarily (for example, to watch a football match) or associate for an extended campaign on behalf of a common cause (for instance, the women's liberation movement), they do not, thereby, turn themselves into a people.

Side by side with the objective element, there is also a subjective basis of peoplehood. It is not enough to have an ethnic link in the sense of past genealogy and history. It is essential to have a present ethos or state of mind. A people is both entitled and required to identify itself as such. Renan's famous reference to a *plébiscite de tous les jours*, in regard to the will to live together and to continue common traditions,[12] is very apposite indeed.

It follows that a people must itself delineate the purview of its common existence and settle criteria for belonging to the group. There is no palce for a *Diktat* from outside in this respect: one people cannot decree that another group is not entitled to peoplehood. Moreover, an individual cannot gate-crash and compel a people to admit him to its fold. The group has to make up its collective mind and resolve whether or not such an individual qualifies.

Is the Right of Self-Determination Granted to All Peoples?

It is often argued that the right of self-determination does not embrace secession from an existing state and that it is, in fact, confined to the process of decolonization (particularly in Afro-Asia).[13] But Art. 1(1) is very explicit on the subject: the right of self-determination is conferred on "all" peoples and not merely on some peoples in non-self-governing territories.

Under Art. 31(1) of the 1969 Vienna Convention on the Law of Treaties, the interpretation of treaties (and the human rights covenants are treaties) is governed by the basic rule that the "ordinary meaning" must be given to the terms of a treaty in their context.[14] This textual approach to the interpretation of treaties is based on numerous precedents in international jurisprudence, such as the advisory opinion on Competence of the General Assembly for the Admission of a State to the United Nations, in which the International Court of Justice stated (in 1950):

> The Court considers it necessary to say that the first duty of a tribunal
> which is called upon to interpret and apply the provisions of a treaty, is
> to endeavour to give effect to them in their natural and ordinary mean-
> ing in the context in which they occur. If the relevant words in their
> natural and ordinary meaning make sense in their context, that is an
> end of the matter.[15]

The ordinary meaning of the term "all," in the context of the right
of all peoples to self-determination, is that of entirety: each and
every people is covered by the expression, irrespective of geographic
or other considerations.

Nevertheless, it may be argued, perhaps, that the term "all" in
Art. 1(1) is not as crystal clear as one may be led to believe and
that, in fact, its meaning in the context is ambiguous. This is a
doubtful argument at best, but in such a case Art. 32 of the Vienna
Convention on the Law of Treaties permits recourse to the preparatory work of the covenants (which, in any event, is allowed in
order to confirm the meaning resulting from the application of the
general rule of interpretation of treaties under Art. 31).[16] However, even if we look into the preparatory work for Art. 1(1) of
the covenants, there is no reason to conclude that the original
intention of the framers of the clause incorporating the right of
self-determination was other than what the text indicates on the
face of it.

The draft resolution that introduced the right of self-determination of "all" people into the covenants was discussed and adopted
by the Third Committee of the General Assembly of the United
Nations, in its Sixth Session of 1951/1952. The deliberations of
the Third Committee plainly demonstrate that it was understood
at the time that the right of self-determination is not necessarily
confined to peoples under colonial rule. By way of illustration,
we may quote the following statement made by the delegate from
India (one of the sponsors of the draft resolution):

> However, the peoples of the Non-Self-Governing Territories were not
> the only ones who should be guaranteed the right of self-determination;
> when putting forward that principle during the First World War, Presi-
> dent Wilson and the representatives of those democratic countries which
> had followed his lead had been thinking of all peoples—those who were
> subject to colonial regimes and those who were not on an equal footing

with the peoples with whom they were associated. Therefore, although there was good reason to make special reference to the peoples of the Non-Self-Governing Territories, it must be recognized that the field of application of the principle of self-determination was wider than that.[17]

In this context it may also be advisable to quote the American delegate, Mrs. Roosevelt, who stated in the Plenary of the General Assembly in its Seventh Session of 1952:

> According to the present text of that paragraph, the right of self-determination should be exercised only by the peoples of Non-Self-Governing and Trust Territories. This is a restriction on the right of self-determination which, in the view of my delegation, falls so far short of the concept expressed in the Charter that we should not endorse it. If a right is valid for one group of peoples, it is equally valid for all peoples.[18]

Patently, the draftsmen of Art. 1(1) of the covenants were aware of the all-inclusive sense of the term "all" when they conferred the right of self-determination on all peoples.

The upshot of the matter is that the right of self-determination is accorded not only to peoples under colonial domination in Africa and Asia, but also to peoples living within independent Afro-Asian nations, as well as to those existing in Europe (for instance, in Scotland or the Ukraine) and in America. Just as a people under colonial domination is entitled to create a new state where none existed before, so can a people living within the framework of an extant state secede from it and establish its own independent country. This is precisely what was achieved by the Bengalis of East Pakistan when they created the new State of Bangladesh. This, too, is what was unsuccessfully atempted by the Igbos of East Nigeria when they tried to creat a new state of Biafra.

Needless to say, when a people endeavors to secede from an existing state, the latter is not apt to accept calmly the prospect of its being carved up between several peoples, and it tends to resist the secession movement. Neither Pakistan nor Nigeria submitted gracefully to the scheme of its dismemberment. Modern international law prescribes a right (self-determination) which is loaded with political and psychological dynamite, but it does not have an answer to the question how that right is to be carried into effect. If a people insists on its right to secede, and the existing state refuses to acquiesce in the implementation of the right at its expense, the confrontation leads almost inevitably to civil war. International law does not encourage civil wars, but it does not prohibit them either. International law is simply indifferent to the phenomenon of civil wars, and in this negative sense may be said to permit them.[19] This, of course, is an unfortunate state of affairs, especially at a time when an interstate war is regarded as a crime against peace.[20] But there has always been a gap between *lex lata* and *lex desiderata*.

It is noteworthy that the right of political self-determination is conferred on peoples everywhere, irrespective of the economic and social conditions in which they live. A people that sits by the fleshpots and enjoys the wealth of the land is still entitled to self-government in an independent state. But self-government implies the requirement that the seceding people is located in a well-defined territorial area in which it forms a majority. When a people is dispersed all over a country—and constitutes a minority in each of its parts—its secession would signify not (legitimate) self-government but (unjustifiable) dominaton of others.

What Is the Meaning of Self-Determination?

Self-determination is reflected, in the first place, in the determination of the self—the formulation of criteria for belonging to a people—and this is the subjective element in the defintion of peoplehood. Self-determination also means that every people is entitled to determine freely its future course.

The right of self-determination has economic, social, and cultural connotations, but its quintessence is the political status of the people concerned. The thrust of self-determination is that a people—if it so wills—is entitled to independence from foreign domination, i.e., it may establish a sovereign state in the territory in which it lives and where it constitutes a majority.

A complex question arises in terms of demarcating the region that has to be taken into consideration when one wants to determine whether a people demanding independence (and entitled to it in theory under the right of self-determination) may implement it in practice against the wishes of other peoples in the area. Frequently, the designation of the geographical boundaries of a region (which may be based on arbitrary yardsticks) predetermines the demographic question as to which people forms a majority in it. The Ukrainians, for instance, are a distinct majority in the Ukraine, but a minority in the USSR as a whole.

The problem came to the fore in the UN debates of the late 1940s and early 1950s in regard to the Ewe tribe in Africa. The members of this tribe—seven hundred thousand all told, at that period—inhabited the coastal plains of West Africa in the Gold Coast, British Togoland, and French Togoland and aspired to unify those areas (in which they formed a majority) into a single "Eweland."[21] Instead, the independent states of Ghana and Togo—whose borders vertically intersect the coastal Ewe population and also incorporate many other tribes in the hinterland—were ultimately established. In British Togoland, a plebiscite was held, on the recommendation of the General Assembly, and, as a result, the territory was united with Ghana. In this plebiscite, the majority in the northern hinterland voted for union, overruling the contrary vote of the southern coastal districts (the Ewes) for separation.[22] Manifestly, had the plebiscite been held in the coastal areas alone, its results would have been totally different.

So far, we have proceeded on the assumption that there is an equal mark between self-determiantion and political independence (or statehood), but such is not the case. Independence is a right (where it is available) and not a duty. Even a people that constitutes a sizable majority in a well-defined territorial area is entitled to waive political independence for economic and other reasons. Thus, the Puerto Rican people has, time and again, freely chosen to decline independence. Instead, it has opted for a special legal status (that of a commonwealth as distinct from a state) under the umbrella of the United States, with the island forgoing political rights for the sake of economic advantages.[23] There is nothing inherently wrong in such a course of action, and Puerto Rico cannot be forced by others to assume independence against its will.

The Middle East Conflict

In Palestine, there are, and there have been for a very long time, two peoples: Jews and Arabs. It is often believed that the Jews, having been expelled from their homeland and scattered in the

Diaspora many centuries ago, have returned to the Holy Land only since the dawn of Zionism late in the nineteenth century. But this is a misconception. At no time did the Jews completely cut off their umbilical cord to the Land of Israel. In fact, in the middle of the nineteenth century, several decades prior to the First Zionist Congress, Jews constituted a majority of the population in the city of Jerusalem and lived in fairly large numbers in other holy places throughout Palestine.

The demographic ratio between Arabs and Jews in Palestine has shifted over the years. Initially, the Arabs were in overall majority. Today the majority is Jewish. But the fundamental reality has not changed, and the land is shared by the two groups. It is the irony of fate that the respective positions of both are exceedingly similar in at least three ways.

1. There are more Jews outside Palestine than inside. There are also more Arabs outside Palestine than inside.

2. It is very difficult to answer the question: "Who is a Jew?" Is he a person who professes Judaism as a religion? Is he an off-spring of the original twelve tribes? Is he a person who speaks Hebrew? All these are indubitably faulty criteria.[24] By the same token, it is very difficult to answer the question: "Who is an Arab?" Is he a person who professes Islam as a religion? Is he an offspring of the original desert tribes of (Saudi) Arabia? Is he a person who speaks Arabic? None of these criteria is plausible.[25]

3. There are many (especially Arabs) who deny that Jews in Palestine belong to a Jewish (as dinstinct from an Israeli) people. Again, there are many (especially Jews) who deny that Arabs in Palestine belong to a Palestinian Arab (as distinct from a Jordanian) people.

It is the tragedy of fate that Arabs and Jews apply to each other arbitrary yardsticks about what constitutes a people, refusing to concede one another's determination of self as sufficient or conclusive. There is no prospect of reconciliation in the Middle East unless and until both sides realize that neither lives in a vacuum and that both are entitled to self-determination. There is a Jewish people (or a part of the Jewish people) in Palestine, and there is an Arab people (or a part of the Arab people) in Palestine. Each must be free to determine its political fate. Neither can dictate to the other its decision. Since both have claims over the same country, and both want to proceed along separate paths, the only solution is partition of Palestine between them.

Such a position has been proposed time and again, and on each occasion it has been rejected by the Arabs within and without Palestine. The most famous instance is that of the Partition Resolution adopted by the General Assembly on 29 November 1947.[26] The Partition Resolution was hardly a matter of record when the Arab leadership in Palestine resolved to oppose it by force. At the outset (from 30 November 1947 to 14 May 1948), civil war raged in Palestine. But, with the establishment of the State of Israel on 15 May 1948, the regular armies of the neighboring Arab states resorted to an armed attack against the Jewish state. The war thus assumed an interstate character and became a crime against peace.

It is all too often alleged that Israel was created by the United Nations in the Partition Resolution. But in fact, owing to Arab resistance, the resolution was washed by bloodshed. Israel emerged as an independent state from the throes of its war of independence. Subsequent to the Arab defeat in the battlefield, a different partition of Palestine was sanctioned by the armistice agreements of 1949.[27]

The 1949 partition of Palestine diverged from the 1947 plan devised by the General Assembly not merely in demarcation of boundaries, but also—and more conspicuously—in that only the Jewish state came into existence in Palestine. The counterpart Arab state was never launched into political orbit, not because the Jews objected (at the time they did not), but because the Palestinian Arabs themselves preferred to forgo the option of independence. Most of them, especially in the West Bank, cast their lot with Jordan. Others lived under Egyptian control in the Gaza Strip, and some chose to live in Israel.

For eighteen years, as long as the Palestinian Arabs in the West Bank and the Gaza Strip were free from Israeli interference and presumably (given the consent of Jordan and Egypt) could establish their own state in Palestine, they showed no inclination to proceed to do so. The idea of creating a third state between the desert and the sea, beside Jordan and Israel, was conceived after the 1967 Six-Day War, when the whole of Palestine had come under Israeli control and the complexion of the political scene had changed.

The so-called Six-Day War is actually in its eleventh year at the time of writing. It has gone through a number of phases of both active hostilities and cease-fire. Some of the rounds of fighting are popularly referred to as separate wars (the War of Attrition and the Yom Kippur War), but they all are manifestations of the same ongoing war. As long as the state of war continues, and even while the shooting is suspended, Israel is entitled to administer the territories that are under its "belligerent occupation." However, as pointed out by Oppenheim, whereas "the occupant . . . has a right of administration over the territory," "there is not an atom of sovereignty in the authority of the occupant."[28] This means that Israel has a right to *imperium* over, rather than *dominium* of, the occupied territories. Sovereignty is not transferred to the occupant, and Israel can only acquire title to any part of the occupied areas as a result of cession duly stipulated in a peace treaty.

By and large, Israel realizes that ultimately it will have to withdraw from the bulk of the West Bank as the price of peace. The interrelated conditions of peace, which Israel envisions, cover various contractual arrangements with the neighboring Arab countries guaranteeing secure and recognized boundaries for all parties. However, in the Israeli scheme of things, such arrangements do not include the establishment of an independent Arab country in the West Bank. Israel's objections to the creation of such a state are generated by actions taken and statements made by Palestinian Arabs in the last few years. Israel fears that the helm of the projected state, should it come into being, would soon fall into the irresponsible hands of military extremists and political adventurers with irredentist aspirations, and that a new conflict would erupt before the ink was dry on the peace treaty terminating the present state of war.

The belligerents in the current Middle East conflict are sovereign states (Israel, on the one hand; Egypt, Syria, and Jordan, on the other), and it will be up to those parties to put an end to their war. The Palestinian Arabs, as such, are not a belligerent party in this interstate war. The issue of an independent Palestinian Arab state did not trigger the war, when it started in 1967, and does not necessarily have to be dealt with in order to produce peace between the belligerent parties. It is a separate problem which could best be resolved against the backdrop of peace rather than in the context of war.

The misfortune of the Palestinian Arabs has generally been that they tend to act on an all-or-nothing impulse. For this very reason, up to the present point, they have achieved precisely nothing. They have an incontrovertible right of self-determination in Palestine. But, by the same token, Palestinian Jews have an equally incontrovertible right of self-determination in the same land. It must be borne in mind that international law has no remedy for the thorny problems that arise in the case of a conflict between equally legitimate rights of self-determiantion of a number of peoples in one and the same territory. Consequently, in many instances, the clash of rights between peoples leads to a clash of arms. The conflict between Arabs and Jews in Palestine is by no means unique. It is not even the only conflict of its kind in the Middle East. The civil wars in Cyprus and Lebanon show how bitter, and how senseless, such conflicts can be.

Time and again, the Palestinian Arabs have attempted to thwart by force the exercise of the Jewish right of self-determination in Palestine. All these efforts have come to naught and, indeed, have had a boomerang effect. Israel is a thriving state while the Palestinian Arabs are in politically worse shape today than they were a generation ago. All the same, even at this late stage, the Palestinian Arabs are not reconciled to the existence of Israel. Their basic charter, the Palestinian National Covenant, in its latest version of 1968, grandiloquently claims the whole of Palestine for the Arabs and disdainfully rejects the rights of the Jews (apart from those Jews who normally resided in Palestine until the beginning of the Zionist "invasion," whatever that means).[29] Such political daydreaming can produce conflict, but so far it has not brought the Palestinian Arabs any closer to attaining self-determination.

In the final analysis, the only way to solve the Palestine problem is through compromise leading to peaceful coexistence of Arabs and Jews. After so many years of purposeless fighting, the Palestinian Arabs must begin to realize that only in the unimpassioned atmosphere of peace can it be expected that such a compromise will be reached. What they need is not a war of liberation but a peace of liberation.

Notes

1. See Yoram Dinstein, "Collective Human Rights of Peoples and Minorities," *International and Comparative Law Quarterly* 25 (1976):102-20.

2. International Covenant on Economic, Social, and Cultural Rights, *United Nations Juridical Yearbook* (1966), pp. 170, 171; International Covenant on Civil and Political Rights, ibid., pp. 178, 179.

3. See L. C. Green, "Self-Determination and Settlement of the Arab-Israeli Conflict," *American Society of International Law, Proceedings* 65 (1971):40, 46.

4. South-West Africa Cases (Preliminary Objections), I.C.J. Report (1962), pp. 319, 329.

5. Legal Consequences for States of the Continued Presence of South Africa in Namibia (South-West Africa) notwithstanding Security Council Resolution 276 [1970], I.C.J. Report (1971), pp. 16, 28-29.

6. Ibid., p. 31.

7. Ibid.

8. Advisory Opinion on Western Sahara [1975], I.C.J. Report, pp. 12, 31.

9. Charter of the United Nations, 1945, *Kitvei Amana* 1, Israel Treaty Series, no. 19, pp. 203, 204, 221.

10. *American Journal of International Law* 67 (1973):389, 391.

11. Ernest Renan, "Qu'est-ce qu'une Nation?" in *Oeuvres complètes* (Paris: Calmann-Lévy, 1947), 1:887, 903-4.

12. Ibid., p. 904.

13. See Rupert Emerson, "Self-Determination," *American Journal of International Law* 65 (1971):459, 464-65.

14. Vienna Convention on the Law of Treaties, *United Nations Juridical Yearbook* (1969), pp. 140, 149.

15. Competence of the General Assembly for the Admission of a State to the United Nations [1950] I.C.J. Report, pp. 4, 8.

16. Vienna Convention on the Law of Treaties, p. 149.

17. UN GAOR, 6th Session, 3rd Committee, 399th meeting (23 January 1952), p. 311.

18. UN GAOR, 7th Session, Plenary, 403rd meeting (16 December 1952), p. 370.

19. See Yoram Dinstein, "The International Law of Civil Wars and Human Rights," *Israel Yearbook on Human Rights* 6 (1976):62, 64.

20. See Yoram Dinstein, "International Criminal Law," *Israel Yearbook on Human Rights* 5 (1975):55, 58.

21. See Louis B. Sohn, ed., *Cases on United Nations Law* (Brooklyn: Foundation Press, 1956), pp. 745-46.

22. See ibid., p. 771.

23. See Jaime Benitez, "Self-Determination in Puerto Rico," *American Society of International Law, Proceedings* 67 (1973):7, 8-10.

24. For recent relevant decisions of the Supreme Court of Israel, which, however, are more helpful in clarifying the issues than in laying the questions to rest, see the Shalit and Tamarin cases excerpted in English in *Israel Yearbook on Human Rights* 2 (1972):317-33.

25. Historically, a distinction has been made between "pure Arabs" and "self-styled Arabs" (*musta-'riba*), namely, local inhabitants assimilated by the conquering Arabs (see *The Cambridge History of Islam* [Cambridge: Cambridge University Press, 1970], 1:60).

26. General Assembly Resolution 181 (2) on the Future Government of Palestine, UN GAOR, 2nd Session, Resolution, p. 131. On the chain of events which led to the resolution and followed upon it, see Yoram Dinstein, "The United Nations and the Arab-Israel Conflict," in John Norton Moore, ed., *The Arab-Israeli Conflict* (Princeton: Princeton University Press, 1974), 2:481, 482-83.

27. Egypt-Israel, General Armistice Agreement, 1949, *Kitvei Amana* 1, no. 1, p. 3; Lebanon-Israel, General Armistice Agreement, 1949, ibid., no. 2, p. 23; Jordan-Israel, General Armistice Agreement, 1949, ibid., no. 3, p. 37; Syria-Israel, General Armistice Agreement, 1949 ibid., no. 4, p. 49.

28. L. Oppenheim, "The Legal Relations between an Occupying Power and the Inhabitants," *Law Quarterly Review* 33 (1917):363, 364.

29. For an English text of the Palestinian National Covenant, see Y. Harkabi, *Palestinians and Israel* (Jerusalem: Keter Publishing House Ltd., 1974), p. 49. The reference is to Art. 6, ibid., p. 53.

11
The Jewish Struggle for Self-Determination: The Birth of Israel

Yonah Alexander

The Early Jewish-Arab Encounter, 1880-1914

One of the fundamental bases of Zionism[1] is the unbroken historical bond between the Jews, the oldest Palestinian people still surviving, and the "land of their fathers," the roots of which go back some four thousand years. Although the vast majority of Jews were scattered to every corner of the earth after the destruction of the Second Commonwealth, continuity of Jewish life in Palestine has been maintained. In addition, during the centuries of exile, the millenial hope for national restoration survived and was expressed in the form of numerous attempts to resettle the Promised Land.[2]

The unique mystical attachment and loyalty of "a people without a country to a country without people"[3] have been reinforced in the Zionist ideology by the fact that the Jews have neither abandoned Palestine nor renounced their title to it. In modern times, an increasing number of *olim* ("immigrants")—influenced by the rise of nationalism in Europe during the nineteenth century,[4] spurred by the brutal pogroms in Czarist Russia[5] and the virulent anti-Semitism rampant in the West,[6] and inspired by the crystalization of a national consciousness advocated by *chovevei Zion* ("lovers of

This chapter is based on material published originally in Yonah Alexander, ed., *International Terrorism* (New York: Praeger Publishers, 1976), Chapter 9. The author wishes to acknowledge with thanks a special permission granted by Praeger Publishers to draw from this material.

Zion")—began to settle in Ottoman Palestine in the 1880s. These early *halutzim* ("Jewish pioneers") purchased and toiled the land, drained its marshes and swamps, reclaimed the uninhabited and barren desert, cultivated and irrigated the exhausted soil, established agricultural settlements, and built new towns.[7] To them, and to the other settlers of the first and second *aliyah* ("immigration"),[8] confrontation with the indigenous Arab population in Palestine was not a major concern, nor did they envision the necessity of having to resort to force in order to secure the right to rebuild a national entity in Zion, their only source of physical and spiritual safety and vitality.[9] Since they regarded their ideology as reasonable, uniquely humane, and even messianic, they saw no inherent and objective reasons for conflict between Jews and Arabs.[10] Indeed, they believed that the aspirations and interests of both people were complementary and interconnected, and that the Arabs in particular would benefit considerably from Jewish achievements.[11]

Dr. Theodor Herzl, the father of the Zionist movement, and his associates and successors[12] who sought in Palestine a political and territorial solution to the Jewish problem[13] concentrated, therefore, on the attainment of two objectives:[14] to convince the Jewish masses in the European Diaspora that such a redemption was both necessary and practical;[15] and to influence the custodians of the Holy Land and the important world powers to permit Jewish settlement there, as well as to secure some kind of autonomous status for those who would hearken to their call and come. Diplomatic interventions with the sultan of the Ottoman Empire, the kaiser of Germany, other European potentates of that time, and the statesmen of the British Empire, whose influence on all areas bordering on the "routes to the East" was burgeoning, were the principal political preoccupations of the early Jewish nationalist functionaries. The achievement of these stated goals, the Zionist leaders assumed, could be done without the slightest detriment to the Arab population in Palestine. Underlying this assumption was Dr. Herzl's guiding pledge: "It goes without saying that we shall respectfully tolerate persons of other faiths and protect their property, their honor, and their freedom with the harshest means of coercion. This is another area in which we shall set the entire world a wonderful example."[16] Committed to this principle, the Zionist movement looked forward to Jews and Arabs living in peace, side by side, within the envisaged Jewish state, enjoying rights and opportunities.

During the same time period, contemporary Arab nationalism revived dreams of independence from the Ottoman Empire. But as soon as the Arab press published reports on the emergence of Zionism as a national ideology, some concern for the fate of Palestine as part of the Arab world began to be articulated.[17] In Palestine itself, opposition to the semilegalized Jewish immigration and settlement took the form of protests by some Arab notables to the Ottoman authorities, who at times acceded to Arab requests to impose various restrictions on Jews. But these demands did not stem from nationalistic motivations, but, rather, were expressions of religious and ethnic assertiveness. In fact, since Palestine was regarded by Turkey as the southern part of the Syrian province, the Palestinian Arabs sought to merge this sector of the Middle East with "greater Syria" on the basis of common political, judicial, social, and economic foundations. It is not surprising, therefore, that no distinct, Arab political-ideological parties developed in Palestine simultaneously with other Arab national movements elsewhere prior to the First World War.

Indeed, any sporadic, small-scale attacks by Palestinian Arabs on the early Jewish settlements in the country occurred primarily because of fear, envy, and greed. That is, sometimes Arab peasants and Bedouin were apprehensive that their rights of ownership and grazing would be threatened by the newcomers. Also, there were Arab raiders who desired to enrich themselves at the settlers' expense.

Since the Turkish administration did little to check such incidents, the Zionist pioneers initially had to rely on hired local Arab and Circassian guards[18] to defend their vulnerable villages. Only in 1907 did some of the settlers form a Jewish armed militia, the Bar Giora, named after a Jewish leader of the rebellion against Rome in the first century. Two years later, it was succeeded by Hashomer (the watchman), which soon provided protection to Jewish settlements in the Galilee and Judea.

British Pledges for Arab Independence Fulfilled—
Promises to the Jews Whittled Down, 1914-1923

When the First World War broke out and Turkey entered the conflict on the side of the Central Powers, Arabs and Jews both appealed to the Allies for assistance in realizing their national aspirations in the Middle East. During the period between July 1915 and March 1916, letters were exchanged between Sherif Hussein of Mecca on behalf of the Arabs and Sir Henry McMahon, the British high commissioner in Egypt, on behalf of the British government. This correspondence culminated in the British promise of Arab independence in the Middle East in return for an Arab agreement to revolt against the Turks. Consequently, Bedouin tribesmen, supported by British funds, arms, and advisers such as the legendary Lawrence of Arabia, began to sabotage Turkish installations. Other Arab units, led by Sherif Hussein and his son Feisal, helped the Allies hasten the disintegration of the Ottoman Empire, already in its death-throes.[19]

About the same time, many Palestinian Jews, jointly with their brethren from other countries, fought alongside British forces in the Middle East in the hope that this effort would lead to Allied support of Zionism.[20] This expectation materialized on November 2, 1917, when Lord Arthur James Balfour, foreign secretary of Britain, declared in a letter sent to Baron Edmond Rothschild, a prominent Jewish leader, "His Majesty's Government views with favor the establishment in Palestine of a National Home for the Jewish people and will use their best endeavors to facilitate achievement of this object."[21]

Regarding this declaration as official British support for Zionist aims in Palestine, Jewish battalions fought within the British army in Palestine in the closing stages of the war. On December 9, 1917, some four hundred years after the Ottoman rule over the Holy Land had begun, the Turks surrendered Jerusalem to General Allenby, and a British military administration was set up in Palestine.

At the San Remo Conference of April 25, 1920, the victorious powers of the First World War, acting as the Supreme Council of the League of Nations, decided to place Palestine in the British sphere of influence.[22] On July 1 of that year, a civil government was established in the country. The League of Nations, on July 24,

1922, approved the final draft of the Palestine mandate and incorporated the Balfour Declaration into the document. It charged the mandatory power with "placing the country under such political, administrative and economic conditions as will secure the establishment of the Jewish National Home."[23]

But the promise given to the Jews in the Balfour Declaration which was originally understood to cover all historic Palestine—on both sides of the Jordan River—was successively whittled down by the British. They created in 1921-1923 the Aemirate of Transjordan, four-fifths of the territory of Palestine assigned by the mandate, in order to accommodate a loyal ally, Abdullah, and thereby fulfill the wartime pledge to his father, Hussein, recognizing the area as Arab and independent.

An Arab–Jewish Dialogue That Failed, 1918–1920

The conclusion of the First World War signaled a brighter era for self-determination of nations, peace, and prosperity in the Middle East. The prospects for mutual recognition of the aspirations of both Arab nationalism and Zionism were forecast by the leaders of these two liberation movements. On March 23, 1918, Sherif Hussein, the exponent of Pan-Arabism (the idea of uniting all Arabic-speaking peoples, Moslems and Christians alike, under one flag), wrote in the daily paper of Mecca, *Al-Qibla*, "We saw the Jews . . . streaming to Palestine from Russia, Germany, Austria, Spain, America. . . . The cause of causes could not escape those who had the gift of deeper insight: They knew that the country was for its original sons, for all their differences, a sacred and beloved homeland."

Stronger support of the Arab nationalist movement for Zionism came on January 3, 1919, when Emir Feisal, son of Sherif Hussein, acting on behalf of the Arab kingdom of Hedjaj, signed a formal agreement with Dr. Chaim Weizmann, president of the World Zionist Organization, which called for "all necessary measures . . . to encourage and stimulate immigration of Jews into Palestine on a large scale, and . . . to settle Jewish immigrants upon the soil." The preamble of the agreement stated,

mindful of the racial kinship and ancient bonds existing between the

Arabs and the Jewish people, and realizing that the surest means of working out the consummation of their national aspirations is through the closest possible collaboration in the development of the Arab state and Palestine, and being desirous further of confirming the good understanding which exists between them, [we] have agreed upon the following . . . .[24]

Feisal's stand was reaffirmed in his subsequent correspondence with Felix Frankfurter, a prominent American Zionist, with the hope of obtaining the assistance of influential world Jewry in achieving the goals of the Arab movement for sovereign independence. On March 3, 1919, he wrote,

We Arabs, especially the educated among us, look with deepest sympathy on the Zionist movement. . . . We will wish the Jews a hearty welcome home. . . . We are working together for a reformed and revised Near East, and our two movements complement one another. The movement is national and not imperialistic. There is room in Syria for us both. Indeed, I think that neither can be a success without the other.[25]

These communications obviously asserted that the Arabs looked upon the Zionists and their envisaged state as a potential ally. Following this signal, the Palestinian Arabs were at first friendly to the idea of a Jewish "national home." Their initial reaction, therefore, was not marked by violence, as most of them showed a lack of political sophistication and expressed little interest in obtaining much more in the way of home rule or exclusive tenure than they had enjoyed under the Turkish regime. The Zionist leaders consistently assured them that their interests would be safeguarded. As Weizmann put it, "cooperation and friendly work with the Arab people must be the cornerstone of all our Zionist activities in the land of Israel."[26]

But these early hopes were shattered by two events. First, the Pan-Arab kingdom, in whose name Feisal spoke, never came into being. Therefore, those Arab leaders who were willing to recognize a Jewish state in Palestine could not implement the Feisal-Weizmann agreement. Second, and perhaps more important, the Palestinian Arabs turned all their efforts against the fulfillment of the Zionist vision. This occurred when an extremist minority faction of Palestinian Arabs assumed control over their own people and introduced terrorism as a way of achieving specific political aims: First, to reduce, if not eliminate, Jewish presence in Palestine and to frustrate Zionist designs to establish a distinct state there; second, to reject any efforts of Jewish-Arab coexistence and cooperation; third, to persuade or force the mandatory power to relinquish its policy as expressed in the Balfour Declaration; and, finally, to achieve national independence in Palestine under Arab control.

These goals were set up at the All-Arab Palestine Conference which met in Jerusalem in January 1919.[27] Palestinian Arabs, jointly with their supporters in the General Syrian Congress, declared on the following June, "We reject the claims of the Zionists for the establishment of a Jewish commonwealth in that part of southern Syria which is known as Palestine, and we are opposed to Jewish immigration into any part of the country. We do not acknowledge that they have a title, and we regard their claims as a grave menace to our national, political and economic life."[28] Similar aims and demands were reiterated by the Third Palestine Arab Congress, meeting in Haifa in December 1920, and by subsequent gatherings during the mandatory period.[29]

Leading and inspiring these ultranationalists was Hajj (Muhammed) Amin Al-Husseini, then president of the Supreme Moslem Council which had managed Moslem affairs in Palestine.[30] The grand mufti of Jerusalem had assembled a personal countrywide religious-political machine and thereby also presided over the Arab Higher Committee (formerly the Supreme Arab Committee) charged with the coordination of the work of Arab nationalists. He and other members of the prominent Husseini family were the only Arab personalities in British Palestine with whom the Zionist leaders did not meet to discuss a basis for mutual understanding, for they bitterly disavowed any proposals that did not entail the total abandonment of Zionist principles. Their constant incitements to violence against the Jewish community in Palestine resulted in the waves of Arab terrorism of the 1920s and 1930s.

The First Wave of Arab Terrorism, 1920–1921

The first wave of Arab terrorism in Palestine was sparked spontaneously. Arab rioters attacked isolated Jewish settlements in Upper Galilee early in 1920. Two villages, Metulla and Tel Hai, succumbed to the overwhelming mob and had to be abandoned. The heroic death of Joseph Trumpeldor, the defender of Tel Hai, and his comrades became a symbol of dedication and sacrifice for future generations of Jews.

Palestinian Arab hostility against Jews spread to Jerusalem, the City of Peace. There, on April 20, thousands of Arab pilgrims who had arrived for the Moslem festival of Nebi Musa were roused to join in an anti-British political demonstration. Soon the march turned into an outburst of anti-Jewish frenzy. Leaders and provocateurs shouted insults against their neighbors (*el Yahood calabana*— "The Jew is our dog") and incited the mob to attack their enemy (*Itbah el Yahood*—"Kill the Jew"). Thereupon, the marchers became an explosive force and went after the "children of doom" with sticks and knives. The Arab police, which was under British control, did not make any attempt to stop the violence and, in some cases, even joined their coreligionists in the wild rioting and plunder.

These disorders claimed the lives of 5 Jews and injured 211 others. Also 4 Arabs died in the incident. British troops who arrived on the scene arrested several hundred Arabs for the night. The following morning, disturbances broke out again when the detainees were released. Order was finally restored several days later, but not before the government was forced to disarm the Arab police, to proclaim martial law, and to ask British troops to assume full control.[31]

The military governor of Jerusalem dismissed the Arab mayor of the city, Mussa Kazim Al-Husseini, for inciting the anti-Jewish rioters. Soon afterward, Al-Husseini was elected as president of the Arab Executive Committee, the leading Palestinian Arab umbrella-organization representing local political parties, which would not cooperate with the British authorities and refused to negotiate with the Jews.

Another member of the prominent Husseini family, Hajj (Muhammed) Amin, at that time the president of the Arab Club in Jerusalem (the organization that supported an all-Syrian unity), was sentenced by a British military court to fifteen years' imprisonment in absentia for his more direct responsibility for the 1920 disturbances. Bowing to Arab pressure, the British allowed him to return to Palestine from his Transjordanian refuge.

To be sure, the authorities in Jerusalem set the tone for an "evenhanded" policy. Thus, Zeev (Vladimir) Jabotinsky, a Zionist leader and one of the commanders of the Jewish Legion of the First World War, was sentenced by the British for fifteen years' imprisonment for his part in organizing the defense of the Jewish quarter of Jerusalem during the 1920 riots. But his sentence was commuted afterward because of strong Jewish protests.

But these developments only tended to bolster the Yishuv's determination that, in order to defend Jewish life, property, and honor, it must rely on Jewish protection. The Haganah (defense), the citizen-soldier militia organization, was thus established in the wake of the 1920 riots. Formed by members of the earlier defense group, Hashomer, and veterans of the Jewish Legion of the First World War, it was soon to face its first test.[32]

On May Day of the following year, an Arab mob took advantage of a clash in the Jewish sector of Jaffa between a government-authorized Jewish labor organization's procession and a counter-parade by illegal Jewish Communists, and unexpectedly attacked both groups. This was followed with the massacre of thirteen Jews by a berserk crowd in the Immigration House in Jaffa. On the outskirts of the city, Joseph Chaim Brenner, a leading Hebrew writer, was murdered, along with the family with whom he was visiting at the time.

A series of reprisals by Haganah members followed in the Jaffa area. A number of people were killed, and many were wounded on both sides. Subsequently, violence spread to other regions in the country. Armed Arabs attacked and looted several settlements. The most serious onslaught befell Petach Tikvah, the oldest Jewish agricultural colony, which traditionally enjoyed good relations with its neighbors. The settlement was able to hold its own against some two thousand attackers until it was saved by an Indian cavalry squadron which happened to be passing by. Another Arab attack on Petach Tikvah was checked by a squadron of British planes and then dispersed by an Indian military unit. Some fifty Arabs and four Jews died in this particular incident.[33]

The Haycraft Commission, sent to Palestine to investigate the causes of the 1920-1921 disturbances, reported "that racial strife was begun by Arabs who were generally the aggressors; that the outbreak was unpremeditated and unexpected; that the general body of Jews was anti-Bolshevist; that the fundamental cause of the riots was a feeling amongst the Arabs of discontent with, and hostility to, the Jews, due to political and economic causes, and connected with Jewish immigration, and with their conception of Zionist policy as derived from Jewish exponents."[34]

Arab Agitation and the Second Outburst of Violence, 1922-1929

In reaction to the 1920-1921 wave of terrorism and the Haycraft report, the mandatory government in Jerusalem sought to appease the Arab nationalists. When they refused to accept the establishment of a legislative council in Palestine, which would have provided a considerable measure of self-government, because it would have meant cooperation with the Jewish community, the mandatory administration formed, in January 1922, the Supreme Moslem Council to administer the affairs of the Moselm community in the country. Hajj Amin Al-Husseini, who, a year earlier, had been appointed the mufti of Jerusalem (religious official who issues rulings in general in response to questions) by Sir Herbert Samuel, the first high commissioner of the civilian administration in Palestine, was elected president. Although Al-Husseini had promised to exercise his great spiritual and social influence to assure peace in Jerusalem, the council soon became the mufti's powerful instrument to fight Arab political opponents, Zionism, and the mandate's policy regarding the establishment of a Jewish "national home" in Palestine.

Several months later, Sir Herbert Samuel announced at a gathering of Arab leaders at Ramleh that Jewish immigration would be reduced. This declaration was formalized with the publication of the British White Paper of June 3, 1922, which proposed establishing a quota on such immigration, to be determined by the economic absorptive capacity of the country.[35] However, the Arab nationalists were not completely satisfied with the document because it did not put an end to the development of the Jewish "national home" in Palestine as envisaged in the Balfour Declaration.

In the following year, the British banned the Haganah as an illegal organization. It went underground and prepared itself to defend the Yishuv in the face of continued Arab agitation reinforced by rising nationalism. But, in the absence of any representative institution in Palestine, resulting directly from Arab objections, the mandatory government permitted the establishment in 1926 of the Va'ad Le'vini (National Council), to serve as a sort of "cabinet" for the Jewish community in the country.

Fortunately, the years 1922-1928 passed without any serious outburst of violence. The Jewish immigration in the country almost doubled, and, when an economic crisis developed in Palestine in 1926-1927, Arab nationalists expected that the Zionist effort to establish a Jewish entity would collapse from within. But the economic conditions improved, and the British strengthened the Palestinian Zionists by recognizing the Jewish Agency as a world Jewish body to advise and cooperate with the mandatory government on matters concerning the "national home." [36] These developments, coupled with an increase in the ferocity of the Arab extremists, suddenly changed the relative peace in the country.

It all began as a consequence of tensions connected with the dispute concerning the Wailing Wall (or Western Wall).[37] The mufti, who fostered the Islamic character of Jerusalem, injected a religious character into his struggle with Zionism when, in 1928, he challenged the right of Jews to bring prayer appurtenances to the Wall in the Old City of Jerusalem, the most sacred site in Judaism. Jews, on the other hand, disputed the right of the Moslem Waqf (the Moslem religious foundation) to build on that part of Haram al-Sharif (the Temple Mount, with the mosques, holy to Islam, of al-Aksa and the Dome of the Rock) immediately overlooking the Wall. A British White Paper was issued in November that favored the Arab position.

On August 23, 1929, Jews obtained permission for and carried out an orderly demonstration to protest this concession and to reaffirm Jewish rights at the Wall. The Arab leadership in the city then incited mobs to participate in a countermarch. Aroused by inflammatory speeches, the protesters burned petitions placed by Jewish worshipers in Wailing Wall services.

Rumors that Jews were planning to appropriate the Haram al-Sharif and to burn down the holy mosques situated there brought to the Old City thousands of Arabs ready to protect their sacred sites. The following day, on the Jewish Sabbath, the mob attacked throughout Jerusalem, including the Mea Shearim quarter inhabited mainly by Orthodox Jews. The Arab police in the city were ineffective, and the British forces were delayed in providing assistance; as a result, the Jewish community suffered badly.

Violence spread to the outlying vicinities of the city, to the Jewish agricultural colonies of Artuf and Motzah. In the latter community, an entire family was slaughtered. Settlements in the southern district of the country, Hulda and Beer Tuvia, were also assaulted. But, in these colonies, the Haganah was able to hold the Arabs at bay.

The most brutal attack that Sabbath day was aimed at the religious center of Hebron, which consisted mostly of older people supported by charitable contributions from abroad and a group of young talmudic academy students. Almost the entire community was wiped out in a terrible ordeal: more than sixty Jews were killed and over fifty wounded, including women and children; the synagogue was profaned; the Jewish clinic (which had provided treatment for both Arabs and Jews) was ransacked; and other Jewish property was destroyed.

On August 28, 1929, another devastating pogrom-type operation took place at Safed, also an old center of Jewish piety. Here, too, the toll was high: 45 Jews were killed or wounded, houses of worship and learning were desecrated, and homes were pillaged and burned. In less than one week, a total of 133 Jews had died, and 339 others had been injured in Jerusalem, Heborn, and Safed. In other mixed cities, such as Gaza, Jenin, Nablus, and Tulkaram, the Arabs expelled their Jewish neighbors from their midst. In different parts of the country, Jews were forced to abandon a total of eleven communities. By the time order was restored, 116 Arabs had also been killed and another 232 wounded.[38]

In the wake of this wave of terrorism, the British government established, in the fall of 1929, a commission headed by Sir Walter Shaw to investigate the reasons for the distrubances. Its report blamed the Arabs for the outbreak of violence, but emphasized their fear of, and opposition to, the continuing development of the Jewish "national home." It recommended, therefore, that Zionist immigration to Palestine should be more tightly controlled.[39]

Sporadic Arab Terrorism, 1930–1936

The years 1930–1936 witnessed a third wave of intermittent

Arab-initiated disturbances and violence. These events unfolded in the wake of an increased Jewish immigration into Palestine, many having left Germany under the impact of Nazi repression and Polish anti-Semitism.

Al-Husseini, who became the most important leader of the Palestinian Arabs after the 1929 riots, increased, with the backing of the extreme political faction of the Supreme Moslem Council, his pressure on the mandatory government to stop the flow of Jewish immigrants. Mobilizing support from coreligionists outside Palestine, delegates from some twenty-two countries met at a Moslem Congress in Jerusalem in December 1931 and warned against the dangers of Zionism. Similarly, the Arab Executive Committee, representing local nationalist parties, in its manifesto of March 1933 asserted that the Zionists had designs to take possession of the country, with the active support of the British, and urged the Arabs to sacrifice themselves in the battle with the "enemy."

This call struck a responsive cord, and the Arabs launched a campaign of violence against the mandatory government. The general strike of October protesting the accelerated Jewish immigration led to anti-British riots in Jaffa, Haifa, and Jerusalem. It resulted in the deaths of twenty-six Arabs and one policeman. The following year, an Arab terror group began to operate against the authorities, but the British forces killed and captured all of its members. Throughout this period, there also had been a number of assassinations of Jews, attacks on Jewish farms, acts of vandalism against orchards and crops, and deliberate maiming of Jewish cattle.[40]

The dramatic events of the 1929 terror and its aftermath shocked the Yishuv. In fact, it rather expected that the national aspirations of the Arabs would be satisfied by the creation of Jordan and the establishment of other new Arab states and, therefore, that they would not object to the establishment of a single Jewish state in the area. After all, the Zionists rationalized, the Arabs had neither a legal nor a moral title to *Eretz Yisrael*. Such a claim, they asserted, was refuted by the fact that the Arab population of Palestine was of a mixed race and did not constitute a distinct "people," and by the failure of the Palestinian Arabs throughout history to fight for independence rather than surrender the land to successive conquerors.

The official Jewish leaders therefore attempted to reach agreements with the more moderate Arab personalities. For example, David Ben-Gurion and Moshe Sharett, representing the Yishuv, met with Musa Alami, a prominent Palestinian spokesman, and agreed that there should be further discussion between the two communities regarding the establishment of a Jewish entity, on both sides of the Jordan River, connected to an Arab federation in the neighboring countries. Ben-Gurion and Musa Alami again met several times in the following year to continue their talks.

Also, unofficial Jewish leaders had attempted to improve relationships with the Palestinian Arabs. The best-known group was Brith Shalom (Covenant of Peace) led by Judah Magnes, then president of Hebrew University and included in a group of noted Jewish scholars of Jerusalem. Founded in 1925, this organization aimed at the establishment of a biracial commonwealth in Palestine, in which both Arabs and Jews would enjoy equal rights without regard to the demographic differences between majority and minority. In the meantime, it promoted active, intellectual and social cooperation between Arabs and Jews in Palestine. It was also instrumental in bringing Jewish and Arab political leaders together on several occasions. An example is the July 18, 1934, meeting between Ben-Gurion and Magnes and the leader of the Istiglal (Arab nationalist party) in Palestine, Abdul Hadi. The latter stated that if the Arabs became united with the aid of the Jews, they would then agree to accept even five to six million Jews in Palestine.

But these contacts consistently failed. Arab apprehension in Palestine was converted into hostility by the more extreme Palestinian leadership orchestrated by the mufti and his followers.

The Arab Revolt, 1936-1939

Encouraged by the failure of the mandatory authority to exercise its police power or moral suasion effectively, particularly when Jewish interests were at stake, and by the inability of the League of Nations to check the aggression of Italian fascism and German nazism (the latter of which had dedicated itself to the "final solution" of the Jewish problem), the militant Arab leadership decided to rise up in open revolt against both the British administration and the Jewish community.

To be sure, two immediate events precipitated the most intensive wave of Arab violence in the pre-1948 period. First, the Arab Higher Committee, the all-embracing body representing the Arab parties in Palestine, was formed in April 1936 under the chairmanship of Hajj Amin Al-Husseini, the mufti of Jerusalem. Despite some internal disagreements, this political machinery enabled the militant nationalists to command greater obedience from the population, and to direct the revolt without challenge from any other Arab leader. Second, the mufti realized that, with the growth of the Jewish population in the country and the determination of the Yishuv to strongly resist Arab violence, terrorism must become a new type of warfare in the form of organized and efficient bands of fighters replacing mob outbursts. Thus, after Al-Husseini set up his storm troops in Green Shirt semimilitary units, the ground for the insurrection was prepared.[41]

The terrifying bloodbath of the rebellion began on April 15, when a mufti group held up ten cars on the Tel Aviv–Haifa highway, singled out three Jews, put them in a truck, and shot them to death. Four days later, an Arab attack in Jaffa resulted in three Jewish fatalities. On April 25, the Arab Higher Committee organized a general strike in the country until their demands for a fundamental change in British policy in Palestine were to be fully met. This strike was accompanied by violence. Jews were assaulted and stoned in various cities. In rural areas, Arab farmers attacked Jewish settlements and the British police. These activities were supplemented by guerrilla warfare carried out by organized Arab units from the hills.

Open support for Palestinian terrorism came almost immediately from the neighboring Arab countries. Their officials justified the bloodshed on the grounds that the Arabs had lost faith in the value of British "pledges and assurances for the future." They also protested the mandatory government's use of force against the Palestinian Arabs. This political support was supplemented by the training of local bands by outside guerrillas, such as Syria's Fawzi al-Qawugji, who also joined the Palestinians in fighting. In fact, the local Arabs were reinforced by volunteers from Lebanon, Syria, and Transjordan. As a result of this escalation, sabotage and murder increased. Roads were mined, railways were damaged, and the oil pipeline between Iraq and Haifa was broken.

This stage of the Arab insurrection came to an end by October, some six months after the outbreak of the revolt, as a result of the intervention of some of the Arab countries. That is, Iraq, Saudi Arabia, Transjordan, and Yemen requested (at Britain's invitation and after a prearranged agreement with her) the Palestinian Arabs to stop the bloodshed, and the violence was halted but only after it had claimed the lives of some eighty Jews and injured some four hundred others.

To investigate these events, the London government established the Palestine Royal Commission headed by Lord Peel. Its report, published in July 1937, declared the Mandate unworkable, and the British pledges to both parties mutually irreconcilable: "To put it in one sentence, we cannot—in Palestine as it now is—both concede the Arab claim to self-government and secure the establishment of the Jewish National Home."[42] The commission therefore recommended the partition of Palestine into a Jewish state and an Arab state that would be united with Transjordan as the best possible solution to the problem. Although this proposal did not meet with full Jewish expectations, the Zionist Congress, meeting in August, decided to enter into negotiations with the British government for the creation of a distinct Jewish entity in Palestine as a decisive step in fulfilling Zionist aims.

On the Arab side, Transjordan's Emir Abdullah favored the partition proposal, hoping to incorporate the Arab portion into his kingdom. Abdullah's supporters among the Palestinian Arabs, such as Rayheb Al-Nashashifi, were inclined to accept this plan, but the strong opposition of the extreme nationalists, led by the mufti of Jerusalem, and the initiation of an internal bloodbath against the Arab moderates, coupled with the resumption of the insurrection with greater vigor, finally shelved the Peel proposal. When the British district commissioner in the Galilee was murdered, the mandatory authorities retaliated by outlawing the Arab Higher Committee on October 1, 1937, for its role in the rebellion. Five of the most important members of the committee were arrested and deported to the Seychelles islands in the Indian Ocean.

The mufti of Jerusalem, who was dismissed by the mandatory authorities from his position as president of the Supreme Moslem Council—which was disbanded—fled the country to Lebanon and then took up residence in Syria. From his exile, Hajj Amin continued to direct the rebellion in Palestine, and his followers resumed operations on a large scale.

Attacks against individual Jews and Jewish settlements were stepped up. A case in point is the October 4, 1938, Tiberias Massacre. Two large Arab units attacked the city of Tiberias for several hours before government troops drove them away. The shooting, stabbing, and burning left nineteen Jews dead and three wounded, including women and children. Violence was also directed at British police stations, as well as at Arab towns where local residents opposed the militant Arab nationalism. But, with the intensification of British military action, coupled with the support provided by the indigenous Arab peace bands established by the authorities to fight the guerrillas, the revolt began to decline in momentum by the spring of 1939.

Meanwhile, in another effort to resolve the Palestine problem, the British government invited the representatives of the Arab and Jewish communities and also, for the first time, delegates of the Arab states to the St. James Round Table Conference held in London in February 1939. Since the Arabs refused to sit down with the Jews at the same table, the British had to meet separately with them and with the Jewish delegation. When the conference ended in a complete deadlock, the mandatory government reverted to ruling Palestine by decree.

Then, on May 17, Malcolm MacDonald, the colonial secretary, published a White Paper enunciating a new policy whereby existing rights of Jews to immigration and land purchases were curtailed and the Balfour Declaration's goals were deferred. It also announced a plan for an independent Palestine in ten years, which would relegate Jews to a permanent minority status.

The White Paper further established that Jewish immigration would be limited to a total of seventy-five thousand during the next five years and that additional Jewish immigration into Palestine would depend on Arab consent. Finally, the document determined that transfer of Arab-owned land to Jewish ownership would be regulated by an interim government.[43]

London's anti-Zionist policy, military realities, the severe economic damage suffered by the Arabs, and a joint appeal by pro-British leaders of the neighboring countries finally convinced the

Arab Higher Committee to end the revolt and urge quiet. The British agreed to permit the guerrillas to escape and made no attempt to disarm the bands. The general strike was called off, and the organized violence ceased, although sniping and other individual attacks still occurred.

By the time World War II broke out in September 1939, the Arab revolt had been virtually suppressed. The toll was frightening: 517 Jews, 3,112 Arabs, and 135 Britons dead; 2,500 Jews, 1,775 Arabs, and 386 Britons injured.[44]

The Jewish Response to the Arab Revolt, 1936-1939

The Jewish losses from the Arab revolt would have been much greater had it not been for the defense efforts of the Yishuv, with some support given by the British authorities, against whom the Arabs also directed their attack. The Jewish Agency, representing the Yishuv, adopted a twofold policy: *havlagah* ("self-restraint") and *haganah* ("self-defense"). This meant a deliberate decision of the Jewish community not to meet Arab terrorism with counter-terrorism, but to take appropriate defensive measures.

More specifically, the Haganah, which was closely linked to the Histadrut (General Federation of Jewish Labor in Palestine), bore the main responsibility for the implementation of this policy.[45] It fortified Jewish villages with barbed-wire fences, redoubts, and searchlights; provided settlements and towns with fighting men; established dozens of stockades and watchtower outposts in areas where no Jewish settlements had previously existed; made available armed escorts to protect vehicles and convoys; constructed new roads to enable greater safety of communications; and gradually organized operations against terrorist bands and their bases.

The mandatory government, in cooperation with the Jewish Agency, formed an auxiliary police known as Ghafirs, or Notrim (Guards), often serving as a cover for the Haganah underground in communications, arms procurement, equipment transportation, and training. These units guarded railways, airfields, and government offices. Protecting villages against incursions by Arab bands was the responsibility of the Jewish Settlement Police, set up by the authorities, and of the Haganah's *peluggot sadeh* ("field companies"). Finally, Special Night Squads, consisting of regular British forces and Haganah members and commanded by Captain Orde Wingate, undertook guerrilla-type operations against the terrorists. Throughout the period of the Arab revolt, the Haganah continued to strengthen its underground forces. It purchased weapons inside and outside the country, developed its own arms industry, and trained its increasing membership. The cost of these activities, and the security expenses in general, were met by *Kofer ha-Yishuv*, a voluntary tax which the Jewish community in Palestine imposed upon itself.

Simultaneously with such defense efforts, Jewish leaders, both official and unofficial, tried to improve relations with the Arab Palestinian community. These attempts were mostly initiated by a few social, business, and labor groups. Several clubs to cultivate closer social relations were sponsored by the League for Arab-Jewish Relations. There were also sporadic instances of Arab-Jewish cooperation by the business leadership of both communities. The Arab chairman of the Nablus Chamber of Commerce participated in a Jewish Nutrition Conference in Tel Aviv, and a number of joint meetings of Arab and Jewish orange growers were held. Histadrut, then an all-Jewish labor organization, launched a parallel Arab labor union, and the two groups cooperated in organizing joint strikes around the country and in initiating joint cooperatives. However, these efforts proved abortive because radical Arab nationalists discouraged and eventually, through intimidation and terror, stopped any contact with Jews. One newspaper correspondent concluded, "Extremist Arab followers of the Mufti . . . are rapidly achieving their aims by eliminating political opponents in Palestine who are inclined toward moderation."[46]

The Jewish leadership also attempted to persuade moderate Arabs from the neighboring countries to begin a dialogue among them regarding the possibility of a peaceful resolution of the opposing nationalistic aims. Thus, Ben-Gurion and Magnes met with George Antonius, a Christian Arab historian and theoretician of the nationalist movement. Eliahu Elath, a representative of the Jewish Agency, held meetings with Faud Bey Hamaz, the foreign minister of Saudi Arabia; Chaim Weizmann saw Dr. Shabander, an adviser to Syria's president; and Magnes met Iraq's Nuri Pasha.

As these contacts also proved fruitless and the Arab revolt in Palestine continued with greater vigor, the Haganah's policy of self-restraint and defense had its critics, particularly among more militant members who owed allegiance to the Revisionists, the extreme nationalist wing of the Zionist movement.[47] Revising an earlier split, they seceded from the Haganah in 1937 and formed the *Irgun Zevai Le'umi* ("National Military Organization") or, in its abbreviated form, Etzel (I.Z.L.), led by David Raziel.[48] It not only advocated a strong defense posture but also insisted on retaliation against Arab terrorists and, at times, even against innocent Arabs. Thus, Etzel bombed Arab marketplaces, cafes, and buses throughout the country, killing scores and wounding hundreds of people. The British response to this wave of violence was severe. For example, in the summer of 1938, the authorities hanged an Etzel member who was captured in an abortive attack on an Arab bus in Galilee.[49]

Despite the activities of Etzel and the constant Arab provocations, the Yishuv's policy of *havlagah* prevailed. But a more militant attitude, particularly toward the British, developed within the Jewish community with the publication of the pro-Arab White Paper of May 1939. The Yishuv denounced this document as not in accord with the Balfour Declaration and the British obligation under the League of Nations mandate. Ben-Gurion asserted at a meeting of the clandestine Haganah, "Until now, we have acted according to the spirit of the law. From now on some of our activities will be directed against the law and with the aim of making that law powerless."[50]

When the British foreign secretary announced an immediate suspension of Jewish immigration to Palestine for six months, beginning on October 1, 1939, Ben-Gurion declared, "The British closed legal entry to Palestine, so the Jews would force their way by the back door."[51]

To facilitate the organization and coordination of illegal immigration, also known as *Aliyah Bet* ("Class B Immigration"),[52] particularly in light of the worsening situation of the Jews in Europe, the Haganah set up a special underground body, the Mosad (the Institution). In addition, the Haganah formed a unit to carry out anti-British operations, including attacks on telephone lines, railroads, and other government property.

As might be expected, Etzel's response to the White Paper was more violent, and many of its activities were directed against the

British authorities. When it called off its operations upon the outbreak of the Second World War, a more extreme splinter wing formed, *Lohamei Herut Yisrael* ("Fighters for the Freedom of Israel") also known as Lehi and the Stern group (named after its first commander).[53] Interestingly, Lehi initially sought to cooperate with Britain's enemies, the Axis powers, in an effort to obtain from them a firm support for the creation of a Jewish state in Palestine.

The Second World War, Violence, and Repression, 1939–1945

Although Arab terrorism ended at the outbreak of the Second World War, the Jews of Palestine were alarmed by the growth of Transjordan's Arab Legion and Frontier Forces, officered and trained by the British, which were also stationed in camps west of the River Jordan. Despite this apprehension, the Yishuv's attention was turned to the struggle against nazism. Some 136,000 volunteers, almost the entire Jewish population between the ages of eighteen and fifty, registered for national service. Nearly 30,000 Palestinian Jews, including members of the Haganah, acting on its orders, joined military units within the framework of the British army, among them the Jewish Brigade. They were equipped and trained by the British and fought alongside the Allies throughout the war. Some of them were recruited for special missions against the advancing Germans in the Middle East in 1941-1942, and for guerrilla action in occupied Europe.

No similar war effort was contributed by the Palestinian Arabs. In fact, the mufti of Jerusalem had established a direct contact with Hitler in Germany and encouraged the faithful in Iraq to join Rashid Ali's pro-Nazi coup against the British in April 1941. In a Berlin broadcast, the mufti declared the following:

> Salaam Aleikum, children of Allah, Moslems of the World; this is your leader talking to you wherever you may be. This is Amin Al-Husseini, calling on you in the name of Allah, besides whom there is no God and Muhammad is his messenger, to take up arms in this Jihad [Holy War] against the infidel British who want to subdue all children of Allah and kill all his soldiers, and against the cunning Jews who desire to rob you

of your sanctuaries and rebuild their Temple on the ruins of our Mosque
of Omar in al-Quds. Children of Allah, this is a Holy War for the glory
and honor of Allah, the merciful and beneficent. If you die in this war,
you will sit in Heaven on the right side of the Prophet. Children of
Allah, I call on you to fight. Heil Hitler.[54]

Although the Iraqi revolt failed, the mufti continued his collaboration with Hitler in planning and executing the "final solution"
of Europe's Jewry. For instance, at a rally in Berlin in November
1943, Al-Husseini declared, "The Germans know how to get rid
of the Jews."

The impact of these activities is illustrated by the deep emo-
tional sympathy of the Arabs for Hitler. In the streets of Palestinian cities, Arab crowds saluted the fuehrer. Moreover, many
Moslems volunteered for Nazi units operating in occupied territories in Russia and Yugoslavia, and for the mufti's legion carrying
out sabotage activities in British Palestine. This wartime assistance
was provided by the mufti in return for Germany's assurances to
liquidate the foundation of the Jewish national home after victory.

Notwithstanding the Jewish and Arab contributions to the war
effort, throughout the period the mandatory government persisted
with its White Paper policy. When the British were about to deport
1,700 illegal immigrants aboard the ship *Patria* in November 1940,
the Haganah sabotaged its departure. The boat sank, and 250 Jews
were drowned in Haifa Bay.[55]

The authorities also continued the cordon-and-search tactic
against the Jewish underground movements. In October 1939,
forty-three Haganah members were arrested for carrying arms and
participating in a military training course. They were sentenced to
five years' imprisonment. In other instances, the British forces discovered hidden arms and ammunition in Jewish villages.[56]

These arms searches and arrests were suspended as the Italian
and German threat to the Middle East became more acute. Thus,
the Haganah cooperated with the British in the invasion of Vichy-
French Syria and Lebanon in 1941. Hundreds of the Haganah's
Palmach (Shock Troops)—permanently mobilized commando
units—were trained in guerrilla tactics by British officers in preparation for a resistance movement in case Palestine were to be occupied by enemy forces.

But, as soon as the war tide turned in favor of the Allies, relations between the Yishuv and the mandatory government deteriorated again. The authorities resumed their arms searches, staged political trials against Haganah members, and blocked attempts of illegal entry into Palestine. In February 1942, the *Struma*, carrying 169 Jewish refugees desiring to reach Palestine, was sunk in the Black Sea.[57]

In response to these events, an extraordinary conference of Zionist leaders from Palestine, the United States, and Europe was held at the Biltmore Hotel in New York. On May 11, 1942, the conference adopted the Biltmore Program demanding the opening of the gates of Palestine for Jewish immigrants and the establishment of the country as an independent Jewish commonwealth. This plan met with strong opposition, particularly from Etzel and Lehi. Supporting a more radical solution, they insisted on a Jewish state within the historical boundaries of the ancient Kingdom of Israel.

Meanwhile, acts of terrorism by Lehi continued intermittently throughout the war. For instance, in January 1942, there were a series of armed robberies and murders of senior British officers in the Tel Aviv area. A month later, Abraham Stern himself was killed. Attempts by members of the group to assassinate the inspector-general of the police and one of his assistants on April 22, as a reprisal, failed.[58]

Lehi did not hesitate to carry out its campaign against the British even outside Palestine. On November 6, 1944, two of its members assassinated Lord Moyne, British resident minister in Egypt, who was known for his anti-Zionist attitude. The assailants were arrested and, subsequently, tried and executed in Cairo on March 22, 1945.[59]

Etzel was also active during the last two years of the war in an attempt to force the British government to reverse its anti-Jewish policy. In 1944, for instance, there were attempted assassinations of British officials, murders of police and military personnel, and attacks on mandatory facilities as well as on police and military installations.[60]

This wave of Jewish violence was strongly condemned by the Yishuv leadership.[61] It called upon the dissident groups to put an end to terrorism, hoping that, with the end of the war approaching, the British would take on a more pro-Jewish disposition. But Etzel and Lehi rejected this request and continued with their violence against the British in the belief that, if they were to destroy British prestige in Palestine, "the removal of their rule would follow automatically."

The Haganah, wishing not to lose its respectability vis-à-vis the mandatory authorities, undertook some strong action against Jewish terrorists, including the surrender to the British police of a number of Etzel and Lehi members.

The mandatory government, on its part, resorted to repressive measures against all those suspected of belonging to Jewish terrorist groups. Thus, in October 1944, the authorities deported 251 suspects to a detention camp in Eritrea. Simultaneously with this response, London also adopted a pronounced pro-Arab policy toward the end of the war by encouraging the creation of the Arab League. It was formally established on March 22, 1945, in Cairo by Egypt, Iraq, Lebanon, Saudi Arabia, Syria, Transjordan, and Yemen. The Arab Higher Committee of Palestine was admitted as a permanent and voting member. The goal of the league became immediately apparent: an eventual unification of all Arab states, including independent Palestine.

The Postwar Disappointment and the Jewish Struggle Against the British, 1945-1947

After the Second World War ended in Europe and the calamity of the Holocaust became known, the Yishuv expected the British government in London to reopen the gates of Palestine to the Jewish survivors gathered in Displaced Persons Camps established by the Allies. But President Harry S. Truman's appeal to London to permit one hundred thousand Jews to immigrate to Palestine was not heeded. The newly elected government, whose leaders, Prime Minister Clement Attlee and Foreign Minister Ernest Bevin, had promised their support for Jewish aspirations before coming into office, stood firmly by the pre-war White Paper restricting Jewish immigration and, in effect, opposing the establishment of a Jewish state in Palestine.

The Yishuv's response was swift. The Mosad, the Haganah's clandestine organization for illegal immigration from Europe, jointly with the Brihah (Flight), another body set up for the purpose of assisting displaced Jews to settle in Palestine, intensified their activities. A few boats with illegal immigrants began to arrive, but most were intercepted by the British navy, and their passengers were interned.

These developments resulted in a unique display of the Yishuv's unity. The three underground organizations—the Haganah (headed by Moshe Sueh), the Etzel (commanded by Menachem Begin), and Lehi (led by Nathan Friedman-Yellin)—decided, in spite of ideological differences between them, to cooperate in a newly formed Jewish Resistance movement. The Haganah contributed to the movement a static force of some forty thousand, consisting of settlers and townfolk; approximately sixteen thousand people attached to a "field army," based on the Jewish Settlement Police; and the Palmach units with a membership of two to six thousand, including reserves. The contributions by the other paramilitary organizations were far smaller. Etzel had a force estimated at between three and five thousand, and Lehi consisted of between two and three hundred members.[62]

Determined to engage in sabotage activities against the mandatory government in order to influence London to change its policy, each of the component units of the movement, under a common authority, carried out separate, specific operations.[63] Thus, the first operation of the movement took place on October 10, 1945, when a Palmach unit breached the walls of the fortified Athlit internment camp and freed 208 illegal immigrants who were held there. On November 1, the Haganah launched a major attack on the Palestine railway system at 153 different points, completely disrupting it. Several coastal patrol boats at Haifa and Jaffa were destroyed. Etzel caused heavy damage to the Lydda station, and the Haifa refineries were sabotaged by Lehi.[64]

On the following day, Kol Israel (Voice of Israel), the underground broadcasting station of the resistance movement, called these activities "an expression of our strength and decision." It also declared: "We lament the British, Arab and Jewish victims who fell in the attack on the railways and ports of Palestine. They are all victims of the White Paper."

A second "warning" to the British government of the consequences that would follow if it did not modify the Palestine policy was given by the Jewish Resistance movement in subsequent months.[65] In a series of operations in February 1946, attacks were directed at police posts, coastguard stations, radar installations, and airfields.[66] Describing these events, Kol Israel in its March 3 broadcast said,

> This last fortnight has seen a renewed intensity in the struggle of the Jewish people against the forces which aim to throttle them and their national aspirations for normal nation-hood in their National Home.
>
> The attack on the Radar Station on Mount Carmel was aimed at destroying one of the principle agents of the Government in its hunt for Jewish refugees. The sabotage of the airfields was the sabotage of a weapon which has been degraded from its glorious fight against the evil forces of Nazism to the dishonorable task of fighting against the victims of Nazism.
>
> Those three attacks are symptomatic of our struggle. In all cases the onslaught was made against the weapon used by the White Paper in its despicable battle to repudiate its undertaking to the Jewish people and the world, and not against the men who use this weapon. It is not our object to cause the loss of life of any Briton in this country; we have nothing against them because we realize that they are but instruments of a policy, and in many cases unwilling instruments.[67]

When London rejected a recommendation for the speedy admission of a hundred thousand Jewish refugees into Palestine, this time offered in the report of the Anglo-American Commission of May 1, 1946,[68] Kol Israel made the following broadcast:

> The Jewish Resistance Movement thinks it desirable to publish the warning it intends to lay before His Majesty's Government. Present British policy is executing a dangerous maneuver and is based on an erroneous assumption: Britain, in evacuating Syria, Lebanon and Egypt intends to concentrate her military bases in Palestine and is therefore concerned to strengthen her hold over the mandate; and is using her responsibility to the Jewish people merely as a means to that end. But this double game won't work. Britain cannot hold both ends of the rope; she cannot exploit the tragic Jewish question for her own benefit as mandatory power, while attempting to wriggle out of the various responsibilities which that mandate confers. From the Zionist point of view, the tepid conclusions of the Commission bear no relation to the political claims of the Jewish people, but even so, in the execution of these pro-

posals, the British Government is displaying a vacillation at once disappointing and discreditable. We would therefore warn publicly His Majesty's Government that if it does not fulfill its responsibilities under the mandate—above all with regard to the question of immigration—the Jewish people will feel obliged to lay before the nations of the world the request that the British leave Palestine. The Jewish Resistance Movement will make every effort to hinder the transfer of British bases to Palestine and to prevent their establishment in the country.

In an attempt to disturb British communications, the Haganah, on the night of June 16, blew up roads and bridges linking Palestine with the neighboring countries.[69] Two days later, five British officers were kidnapped from a military club in Tel Aviv.[70] On June 23, Kol Israel announced that three of the officers would be kept as hostages for two Etzel members who were under sentence of death. Subsequently, the British high commissioner granted an amnesty to the two resistance members.[71]

In light of these events, the mandatory government decided to take firm steps against the Yishuv's leadership.[72] On June 29, also known by the Jewish population as "Black Saturday," the authorities arrested many Jewish leaders and conducted searches for arms caches in dozens of settlements. In the following days, thousands of suspected Palmach members were interned, and the British continued with their searches for weapons throughout the country.[73] Also, in a stiffening shift of its policy, London determined to intern all apprehended illegal immigrants in refugee camps in Cyprus rather than in Palestine as it had been done previously.[74]

But the unity of the Jewish Resistance movement collapsed on July 22, 1946. In one of the most dramatic actions of that year, Etzel blew up one wing of the King David Hotel in Jerusalem, the wing that contained the British military headquarters in Palestine and all offices of the government secretariat except those of the high commissioner. The total casualties were ninety-one killed and forty-five injured, including soldiers and civilians (British, Arab, and Jewish). On the following day, the "Voice of Fighting Zion," Etzel's clandestine radio, declared that "the tragedy was not caused by Jewish soldiers, who carried out their duty courageously and with self-sacrifice, but by the British themselves, who disregarded a warning and refused to evacuate the building."[75]

This action was strongly denounced by the Jewish Agency. It

requested Etzel and Lehi to halt their terror activities against the British, but the dissident groups continued with their violence. They ambushed and killed British policemen and soldiers, attacked government installations and army camps, blew up railways, and mined roads. In a daring operation, they freed their comrades from the Acre fortress prison.[76] Etzel even extended its sabotage beyond Palestine. On October 1, 1946, the British embassy in Rome was badly damaged by bomb explosions.[77]

Realizing that it could not bring about the formation of a new, more-moderate Jewish leadership in Palestine, the mandatory government released many Jewish Agency and Haganah members. A new London-initiated proposal, the Morrison-Grady plan of July 1946 (named after Herbert Morrison, lord president of the Council, and Henry F. Grady, an American special envoy), would have divided Palestine into semiautonomous Jewish and Arab sectors with a central British authority retaining the supreme power for another four years. The proposal was rejected by both Jews and Arabs.

The United Nations Debate, 1947

Unable to find a satisfactory solution to the mounting violence in Palestine, and in the absence of any willingness on the part of the two Palestinian communities to accept various proposals for the future of the mandate,[78] Britain asked on April 2, 1947, for a special session of the United Nations General Assembly to consider the question of "constituting and instructing a special committee to prepare for consideration of the questions of Palestine."[79]

The Arab members of the United Nations objected to the terms of the British request because they implied recognition of Jewish claims, and the Arabs therefore demanded that the forthcoming meeting alternatively consider the questions of the termination of the mandate over Palestine and the declaration of independence.[80]

But, when the special session of the United Nations General Assembly convened on April 25, 1947,[81] the British item was placed on the agenda. The Assembly agreed to hear the cases of the Jewish Agency for Palestine, the Arab Higher Committee, and other interested nongovernmental parties.[82]

The Jewish representatives complained of the British restrictions on immigration to Palestine. The Arab delegates, on the other hand, stated that the Balfour Declaration had been made without consent or knowledge of the people most directly affected—the Arabs of Palestine. Subsequently, the special Assembly set up a United Nations Special Committee on Palestine (UNSCOP)[83] to prepare the Palestine item for consideration by the forthcoming regular Assembly. The Arab countries announced that they would boycott UNSCOP.

After intensive investigation of the various aspects of the problem, UNSCOP, on August 31, 1947, issued its report to the General Assembly.[84] It unanimously resolved that the mandate should be terminated. The majority recommended that Palestine should be divided into an Arab state and a Jewish state, with international status for Jerusalem, all of which should be linked in an economic union. They further recommended that the Arab and Jewish states should become independent after a transitional period of two years, beginning September 1, 1947, during which the United Kingdom would progressively transfer the administration of Palestine to the United Nations; that Jerusalem should be placed under an international trusteeship system with the United Nations as the administrating authority; and that provisions for preservation of, and free access to, the holy places would be contained in the constitutions of both the Arab and Jewish states. As a preferable alternative to the partition of Palestine, a minority recommendation proposed a single, independent federal state, comprising independent Arab and Jewish states, with Jerusalem as its capital.[85]

The Arab states and the Arab Higher Committee immediately rejected UNSCOP's recommendations. When Great Britain informed the regular session of the General Assembly on September 29, 1947, that it had decided to evacuate Palestine, the Arab Higher Committee proposed an alternative plan to the UNSCOP report, with these recommendations: an Arab state should be established in the whole of Palestine; this state would respect the rights and fundamental freedoms of all persons before the law; the Arab state would protect legitimate rights and interests of all minorities; and the Arab state would recognize freedom of worship and access to holy places, including Jerusalem.

But this proposal for the future constitutional organization of Palestine was not accepted by the United Nations or the Jewish party. Rather, the General Assembly in its November 29, 1947, session, adopted Resolution 181 (II) on the "Plan of Partition with Economic Union of Palestine," as recommended by UNSCOP.[86] It established the United Nations Palestine Commission to implement the resolution, and the Security Council was to assist in implementation, as well as to take additional measures, if necessary, to maintain peace in the area.

Although this recommendation fell short of the Balfour Declaration, which, according to the Jewish Agency, referred to the whole of Palestine, the Yishuv readily accepted the partition plan. The major reservation registered by the Agency stated that, since West Jerusalem was heavily populated by Jews, it should become the capital of the Jewish state and not be placed under an international administration as proposed by the resolution.

The Arab delegates at the United Nations asserted that they would oppose the implementation of the partition plan. Several weeks later, on December 14, 1947, the Arab League, at the conclusion of its Cairo conference, released letters sent to the United Nations, the United Kingdom, and the United States warning that the partitioning of Palestine would be considered a "hostile act towards 400 million Moslems." Britain, alone, capitulated to this pressure, declaring that it would not cooperate in the implementation of the United Nations resolution.

The Arab Armed Insurrection
and the Jewish Response, 1947–1948

Since the scene in Palestine from the end of the Second World War up to the United Nations vote of November 29, 1947, was dominated by British-Jewish confrontations,[87] a strange lull in relations between Arabs and Jews settled in during this period. But, as soon as news of the General Assembly's recommendation reached the country, a wave of Arab terrorism began, followed by an armed insurrection and culminating in a military invasion of the newly born State of Israel some six months later. Thus, on November 30, the morrow of the United Nations resolution, a bus was fired on by Arabs, and five Jews were killed. The Arabs proclaimed a general strike, and, on the next day, a mob of some two hundred youths broke their way into the Jewish commercial section of

Jerusalem, smashed windows, looted shops, set goods on fire, and stabbed a number of people.[88] Riots also took place in Haifa and the mixed quarter between Tel Aviv and Jaffa, and convoys were attacked in different parts of the country. Dozens of Jews lost their lives in these incidents.[89] On December 30, some two thousand Arab employees of the oil refineries in the Haifa-Acre area attacked their Jewish colleagues and massacred forty-one of them.[90]

The situation in the country approached administrative chaos and political anarchy. The British did not make any serious efforts to prevent the intensification of Arab terrorism. In mid-January 1948, an Arab bomb planted in a postal delivery truck exploded in the heart of the Jewish business center of Haifa, causing nearly fifty casualties.[91] Several days later, in the Hebron hills, a group of thirty-five men, composed almost entirely of Hebrew University students, was murdered to the last man, and their bodies were mutilated by their attackers.[92]

In addition to Palestinian Arab armed bands, led by local leaders such as Abd al-Qadir Al-Husseini and supported financially by the neighboring states, the Arab League also began recruiting volunteers for an "irregular" Arab force for the purpose of participating in the Palestine struggle. Hajj Amin Al-Husseini, the former mufti of Jerusalem who had escaped arrest after the Second World War and settled in Egypt, was particularly active as president of the Arab Higher Committee in this effort.

Early in 1948, the Arab Liberation Army or Army of Deliverance (*Jeish al-Ingadh*), commanded by Fawzi al-Qawugji who once before had headed volunteers to assist the guerrillas during the Arab revolt, sent some five thousand men, mostly Iraqis, Syrians, and Lebanese, into Palestine.[93] Only after the force had been entrenched in the country did an increasing number of Palestinian Arabs join in. The army used small units to attack specific targets, usually Jewish settlements or convoys moving between settlements in northern and central Palestine. Other volunteers were sent to the southern part of the country by Egypt's Moslem Brotherhood, an ultraconservative religious and political organization.

Jewish response to the wave of Arab terrorism and its escalation into an organized armed insurrection was swift. While the Haganah focused on defensive actions, Etzel and Lehi, which continued to operate independently, did not exclude strong retaliation. Thus, on December 11, 1947, six Arabs were killed and thirty wounded when bombs were thrown at Arab buses in Haifa; there were also many casualties in an attack on an Arab village near the city. Two days later, eighteen Arabs died and sixty were injured in several attacks in Jerusalem, Jaffa, and the Lydda area. Houses blown up in an Arab village near Safad on December 18 left ten people dead.[94]

In an attack on Balad-ei-Sheikh on the slopes of Mount Carmel on January 1, 1948, apparently in retaliation for the oil refinery massacre in the previous month, many Arab villagers were killed and wounded.[95] On the same day, ten Arabs were killed in a Jaffa cafe explosion.[96] During the same month, there were heavy Arab casualties in Etzel and Lehi attacks on the Arab National Committee in Jaffa, an Arab-owned semiramis in Jerusalem, and Arab crowds in various cities.[97]

As terrorism increased daily in the country, the United Nations Palestine Commission sent its First Special Report to the Security Council on February 16, 1948. It criticized "powerful Arab interests" in and out of Palestine for "a deliberate effort to alter [the Partition Plan] by force," and "certain elements of the Jewish community" for "irresponsible acts of violence which worsen the security situation." The commission called on the Security Council to establish "an adequate non-Palestinian force which will assist law-abiding elements in both Arab and Jewish communities." Without such a force, the report warned, there will be "uncontrolled, widespread strife and bloodshed" at the termination of the mandate. Finally, it also quoted official British figures on casualties in Palestine during the period November 30, 1947–February 1, 1948: 869 killed; including 427 Arabs, 381 Jews, 46 British, and 15 others.[98]

The Security Council, aware of the seriousness of the situation, had conducted a long series of debates on the question of maintaining peace in Palestine.[99] But during the same period, both sides continued with violence and counterviolence. Moreover, there was apparently some British involvement on the side of the Arabs. For instance, on February 1, the editorial offices of the *Palestine Post*, a Jewish-sponsored English newspaper in Jerusalem, was demolished by the explosion of a British armored car loaded with explosives and parked outside the building. Some twenty people were injured.[100] Similarly, on February 22, British armored cars parked near an apartment building on Ben Yehudah Street in the Jewish sector of Jerusalem exploded, destroying several houses and killing more than fifty residents.[101]

In light of these and other incidents, the general feeling prevailing within the Jewish community was that, on the whole, the authorities intervened on behalf of the Arabs. Etzel delivered a warning to the British stating that, since London was interested in kindling the fight between Arabs and Jews in order to remain in Palestine, it would direct its activities against the authorities inside and outside Palestine until "freedom is achieved." Etzel, as well as Lehi, were subsequently involved in blowing up trains in the country, sending letter- and parcel-bombs to England, and placing explosives in a government office in London.[102]

London immediately denounced these actions and condemned the Jewish Agency for its failure to take steps to suppress "Jewish terrorism." In a statement addressed to the Agency, the government concluded that the

> Haganah have from time to time foiled the terrorist groups, but there still remains no method of dealing effectively with these people except the use of the machinery provided by the law. The Government, confronted with the deliberate policy of the Jewish Agency to render their task as difficult as possible, desires to bring once more to the attention of the Jewish community the fact that the continuance of indiscriminate murder and condoned terrorism can lead only to forfeiture by the community of all right in the eyes of the world to be numbered among civilised people.[103]

Early in March, the Vaad Haleumi (National Council of Palestinian Jews), in accordance with the United Nations Partition Resolution, had set up an interim government to serve as a provisional organ of the Jewish state following the termination of the British mandate. The Arab response to this unilateral political act was more violence. Jerusalem was besieged by Arab irregulars and cut off from the coast, and Jewish settlements in the Galilee were attacked by Arab volunteers. Clashes between Arabs and Jews near Tel Aviv resulted in the deaths of seventeen Haganah members and fifteen Arabs. On March 11, a device was smuggled into the courtyard of the Jewish Agency headquarters in Jerusalem, in a car belonging to the American consulate and driven by an Arab driver. The explosion wrecked a section of one of the wings and caused thirteen deaths and other casualties.[104] Toward the end of the month, Arabs carried out persistent raids on highways, blocking traffic and movement of people.

Lehi, during this period, was particularly active. In one operation, it heavily damaged the Haifa headquarters of an Arab military group under the direction of Iraqi and Syrian officers. In the same city, Lehi used explosives to destroy vehicles in the Arab sector, killing seventeen and injuring one hundred. Its units also mined a Haifa-Cairo train and caused a heavy toll in dead and wounded.[105]

In April, the Arab boycott policy against the Jews of Palestine, which was formally adopted by the Arab League Council on February 12, 1945, was further intensified. The government of Iraq stopped delivery of oil through the pipeline from Iraq to the refineries in Haifa.

Encouraged by this display of support by neighboring countries, the local Arabs blockaded the Jewish quarter of the Old City of Jerusalem, cutting off the supplies of food, water, and medicine to the noncombatant residents of that sector.[106] A medical convoy, consisting of seventy-five Jewish doctors, nurses, and teachers, was attacked on its way to the Hadassah Medical Hospital on Mount Scopus, and most of them were killed. Other units were ambushed elsewhere, such as the relief convoy of forty-six people which was destroyed near Yechiam, a kibbutz in the Galilee.[107]

In spite of these setbacks, the Haganah was able, during the month of April, to establish control rapidly over the entire area allotted to the Jewish state in the United Nations partition plan. It opened the road to Jerusalem by occupying Arab areas on both sides of the road, routed the Qawugji forces in the Jezrael Valley, and drove the Arab units from Safed, Tiberias, and Haifa.

Etzel and Lehi, meanwhile, continued to operate unilaterally, and sometimes jointly, against both the Arabs and the British. On April 6, a military camp at Pardes Hanna near Haifa was attacked, and several British soldiers were shot, some in the back. This incident brought a strong denunciation from the colonial secretary in London who declared that it was "cold-blooded murder for its own sake and nothing else" and added, "Such senseless crimes, committed by members of a community which aspires to recognition by the world for acceptance into the community of nations, continue to blot the record of the Jews of Palestine."[108]

A more dramatic incident took place on April 9 during a combined military operation of Etzel and Lehi against the Arab village of Deir Yassin near Jerusalem. Some two hundred Arab civilians, most of them women and children, died when they failed to heed the repeated loudspeaker warnings in Arabic advising them to evacuate the village.[109] This tragedy was unreservedly condemned by the Haganah and all responsible leaders of the Yishuv.

The Arab reaction was bitter. Dr. Husein Khalidi, secretary of the Arab Higher Committee of Palestine, stated that there were two hundred and fifty dead at Deir Yassin, including twenty-five pregnant women, fifty-two mothers "with sucklings up to a few months old" and about sixty other women and girls.[110] He also asserted, "We realize that the Jews have been treated in this manner by the Nazis. We know of their suppressed hatred of their persecutors. But now their hatred is directed against the Arabs, among whom the Jews lived for thirteen centuries. . . . The Arab reaction is not for me to say, but there will be no reprisals."[111] Clearly, this and similar statements by the Arab leadership influenced passions and, in fact, increased the panic among the Arab population resulting in a mass exodus in subsequent weeks.

At the United Nations, meanwhile, diplomatic activity continued. The second special session of the General Assembly, which began on April 16, rejected a U.S. plan for a temporary trusteeship for Palestine as a move to stop violence there. The Arabs favored the plan because it implied a single rather than a partitioned state; the Jews opposed it, holding that the trusteeship proposal was untenable and would negate the Partition Resolution.

The Security Council, on its part, was fully aware of "the increasing violence and disorder in Palestine," and adopted, on April 1, a resolution that called upon the antagonistic Arab and Jewish armed groups "to cease acts of violence immediately."[112] Having failed to achieve this truce, the Security Council, on April 17, called again on the parties to stop all confrontations, to refrain from provocative political activity, and to safeguard the holy places.[113] On April 23, the Security Council created a Truce Commission, composed of representatives of the United States, France and Belgium, to assist in carrying out the proposed cease-fire arrangements.

As the United Nations was unable to stop the bloodshed, Golda Meyerson (who later became Golda Mier) met secretly, on behalf of the Jewish Agency, with King Abdullah of Transjordan on the night of April 30 in an attempt to avert what seemed to be a threatened invasion by the neighboring countries. Although the Arab monarch was prepared to recognize some sort of autonomy for Palestinian Jews, he could not resist both British and Pan-Arab pressure advising him against concluding a separate agreement with the Jewish Agency. The dialogue thus failed, and the parties braced themselves for the inevitable confrontation.

The final two weeks of the pre-state period were costly to the Yishuv. Transjordan's army, better known as the Arab Legion and commanded by British officers, entered the fighting in and around Jerusalem. In one of its military operations, the Arab Legion cordoned off Kfar Etzion on the Hebron-Jerusalem road. After the inhabitants surrendered, they were murdered by Arab villagers. Only 4 out of 110 men and women who were in Kfar Etzion at the time managed to escape. The other three Jewish settlements in the region were also overwhelmed by the superior Jordanian forces.[114]

On May 14, 1948, the Palestine mandate ended, and the British completed the withdrawal of their forces. That day, the Jewish Provisional State Council proclaimed the birth of *Medinat Yisrael* ("State of Israel"). The Proclamation of Independence of the State of Israel made a special plea: "In the midst of wanton aggression . . . we extend the hand of peace and good neighborliness to all the neighboring States and their peoples and invite their cooperation and mutual assistance." It also called "upon the Arab inhabitants of the State of Israel to preserve the ways of peace and play their part in the development of the State on the basis of full and equal citizenship and due representation in all its bodies and institutions—provisional and permanent."

The Arabs responded to this appeal by sending invasion forces from Egypt, Iraq, Jordan, Lebanon, and Syria in order to guarantee the abrupt and conclusive demise of the Jewish state on the very first day of its existence. Azaam Pasha, the secretary general of the Arab League, outlined its purpose: "There will be a war of extermination and a momentous massacre which will be spoken of like the Mongolian Massacres and the Crusades."[115]

But the infant state survived the first onslaught. Now, thirty years later, Israel, having fought three additional bloody wars—in 1956, 1967, and 1973—is still struggling for its right to self-determination and life as a distinct nation.

Notes

1. For the basic ideology of Zionism by the founder of the Zionist movement, see Theodor Herzl, *The Jewish State* (New York: Scopus Publishing Company, 1943); *Old New Land (Altneuland),* trans. from German, with revised notes, by Lotta Levensohn (New York: Herzl Press, 1960); *The Complete Diaries of Theodor Herzl,* ed. Raphael Patai, trans. Harry Zohn, 5 vols., (New York: Yoseloff, 1960); and *The Diaries,* trans. and ed. Marvin Lowenthal (New York: Grosset and Dunlap, 1962). For works related to Zionism by other Zionist leaders, see Nahum Sokolow, *History of Zionism* (London: Longmans, Green and Co., 1919), Vol. 1; Arthur Ruppin, *The Jewish Fate and Future* (New York: Macmillan, 1940); Chaim Weizmann, *Trial and Error: The Autobiography of Chaim Weizmann* (New York: Harper and Brothers, 1949); David Ben-Gurion, *The Rebirth and Destiny of Israel* (New York: Philosophical Library, Inc., 1954); Louis Lipsky, *A Gallery of Zionist Profiles* (New York: Farrar, Strauss, and Ciroux, 1956); and Nahum Goldman, "Zionism: Ideal and Realism" (a speech delivered in Basel on Sept. 24, 1967, marking the 70th anniversary of the First Zionist Congress), in *Confrontation: Viewpoints on Zionism* (Jerusalem: World Zionist Organization, 1970). For a brief analysis of "Jewish" or "Israeli" nationalism, see Israel Kolatt, "Theories on Israel Natonalism," in *Confrontation: Viewpoints on Zionism* (Jerusalem: World Zionist Organization, 1969).

2. See, for instance, *The Historical Connection of the Jewish People with Palestine* (Jerusalem: Jewish Agency for Palestine, 1936).

3. Israel Zangwill, "The Return to Palestine," *New Liberal Review* 2 (December 1901), p. 627.

4. See Ben Halpern, "Zionism and Israel," in Benjamin Rivlin and Joseph S. Szyliowicz, *The Contemporary Middle East: Tradition and Innovation* (New York: Random House, 1965), pp. 276-82, for a comparison between Zionism and other nationalisms and for an analysis of the reasons for the unique characteristics of Jewish nationalism.

5. See Simon M. Dubnow, *History of the Jews in Russia and Poland,* 3 vols. (Philadelphia: Jewish Publications Society, 1916-1920), and L. Greenberg, *The Jews in Russia* (New Haven: Yale University Press, 1951), Vol. 2.

6. See James Parks, *Antisemitism* (London: Vallentine Mitchell, 1963),

and A. Roy Eckardt, *Elder and Younger Brothers* (New York: Charles Scribner's Sons, 1967).

7. Among the earliest pioneers were students from Eastern Europe belonging to an organization called BILU (initials of the Hebrew words *Beth Yaacov Luhu Venelha*—"House of Jacob, come ye, and let us walk" [Isaiah, 2:5]). See, for example, Leon Pinsker, *Auto-Emancipation: A Call to His People by a Russian Jew* (London: Rita Searl, 1947); David Ben-Gurion, *Rebirth and Destiny of Israel*, pp. 270-72; and Alex Bein, *The Return to the Soil* (Jerusalem: Youth and Hechalutz Department, World Zionist Organization, 1952).

8. The Jewish population in Palestine in 1882 reached 24,000. During the first *aliah*, 1882-1903, some 25,000 Jews immigrated to Palestine. In the second *aliah*, 1904-1914, nearly 40,000 immigrants arrived.

9. For background accounts on Arab-Jewish relations, see, for example, Michael Assaf, *History of the Arabs in Palestine*, Vol. 3, *The Arab Awakening and Flight—Nations and States Contend for Palestine, 1876-1948*, in Hebrew (Tel Aviv: Tarbut We-Hinukh, 1967); Shimon Shamir, *A Modern History of the Arabs in the Middle East*, Hebrew (Tel Aviv: Reshofim, 1965); and Aaron Cohen, *Israel and the Arab World* (London: W. H. Allen, 1970).

10. See "The Spiritual and Pioneering Mission of Israel: The Eternity of Israel," *Ayanot*, Hebrew (1964), p. 74. See also statement by David Ben-Gurion before Knesset, January 2, 1956, as quoted in *Israel Peace Offers* (Jerusalem: Ministry of Foreign Affairs, 1958), p. 56; and Martin Buber, "Zion and Youth" (1918) in *Mission and Destiny* 2 (Hebrew), p. 219.

11. See, for example, Cmd. 1700, p. 8; *Financial Aspects of Jewish Reconstruction in Palestine: How the Arabs Have Benefited through Jewish Immigration* (London: Jewish Agency for Palestine, 1930); and *Zionism and the Arab World* (New York: Jewish Agency for Palestine, 1946).

12. For works related to Zionism, see note 1. For diagnoses of Zionism's founders relative to the processes dominating Jewish life in the Disaspora, see, for example, Martin Buber, "Aus einer Rede," *Die Welt* (March 29, 1912), reprinted in *Juedische Bewegung* (Berlin: Juedische Verlag, 1916), p. 195; A. D. Gordon, "The Congress" (1913), in *The Nation and Labor*, Hebrew (1952), p. 198; Ber Borochov, *On Zionist Theory* (1915), in his *Writings*, Hebrew, Vol. 1, p. 2; Chaim Weizmann, "The Jewish People and Palestine," statement made before the Palestine Royal Commission in Jerusalem, on November 25, 1936; and David Ben-Gurion, "From Class to People," *Ayanot* (1955), p. 23.

13. Theodor Herzl stated that "the Jewish Question exists wherever Jews live in perceptible number. Where it does not exist, it is carried by Jews in the course of their migration" (*The Jewish State*, Hebrew [1896], Vol. 1, pp. 21-22). For a recent analysis, see Jacob Neusser, "Zionism and the Jewish Problem," in *Confrontation: Viewpoints on Zionism* (Jerusalem: World Zionist Organization, 1970), pp. 3-14.

14. For the Zionist objectives as formulated in the first Zionist Congress, see *Protokoll des I. Zionistenkongresses in Basel vom 29 bis 31 August 1897* (Prog., 1911), p. 131. See also *Constitution of the Zionist Organization* (Jerusalem: World Zionist Organization, 1938); Israel Cohen, *The Zionist Movement* (New York: Zionist Organization of America, 1947); Gavriel Stern, "70th Anniversary of the First Zionist Congress," *Israel Horizons* 15, Nos. 9 and 10 (November-December 1967), pp. 20-23; K. Israel, "The Zionist Movement and the Jerusalem Programme 1968," in *Confrontation: Viewpoints on Zionism* (Jerusalem: World Zionist Organization, 1970), pp. 3-12; and Eliezer Schweid, "Israel as a Zionist State," in *Confrontation: Viewpoints on Zionism.*

15. Some Jews rejected the concept of unity of the Jewish people with Palestine as a beacon of national security. For anti-Zionist works, see, for instance, Morris R. Cohen, *Zionism: Tribalism or Liberalism* (New York: American Council for Judaism, 1946); Alfred M. Lilienthal, *What Price Israel* (Chicago: Henry Regnery Company, 1953); Moshe Menuhin, *The Decadence of Judaism in Our Time* (New York: Exposition Press, 1965); Benjamin Matov, "Zionist and Anti-Semite: 'Of Course!'" *Issues* (Spring 1966), pp. 21-26; and Jakob J. Petuchowski, *Zion Reconsidered* (New York: Twayne Publishers, 1967).

16. "Diary" (June 1895), in Borochov, *Writings*, Hebrew, Vol. 2, p. 71.

17. Anis Sayegh, in her study *Palestine and Arab Nationalism* (Beirut: Palestine Liberation Organization Research Center), reports that during this period the first articles attempting to expose the "Zionist plot" appeared in *Al-Manor* (Cairo) and *Al-Carmel* (Haifa). For a pro-Arab anthology of readings of the history of Zionism and Palestine from 1897 until the establishment of Israel, see Walid Khalidi, *From Haven to Conquest* (Beirut: Institute for Palestine Studies, 1971); see also Nevill Mandel, "Turks, Arabs, and Jewish Immigration into Palestine," *St. Anthony's Papers, Number 17: Middle Eastern Affairs*, No. 4 (Oxford: Oxford University Press), p. 80, and Nagib Azoury, *Le Reveil de la nation Arabe* (Paris: 1905).

18. Circassians are members of a Moslem ethnic group from the Caucasus region who were transported to Palestine in the mid-nineteenth century by the Ottoman Turks.

19. For a general discussion of the period, see Suleiman Mousa, *T. E. Lawrence: An Arab View*, trans. Albert Butros (New York: Oxford, 1966).

20. Some Palestinian Jews, at least initially, favored wartime cooperation with the Central Powers. See Alexander Aaronsohn, *With the Turks in Palestine* (New York: Houghton Mifflin, 1916), for a personal narrative of a well-known Palestinian Jew concerning the early part of World War I in Palestine; see also Yigal Allon, *Shield of David* (New York: Random House, 1970), pp. 32-34.

21. For text, see United Kingdom, *Balfour Declaration*, November 2, 1917, quoted in report of Royal Commission, Cmd. 5479, (London, 1937),

p. 16. For resolutions, statements, and views by Jewish organizations relating to the Balfour Declaration, and for press comments, see *Great Britain, Palestine, and the Jews: Jewry's Celebration of Its National Charter* (New York: George H. Doran Company, 1918). See also Blanche Elizabeth Dugdale, *The Balfour Declaration: Origins and Background* (London: Jewish Agency for Palestine, 1940); Leonard Stein, *The Balfour Declaration* (New York: Simon and Schuster, 1961); and Richard H. S. Crossman, "The Balfour Declaration, 1917-1967," *Midstream* 13, No. 10 (December 1967), pp. 21-28.

22. This was done in accordance with the wartime secret Sykes-Picot Treaty of May 9, 1916, whereby Britain and France agreed to divide the eastern Middle East between them. For an examination of the British and French roles in the Middle East, see Jukka Nevakivi, *Britain, France, and the Arab Middle East, 1914-1920* (London: Oxford University Press, 1969); John Morlowe, *Arab Nationalism and British Imperialism* (New York: Praeger, 1961); and Elizabeth Monroe, *Britain's Moment in the Middle East, 1914-1956* (Baltimore: Johns Hopkins, 1963). For an interpretation of Britain's Palestine promises, see Fayez Sayegh, "Two Secret British Documents," *Hiwar* (Beirut), No. 8 (January-February 1964), pp. 17-32, and *Times* (London), April 16, 1964.

23. See United Kingdom, "Final Drafts of the Mandates for Mesopotamia and Palestine for the Approval of the Council of the League of Nations" (London, 1921), Cmd. 1500, and Cmd. 1785, pp. 1-11, for official documents of the mandate. See also Albert M. Hyamson, *Palestine under the Mandate 1920-1948* (London: 1950), for a Zionist view by a former mandatory official. For other works, see Norman and Helen Bentwich, *Mandate Memories, 1918-1948* (New York: Shocken, 1965), and Edwin Samuel, *A Lifetime in Jerusalem: The Memoirs of the Second Viscount Samuel* (Jerusalem: Israel Universities Press, 1970).

24. Quoted in report of Royal Commission, Cmd. 5479 (London, 1937), pp. 19-20, and the Jewish Agency for Palestine, *Documents Relating to the Palestine Problems* (Jerusalem, 1945), pp. 17-18.

25. Quoted in Chaim Landau, ed., *Israel and the Arabs* (Jerusalem: Central Press, 1971), p. 48. See also letter by Sir Henry MacMahon in London *Times*, July 23, 1937; Chaim Weizmann's speech to the Zionist Congress 1931, quoted in Jewish Agency for Palestine, *Memorandum to the Palestine Royal Commission* (Jerusalem, 1936), pp. 87-89; and N. Mandel, "Attempts at an Arab-Zionist Entente, 1913-1914," *Middle Eastern Studies* 1, No. 3 (April 1965), pp. 238-67.

26. *Speeches*, Hebrew (1937), Vol. 1, p. 141.

27. ESCO Foundation for Palestine, *Palestine: A Study of Jewish, Arab, and British Policies* (New Haven: Yale University Press, 1947), Vol. 1, p. 473 (later referred to as ESCO, *Palestine Study*).

28. Quoted by George Antonius, *The Arab Awakening*, 3rd ed. (Beirut: Khayats, 1955), p. 441.

29. For details, see Issa Sifri, *Arab Palestine between the Mandate and Zionism* (Jaffa, 1937); Robert John and Sami Hadawi, *The Palestine Diary*, Vol. 1, 1914-1945 (Beirut: Palestine Research Center, 1970); Don Peretz and others, *A Palestine Entity* (Washington, D.C.: Middle East Institute, 1970), pp. 1-21; and A. Kayal, ed., *Documents on Palestinian Resistance to the British Mandate and Zionism, 1918-1939* (Beirut: Institute for Palestine Studies, 1969).

30. Maurice Pearlman, *Mufti of Jerusalem: The Story of Haj Amin Al Hussein* (London: Gollancz, 1947); Eliahu Elath, *Haj Mohammed Amin El-Husseini*, Hebrew (Tel Aviv: Reshafim, 1968); and *Ha'aretz* (Tel Aviv), March 1, 2, and 6, 1970.

31. ESCO, *Palestine Study*, pp. 132-33.

32. For details, see, for instance, Munya Mardor, *Haganah* (New York: New American Library, 1966).

33. ESCO, *Palestine Study*, pp. 269-70.

34. Ibid., p. 271.

35. Weizmann, *Trial and Error*, p. 342.

36. See *The Hope-Simpson Report* (Jerusalem: Government Press, 1929), pp. 53-54 and 78-79.

37. See, for example, Jewish Agency for Palestine, *Memorandum on the Western Wall* (Jerusalem: Azriel Press, June 1930); ESCO, *Palestine Study*, pp. 608-9; and United Kingdom, *International Commission for the Wailing Wall Report, December, 1930* (London: His Majesty's Stationary Office, 1931).

38. *A Survey for Palestine*, prepared in December 1945 and January 1946 for the information of the Anglo-American Committee of Inquiry (Jerusalem: Government Press, 1946), Vol. 1, p. 24. See also Arye Hashavia, "This Month— Forty Years Ago, the Hebron Massacre" (Jerusalem: Prime Minister Office, 1969).

39. See Cmd. 2530. For another proposal to limit Jewish immigration, see *The Hope-Simpson Report*.

40. See *A Survey for Palestine*, pp. 30-31.

41. See Leila S. Kadi, *Basic Political Documents of the Armed Palestine Movement* (Beirut: Palestine Liberation Organization, December 1969).

42. United Kingdom, Palestine Royal Commission, *Report*, Cmd. 5479, July 1937 (London: His Majesty's Stationary Office, 1937), pp. 110-11.

43. For an excellent analysis of Arab, Jewish, and British policies from 1936 leading to the breakdown of the mandate, see Jacob C. Hurewitz, *The Struggle for Palestine* (New York: Greenwood Press, 1968).

44. See *A Survey for Palestine* and ESCO, *Palestine Study*.

45. For details, see Mardor, *Haganah*; and Ephraim Dekel (Krasner), *Shai: Historical Exploits of Haganah Intelligence* (New York: Yoseloff, 1959).

46. *New York Times,* October 15, 1938. For Arab attitudes, see, for instance, Cmd. 3530, 5479, 5854, 6808, and 7044.

47. The Revisionists established the World Union of Zionists Revisionists in 1925 and a youth movement, Betar (Brith Trumpeldor). In 1935, it seceded from the official Zionist Organization, only to rejoin it in 1946. Its leader was Zeev (Vladimir) Jobotinsky; see his presentation in *The Story of the Jewish Legion* (New York: Ackerman, 1945).

48. The first split occurred in 1931 when these dissidents left the Haganah. However, most of them rejoined it in 1936. For details on Etzel by commanders who succeeded Raziel, see Yaacov Meridor, *Long Is the Road to Freedom* (New York: United Zionists Revisionists, 1961), and Menachem Begin, *The Revolt: Story of the Irgun* (New York: Henry Schuman, 1951).

49. *Keesing's Contemporary Archives* 3 (1937-1940), pp. 3177A, 3312A, 3513, 3642B.

50. Quoted by Michael Bar-Zohar, *The Armed Prophet: A Biography of Ben-Gurion* (London, 1967), p. 53.

51. Ibid., p. 74.

52. For details, see Bracha Habas, *The Gate Breakers* (New York: Yoseloff and Herzl, 1963), and Jon and David Kimche, *The Secret Roads* (New York: Farrar, Straus, and Cudahy, 1955).

53. For an insight into the workings of Etzel and Lehi, see Jerold Frank, *The Deed* (New York: Simon and Schuster, 1963). For a description by a former member of Lehi on some of the organization's activities, see Avner, pseud., *Memoirs of an Assassin* (New York: Yoseloff, 1959). See *The "Activities" of the Hagana, Irgun, and Stern Bands* (New York: Palestine Liberation Organization, n.d.), and "Zionist Terrorism," UN Doc. A/C.6/C.876, November 22, 1972, for Arab perspectives.

54. Quoted in American Professors for Peace in the Middle East, *Newsletter* (October 1969). See also Joseph B. Schechtman, *The Mufti and the Fuehrer* (London: Yoseloff, 1965), and Seth Arsenian, "Wartime Propaganda in the Middle East," *Middle East Journal* 2 (October 1948), pp. 417-29.

55. See Munya Mardor, *Strictly Illegal* (London: Robert Hale, 1964), p. 56 ff.

56. *A Survey for Palestine,* pp. 58, 61, and 63.

57. See Thierry Nolin, *La Haganah: L'armée secrète d'Israel* (Paris: Ballard, 1971), pp. 159-63.

58. *Keesing's Contemporary Archives* 4 (1941-1942), p. 6798A.

59. "The Assassination of Lord Moyne," *Jewish Agency's Digest of Press and Events* (November 11, 1944), pp. 1-3. For a basic study, see Frank, *The Deed,* and his article "The Moyne Case: A Tragic History," *Commentary* 2

(December 1945), pp. 64-71. See also Issac Zaar, *Rescue and Liberation* (New York: Bloch, 1954), pp. 38-43; J. Bowyer Bell, *The Long War* (Englewood Cliffs, N.J.: Prentice-Hall, 1969), pp. 12-13, and "Assassination in International Politics: Lord Moyne, Count Bernadotte, and the Lehi," *International Studies Quarterly* no. 1 (1972), pp. 59-82; and *Ha'aretz,* March 26, 1975.

60. *A Survey for Palestine,* pp. 63 and 72, and *Keesing's Comtemporary Archives* 5 (1943-1945), p. 6798.

61. For details, see *Palcor News Agency Cables* (March 27, April 13, November 20 and 22, 1944). Arab reactions are cited in *Jewish Agency's Digest of Press and Events* (April 10 and November 21, 1944).

62. See report of the *Anglo-American Committee of Inquiry on Palestine,* Cmd. 6808 (1946), pp. 40-41.

63. For activities prior to the merger of these groups, see Valia Hirsch, "The Truth about the Terrorists," *Today* 1 (January 1945), pp. 10-12, and Frank Gervasi, "Terror in Palestine," *Colliers'* 116 (August 11, 1945), pp. 64-65.

64. See George Kirk, *Survey of International Affairs: The Middle East, 1945-1950* (London: Royal Institute of International Affairs, 1951), p. 195, and *Hamaas* (Lehi's publication), No. 2 (November 1945).

65. See *Palcor News Agency Cables* (November 29, 1945), and *Jewish Telegraphic Agency* (December 26, 1945).

66. *Herut* (Etzel's publication), No. 55 (February 1946).

67. *Eshnav* (Publication of the Jewish Resistance Movement), No. 116 (March 4, 1946). For other activities by the movement, see *Palcor News Agency Cables* (April 4 and 24, 1946).

68. This commission was formed by the British government in November 1945 for the purpose of involving the United States in the responsibility for a solution to the Palestine problem; see report of the *Anglo-American Committee of Inquiry.*

69. R. D. Wilson, *Cordon and Search: With 6th Airborne Division in Palestine* (Aldershot: Gale and Polden, 1949), p. 262.

70. *Keesing's Contemporary Archives* 6 (1946-1948), p. 7983.

71. Itzhak Gurion, *Triumph on the Gallows* (New York: Brit Trumpeldor of America, 1950), pp. 80-81.

72. Prior to this action, the British, for instance, imposed all-night curfews; see *Palcor News Agency Cables* (April 30, 1946).

73. *New Palestine News Reporter* (July 12, 1946), and *Palcor News Agency Cables* (July 30, 1946).

74. Emanuel Celler stated in the United States that "terrorism in Palestine is a symbol of despair resulting from British action and would be a tragedy if the British used it as a pretext to deny entrance of 100,000 Jews into Palestine" (*Congressional Record* [July 24, 1946], pp. 9944-45).

75. *Keesing's Contemporary Archives* 6 (1946-1948), p. 8103. See also Begin, *The Revolt*, pp. 212-20.

76. *Palcor News Agency Cables* (October 9 and 30, and November 7, 1946), and *Keesing's Contemporary Archives* 6 (1946-1948), p. 8222.

77. *Palcor News Agency Cables* (November 12, 1946), and Begin, *The Revolt*, p. 234.

78. See, for example, *Jewish Telegraphic Agency* (February 9, 1947), and *Palcor News Agency Cables* (February 11, 19, 20, March 3, and 12, 1947).

79. U.N. Doc. A/286.

80. U.N. Doc. A/287-291, April 22, 1947.

81. For excellent presentation of the Palestine question as discussed by the special session of the General Assembly, see Jacob Robinson, *Palestine and the United Nations: Prelude to a Solution* (Washington, D.C.: Public Affairs Press, 1948).

82. When the Charter of the United Nations came into force on October 24, 1945, the Arab States of Egypt, Iraq, Lebanon, Saudi Arabia, and Syria were among the original members of the world organization.

83. Members of UNSCOP were Australia, Canada, Czechoslovakia, Guatemala, India, Iran, the Netherlands, Peru, Sweden, Uruguay, and Yugoslavia.

84. U.N. Doc. A/364.

85. The minority proposal was submitted by India, Iran, and Yugoslavia.

86. The Assembly vote was 33 to 13 with 10 abstentions.

87. See, for instance, *Palcor News Agency Cables* (May 15 and August 4, 1947); *New York Times*, August 1, 1947; and *Sunday Times* (London), September 4, 1947.

88. *Palestine Post*, December 3, 1947.

89. See, for example, *New York Times*, December 11, 12, and 13, 1947.

90. *Palestine Post*, December 31, 1947.

91. Ibid., January 15, 1948.

92. Ibid., January 20, 1948.

93. See Al-Qawugji's "Memoirs, 1948, Part I," *Journal of Palestine Studies* 1 (Summer 1972), pp. 25-28, and Part II of his "Memoirs," *Journal of Palestine Studies* 2 (Autumn 1972), pp. 3-33.

94. *Keesing's Contemporary Archives* 6 (1946-1948), p. 9237.

95. Ibid.

96. *New York Times*, January 2, 1948.

97. *Keesing's Contemporary Archives* 6 (1946-1948), p. 9238.

98. U.N. Doc. S/616.

99. U.N. Doc. S/PV.253, February 24, 1948.

100. *Palestine Post*, February 2, 1948.

101. Ibid., February 23, 1948.

102. Ibid., February 29, 1948, and *New York Times*, February 21, 22, 23, and 24, 1948.

103. *Keesing's Contemporary Archives* 6 (1946-1948), p. 9238.

104. See Netanel Lorch, *The Edge of the Sword: Israel's War of Independence, 1947-1949* (New York: Putnam, 1961), p. 63.

105. *Keesing's Contemporary Archives* 6 (1946-1948), p. 9239.

106. The siege of Old Jerusalem ended on May 28, 1948, when the Jewish quarter surrendered to the Arab Legion; see Harry Levine, *Jerusalem Embattled* (London: Gollancz, 1950), and John Bagot Glubb, *A Soldier with the Arabs* (London: Hadder and Stoughton, 1957), pp. 129-30.

107. See Lorch, *Edge of the Sword.*

108. *Times*, April 7, 1948, and *Keesing's Contemporary Archives* 6 (1946-1948), p. 9239.

109. See "Dir Yassin," *West Asia Affairs* (Summer 1969), pp. 27-30; *New York Times*, April 10, 11, and 12, 1948; Edgar O'Ballance, *The Arab-Israeli War, 1948* (New York: Praeger, 1957), p. 58; Arthur Koestler, "The Other Exodus," *Spectator* (May 18, 1961); and Christopher Sykes, *Crossroads to Israel* (Cleveland: World, 1965), pp. 416-17.

110. *New York Herald Tribune*, April 12, 1948.

111. Quoted by Guy Ottewell, "Deir Yassin: A Forgotten Tragedy with Present-Day Meaning," *Perspective* (April 1969), p. 6.

112. U.N. Doc. S/PV.277.

113. U.N. Doc. S/723.

114. See Lorch, *Edge of the Sword*, p. 129; Edgar O'Gallance, *The Arab-Israeli War, 1948* (London: Faber and Faber, 1956), pp. 65-66; and Dov Knohl, *Siege in the Hills of Hebron: The Battle of the Etzion Bloc* (New York: Yoseloff, 1958).

115. BBC news broadcast, May 15, 1948.

Part 6

International Law and
the United Nations

.

12
Self-Determination:
A Legal-Political Inquiry

Robert A. Friedlander

On January 8, 1918, President Woodrow Wilson delivered his Fourteen Points Address before the United States Congress and thus dramatized to the twentieth century the concept of national self-determination.[1] The entire speech was merely intended to be a presidential statement of Allied war aims, but war-weary peoples everywhere, in addition to idealistic American commentators, interpreted Wilson's address as the official statement of the basic principles to be adopted in the forthcoming peace settlement.[2] Similar views were expressed by the governments of the Central Powers when they sued for an armistice in that same year based upon the Fourteen Points.[3] The Allies themselves accepted self-determination only insofar as it applied to the disintegration and dissolution of the German, Austro-Hungarian, Turkish, and former Russian empires. There was no intention of applying the principle to their own colonies and subject peoples.[4]

Although self-determination has long been associated with the Fourteen Points Address, nowhere in that speech can the phrase itself be found.[5] In actuality, the concept was first mentioned in a memorandum prepared by the British Foreign Office during the

The author is indebted to Professor M. Cherif Bassiouni of DePaul University for his advice and encouragement in the preparation of this article.

This chapter was originally published in *Detroit College of Law Review*, Issue 1, Volume 1975, pp. 71-91. Reprinted by special permission.

fall of 1916, the purpose of which was to suggest a basis for future territorial settlements. It is an essential condition of peace, the memorandum declared, that full scope must be given to national aspirations whenever practicable, and that "the principle of nationality should therefore be one of the governing factors in the consideration of territorial arrangements after the war." [6]

As a catchword, it was utilized by the Allied Supreme War Council on December 22, 1918, which in discussing war aims resolved to "continually repeat our readiness to accept the principles of self-determination." [7] It is true that six of the Fourteen Points sought to apply the principle of nationality to specific territories, "and a seventh urged recognition of the interests of the populations concerned" in any future colonial settlements. [8] But Wilson's own use of the phrase so closely associated with his name came after January 8, 1918, [9] and was not even mentioned in subsequent addresses of amplification and modification. However, by the following year, the term self-determination had entered into general use and was commonly attributed to the American president and his Fourteen Points. [10]

The Paris Peace Conference of 1919 did more violence than justice to the concept of self-determination, and the term did not appear in any of the peace treaties or in the Covenant of the League of Nations. [11] According to Secretary of State Robert Lansing, a generalized application of the concept would be political dynamite which could only result in "misery" and "calamity." [12] The Allies never really accepted Wilson's entire Fourteen Point program and reserved to themselves the power to interpret the meaning of self-determination as it applied to specific territories. Nonetheless, the Allied leadership failed to make this clear, either to their enemies or to their own citizenry, with the result that self-determination as a concept had become misinterpreted even before it was given practical implementation by the victorious Allied Powers.

Originally put forward as a philosophical *principle* to be considered in any forthcoming peace settlement, self-determination was transformed by the Wilsonian pronouncements into a universal human *right*. [13] But the failure to distinguish between a principle and a right led to public confusion and private misunderstanding within the Allied camps and raised false hopes among subject peoples both in Europe and the non-European world. [14] At Paris, self-determination underwent a further transformation from that of a right to that of a *remedy*. It was primarily utilized as a justification for legitimizing the newly formed Eastern European states, and it is one of the ironies of history that the phrase was turned by Adolf Hitler against several of those very states during the 1930s in order to justify his expansionist and annexationist policies.[15] It was not, however, applied to colonial populations, for the victorious Allies had empires to preserve and territorial ambitions to fulfill. The resulting mandate system[16] was a less than perfect compromise between Wilsonian idealism and the harsher realities of international power politics. Small wonder then that self-determination, to use the words of one scholar, became a "political programme," misapplied after World War I and misunderstood since.[17]

As a result of this background, the so-called right of self-determination has been subjected to much criticism for being largely political and somewhat moral, but having no legal validity within the law of nations.[18] There are those who argue, however, that although self-determination does not constitute part of customary international law, it is still a formative legal principle of the law of nations because of its recognition by the United Nations Charter and due to post-1945 United Nations declarations.[19] However, it should be noted that not only has there been a change of position from antagonism to acceptance among legal commentators as a result of Afro-Asian and Communist bloc pressures within the United Nations,[20] but also a strong case can be made that the United Nations has in fact formalized self-determination as an important principle of contemporary international law.[21]

In recent years, numerous analysts have interpeted the principle of modern-day self-determination to be an evolutionary phenomenon with deep historical roots. Some feel that its origins can be traced back to the Greek city-state with the idea of self-government as the primary source.[22] There are also those who date the earliest beginnings from the Peace of Westphalia in 1648, when a limited principle of "religious equality" was given the sanction of international law.[23] Others believe that the concept of self-determination evolved from the American Declaration of Independence and the French Declaration of the Rights of Man and of the Citizen, wherein civil and juridical equality was demanded and achieved through the exercise of popular sovereignty.[24] Still others attribute its conception to the French Emperor Napoleon III, who embraced the principle of the "awakening of nationalities" as part of his ideological program and made effective use of the plebiscite as a political corollary.[25] Winston Churchill, writing a decade after the Paris Peace Conference, credits the Italian nationalist ideologue, Mazzini, with the first practical implementation of the principle. According to Churchill, the phrase itself belongs to the Prussian philosopher, Johann Fichte.[26]

The above analysis assumes that self-determination is a traditional legal principle applicable to the law of nations and that twentieth-century phraseology does not detract from the historic validity of the concept. Some commentators, however, more cautious in their approach, prefer to interpret self-determination as a revolutionary idea associated with the political collapse of the Eastern European empires at the end of the First World War.[27] Whether or not self-determination is actually an inherent right,[28] there can be no doubt that it has become a cardinal doctrine of the United Nations dating from the very beginning of the world organization.

With the resurrection of the Wilsonian ideal of a "general association of nations" following the Second World War, it was inevitable that the concept of self-determination which had become associated with Wilson would likewise be revived. The United Nations Charter signed at San Francisco on June 26, 1945, twice refers to "the principle of equal rights and self-determination of peoples."[29] Seven years later, on December 16, 1952, the United Nations General Assembly adopted several resolutions proclaiming that "the States Members of the United Nations shall uphold the principles of self-determination of all peoples and nations," urging "respect for the right of self-determination of peoples and nations," and counseling "ways and means of ensuring international respect for the right of peoples to self-determination."[30]

In 1960, the Assembly adopted a Declaration on the Granting of Independence to Colonial Countries and Peoples which acknowledged "a right" on behalf of "all peoples" to self-determination.[31] Taken in context with a preceding resolution condemning "all manifestations and practices of racial, religious and national hatred in the political, economic, social, educational and cultural spheres of the life of society as violations of the Charter of the United Nations and the Universal Declaration of Human Rights,"[32] the combined effect was to imply an international guarantee of popular sovereignty[33] for disaffected groups everywhere. Perhaps realizing the disruptive potentialities of this sweeping approach, the General Assembly, as an apparent afterthought, added a caveat that "any attempt at the partial or total disruption of the national unity and the territorial integrity of a country is incompatible with the purposes and principles of the Charter of the United Nations."[34] The obvious irreconcilability between the two statements led at least one critic to wonder if there was "even a clear understanding in this august body of what exactly they were resolving about."[35]

No caveat was applied, however, to the General Assembly's resolution of October 1966, proclaiming "the inalienable right of the people of South-West Africa to freedom and independence."[36] Nor was there any confusion over the intent of the Assembly's action. It was the direct result of an adverse ruling by the International Court of Justice on a complaint brought by Ethiopia and Liberia against the government of South Africa, seeking to have the world tribunal affirm that the Territory of South-West Africa was still subject to Mandatory controls originally imposed by the League of Nations. The decision in favor of South Africa[37] angered the anti-colonial majority in the Assembly, and a new militancy swept the Afro-Asian bloc. Calling upon the "inalienable right" of South-West Africa "to self-determination, freedom and independence in accordance with the Charter of the United Nations," the General Assembly terminated the mandate on its own authority and placed it, at least in theory, under United Nations responsibility.[38]

In December 1966, the principle of self-determination was further reinterpreted and greatly expanded by two international covenants—the International Covenant on Economic, Social, and Cultural Rights and the International Covenant on Civil and Political Rights. Using identical language, they emphatically state that "all peoples have the right of self-determination. By virtue of that right, they freely determine their political status and freely pursue their economic, social and cultural development." Moreover, those nations having responsibility for administering non-self-governing and trust territories are required "to promote the realization of the right of self-determination," and "to respect that right, in conformity with the provisions of the United Nations Charter."[39]

This admonition was dramatically implemented by the General Assembly in May 1967. After once again reaffirming the right of South-West Africa to "freedom and independence," the Assembly created a United Nations Council for the Territory and gave to the council full administrative powers, while at the same time calling for the withdrawal of South Africa from its mandate.[40] One year later, in June 1968, the United Nations General Assembly created by resolution the Territory of Namibia, formerly South-West Africa, to be administered by the United Nations until such time as the Namibians were ready for self-government.[41] However, the government of South Africa ignored United Nations demands that it withdraw from the territory and refused to recognize any of the United Nations actions taken after the 1966 decision of the International Court of Justice. The result was a political stalemate which the Security Council subsequently sought to break by seeking from the Court an advisory opinion in July 1970 on "the legal consequences of the continued presence of South Africa in Namibia."[42]

In the controversial opinion handed down in June 1971, the Court concluded that "South Africa's presence in Namibia is illegal and its acts on behalf of or concerning Namibia are illegal and invalid." According to the world tribunal, "the injured entity is a people," and therefore entitled to the right of self-determination.[43] But nowhere in the opinion is a definition to be found as to *what* exactly constitutes "a people" or a statement as to *when* a collectivity may exercise the right of self-determination. And, as yet, almost no one has commented upon the future implications of the United Nations' unprecedented act in granting itself the power to determine the "rights" of a particular people and in being sustained in its action by the International Court of Justice.[44]

With this background, the General Assembly at its Twenty-Fifth Session (1970) unanimously passed a Declaration of Principles of International Law concerning Friendly Relations and Cooperatiom among States in Accordance with the Charter of the United Nations. The length of the title is indicative of the scope of the resolution. After proclaiming that self-determination is a basic principle of international law pertaining to friendly relations and cooperation between states, the declaration goes on to proclaim the right of "all peoples" to determine their own destiny without external interference, and that every state is obliged to refrain from any forcible action which would deprive said peoples of their inherent right. Furthermore, all states are urged to promote the "self-determination of peoples" as "a significant contribution of international law." The disintegrating possibilities of this declaration are staggering. Whether or not the Assembly was actually aware of the implications of its resolution is open to serious question, for the same document emphatically declares, as another basic principle of international law, that "the territorial integrity and political independence of the state are inviolable."[45] If this is so, then how can it be reconciled with the doctrine of self-determination? Or was the Assembly consciously proclaiming a double standard—one that applies to those states still classifiable as colonial powers and another standard for the newly independent Third World nations, many of which until their independence (and after) had no sense or tradition of national identity?

Despite growing reservations as to the wisdom of the Assembly's course with respect to self-determination, it reaffirmed its militant views in the Optional Protocol of December 1971.[46] A year later, the Assembly equated colonial rule with racist regimes. It denounced both terrorist acts and repressive government as denials of the principle of self-determination and as inimical to the right of political independence on the part of subject peoples everywhere.[47] Nevertheless, division within the United Nations ranks grew stronger as the language of the resolutions grew tougher.[48]

A significant number of international lawyers are of the opinion that the "right" of self-determination can only be exercised *one time* by a particular people within a specific geographic area. Thus, if a unitary or federal state has come into being as a result of self-determination, that state cannot be further subdivided on the same basis. For example, the South in the American Civil War and Biafra in the Nigerian Civil War under this theory were *not* exercising a legal right to self-determination. The one-time-only rule is, of course, dependent upon the original state not discriminating against one of its constituent peoples.[49] That limitation is an important one if self-determination is to be a viable concept.

Curiously, the Universal Declaration of Human Rights[50] omits altogether any mention of the principle of self-determination, which may be one of the reasons why the United Nations, after its ranks were swelled by former colonial and newly independent states, found it necessary to add further international covenants.[51] The United Nations resolutions became even more puzzling with the assertion by Secretary-General U Thant on January 4, 1970, that "as an international organization, the United Nations has never accepted and does not accept and I do not believe it will ever accept the principle of secession of a part of its Member State."[52] Following this line of reasoning, what remains is the "right" of a colonial people to decolonization, but as to the "right" of a particular population of an established state to secure political independence from a larger national entity, the United Nations resolutions are apparently inapplicable.[53] Evidently, the best that can be contemplated is a greater measure of autonomy for separate identifiable groups within the framework of a federal state structure.[54]

Even though they are not directly binding upon the United Nations membership, the International Covenant on Civil and Political Rights and the Covenant on Economic, Social, and Cultural Rights may be considered as authoritative interpretations of the Charter.[55] Whether or not self-determination has evolved by way of United Nations "law" into an international legal right is still a matter of considerable debate.[56] Several member states have formally denied that it represents any legal principle whatsoever,[57] and a number of reputable scholars have vigorously asserted that it has never been nor is it even capable of becoming a general rule of international law.[58] The best that can be said of the present-day concept of self-determination is its definition as "the freedom of the people of an entity, with respect to their own government, to participate in the choice of authority structures and institutions and to share in the values of society."[59] There also should be an identifiable link between people and territory so that the population asserting its rights is inextricably connected with the geographic area which it seeks to control.[60] Given the nature of the contemporary international community and the desire of the United Nations to preserve the political structures of its newer, anti-colonial membership (as evidenced, for example, in the Congo and Nigeria), self-determination remains as much a political program now as it was in the Wilsonian era.

Surprisingly, there has been almost no attempt to indicate the degree of disaffection necessary to formalize the process. Where does integration end and autonomy begin? When does autonomy cease and independence become desirable? If caution is exercised by the disaffected minority, then is self-determination merely "the right of a group to adapt their political position in a complicated world to reflect capabilities and changing opportunities"?[61] If, however, the disaffected minority feels itself so oppressed that it can no longer maintain its special identity, then does self-determination become a watchword for political revolution? And if so, does success or failure depend upon legal rights, or upon outside allies and military strength?[62]

In the final analysis, the definition of the problem depends upon the nature of the problem area. Each separate and distinct population within a given national entity is more or less unique in its own setting, and therefore minority rights have to be balanced against majority interests. What standards, then, are to be applied in judging the claims of those attempting to assert the right to control their own political, economic, and cultural destiny? One perceptive analyst has proposed the following criteria for evaluation:

> Constitutional boundaries, geographic boundaries, historical relations, economic viability and sociological and psychological factors. Have the people historically constituted a nation? Do they share a common ethnic, religious or linguistic identity? Are the old and new entities economically viable? Do the people live within a common geographic area? Do they share common institutions and political authority or common awareness as a people?[63]

It is quite unlikely that any particular group will be able to meet all the criteria proposed above. That being the case, the question now becomes how many factors must be applicable before a dissident "people" can claim an independent "right" to determine its future? Or for that matter, what are the qualifications required to constitute a "people" in the juridical sense? The answer, of course, is that there is no precise formula by which a "people" can be identified or by which a "right" can be established, and the possibilities of self-determination as a disintegrating concept are almost unlimited. The Blacks in the United States, the French in Canada, the Georgians in Russia, the Basques in Spain, the Berbers in Morocco, the Indians in Brazil are only a few of the endless number of examples that can be cited as ethnic, linguistic, and racial minorities that have, at one time or another, been subservient to the dominant majority.[64]

One alternative to secession which has been utilized by a number of nation-states in order to safeguard the rights (and privileges) of identifiable minority groups is that of autonomous guarantees preserved by constitutional limitations. The most successful examples of balancing minority and majority interests are Switzerland and Canada where, not altogether accidentally, bilingualism has played a historically significant role. In these two countries, dissent is not only tolerated within the governmental system, but individual and community rights (particularly language and religion) which set the minorities apart are constitutionally recognized and juridically enforced.[65] Yet it cannot be said that federation and autonomy have always been able to provide an effective solution, particularly with respect to the Asian and African nations whose political independence derived from the disruptive experience of revolution and sudden decolonization.

Both Nigeria and Pakistan were quasi-federal regimes which granted in theory certain autonomous rights to their potentially dissident minorities.[66] Both states also were basically artificial creations. The "winds of change" hastened the British departure from East-Central Africa and left in their wake several self-governing federations, none of which ultimately survived. Nigeria had been considered a model of enlighteneed colonial rule, and, of all the former British African colonies, it was widely believed that Nigeria had the greatest potentiality for the future. Pakistan was largely a by-product of the Indian liberation movement, and its emergence as a nation-state had been the unanticipated result of revolution and civil war.[67] Geographical separation offered a rare opportunity in federation and autonomy for that bifurcated state, but as with Nigeria the temptations for exerting control over the subservient minority region proved too great for the dominant majority region to overcome. In each case, linguistic, cultural, and ethnic differences, and the deprivation of civil and political rights, finally led to secession and civil war with the rebel leadership proclaiming their independence in accordance with the principle of self-determination.[68]

Although it might even be argued that neither state was, in truth, a cohesive national entity, there the similarity ends. Biafra (the secessionist Nigerian territory) was extended formal recognition by only five states, and the first government to do so, Tanzania, acted a full eleven months after the Biafrans had raised the standard of rebellion. None of the five recognizing states ever established formal diplomatic relations, the United Nations never considered the issue, and the Organization of African Unity gave strong support to the regular Nigerian government.[69] Most revealing was the statement by Ethiopian Emperor Haile Selassie, a member of the OAU Consultative Committee, who forthrightly declared: "The organization of African Unity is both in word and deed committed to the principle of unity and territorial integrity of its member states. . . . *The national unity and territorial integrity of member states is not negotiable. It must be fully respected and preserved"*[70] (emphasis added). If this declaration is meant to represent the official policy of the OAU, then the member-states of that organization have refused to accept or even to recognize one of the fundamental tenets of the United Nations. The principle of self-determination is apparently now that of *selective* self-determination, to be applied only in non-African or perhaps non–Third World situations. In other words, it is purely a political concept, and should be regarded in that light whenever rebellion or secession occurs within the confines of a nation-state.

East Pakistan was not only separate and distinct in the physical sense from West Pakistan but differed linguistically and racially as well. For example, 98 percent of the population spoke Bengali and less than 2 percent spoke Urdu, Pakistan's principal language.[71] The Moslem religion and animosity toward India provided the major bonds between the two territories, and their association was a tenuous one from the very beginning. Moreover, at the time of secession, numerous violations of the principles set forth in the Universal Declaration of Human Rights as well as of the provisions contained in the two international covenants and Optional Protocol were being committed by the Pakistan central government. Nevertheless, in the beginning, the Security Council did nothing, the Economic and Social Council held a June 1971 meeting on the report of atrocities taking place in East Pakistan but refrained from acting until July and then limited itself to dealing with United Nations relief operations, while the secretary-general waited four months before deciding that Pakistan's civil war threatened international peace and security. Only after the outbreak of full-scale hostilities between India and Pakistan did the Security Council and the General Assembly permit formal consideration of the conflict.

Needless to say, it was Indian military intervention and not United Nations inaction and debate which finally decided the issue. Bangladesh (the secessionist East Pakistan territory) had proclaimed its independence and the right of self-determination in April 1971, and within eleven months forty-seven states granted formal recognition.[72]

United Nations noninvolvement with the East Pakistan crisis was at least consistent with its 1970 declaration, statements of Secretary-General U Thant,[73] and interpretations put forward by sympathetic scholars to the effect that "the United Nations would be in an extremely difficult position if it were to interpret the right of self-determination in such a way as to invite or justify attacks on the territorial integrity of its own members."[74] It was not the "right" of a national self-determination which triumphed in East Pakistan but Indian military might.[75] Bangladesh succeeded where Biafra failed because it had the strong support of an effective political ally.

From its Wilsonian origins, the concept of self-determination has been more an instrument of international politics than a humanitarian principle associated with the law of nations. It was as much a disintegrating force as it was a unifying factor,[76] and its destructive potentialities were tragically revealed by the German expansionist doctrine of the 1930s.[77] With the revival of Wilsonian idealism during the Second World War, as symbolized by the proclamation of the Atlantic Charter on August 14, 1941, and the declaration of the United Nations on January 1, 1942, the concept of national self-determination once again became a major Allied war aim. By implication, it was also to be a basic tenet of the forthcoming peace settlement, although rejected by Winston Churchill with respect to the British Empire. (His interpretation of the Atlantic Charter was that it served merely as "a guiding signpost, expressing a vast body of opinions among all the Powers now fighting together.") The Dumbarton Oaks proposals and the subsequent Charter of the United Nations, signed at San Francisco on June 26, 1945, formalized "self-determination of peoples" as an established principle of international relations.[78]

Though twice mentioned in the United Nations Charter,[79] the principle of self-determination is conspicuously absent from the Universal Declaration of Human Rights approved by the United

Nations General Assembly on December 10, 1948.[80] Self-determination as a war aim looking toward the liberation of formerly independent states had ceased to serve a useful function in the immediate postwar world; but as a justification for rebellion and decolonization it took on an entirely different meaning. In 1948, there were only three self-governing African nations (one of which had been subject to military conquest)—Ethiopia, Liberia, and the Union of South Africa. A dozen years later, at the time of the Declaration on the Granting of Independence to Colonial Countries and Peoples,[81] there were twenty independent African states.[82]

Decolonization had become a significant factor in world politics, and self-determination was to provide its legal and moral rationale. Once independence was achieved, however, the danger of further political disintegration due to racial, cultural, economic, and religious antagonisms places self-determination in a new and disadvantageous light. Thus, the interpretations of territorial inviolability put forward by the United Nations international covenants,[83] Secretary-General U Thant,[84] and the Organization of African Unity[85] were meant to draw a careful distinction between self-determination as applied to colonial regimes and self-determination as applied to self-governing "nations." The principle was distorted in the practice, and the net result has been to turn it into an ideological weapon which, though purporting to champion popular sovereignty on a global scale, actually serves to perpetuate the deep divisions between the countries of the Third World and their former colonial masters.[86] Whatever the value of self-determination as a moral force,[87] its legal validity must now be called into question.

A citizen, according to Socrates, binds himself by an implied contract with the state in that his actions are to be subject to state control. If the individual does not agree to abide by the laws thus imposed, he is free to go elsewhere and to place himself under another sovereign authority.[88] To the Greeks of the Golden Age citizenship involved allegiance to a particular collectivity and not to a national ideal. The concept of kingship on the other hand reflected neither nationality nor nationhood, for the king in his own person represented the nation-state with the citizen owing absolute obedience to the monarch and not to the national entity. It was the eighteenth-century American and French revolutions that combined the concept of democratic legitimacy with the principle of nationality.[89]

Nevertheless, national identity during the Revolutionary era was as much a consequence of indigenous reaction to foreign conquest as it was the influence of revolutionary idealism. But the national unification movements of the mid-nineteenth century derived their successes from victories on the battlefield and not from debates in legislative chambers. Military force created the new national boundaries of late nineteenth-century Europe just as territorial ambitions, strategic necessity, and power politics were mainly responsible for the creation of new states and the disintegration of colonial empires following the First World War. The transformation of self-determination from an international principle to a human right after the Second World War was largely a consequence of the decolonizing process brought about by the war itself. Yet the history of the past decade has demonstrated that self-determination is a two-edged sword—cutting the bonds with a former colonial master has been treated as a juridical right satisfying the legitimate aspirations of the subject group; however, any attempt on the part of a repressed minority to break away from an established polity is still considered to be a revolutionary act with all its attendant consequences.

A complicating factor in the contemporary world has been that of partition. This is a relatively modern phenomenon due largely but not exclusively to the Cold War and to the continuing crisis in Southeast Asia.[90] Partition is basically a geopolitical device, often effectuated by the great powers, and in some cases it has severely distorted the concept of nationality. Divisions imposed from the outside along with the alteration of national frontiers have brought into being essentially artifical entities, and in many cases have created new minorities where none previously existed. Partition when applied to historic sovereignties is thus likely to foster irredentism as a concomitant protest, and it is precisely in these areas where self-determination will have its greatest future impact.[91]

If nothing else, self-determination has proved to be a dynamic twentieth-century political force. In theory, it stands for popular sovereignty on a global scale. In practice, it has provided the juridical justification for the creation of new states and a legal rationale for revolution within the confines of established polities. But many questions still remain unanswered. What is the extent of its application? Should it be an absolute and unlimited right or a carefully defined principle held in check by overriding national concerns and international considerations? Is it merely a corollary of democratic theory or a moral force transcending political systems and territorial boundaries? And at what point does the process finally come to a halt?[92]

Whatever the answer, the effectiveness of self-determination has historically depended upon the particular area and the particular peoples involved. It has never been universally applied and is more an ideological weapon than a practical political device.[93] As a general principle of international law it has secured widespread acceptance. As a fundamental human right it is even now a questionable doctrine.[94]

Notes

1. 1 *Public Papers of Woodrow Wilson: War and Peace*, Sect. 2, at 155-62 (R. Baker and W. Dodd, eds., 1925).

2. R. Osgood, *Ideals and Self Interest in America's Foreign Relations* (1953); T. Bailey, *Woodrow Wilson and the Lost Peace* (1944).

3. H. Rudin, *Armistice 1918* (1944); "Correspondence between the United States and Austria-Hungary Regarding an Armistice," 13 *Am. J. Int'l L.*, 73, 73-79; "Correspondence between the United States and Germany Regarding an Armistice," id., 85, 85-96.

4. Russia since the Bolshevik Revolution of November 1917 was technically not an enemy but was definitely a source of great concern to the Allies.

5. On the confusion of both legal scholars and historians as to the origin of the phrase, see Woolsey, "Two Treaties of Paris," 13 *Am. J. Int'l L.*, 81, 83 (1919); Woolsey, "Self-Determination," id., 302-3; 1 J. Verzijl, *International Law in Historical Perspective*, 321 (1968); A. Milot, *Les Mandats international*, 5 (1924); 4 W. Churchill, *The World Crisis*, 209 (1929); Garraty, "Failure After Versailles," in *The American Story*, 313-14 (E. Miers ed., 1956); W. Leuchtenberg, *The Perils of Prosperity, 1914-1932*, at 48 (1958); Mustafa, "The Principle of Self-Determination in International Law," 5 *Int'l Law*, 479 (1971); McWhinney, "Nationalism and Self-Determination and Contemporary Canadian Federalism," in 3 *Miscellanea W. J. Ganshoff Van Der Meersch*, 221 (1972).

6. 1 D. Lloyd George, *Memoirs of the Peace Conference*, 11-12 (1939).

7. *Woodrow Wilson: Life and Letters,* 426 (R. Baker, ed., 1939); 1 Department of State, Foreign Relations of the United States, 1918 Russia Supp. 1, at 330-31 (1931).

8. See numbers 5, 6, 9, 10, 11, 12, and 13; J. Blum, *Woodrow Wilson and the Politics of Morality,* 148 (1956), states that eight points "advanced the principle of self-determination."

9. 2 Lloyd George, supra note 6, at 495, is one of the few participants or scholars to point this out.

10. Woolsey, "Two Treaties of Paris," supra note 5, at 83, and Woolsey, "Self-Determination," supra note 5, at 302, are illustrative of this.

11. 2 *Major Peace Treaties of Modern History, 1648-1967,* at 1265-1553 (F. Israel ed., 1967); 3 id., at 1535-2213; 4 Churchill, supra note 5, at 211, argued ten years after Paris that only about 3 percent of Europe's population was placed under governments they opposed, claiming "the map of Europe has for the first time been drawn in general harmony with the wishes of its people." A contrary view is expressed in Brown, "Self-Determination in Central Europe," 14 *Am. J. Int'l. L.,* 235, 237-38 (1920).

12. R. Lansing, *The Peace Negotiations: A Personal Narrative,* 97-98 (1921).

13. These include the Fourteen Points of January 8, 1918; Wilson's address to Congress on February 11, 1918; the Mount Vernon speech of July 4, 1918; the New York speech of September 27, 1918. See also M. Pomerance, "The United States and Self-Determination: Perspectives on the Wilsonian Conception," 70 *Am. J. Int'l. L.,* 1, 2 (1976).

14. See A. Cobban, *The Nation State and National Self-Determination,* 58 and 64-65 (1969).

15. Id., at 57-75 and 93-97; see also Brown, supra note 11, at 235; Milot, supra note 5.

16. For a brief discussion of the mandate system, see 1 D. O'Connell, *International Law,* 363-70 (1964); 1 L. Oppenheim, *International Law,* 212-22 (8th ed., H. Lauterpacht, 1958). An extensive analysis can be found in Milot, supra note 5; Q. Wright, *Mandates under the League of Nations* (1930); Slonim, "The Origins of the South West Africa Dispute: The Versailles Peace Conference and the Creation of the Mandate System," 6 *Can. Y.B. Int'l. L.,* 115 (1968).

17. 1 Verzijl, supra note 5, at 558; V. Van Dyke, *Human Rights, the United States, and the World Community,* 81 (1970), assessing post–World War II developments, claims "the word 'self-determination' has become a weapon used in political struggles because it has appeal, whether or not it is apt." He also points up the confusion since the ending of World War II as to whether self-determination represents a right or a principle (id., at 78-79); Greenspan, "Human Rights in the Territories Occupied by Israel," 12 *Santa*

Clara Law, 377, 394 (1972), asserts "the truth is that the purported right of self-determination is an exceedingly vague and undefined concept."

18. 1 Verzijl, supra note 5, at 321-25 and 557-58; I. Brownlie, *Principles of Public International Law,* 483 (1966); Green, "Self-Determination and Settlement of the Arab-Israeli Conflict," 65 *Proc. Amer. Soc. Int'l. Law,* 40 (1971); see Mustafa, supra note 5, at 487.

19. Brownlie, supra note 18, at 483; Bassiouni, "'Self-Determination' and the Palestinians," 65 *Proc. Amer. Soc. Int'l. L.,* 31, 33 (1971); 1 G. Schwarzenberger, *A Manual of International Law,* 67 (4th ed., 1960). The latter goes on to note the "potentialities of the principle as an optional principle of international law."

20. Brownlie, supra note 18, at 483; Abi-Saab, "Wars of National Liberation and the Laws of War," 3 *Annales d'études internationales,* 93, 98-99 (1972).

21. According to one noted authority, the development of human rights in the international arena has made its greatest strides as part of customary international law by way of self-determination (Lauterpacht, "Some Concepts of Human Rights," *Howard L. J.,* 264 [1965]).

22. Bassiouni, supra note 19; C. Tornaritis, *The Right of Self-Determination with Special Reference to the Republic of Cyprus,* 2 (1973); Toynbee, *Hellenism* (1959), implies this throughout. Athens, of course, provides the best example.

23. Gross, "The Peace of Westphalia, 1648-1949," 42 *Am. J. Int'l. L.,* 20, 22-24 (1948), strongly hints that the evolution of self-determination as a human right dates from these treaties. Professor Mirabelli, quoted in id., n.22., views "the equality of confessions" as an "international agreement" which overrode the wishes of the ruler. See also Bassiouni, supra note 19; I. Claude, *National Minorities,* 6-7 (1955); Tonaritis, supra note 22, at 2. A close reading of the Treaty of Westphalia makes this interpretation suspect (see 1 Israel, supra note 11, at 7).

24. Cf. R. Aron, *Peace and War,* 81-82 (1966); Bos, "Self-Determination by the Grace of History," 15 *Netherlands Int'l. L. Rev.* 362 (1968); Cobban, supra note 14, at 114, which adds the caveat that "it had been a simple corollary of democracy"; East Pakistan Staff Study, "Right of Self-Determination in International Law," 8 *Int'l. Comm. Jurists Rev.,* 23, 43 (1972); U.N. Comm'n. on the Racial Situation in the Union of South Africa, Report, UN GAOR, Supp. 16, UN Doc. A/2505 (1952).

25. 1 Verzijl, supra note 5, at 321; Woolsey, "Self-Determination," supra note 5, at 302; Cobban, supra note 14, at 114.

26. 4 Churchill, supra note 5, at 208-9; Cobban, supra note 14, at 42, seems to share his view of Mazzini's role.

27. 1 Verzijl, supra note 5, at 321; Woolsey, "Two Treaties of Paris,"

supra note 5, at 83, a contemporary view, describes the territorial adjustments proposed by the Paris Peace Conference as "fairly revolutionary"; Van Dyke, supra note 17, at 86, suggests that self-determination became a "powerful force in world affairs mainly as a result of the speeches of Woodrow Wilson"; cf. Emerson, "Self-Determination," 60 *Proc. Amer. Soc. Int'l. L.,* 135, 137 (1966); Schoenberg, "Limits of Self-Determination," 6 *Israel Y.B. on Human Rts.,* 91 (1976).

28. Brown, supra note 11, at 235, refers to the "right of self-determination," as a "fundamental principle of international law and order." Cf. Schwelb, *Human Rights and the International Community,* 132 (1964); Sukovic, "Principle of Equal Rights and Self-Determination of Peoples," in *Principles of International Law concerning Friendly Relations and Cooperation,* 323 (M. Sahovic ed., 1972), claims that following promulgation of the UN Charter, self-determination was no longer a mere principle but an absolute legal right. Van Dyke, supra note 17, at 78, draws a careful distinction between self-determination as a principle and self-determination as a human right. Greenspan, supra note 17, at 395, states that a principle may lay the foundation for creating a right, but cannot be equated with the right itself. There must be an adequate degree of definition before a right can be said to exist. For a sweeping definition as to what constitutes a human right, see Virally, "Droits de l'homme et théorie générale du droit international," 6 *Human Rts. J.,* 76 (1973).

29. UN Charter, Art. 1, ¶2, and Art. 55. It is frequently overlooked by commentators, although of fundamental importance, that self-determination has to be asserted as a *collective* concept (see Dienstein, "Terrorism and Wars of Liberation Applied to the Arab-Israeli Conflict: An Israeli Perspective," 3 *Israel Y.B. on Human Rights,* 78, 79-81 [1973]).

30. The Right of Peoples and Nations to Self-Determination, G.A. Res. 637 A-B-C, 7 UN GAOR Supp. 20, UN Doc. A/2361 (1952).

31. Declaration on the Granting of Independence to Colonial Countries and Peoples, G.A. Res. 1514, 15 UN GAOR Supp. 16, UN Doc. A/4684 (1960); see also opinion by the International Court of Justice, Legal Consequences for States of the Continued Presence of South Africa in Namibia (South-West Africa) notwithstanding Security Council Resolution 276 [1970], I.C.J., 16; 66 *Am. J. Int'l. L.,* 157 (1972), hereinafter cited as Namibia Case.

32. Manifestations of Racial and National Hatred, G.A. Res. 1510, 15 UN GAOR Supp. 16, UN Doc. A/4684 (1960).

33. Popular sovereignty may be defined as a concept of sovereign authority wherein power derives from an identifiable group, people, or nation and whereby the governing entity acts in a trusteeship capacity with the consent of the governed. Cf. J. Stein (ed., unabridged ed.) *The Random House Dictionary of the English Language* (1967); Yick Wo v. Hopkins, 118 U.S. 356, 370 (1886).

34. Supra note 31, G.A. Res. 1514.

35. 1 Verzijl, supra note 5, at 323. Another commentator observed that of the more than three dozen General Assembly resolutions dealing with self-determination, "the formulae have been so vague as to confuse substantive legal content" (Spencer, "The Impact of International Law on Political and Social Processes within the African Context," 66 *Proc. Amer. Soc. Int'l. L.,* 56, 57 [1972]). An earlier critic likewise complained that "these utterances take no account of reason, or justice, or practicality, they simply bespeak desires" (Eagleton, "Self-Determination in the United Nations," 47 *Am. J. Int'l. L.,* 88, 89 [1953]).

36. Question of South-West Africa, G.A. Res. 2145, 21 UN GAOR Supp. 16, UN Doc. A/6316 (1966).

37. South-West Africa Cases [1966], I.C.J., 6.

38. Supra note 36.

39. International Covenant on Economic, Social, and Cultural Rights, International Covenant on Civil and Political Rights and Optional Protocol to the International Covenant on Civil and Political Rights, G.A. Res. 2200, 21 UN GAOR Supp. 16, UN Doc. A/6316 (1966); see also comment by the International Court of Justice, Namibia Case, supra note 31, at ¶ 52.

40. Question of South-West Africa, G.A. Res. 2248, 21 UN GAOR (Fifth Special Session) Supp. 1, UN Doc. A/6657 (1967).

41. Question of South-West Africa, G.A. Res. 2372, 22 UN GAOR Supp. 16 A, UN Doc. A/6716/Add. 1 (1968).

42. Resolution of the Security Council requesting an advisory opinion from the International Court of Justice on the question, What are the legal consequences for states of the continued presence of South Africa in Namibia, notwithstanding Security Council Resolution 276 (1970)? S.C. Res. 284, 25 UN SCOR (S/INF/25), UN Doc. S/9863 (1970).

43. I.C.J., Namibia Case, supra note 31, at ¶ 127. For a careful analysis of the opinion, see Gordon, "Old Orthodoxies amid New Experiences: The South West Africa (Namibia) Litigation and the Uncertain Jurisprudence of the International Court of Justice," 1 *Denver J. Int'l. L. and Policy,* 65, 72-92 (1971); Murphy, "Whither Now Namibia," 6 *Cornell Int'l. L. J.* (1972). The South African response is presented in Department of Foreign Affairs, *South West Africa Advisory Opinion 1971* (1972), and Information Service, Republic of South Africa, *South West Africa Case* (n.d.).

44. But see Department of Foreign Affairs, Republic of South Africa, supra note 43, at 11, which claims the Assembly was impliedly asserting unlimited powers. Twelve years earlier, the International Court declared that it was not part of its juridical function to apply the principle of self-determination to the Goa controversy (Case concerning Right of Passage over Indian Territory [Portugal v. India], [1960] I.C.J., 6).

45. Declaration of Principles of International Law concerning Friendly Relations and Cooperation among States in Accordance with the Charter of the United Nations, G.A. Res. 2625, 25 UN GAOR Supp. 28, UN Doc. A/8028 (1970).

46. Importance of the Universal Realization of the Right of Peoples to Self-Determination and of the Speedy Granting of Independence to Colonial Countries and Peoples for the Effective Guarantee and Observance of Human Rights, G.A. Res. 2787, 26 UN GAOR Supp. 29, UN Doc. A/8429 (1971).

47. Measures to Prevent International Terrorism which Endangers or Takes Innocent Human Lives or Jeopardizes Fundamental Freedoms, and Study of the Underlying Causes of those Forms of Terrorism and Acts of Violence Which Lie in Misery, Frustration, Grievance, and Despair and Which Cause Some People to Sacrifice Human Lives, Including Their Own, in an Attempt to Effect Radical Changes, G.A. Res. 3034, 27 UN GAOR Supp. 30, UN Doc. A/8730 (1972).

48. See particularly the Assembly declarations of January 12, 1973, Importance of the Universal Realization of the Right of Peoples to Self-Determination and of the Speedy Granting of Independence to Colonial Countries and Peoples for the Effective Guarantee and Observance of Human Rights, G.A. Res. 2955, 27 UN GAOR Supp. 30, UN Doc. A/8730 (1972); and the Assembly declaration of the same title of November 30, 1973, at G.A. Res. 3070, 28 UN GAOR Supp. 30, UN Doc. A/9030 (1973). The double standard on self-determination is nowhere more apparent than in the UN Draft Definition of Aggression of April 1974, which specifically exempts "peoples under colonial and racist regimes or other forms of alien domination" from inclusion in the category of aggressive acts (UN press release L/2092 [April 12, 1974]).

49. See the discussion in East Pakistan Staff Study, supra note 23, at 48-86 and 49-50; Humphrey, "The International Law of Human Rights in the Middle Twentieth Century," in *The Present State of International Law*, 103 (M. Bos., ed., 1973); Bowett, "Self-Determination and Political Rights in Developing Countries," 60 *Proc. Amer. Soc. Int'l. L.*, 129, 130 (1966); Mustafa, supra note 5; Modeen, "The International Protection of the National Identity of the Aaland Islands," 12 *Scand. Studies L.*, 177, 181-82 (1973); Novogrod, "Internal Strife, Self-Determination, and World Order," in 1 *A Treatise on International Criminal Law*, 211 (M. Bassiouni and V. Nanda, eds., 1973), sharply criticizes the newly-independent African states for their official anti-secessionist attitudes. His criticism is blunted, however, by a failure to mention either the rule or its exception.

50. Universal Declaration of Human Rights, G.A. Res. 217A, 3 UN GAOR Supp. 2, UN Doc. A/555 (1948).

51. See supra note 39.

52. Quoted by Emerson, "Self-Determination," 65 *Am. J. Int'l. L.*, 459, 464 (1971).

53. Id., at 465-77; J. Fawcett, *The Law of Nations*, 37 (1968), wryly observes "a cynic might conclude that in U.N. politics some people have a greater right of self-determination than others." In the eyes of Professor Humphrey, the United Nations has adopted the questionable position that though "all peoples have the right of self-determination, only colonial countries *are* peoples" (Humphrey, supra note 49, at 103).

54. East Pakistan Staff Study, supra note 24, at 45-46.

55. A similar interpretation has been put upon the Universal Declaration of Human Rights, also unanimously adopted (see Sohn, "The Universal Declaration of Human Rights," 8 *J. Int'l. Comm. of Jurists*, no. 2, at 23 [1967]; Sohn, "Protection of Human Rights through International Legislation," in *Problèmes de protection internationale des droits de l'homme*, 325 [K. Vasak ed., 1969]). Scholarly opinion, however, has divided over the question of whether the human rights provisions contained in the Charter (including self-determination) imposes legal obligations on the UN member states (see Schwelb, "The International Court of Justice and the Human Rights Clauses of the Charter," 66 *Am. J. Int'l. L.*, 337, 338-41 [1972]; Bassiouni, "Unlawful Seizures and Irregular Rendition Devices as Alternatives to Extradition," 7 *Vand. J. Transnat'l. L.*, 25, 52-55 [1973]. The International Court of Justice holds that "an international instrument has to be interpreted and applied within the framework of the entire legal system at the time of the interpretation" (I.C.J., Namibia Case, supra note 31, at ¶53).

56. For an affirmative answer see Higgins, "The United Nations and Lawmaking: The Political Organs," 64 *Proc. Amer. Soc. Int'l. L.*, 37 (1970). Schwelb, supra note 55, at 338-41, summarizes both positive and negative views. Confusion over the applicability of UN covenants and Assembly resolutions has led one exasperated authority to remark with respect to self-determination that "it is one of the most hallowed principles of the United Nations and, like all the hallowed principles of the United Nations, tends to be completely disregarded" (Green, supra note 18, at 55).

57. Brownlie, supra note 18, at 484.

58. See, e.g., 1 Verzijl, supra note 5, at 323, 326, and 557; Green, supra note 18. The former views both the substantive contents of self-determination and the extent of its operation as "floating on air."

59. Moore, "The Control of Foreign Intervention in Internal Conflict," 9 *Va. J. Int'l. L.*, 209, 247 (1969).

60. See the interesting discussion in Bassiouni, supra note 19. On the importance of territory, cf. H. Lauterpacht, *Recognition in International Law*, 30 (1948).

61. Fisher, "The Participation of Microstates in International Affairs," 62

Proc. Amer. Soc. Int'l. L., 164, 166 (1968). See particularly the problems raised by Franck and Hoffman, "The Right of Self-Determination in Very Small Places," 8 *N.Y.U.J. Int'l. L. and Pol.,* 331 (1978).

62. Cf., for example, the remarks of Moore, supra note 59, at 209; Emerson, supra note 52, at 459; Brown, supra note 11, at 235; Woolsey, supra note 5, at 302. Novogrod, "Internal Strife, Self-Determination, and World Order," 23 *Jag. J.,* 63, 70 (1968-69), claims "the essential task is to determine the dividing line between civil strife which is basically criminal and that which is an expression of the will of the people."

63. Criteria suggested by T. Mensah, "Self-Determination under United Nations Auspices," (Ph.D. dissertation, Yale Law School, 1963), 282-329; also cited in Moore, supra note 59, at 249; cf. the categories listed in East Pakistan Staff Study, supra note 24, at 47; the questions raised by Greenspan, supra note 17, at 395-96; and Nyar, "Self-Determination beyond the Colonial Context: Biafra in Retrospect," 10 *Texas Int'l. L. J.,* 321, 339-40 (1975).

64. See the comments of Cobban, supra note 14, at 144-47; Brown, supra note 11; 1 Verzijl, supra note 5, at 322-24. Religious minorities such as the Catholics in Northern Ireland or the Moslems in India cannot be excluded from claiming special political rights under this all-embracing principle. The question of what constitutes a people is summed up by the East Pakistan Staff Study, supra note 24, at 47, with the statement that "the fact of constituting a people is a political phenomenon, that the right of self-determination is founded on political considerations and that the exercise of that right is a political act."

65. See K. Wheare, *Modern Constitutions* (1966), especially at 87-88; 1 *Le Droit dans la vie familiale,* xiii-xxx and 3-25 (J. Boucher and A. Morel, eds., 1970); Sussman, "Bilingualism and the Law in Canada," 6 *Int'l. Symposium on Comparative Law,* 9 (1969); Dutoit, "Droit et pluirlinguisme en Suisse," id., 39; Caparros, "Le droit face au bilinguisme: comparative conclusion," id., 107; McWhinney, "Federalism, Biculturalism, and International Law," 3 *Can. Y.B. Int'l. L.,* 100 (1965). The USSR, on the other hand, provides significant autonomy to its constituent republics in theory, but very little in practice (see American Bar Association, *A Contrast between the Legal Systems in the United States and the Soviet Union* [1968]; J. Triska, *Constitutions of the Community Party States* [1968]). The unique relationship between the bilingual Commonwealth of Puerto Rico and the United States presents another alternative, though the arrangement is not without its difficulties (see Panel, "The Applicability of the Principle of Self-Determination to Unintegrated Territories of the United States: The Cases of Puerto Rico and the Trust Territory of the Pacific Islands," 67 *Proc. Amer. Soc. Int'l. L.,* 1 [1973]). Professor Cabranes prefers the Spanish term of "Free Associated State" to the English word "Commonwealth" (id., at 2).

66. For the original Nigerian Federal System and its subsequent modifications, see the comments and documents in 8 *Constitutions of the Countries of the World,* Kasunmu, "Nigeria," 1-9 (A. Blaustein and G. Flanz, eds., 1972). The original nature of the Pakistan Federation and its subsequent modifications is discussed in 1 *Blaustein and Flanz,* Blaustein, Augenstein, and Kornhauser, "Bangladesh."

67. Cf. J. Coleman, *Nigeria: Background in Nationalism* (1958); J. Cameron, *The African Revolution* (1960); F. Moraes, *India Today* (1960); K. Callard, *Pakistan: A Political Study* (1957); Pearson and Tonsich, "The Partition of India and Pakistan: The Emergence of Bangladesh," in *The Problem of Partition: Peril to World Peace,* 133 (T. Hachey, ed., 1972).

68. Cf. the excellent analyses of East Pakistan Staff Study, supra note 24; Nanda, "Self-Determination in International Law: The Tragic Tale of Two Cities," 66 *Am. J. Int'l. L.,* 321 (1972); Nanda, "A Critique of the United Nations Inaction in the Bangladesh Crisis," 49 *Den. L. J.,* 53 (1972); Franck and Rodley, "The Law, the United Nations, and Bangladesh," 2 *Israel Y.B. on Human Rights,* 142 (1972); Ijalaye, "Was 'Biafra' at Any Time a State in International Law?" 65 *Am. J. Int'l. L.,* 551 (1971); Nyar, supra note 63.

69. Ijalaye, supra note 68, at 553-56; see also Mowls, "Infringement of Human Rights in Biafra and the Response of the United States and the United Nations," in *International Protection of Human Rights, Hearings before the Subcommittee on International Organizations and Movements of the House Comm. on Foreign Affairs,* 93rd Cong., 1st Sess., 877 (1973). The Assembly of the Organization of African Unity meeting in its Fourth Session between September 11 to 14, 1967, approved a "Resolution on the Situation in Nigeria" which generally condemned any act of secession occurring within a member state and specifically denounced the Biafran rebellion (6 *Int'l. Legal Materials,* 1243 [1967]).

70. Quoted in Ijalaye, supra note 68, at 556; the emphasis is mine. Former UN Secretary-General U. Thant sought to emphasize the humanitarian aspect as distinct from the political issues (De Schutter, "Humanitarian Intervention: A United Nations Task," 3 *Cal. West. Int'l. L. J.,* 21, 36 [1972]).

71. 2 *Encyclopedia Britannica, Macropaedia,* 690, col. 2 (15th ed., 1974).

72. See the discussion in East Pakistan Staff Study, supra note 24, at 23; Nanda, "Self-Determination," supra note 68; Nanda, "A Critique of the United Nations Inaction," supra note 68; Niksch, "The Violations of Human Rights in East Pakistan in 1971 and the U.S. and U.N. Response," in *International Protection of Human Rights,* supra note 69, at 913; Franck and Rodley, supra note 68, at 142.

73. See supra notes 45 and 52.

74. Van Dyke, supra note 17, at 102.

75. Franck and Rodley, "After Bangladesh: The Law of Humanitarian

Intervention by Military Force," 67 *Am. J. Int'l. L.,* 275 (1973); cf., Note, "Bangladesh," 14 *Harv. Int'l. L. J.,* 565 (1973); Friedman, Comment, in *Humanitarian Intervention and the United Nations,* 114 (R. Lillich ed., 1973).

76. This was clearly perceived by Brown, supra note 11, written only one year after the Paris Peace Conference. Speaking along the same lines in 1952, Mrs. Eleanor Roosevelt warned that "the principle of self-determination of peoples given unrestricted application could result in chaos" (27 *State Dept. Bulletin,* 919 [December 8, 1952]).

77. Cobban, supra note 14, at 96, observes that except where they worked to Germany's direct advantage, Hitler's arguments were "consistently hostile to the principle of self-determination."

78. See the comments of L. Goodrich, E. Hambro and A. Simons, *Charter of the United Nations,* 29-35 (3rd rev. ed., 1969); N. Bentwich and A. Martin, *A Commentary on the Charter of the United Nations,* xiii-xv (1951); 1 Oppenheim, supra note 16, at 738 and 872-73. Churchill's statement is quoted in id., at 873 n.2.

79. See supra note 29.

80. See supra note 50; Van Dyke, supra note 17, at 77, states: "Neither the Charter of the United Nations nor the Universal Declaration of Human Rights suggests that questions about self-determination and minorities should figure in discussions of human rights."

81. See supra note 34.

82. United Nations, *Y.B. on Human Rights 1960,* at iii-iv (1962).

83. See supra note 39.

84. See supra note 52.

85. See supra note 70.

86. Professor Van Dyke insists that "if self-determination is a right only for the inhabitants of colonies, the United Nations and its various members have a better chance of avoiding involvement in efforts to re-draw boundary lines over much of the world" (Van Dyke, supra note 17, at 102). A case in point is the Cyprus controversy which dramatically demonstrates the restrictive barriers created by the one-time-only rule. For a general background, cf. Kyriakides, "Cyprus: Constitutional Chronology," 2 *Blaustein and Franz,* supra note 66; Tornaritis, supra note 22.

87. Aron, supra note 24, at 728-29. Professor Sohn has called it "an idea that revolutionized the world" (Sohn, Comment, "Radical Perceptions of International Law and Practice," 66 *Proc. Amer. Soc. Int'l. L.,* 162, 173 [1972]); Note, "Towards Self-Determination—A Reappraisal as Reflected in the Declaration on Friendly Relations," 3 *Ga. J. Int'l. and Comp. L.,* 145 (1973), presents a similarly optimist but largely uncritical view.

88. Plato, *The Crito.*

89. Aron, supra note 24, at 81 and 375.

90. Prominent examples of partition include Ireland (pre–World War II), the Indian Subcontinent, the Indochinese peninsula, Palestine, Korea, and Germany; cf. *Divided Nations in a Divided World* (G. Henderson, R. Lebow, and J. Stoessinger, eds., 1974).

91. See especially the studies contained in Hachey, supra note 67. Surprisingly, there is no mention at all of self-determination by any of the authors. Many political scientists argue that the concept of partition is applicable solely to unitary states and prefer to substitute the term secession when referring to federal structures.

92. A Leningrad apartment house in the desperate days of the Russian Civil War petitioned President Wilson for the right of self-determination. Throughout the month of October 1973, both the *Washington Post* and the *Washington Star-News* enthusiastically proposed "self-determination" for the District of Columbia.

93. Humphrey, supra note 49, at 104, refers to a direct causal relationship between self-determination and the "increasing politicization of human rights in the United Nations." A. Rigo Sureda, *The Evolution of the Right of Self-Determination: A Study of United Nations Practice*, 261 (1973), maintains that "self-determination has come to mean emergence as an independent state by getting rid of colonial rule."

94. Professor Bos emphatically declares that "nothing is gained by an identification of self-determination and human rights" (Bos, supra note 24, at 372). Admittedly, Portuguese President Antonio de Spinola's statement published in the *Government Gazette* on July 24, 1974, which acknowledged "in accordance with the United Nations Charter, the recognition by Portugal of the right to self-determination" of her overseas territories, strengthens the case for self-determination as a collective human right (statement quoted in the *Chicago Tribune*, July 25, 1974). Nonetheless, the overall historical record is hardly persuasive. For sweeping UN claims made before the Portuguese military takeover, see the Joint Statement of 9 May 1974 by the chairman of the Special Committee on the Situation with Regard to the Implementation of the Declaration on Granting Independence to Colonial Peoples, the chairman of the Special Committee on Apartheid, and the president of the United Nations Council for Namibia reaffirming the objective of total and complete independence of Angola, Mozambique, and the other territories in Southern Africa (UN Doc. A/Ac.109/447).

13
Self-Determination:
A United Nations Perspective

Seymour Maxwell Finger
Gurcharan Singh

The three decades following World War II have been marked by many unprecedented developments which have materially changed the world political environment. Of these, the liquidation of the Western colonial empires and the emergence of more than sixty new nations in Asia and Africa are of cardinal significance for students of international politics. Neither Woodrow Wilson nor Lenin, "two unlike partners," who "met at this point of national self-determination,"[1] could have anticipated the speed and extent of the colonial revolution. Even those who drafted the Charter of the United Nations did not inspire much hope in this direction—despite some conceptual improvement in the Charter over the Covenant of the League of Nations. Nevertheless, the era of Western colonialism is almost coming to an end, despite some remaining outposts in southern Africa. Many new multinational and polyethnic political entities have emerged as powerful forces in the world arena. In this process, the ethical and political principles of self-determination have been transformed into a major political weapon. Indeed, in its present reincarnation, it can be misconstrued as a universal legal norm. The following analysis will focus on the changing ramifications of self-determination in the contemporary world.

The Dynamics of Self-Determination

The scope of the League of Nations mandate system was limited to territories taken from defeated enemies and only supervisory competence was conceded to the League. Nevertheless, it marked the "beginning of systematic international intrusion into the workings of colonialism."[2] While the trusteeship system represents some conceptual improvement over the mandate system, the dynamics of interplay of forces had also changed a great deal between 1919 and 1945. The myth of Western supremacy was shattered. Japan, even though defeated in 1945, had inflicted a crushing blow to the Western colonialism in Asia. Western-educated elites in Asia and Africa had undermined colonial authority by preaching the right of self-determination, which had acquired a new talismanic connotation for the people aspiring for independence. Liberal elements within the Western world were raising serious questions about the legitimacy of colonialism. In fact, "the whole structure of imperialism was threatened by 'rising tide of color' in such ancient centers of civilization as China, India and Egypt."[3] Despite American assurances to Winston Churchill at the Yalta Conference about the limited scope of the proposed trusteeship machinery, anti-colonial forces were gathering increasing strength. As pointed out by Inis Claude, Jr.:

> The critical difference between the political context of 1945 and that of the early League era lies in the fact that widespread attack upon the very existence of the colonial system had gathered momentum by the end of World War II. . . . Colonialism had become a global question, and the political arena within which it was discussed had been enlarged to include active and vociferous participants from both sides of the colonial fence.[4]

In the words of Rupert Emerson, "India's independence and the total removal of China from the Western sphere established a world in which the old signposts no longer served as useful guides, and had even become dangerously misleading."[5]

Chapter 11 of the Charter on Declaration Regarding Non-Self-Governing Territories, which has been used by the anti-colonial forces in the United Nations to demand the speedy end of colonialism, speaks neither of self-determination nor of colonialism. The principle of self-determination, enshrined in Arts. 1(2) and 55 of the Charter, does not explicitly address itself to the wider problem of colonialism. Nevertheless, the anti-colonial coalition used the international arena to launch an all-out diplomatic attack on colonialism by expanding the implications of Chapter 11 of the Charter and "by outflanking the Trusteeship System."[6] They waged an aggressive campaign "to override claims of domestic jurisdiction, and restrictive interpretations of the commitments in Chapter XI."[7]

The process of decolonization, which has radically changed the political map of the world, coincided with the development of the United Nations, though the direct role of the United Nations in this transformation has been modest.[8] In fact, the main contribution of the United Nations lies in "the creation of a climate of opinion which has given the decolonization movement a considerable impetus."[9] Moreover, the United Nations provided the necessary parliamentary framework to experiment with the trade-union style of diplomacy and to organize a kind of small-power pressure group as a countervailing force to humble Western colonialism in international assemblies.

The Afro-Asian countries, while increasing their numerical strength in the United Nations, signaled a major diplomatic offensive in the Bandung Conference held in 1955. The conference declared that "colonialism in all its manifestations is an evil which should speedily be brought to an end." During the Fifteenth General Assembly in 1960, the colonial question was placed in a new dimension. Seventeen former colonial territories joined the ranks of independent nations and were admitted to the United Nations in that year. By this time, "almost one billion people, inhabiting more than 20 percent of the world's land area, had gone from dependence to independence. . . . These new nations proudly swelled the ranks of the United Nations by thirty-three, and there was a promise of more on the way."[10]

While Western colonialism was in retreat, the anti-colonial forces were impatient with the pace of decolonization. This was reflected in the Fifteenth General Assembly's Declaration on the Granting of Independence to Colonial Countries and Peoples. It declared, inter alia, that "all peoples have the right to self-determination" and that "the subjection of peoples to alien subjugation, domination and exploitation constitutes a denial of fundamental human rights, is contrary to the Charter of the United Nations and is an impediment to the promotion of world peace and cooperation."[11] Besides expanding the implications of Chapter 11 of the Charter, the champions of decolonization "relied upon the principle of self-determination embodied in Articles 1 and 55 of the U.N. Charter to buttress their argument that all forms of colonialism were contrary to the Charter and inherently dangerous to world peace."[12] In the opinion of Rupert Emerson, it was "a virtual amendment to the Charter, branding all colonialism as illegitimate as the Charter's Article 73 did not."[13] He also pointed out that "although the U.N. might help to make it so, self-determination is not a right which finds any place in international law."[14]

At any rate, in their zeal for complete decolonization, the anti-colonial forces tended to apply self-determination "across the board to all colonial territories."[15] This was so, despite the frightening experience with the Belgian Congo's sudden independence and consequent bloodshed. It may, however, be mentioned that the uncompromising attitude of Portugal and the white minority regimes in South Africa and Southern Rhodesia provided further ammunition to the militants among the anti-colonial group. South Africa's rigid policy of racial segregation and her intransigence in the case of South-West Africa (Namibia) were cited as added justifications for this militancy. Therefore, the anti-colonial powers "have tended to regard themselves as crusaders, doing battle against the forces of entrenched privilege and oppressive exploitation."[16] Thus, mutual recrimination rather than mutual consultation characterized the situation. In this atmosphere, the voices which would counsel patience and still speak in terms of peaceful transformation were very much subdued.

The following year, the Assembly, expressing its regret over the poor response to the declaration, established a special committee composed of seventeen members to examine the implementation of the declaration. In 1962, the Assembly, expressing its "profound regret" at the failure to implement the declaration and deploring the "deliberate refusal of certain administering Powers to cooperate," increased the membership of the special committee from seventeen to twenty-four and reaffirmed its mandate.[17]

It was not difficult for the Committee of Twenty-Four to mobilize overwhelming support for the adoption of resolutions against the colonial powers, but the results were not encouraging. Instead of meaningful negotiations and consultations to arrive at a consensus, the committee took extreme positions—which reflected its impatience with the hard core of colonialism represented by Portugal, South Africa, and Southern Rhodesia. The climax of this militancy was reflected in the program of action in connection with the tenth anniversary of the Declaration on the Granting of Independence to Colonial Countries and Peoples. As observed by one of the authors in an earlier article: "Not only did this program carry forward all of the unworkable recommendations of previous sessions, but it added an endorsement of armed struggle and declared that 'Member States shall render all necessary moral and material assistance to the peoples of colonial Territories in their struggle to attain freedom and independence.'"[18] Consequently, the United States and the United Kingdom decided to withdraw from the Committee of Twenty-Four. It may, however, be added that

It was not the United States view that peoples should be denied the right to resort to any means at their disposal, including violence, if armed suppression by a colonial power required it. Indeed, the United States itself was obliged to resort to violence in order to gain independence. The difficulty lay in giving a general endorsement by the United Nations—an organization dedicated to peace—to such violence (which) could hardly be reconciled with the requirements of the Charter of the United Nations.[19]

Another objection raised by the United States, the United Kingdom, and other Western members was the tendency of the majority in the Committee of Twenty-Four to regard independence as the only acceptable form of self-determination for dependent territories. Thus, the majority disregarded the provisions of General Assembly Resolution 1541 (15) which stated, in its Annex, Principle 6, that self-government could be deemed to have been attained if any of the three conditions were fulfilled: (1) emergence as a sovereign state, (2) free association with an independent state,[20] or (3) integration with an independent state. This militancy can be explained in terms of divergent perceptions and mutual suspicion of each other's motivations. Therefore, the anti-colonial coalition opposed even genuine cases of "free association" or "integration," fearing that these were disguised pretexts for keeping colonial control over certain areas.

In any case, the anti-colonial forces used the parliamentary arena of the United Nations to inflict moral and political humiliation upon Western colonialism, and to challenge its legitimacy. Though "war of liberation" did not fit in the Gandhian vocabulary, India had to use force to "liberate" Goa. India's action was condemned by the Western powers but acclaimed by the anti-colonial group. India's argument that (1) Goa was an integral part of India, "illegally occupied by right of conquest by the Portuguese," (2) "Portugal has no sovereign right over this territory," (3) "there is no legal frontier—there can be no legal frontier—between India and Goa," and (4) "there can be no question of aggression against your own frontier, or against your own people, whom you want to liberate," received overwhelming support.[21] In fact, India's defense minister, V. K. Krishna Menon, went a step further and justified India's action in terms of the developing international law, thereby challenging the colonial titles. He further stated that India regarded colonialism as "permanent aggression."[22] India's "Western critics conceded that they could not expect to win . . . a political verdict unfavorable to India."[23]

The Reincarnation of Self-Determination

During this struggle between colonialism and national self-determination at the United Nations, the anti-colonial powers were successful in expanding the application of Chapter 11 and other stipulations embodied in the Charter regarding non-self-governing territories and trust territories. In this process, they buttressed their arguments with reference to the principle of self-determination embodied in Arts. 1 and 55 of the Charter. However, it would be misleading to think that the scope of self-determination has been expanded beyond limits. On the contrary, in its "present incarnation, the loudly proclaimed right of all peoples to self-determination must actually be read to mean that all overseas colonial peoples have a right to be liberated from the overlordship of their alien white masters."[24] That is why the champions of self-determination virtually ignored similar claims of the Biafrans in Nigeria, the Kurds in Iraq, the Karens in Burma, the Croatians in

Yugoslavia, the Nagas in India, the Somalis in Kenya and Ethiopia—to cite a few examples. They also assumed an evasive silence during Soviet interventions in Hungary and Czechoslovakia and the Chinese annexation of Tibet—not to mention the Formosans right to self-determination. On this point, the following observations are pertinent:

1. In this connection oppression of white men by white men is viewed by many Asians and Africans as different and perhaps less deplorable than the oppression of colored men by white men.

2. Following a liberation achieved in the name of the principle of national self-determination, the successor governments are often plagued by the problem of a continuing demand for national self-determination on the part of groups comprising the nations.[25]

It is needless to add that the anti-colonial forces at the United Nations have been functioning on the basis of consensus, like any other political coalition or a trade union. As such, for the sake of Afro-Asian unity and continued Latin-American and Soviet bloc's support in the struggle over colonialism, they compromised over the issues involving intraregional and intranational disputes. By the same token, claims for self-determination (based on distinct ethnicity, religion, culture, or language) coming into conflict with the territorial integrity of an existing state were ignored. On this issue, a widely held African view was summarized in a memorandum on the Somali question by the Kenya delegation to the Addis Ababa Conference in 1963: "The principle of self-determination has relevance where foreign domination is the issue. It has no relevance where the issue is territorial disintegration by dissident citizens."[26] In the same vein, the General Assembly has refused to accept the desire of the people of Mayotte, one of the Comoro Islands, to continue association with France. Instead, it has endorsed the claims of the Comoro Islands government to hold Mayotte, contrary to the will of its inhabitants as clearly expressed in a referendum.

It should also be noted that the Assembly consistently supported Indonesian claims to West Irian, despite the fact that its people were ethnically and culturally distinct. Its incorporation into Indonesia is more easily understood in terms of the general tendency to endorse succession by an African or Asian government to any territory formerly administered by a colonial power than to any overwhelming evidence produced by the secretary-general's representative.[27] On the other hand, the Indonesian invasion of East Timor, formerly a Portuguese territory, occasioned divided reactions among Third World countries, depending on their political sympathies. It will be interesting to see the reaction of members of the Trusteeship Council, the Security Council, and the General Assembly to the referendum in the Mariana Islands, whose people voted for detachment from the Trust Territory of the Pacific Islands and association with the United States.

This conflict between the claim for self-determination by a distinct minority (whether French Canadians, the Biafrans, the Kurds, the Karens, or the Croatians) and the territorial integrity of an existing state is not entirely new. Indeed, India was partitioned in 1947 on the basis of Muslim self-determination.

The partition of Palestine was another attempt to satisfy two conflicting claims for self-determination. The subsequent outbreak of four wars and the continued unsettled situation in the area are obvious evidence that this attempt to deal with the problem of the two conflicting nationalisms has still not resolved the issue. The literature on this situation is so voluminous that it would be superfluous to cite or summarize it here. For purposes of this essay, it suffices to record the General Assembly's decision to grant the Palestine Liberation Organization observer status and its endorsement of the "inalienable right" of the Palestinians to self-determination. Even Israel has accepted this "right," but has argued that such self-determination should be realized through Jordan, which could presumably incorporate the major part of the West Bank through negotiations with Israel, e.g., the Allon Plan. Politically, the Palestinian Arabs have been accepted by the Afro-Asian majority as one of their own; the Israelis have not. While this means that the General Assembly majority, including the Soviet bloc, will support the Arabs, it is most doubtful that the United Nations could or would enforce a decision to establish a new, independent Palestinian Arab state. Here too, the issue is likely to be decided, if and when it is decided, by negotiation among the parties and perhaps future shows of strength, rather than juridical edict or resolutions of the General Assembly or the Security Council.

As the era of Western colonialism is coming to an end, the question of self-determination is assuming new dimensions. As pointed out by Robert Lansing, "the phrase is simply loaded with dynamite. It will raise hopes which can never be realized."[28] It is often easier to identify the "self" against an "alien" rule, but it is difficult to reconcile self-determination with the countervailing principle of respect for the territorial integrity of an existing state—old or new. In fact, one claim can lead to another, just like opening a Pandora's box. This can take us back to where the thirteen American colonies started to form a "more perfect union." In a very insightful study on self-determination, though focused on the "Wilsonian Conception," Michla Pomerance makes the following interesting observations:

1. the concept of self-determination was not, and can never be, an ideal capable of universal application,

2. the identification of the "self" was not only "space-bound" but also "time-bound,"

3. the basic question of whose claim to self-determination will receive priority over whose claim to territorial integrity remains unresolved,

4. self-determination was, after all, most often "determined" by the "selves" concerned, rather than received by them as a gift.[29]

The last observation makes the validity and success of a claim, quite realistically, contingent upon the momentum of support and forceful assertion by whatever means—peaceful or violent. East Pakistan's secession from Pakistan and the emergence of Bangladesh as a new nation is a more recent case in point. East Pakistan's initial demand for complete autonomy was perceived by the military rulers of Pakistan as a threat to the territorial integrity of Pakistan. Therefore, West Pakistan's response was in the form of a massive military crackdown on the "troublemakers." Without India's military intervention, East Pakistan's transformed claim from autonomy to complete independence would have had only a little better chance of success than the Biafrans' claim against Nigeria.

Ved Nanda, in his appraisal of this conflict, suggested that "as the era of colonialism comes to a close, claims to self-determination in non-colonial situations are likely to increase" and "it may not be wise for the world community to reject all such claims."[30] In his opinion, the situation in East Pakistan had "approached the parameters of a colonial situation," for the following reasons: (1) economic exploitation; (2) ethnic, linguistic, and cultural differences; (3) a thousand miles of physical separation between East and West Pakistan; (4) the use of excessive military force to stifle dissent, approaching "selective genocide"; (5) the deprivation of human rights to a majority of Pakistanis; and (6) an overwhelming majority determination by vote of the future political directions. Using these factors as the basic criteria, he suggested that

> a decision can be made to place the demands of self-determination above those of "territorial integrity" and of a "non-intervention" stand on the part of the United Nations. For where violence is perpetrated by a minority to deprive a majority of political, economic, social, and cultural rights, the principles of "territorial integrity" and "non-intervention" should not be permitted to be used as a ploy to perpetuate the political subjugation of the majority.[31]

The above appraisal brings us closer to the present situation in South Africa and Southern Rhodesia, where white minority regimes are trying to preserve their privileged positions against the natives' demand for majority rule or self-determination. A recent editorial in the *New York Times*, inter alia, emphasized the following points:

> Mr. Vorster's Afrikaner minority may be able to repress the country's huge black majority for decades more, but not forever; and the time left for peaceful change will rapidly shrink if the last remnants of legitimacy are withdrawn from its Government by other nations.

> Violence and economic deprivation are tolerated too much in our own land. But racism stands condemned as intolerable. Official racism that seeks to root political power in the doctrine of the permanent inferiority of men and women of a different color is the evil inheritance of white men everywhere and they are pledged to expunge it.[32]

Conclusion

The era of Western colonialism is almost coming to an end, despite some remaining outposts in southern Africa. During this struggle over colonialism, the anti-colonial forces at the United Nations launched an all-out attack on Western colonialism by expanding the implications of Chapter 11 of the Charter and by "outflanking the Trusteeship System." In this struggle, they received a kind of "spiritual inspiration" from the principle of self-determination enshrined in Arts. 1(2) and 55 of the Charter. Therefore, they tended to apply it across the board to all colonial territories. The United Nations General Assembly provided the necessary parliamentary framework for the Afro-Asian group—in political coalition with the Latin-Americans and the Soviet bloc—to inflict moral and political humiliation on Western colonialism, and challenge the very legitimacy of the colonial titles everywhere.

Opinions might differ whether, in this process, the ethical and political principles of self-determination have been transformed into a universal legal norm or not. It would, however, be misleading to believe that, even in its present reincarnation, the practical application of self-determination has been expanded beyond limits. It sounds paradoxical, but on the demise of old colonial empires many new multinational and polyethnic political entities have emerged, with disturbing indications of the political phenomenon defined as "intrastate imperialism." It is not surprising, therefore, that forces of separatism exist in many of these new political entities, as well as in some older ones. These forces can neither be "wished away" nor "steamrolled" to nonexistence. These new claims, prima facie, come into conflict with the territorial integrity of many existing states. Yet there are situations where the principle of territorial integrity may have to give in to the principle of self-determination or find a way to compromise with it.

At any rate, the application of self-determination is likely to be highly selective. Since it is "loaded with dynamite," as Robert Lansing observed, it is not likely to be offered as a gift. The price may invariably have to be paid in the form of human life. In this process, the United Nations may not be instrumental in resolving major conflicts, but it is likely to get involved in many of them—

indeed, in certain cases, it may be called upon to function as a "receiver in bankruptcy." Ved Nanda's candid suggestions that "as the era of colonialism comes to a close, claims to self-determination in non-colonial situations are likely to increase" and that "it may not be wise for the world community to reject all such claims" are not likely to find much favor with the champions of the territorial integrity of the existing states—at any cost!

Nevertheless, the world community will have to deal with these new claims sooner or later, and possibly work out a modus vivendi to reconcile the two conflicting but valid claims. The quest of a national minority for the recognition and maintenance of its distinct identity at the vertical level has to be reconciled with the struggle of a preponderant majority to maintain the territorial integrity at the horizontal level. Despite the emphasis on class-based identities in many societies, ethno-cultural identities still remain powerful catalytic agents in group mobilization.[33] Political innovations may have to be worked out in the forms of loose federations, confederacies, and commonwealths, where national minorities would enjoy freedom in their own little ethno-cultural republics while remaining an integral part of the larger commonwealth.

Notes

1. Rupert Emerson, *From Empire to Nation* (Boston: Beacon Press, 1966), p. 3. Emerson points out that "the principle of self-determination derives from a familiar set of doctrines, whose apparent simplicity conceals a multitude of complications." The complexity becomes "most serious when the doctrine is brought down from abstraction to working reality and when the effort is made . . . to translate it from ethical and political precepts to binding legal norms" (ibid., p. 197).

Michla Pomerance suggests a very simple definition of self-determination "as freedom from alien rule," but points out the necessity of defining "what is 'self' and what is 'alien.'" She also observes that this concept has been "associated in the popular mind with Woodrow Wilson, although, in fact, he cannot claim true paternity but only foster-fatherhood." This expression borrowed from a German term *selbstbestimmungsrecht*, "gained political currency in Socialist circles from the turn of the century. . . . Popularization of the term even then owed more to the Bolsheviks than to Wilson." The Bolshevik slogan was: "Peace without annexations and indemnities on the basis of the self-determination of peoples" (see Michla Pomerance, "The United States and Self-Determination: Perspectives on the Wilsonian Conception," *American Journal of International Law* 70 [January 1976] :1-2).

2. Inis L. Claude, Jr., *Swords into Plowshares: The Problems and Progress of International Organization* (New York: Random House, 1964), p. 3.

3. Emerson, *From Empire to Nation*, p. 4.

4. Claude, *Swords into Plowshares*, p. 329.

5. Emerson, *From Empire to Nation*, p. 4.

6. Claude, *Swords into Plowshares*, p. 332.

7. Ibid. The Trusteeship Council has been dealing with the questions of trust territories, while the General Assembly took up the wider colonial issues. Eleven territories, which had either been former mandates or ex-enemy territories, were placed under the trusteeship system. Of these, ten have already achieved self-determination, leaving only the U.S.-administered Pacific Islands, where negotiations to end the trusteeship are now in process. The problem of South-West Africa (Namibia) administered by the Republic of South Africa is the only remaining League of Nations Mandate that has neither achieved independence nor been placed under the international trusteeship system. Besides, at the first session of the General Assembly in 1946, seventy-four territories were identified that had "not yet attained full measure of self-government." Consequently, Australia, Belgium, Denmark, France, the Netherlands, New Zealand, the U.K. and the U.S. agreed to transmit information on the enumerated territories to the General Assembly. Since Spain and Portugal were not members of the UN at that time (they were admitted in 1955), their colonies were added to the list in December 1960. Southern Rhodesia was added to the list in 1962. The government of Portugal under Dr. Salazar refused to transmit any information to the General Assembly, claiming that the overseas territories under their jurisdiction were not the colonies but the overseas provinces of Portugal.

8. Philippines, India, Pakistan, Burma, and Ceylon achieved independence much before the UN started consideration of the colonial issues in any significant manner. At any rate, more than sixty former colonial territories in Asia and Africa have joined the ranks of independent nations. The membership of the UN has increased from 51 in 1945 to 149 in 1977, with Vietnam's admission in September 1977.

9. David W. Wainhouse, *Remnants of Empire: The United Nations and End of Colonialism* (New York: Council on Foreign Relations, 1964), p. 5.

10. Ibid., p. 9.

11. G.A. Resolution 1514 (15), December 14, 1960 (adopted unanimously by a vote of 89 to 0 with 9 abstentions).

12. Wolfgang Friedmann et al., *International Law: Cases and Materials* (St. Paul, Minn.: West Publishing Company, 1969), p. 233.

13. Rupert Emerson, *Self-Determination Revisited in the Era of Decolonization* (Harvard University, Center for International Affairs, Occasional Paper, no. 9, December 1964), p. 29.

14. Emerson, *From Empire to Nation*, p. 303.

15. Wainhouse, *Remnants of Empire*, p. 5.

16. Claude, *Swords into Plowshares*, p. 337.

17. G.A. Resolution 1810 (17).

18. Seymour M. Finger, "A New Approach to Colonial Problems at the United Nations," *International Organization* (Winter 1972):145 (refers to General Assembly Resolution 2621 [25], October 12, 1970).

19. Ibid., pp. 145-46.

20. Editor's note; e.g., Puerto Rico or Pacific Islands.

21. SCOR, 987th meeting (December 18, 1961), pp. 10-11.

22. See Emerson, *Self-Determination Revisited*, p. 21.

23. Inis L. Claude, Jr., *The Changing United Nations* (New York: Random House, 1967), p. 97.

24. Emerson, *Self-Determination Revisited*, p. 63.

25. Ivo D. Duchacek, *Nations and Men* (Hinsdale, Ill.: Dryden Press, 1975), p. 80.

26. As cited by Friedmann et al., *International Law*, p. 233.

27. It appears that this general tendency among the Third World countries is influenced by their past experience with Western colonialism. They suspect that self-determination of smaller communities or their association with a former colonial power would provide new sanctuaries for Western colonialism. This suspicion and fear is often used as an excuse to fend off even genuine demands for self-determination by distinct but smaller political entities.

28. Robert Lansing, "Self-Determination," in *Saturday Evening Post* (April 9, 1921).

29. Pomerance, "United States and Self-Determination," pp. 9-10.

30. Ved P. Nanda, "Self-Determination in International Law," *American Journal of International Law* 66 (April 1972):322.

31. Ibid., p. 336.

32. *New York Times*, October 23, 1977.

33. See Nathan Glazer and Daniel Moynihan, "Why Ethnicity," *Commentary* (October 1974):37-38.

Part 7

Self-Determination:
Future Prospects

14
Self-Determination
and World Order

Harold S. Johnson
Baljit Singh

The concept of self-determination has become closely linked with the nature and scope of the international community. Its central focuses have been the sovereignty of a people as a nation, the status of national units within the international system, and the style of international relations. Self-determination has come to mean independence from alien rule. It postulates that sovereignty rests with the people who are thus free to monitor the territorial limits within which they desire their sovereignty to be active. In order for a people to be free, they must be able to organize their future independently from others. Self-determination therefore is the process by which a people determine their own soveriegn status.

I

An inventory of the activities of the United Nations during the past several decades reveals a significant and often dominant involvement of that organization in issues related to the concept of self-determination. Indeed, the expansion of the membership to almost triple its original size is a monument to the principle. With the adoption of the Declaration on the Granting of Independence to Colonial Countries and People in 1960, it may be maintained that what had been a principle is now a right, appertaining to all peoples and all nations, without which neither they nor their individual members can be considered free.

But a belief in self-determination can have anarchical implications within the international system. It suggests an opportunity for a group of individuals to disregard all established political relationships in a search for new ones. It further suggests that the aspirations of one group may often conflict with those of another. Thus, a desire to be self-determining directly challenges the order within the international system.

The International Covenants on Human Rights define self-determination as the right of peoples to determine their status and to pursue their economic, social, and cultural developments without foreign interference. The questions arise as to who may enjoy self-determination and under what circumstances may it be exercised. These are of direct international concern. Internationally, the right has been claimed only for those groups that the international community has been willing to recognize as nations. The latter have been defined by their potential to become independent, measured by factors more relevant to statehood than nationhood, and a people has been recognized as a nation only when it has been judged to be eligible for statehood. To date, therefore, self-determination actually has meant a right to recognition as a state and the distribution of territory among nations that have this capacity. Each people that has occupied a specific territory and has been able to form a government has acquired the basis for such recognition. Nationalist aspirations themselves have not always been honored by the international community until they have acquired a certain success and therefore could no longer be ignored. The issue has rested primarily on which nations the international community has been willing to recognize as sovereign.

Paradoxically, the Charter of the United Nations not only asserts a respect for the principle of equal rights and self-determination of peoples but states that in the pursuit of this principle there shall be respect for the sovereign equality and territorial integrity of its members. The anti-colonial powers attempted to avoid this conflict by not recognizing the sovereignty of the administering or colonial powers over their non-self-governing territories, claiming a right only for those peoples or nations that have been under foreign or alien domination. The right has further been claimed for victims of aggression, should the United Nations be in a position to take effective action.

The intention has been to give the people of a territory a right to determine their own future status. The anti-colonial powers believed that a dependent people or nation should be assisted in the exercise of self-determination, but once they had achieved independent status there might be no external intervention. In this context, self-determination has concerned a change of sovereign status but not how sovereignty has been exercised thereafter.

It is one thing to claim that self-determination of peoples should govern the relations that exist between states and another to suggest that it should also govern relations within a state between the people and its government. If the right were limited to those people who were already organized as a state, there would be no problem; such a claim is a claim to national sovereignty or equal status and treatment vis-à-vis other states. If it were extended to those people who were dependent because they had lost a previous status for which they claim restoration, the problem would be confined. Such an application of the right would rest with people who constitute a majority within a given territory. The main difficulty in extending universal application of the right of self-determination arises when a minority within a given region develops national aspirations that conflict with those of the rest of the community; under which circumstances may it exercise a right of self-determination?

The sponsors of the various resolutions asserting a right to self-determination have maintained that secession is contrary to the spirit of the Charter of the United Nations, that for strictly local groups there is no right of secession, and that the right of self-determination is not applicable to territories that are an integral part of a national entity.

Rupert Emerson has clearly stated that "if the right to self-determination is to be made an operative one under international law and an orderly one within the confines of an organized international society, an essential condition is surely that the peoples or territories to which it applies are demarcated with at least reasonable clarity."[1] The more strictly the people to whom the right may be applied are defined, the more easily the right can be stated with reasonable precision and given institutional expression.

II

The circumstances under which the exercise of a right to self-determination has been possible have been both domestic and international. In the domestic case, the inhabitants have set aside their previous sovereign status by revolutionary means. Internationally, the circumstances have been either military or ideological. The anti-colonial movement gradually produced the change that put in doubt the legitimacy of the sovereignty of a metropolitan state over a colony or dependent territory, or at least whether this sovereignty was subject to termination at the will of the people of the dependent territory. It has been maintained by the anti-colonial powers that sovereignty in dependent areas belongs directly to the people and that they should be allowed to exercise it in determining their own status. The United Nations has tried to establish a claim for self-determination on behalf of these territories and has tried to assist them in acquiring the opportunity to exercise it by intervention. The Declaration on the Granting of Independence to Colonial Countries and Peoples in December 1960 resolved that the subjection of peoples to alien governance was contrary to the Charter, and it recommended that political power in all dependent territories be transferred to the people in accordance with their freely expressed will.

Since 1961, a special committee (now with twenty-four members) has studied the application of the declaration and has made recommendations to the General Assembly. The special committee developed into a steering committee for much of the activity of the parent body in its review of non-self-governing territories. Its reports have been of increasing size, exceeding in length those from any previous or existing subsidiary organ. It has progressively concerned itself with as many as sixty-seven trust and non-self-governing territories. Its mandate has allowed it to hear petitioners directly and to make recommendations territory by territory, determining for itself the status of each territory, the circumstances under which the territory was to become self-determining, and the seriousness of any delay in the face of a general threat to international peace and security. In 1962, the special committee was further authorized to directly appraise the Security Council of any developments in the dependent territories that might threaten international security, in response to which the committee has consistently drawn attention to situations in the dependent territories in southern Africa.

During its tenure, the special committee has recommended deadlines for the accession to independence of those territories it has identified where independence is in accordance with the wishes of the people. Particular attention has been paid to the small territories, with recommendations for appropriate means by which to enable the populations to exercise fully their recognized right. In regard to small territories, it has been repeatedly emphasized that inadequacy of political, economic, social, or educational preparedness was not to serve as a pretext for delaying independence. However, in the special committee's review of the sparsely populated islands in the Atlantic, Pacific, and Indian oceans, alternate means for attaining the objectives of the 1960 declaration have been sought. Self-government by means other than independence have been considered.

When the Cook Islands became self-governing in 1965, they opted to remain in association with New Zealand, responsible for their own internal affairs and free to alter their status without reservation. The issue before the special committee was whether under these circumstances an act of self-determination had taken place in accordance with the principles of the United Nations Charter. The issue focused on whether a right of self-determination was to be implemented in reference to the status of a people or territory or the means by which the status was to be determined. If the former were to be recognized, the question remained whether a people were self-determining if they achieved any degree of self-government short of independence. A number of delegations, especially relative to issues concerning the small territories, have returned for guidance to earlier resolutions[2] that indicated a full measure of self-government was satisfied either "by emergence as a sovereign independent State," "free association with an independent State," or "integration with an independent State."

An emphasis on the national unit has been evident in the claims for self-determination, but different interpretations of the concept of self-determination reflect a conflict in the meaning assigned to national status with a resulting clash between competing national interests. The anti-colonial powers have recognized the clash as warranted if it is intended to liberate a dependent people that form a majority within a given territory. In 1965, the General Assembly went so far as to invite all states to provide material and moral assistance to the national liberation movements in colonial territories, thus in effect granting an international status to "legitimate" nationalist movements. In 1966, the General Assembly resolved that the right of oppressed peoples to use force in their struggle for independence could not be denied, extending to them a right to seek and receive all support in their struggle.[3] The implication was that assistance to national liberation movements would not be considered intervention in the domestic affairs of a state. At the same time, the nonadministering and anti-colonial powers within the United Nations have received the organization's endorsement to declare the continuation of colonial rule a threat to international peace and security.

The number of territories under colonial rule has rapidly decreased, an indication that the circumstances in each of the remaining cases may suggest an adjustment in the concept of self-determination and in the means for its implementation. The territories that are still dependent are several "hard-core" colonial areas in southern Africa, as well as the numerous small, sparsely populated territories in the three major oceans and the Caribbean. The white minority groups in southern Africa have refused to relinquish their control and continue to defy efforts to establish self-government and majority rule in Southern Rhodesia or South-West Africa. It is even questionable whether the anti-colonialists will permit the Republic of South Africa itself to enjoy immunity from the claims of its black inhabitants under the guise of domestic jurisdiction.

III

Self-determination, as a concept, was not at first national but was rather an extension of popular sovereignty and was, therefore, territorial. It allowed the people of a given territory to determine their own government. This aspect has not been completely discarded. In assessing the "claimed" universality of the principle, the colonial powers and their allies have suggested that if the right were universal it could not be confined to dependent areas but ought to be extended to all people, regardless of where they lived, who were denied full participation in the affairs of their government. The colonial powers have stressed the concept of the nation-state as an open society of free citizens based on laws. Self-determination would be internal as well as external. It would relate to the continued opportunity for people within a territory to remain in control of their own destiny, not only relative to other peoples but relative to groups within their own state.

After the French Revolution, the nationalist principle became dominant in Western Europe. It was believed that people exercising their sovereignty would do so on a national basis, although it never became possible to identify in precise terms the distinctive attributes of a nation. Of all the factors that seemed to aid in shaping a national base, the most significant came to be the existence of a common political sentiment. A nation by identity was a people *willing* to be so identified. Those who held back or attached reservations, whose aspirations were in conflict with those of the majority and the state they represented and controlled, were labeled a national minority. The inability of such groups to associate their destiny with that of the single nation stimulated an aspiration for a status that would provide a more equal opportunity to advance a separate interest.

Wherever there is a disharmony within an established political system, any disassociated group may desire a separate status. No group is in itself stable. Since statehood may become the goal, the international community is an equally unstable environment. In a recent article, Anthony H. Birch observed that "the rise of resurgence of minority nationalist movements has become so widespread in the last decade that it is no longer necessary to begin a paper on the subject with a list of examples."[4] Almost every state at some time in this century has experienced pressure from a minority with sufficient strength to undermine the solidarity of the state itself.

In Renaissance Europe, nationalism was integrative. The emerging dynastic states facilitated the centralization of loyalty. The state created the nation; state and nation were synonymous. Nationalism became the belief in the predominance of the nation-state. An overcommitment at times resulted in a preference for the competitive interests and the exaltation of one's nation over those of all other nations and caused nationalism to become imperialistic. The enthusiasm of the French under Napoleon led to a religious zeal to extend the benefits of being French throughout nineteenth-century Europe and, as late as 1960, characterized the French position in Algeria.

Modern nationalism is not integrative. It is equated less and less with loyalty to the state, focusing on loyalty to a group "non-national" in scope. Various "subnational" groups become active as nationalist movements but have fewer of the traditional character-istics associated with a national identity other than the conscious-ness that its members' needs are not considered equal by the mem-bers of the larger unit.

The empires of nineteenth-century Eastern Europe were dis-mantled because they were identified as multinational. As states, they encompassed peoples whose loyalties were divided. National self-determination recognized a basis for regrouping and placing sovereignty. It did not anticipate that when any group within a state felt itself to be alienated it would press a claim eroding loyalty traditionally placed at a level above itself.

Thus, nationalism gave stimulus to subjugated groups to estab-lish claims for "national" liberation. Self-determination has con-tinued to mean the right of subjugated peoples, as nations, to liberation. When self-determination was identified with nationality, the problem became that of defining a nation. It was not always possible to extend an opportunity to a nation so long as there were limited bases upon which to identify the unit. This emphasis on national unity is still evident in the claims for self-determina-tion today. The different interpretations, however, reflect a con-flict in the definition of a nation. The desire to liberate dependent areas from colonial administration often led to claims that they form part of the national territory of previously liberated areas, e.g., West Irian as part of Indonesia.

The principle of *national* self-determination evolved from an assertion of the sovereignty of the people, in order to justify its use, to a clash between two peoples over the same territory. In its earlier environment, the principle justified the transfer of sover-eignty over a definite territorial entity that had been detached from the control of its previous sovereign. This was true until the peace settlements following the First World War, when the focus shifted from the assignment of territory on the basis of nationality to competing claims based on nationality. The justification for the claim was no longer centered in the area itself, and the result would associate the people of a given territory with those of another. Only the wishes of the people could determine with which group it should be associated.

National self-determination under anti-colonial influence continued to focus on the achievement of national independence, but it did not remain a simple clash between the interests of a subordinate group and those of its oppressors, in the form of the administering powers. It became, at least in one case (Kashmir), a clash between national groups (India and Pakistan) on the same level. Both have sovereignty and claim the people or territory in question in fulfillment of national aspirations that are not necessarily centered in the territory in dispute.

National self-determination became an assertion of a people with a national identity of their right to determine their own sovereign status. The right followed from the identity. Dependent peoples, whether in non-self-governing territories or in minority status, have asserted nationality in anticipation of emancipation.

IV

The most revolutionary element within the concept of self-determination, regardless of the unit to which it is applied, is the collective self-consciousness that separates the "we" from the "they." The psychological focus that generates this awareness both determines the group and distinguishes it from others. It is the latter process that operates against the status quo. Once the psychological aspects of the concept are recognized, the concept of self-determination defies classification within any rigid structuring of the international system. It becomes the basis for the system, redistributing political control among those self-defined units able to demand attention. There is no legitimate structure. The structure will be determined by the nature of the groups that demand access to a decision-making role. If an existing structure fails to accommodate this need, the alienated group will press for its modification.

Chong-Do Hah and Jeffrey Martin define nationalism as consisting of "organizationally heightened and articulated group demands directed toward securing control of the distributive system in a society."[5] Their thesis focuses on the concept of relative deprivation as effecting a synthesis between integration and conflict theories of nationalism. They propose that levels of nationalism parallel stages of modernization. Modernization is viewed as generating nationalism indirectly by integrating groups at the societal level, and directly by causing relative deprivation. All are primarily phenomena of transitional societies.

In the past two decades, the Institute for World Order has sponsored a number of studies concerned with a global transformation. In 1965, supporters of this movement met at Bellagio, Italy, for a symposium devoted to "Conditions of World Order." The conference chairman, Raymond Aron, distinguished among five different meanings given to world order by the conference participants. According to a summary by Stanley Hoffman:

> Two of the meanings were purely descriptive: order as any arrangement of reality, order as the relations between the parts. Two were analytical—partly descriptive, partly normative: order as the minimum condition for existence, order as the minimum condition of coexistence. The fifth conception was purely normative: order as the condition for the good life.[6]

Aron chose the fourth conception as the most desirable: world order as an inquiry into the conditions under which peoples in the world would "be able not merely to avoid destruction, but to live together relatively well in one planet."

The concept of self-determination, as it has evolved during the past two decades, suggests the above conception to be incomplete. An international system ordered on the basis of coexistence has many of the attributes of the traditional nation-state system, which self-determination came to question. Hah and Martin's framework recognizes developmental aspects within the international environment which pressure for a new system or world order.

Not all aspects of the concept of self-determination are mutually compatible. Nations may claim a right to self-determination, but when may a people claim the status as a nation? Does the right of self-determination extend to the right of various interests to merge their destinies within a national unit, potentially to challenge their subordinate status within the territory of a competitive national unit claiming an equal right to remain integral? Is self-determination functional only when a people, as a nation, become independent rather than self-governing? If the latter is acceptable, what are the continuing characteristics of the polity that will assure that they shall remain secure in their control over their destiny?

Is self-determination, as a process, an act conditioned in time or a series of characteristics that allow a continuation of alternatives to remain available in determining a people's destiny?

Self-determination is not defined by any predetermined concept of world order. Self-determination itself is becoming the basis for the international system. Embedded in its evolution is the desire of human beings to have an equal opportunity for control of the international environment. At the root of this concept and world order is the broader issue of human rights. World order will come to mean the granting of equal opportunity, with no group or individual more "equal" than another.

Notes

1. Rupert Emerson, "Self-Determination," *American Journal of International Law* 65, no. 3 (July 1971):462.

2. General Assembly resolutions 742 (8), 27 November 1953, and 1541 (15), 15 December 1960.

3. General Assembly Resolution 2160 (21), 30 November 1966.

4. Anthony H. Birch, "Minority Nationalist Movements and Theories of Political Integration," *World Politics* 30, no. 3 (April 1978):326.

5. Chong-Do Hah and Jeffrey Martin, "Toward a Synthesis of Conflict and Integration Theories of Nationalism," *World Politics* 27, no. 3 (April 1975):362.

6. Stanley Hoffman, "Report of the Conference on Conditions of World Order—June 12–19, 1965, Villa Serbelloni, Bellagio, Italy," *Daedalus* (Spring 1966):455-78.

Selected
Bibliography

Books:

Alexander, Yonah. *The Role of Communications in the Middle East Conflict: Ideological and Religious Aspects.* New York: Praeger Publishers, 1973.

_____, ed. *Terrorism: National, Regional, and Global Perspectives.* New York: Praeger Publishers, 1976.

Alexander, Yonah; Browne, Marjorie Ann; and Nanes, Allan S., eds. *Control of Terrorism: International Documents.* New York: Crane, Russak, 1979.

Alexander, Yonah, and Kittrie, Nicholas, eds. *Crescent and Star: Arab-Israeli Perspectives on the Middle East Conflict.* New York: AMS Press, 1972.

Avineri, Shlomo, ed. *Israel and the Palestinians: Reflections on the Clash of the Two National Movements.* New York: St. Martin's Press, 1971.

Bell, J. Bowyer. *The Myth of the Guerrilla: Revolutionary Theory and Malpractice.* New York: Knopf, 1971.

_____. *On Revolt: Strategies of National Liberation.* Cambridge, Mass., and London: Harvard University Press, 1976.

_____. *Terror Out of Zion: The Violent and Deadly Shock Troops of Israeli Independence, 1929-1949.* New York: St. Martin's Press, 1977.

Bocca, Geoffrey. *The Secret Army.* Englewood Cliffs, N.J.: Prentice-Hall, 1968.

Borisov, J. *Palestine Underground: The Story of Jewish Resistance.* New York: Judea Publishing Co., 1947.

Brossard, J. *L'accession à la souveraineté et le cas du Québec.* Montreal: Les presses de L'Université de Montréal, 1976.

Buchheit, Lee C. *Secession: The Legitimacy of Self-Determination.* New Haven, Conn.: Yale University Press, 1978.

Cameron, David. *Nationalism, Self-Determination, and the Quebec Question.* Toronto: Macmillan Co. of Canada, 1974.

Chailand, Gerald. *The Palestinian Resistance.* Baltimore: Penguin Books, 1972.

Cheffins, Ronald I. *The Constitutional Process in Canada.* 2nd ed. Toronto: McGraw-Hill Co. of Canada, 1975.

Clark, Michael K. *Algeria in Turmoil.* New York: Praeger Publishers, 1959.

Cobban, Alfred. *The Nation State and National Self-Determination.* Rev. ed. New York: Thomas Y. Crowell Co., 1970.

Cockram, Gail-Maryse. *South West African Mandate.* Cape Town, Wynberg, and Johannesburg: Juta and Co., 1976.

Crozier, Brian. *South-East Asia in Turmoil.* Baltimore: Penguin Books, 1965.

_____. *Ulster: Politics and Terrorism.* London: Institute for the Study of Conflict, 1973.

Curtis, Michael, et al., eds. *The Palestinians: People, History, and Politics.* Edison, N.J.: Transaction Books, 1975.

Dangerfield, George. *The Damnable Question: One Hundred and Twenty Years of Anglo-Irish Conflict.* Boston and Toronto: Little, Brown and Co., 1976.

Dobson, Christopher. *Black September: Its Short, Violent History.* New York: Macmillan, 1974.

Duchacek, Ivo D. *Nations and Men.* Hinsdale, Ill.: Dryden Press, 1975.

Duignan, Peter, and Gann, L. H., eds. *Colonialism in Africa 1870-1960.* Vol. 2, *The History of Politics of Colonialism 1914-60.* Cambridge: Cambridge University Press, 1970.

Emerson, Rupert. *From Empire to Nation: The Rise to Self-Assertion of Asian and African Peoples.* Boston: Beacon Press, 1962.

_____. *Self-Determination Revisited in the Era of Decolonization.* Cambridge, Mass.: Harvard University Press, 1964.

Fanon, Frantz. *Toward the African Revolution: Political Essays.* Trans. by Haakon Chevalier. New York: Grove Press, 1969.

Friedlander, Robert A. *Terrorism: Documents of International and Local Control.* 2 vols. Dobbs Ferry, N.Y.: Oceana Publications, 1979.

Gibson, Richard. *African Liberation Movements: Contemporary Struggle against White Minority Rule.* New York: Oxford University Press, 1972.

Grundy, Kenneth W. *Guerrilla Struggle in Africa: An Analysis and Preview.* New York: Rand McNally, 1972.

Hachey, Thomas, ed. *The Problem of Partition: Peril to World Peace.* New York: Rand McNally, 1972.

_____. *Voices of Revolution: Rebels and Rhetoric.* Hinsdale, Ill.: Dryden Press, 1973.

Harkabi, Yehoshafat. *The Arab's Position in Their Conflict with Israel.* Jerusalem: Israeli Universities Press.

Henderson, Gregory; Lebow, Richard N.; and Stoessinger, John G., eds. *Divided Nations in a Divided World.* New York: David McKay Co., 1974.

Hodges, Donald Clark. *National Liberation Fronts: 1960-1970.* New York: William Morrow and Co., 1972.

Hodges, Donald Clark, and Abu-Shanab, Robert Elias. *National Liberation Fronts 1960-1970: Essays, Documents, Interviews.* New York: William Morrow and Co., 1972.

Horne, Alistair. *A Savage War of Peace: Algeria, 1954-1962.* Harmondsworth, Eng.: Penguin Books, 1979.

Hutchinson, Martha C. *Revolutionary Terrorism: The FLN in Algeria, 1954-1962.* Stanford, Calif.: Hoover Institution Press, 1978.

Johnson, Harold S. *Self-Determination within the Community of Nations.* Leiden: A. W. Sijthoff, 1967.

Kedouri, Elie, ed. *Nationalism in Asia and Africa.* New York and Cleveland: World Publishing, 1970.

Laffin, John. *Fedayeen.* New York: Macmillan, 1973.

Laqueur, Walter. *Guerrilla: A Historical and Critical Study.* Boston: Little, Brown and Co., 1976.

_____. *The Guerrilla Reader: A Historical Anthology.* New York: New American Library, 1977.

Mallory, J. R. *The Structure of the Government of Canada.* Toronto: Macmillan Co. of Canada, 1971.

Miller, Norman, and Aya, Roderick, eds. *National Liberation: Revolution in the Third World.* New York: Free Press, 1971.

Morton. W. L. *The Canadian Identity.* Menasha, Wis.: University of Wisconsin Press, 1961.

Ofuatey-Kodjoe, W. *The Principle of Self-Determination in Internatonal Law.* New York: Nellen Publishing Co., 1977.

Pearcy, Etzel G. *World Sovereignty.* Fullerton, Calif.: Plycon Press, 1977.

Pryce-Jones, David. *The Face of Defeat: Palestinian Refugees and Guerrillas.* London: Weidenfeld and Nicholson, 1972.

Riseborough, Donald J., ed. *Canada and the French.* New York: Facts on File, 1975.

Russell, Peter. *Nationalism in Canada.* Toronto: McGraw-Hill Co. of Canada, 1966.

Sahovic, Milan, ed. *Principles of International Law concerning Friendly Relations and Cooperation.* Dobbs Ferry, N.Y.: Oceana Publications, 1972.

Seton-Watson, Hugh. *Nations and States: An Enquiry into the Origins of Nations and the Politics of Nationalism.* Boulder, Colo.: Westview Press, 1977.

Smiley, D. V. *Canada in Question: Federalism in the Seventies.* 2nd ed. Toronto: McGraw-Hill Ryerson, 1976.

Stevens, F. S., ed. *Racism: The Australian Experience.* Vol. 3, *Colonialism.* New York: Taplinger Publishing Co., 1972.

Stone, Julius. *Conflict through Consensus: United Nations Approaches to Aggression*. Baltimore and London: Johns Hopkins University Press, 1977.

Suhrke, Astri, and Noble, Lela Garner, eds. *Ethnic Conflict in International Relations*. New York: Praeger Publishers, 1977.

Sureda, A. Rigo. *The Evolution of the Right of Self-Determination*. Leiden: A. W. Sijthoff, 1973.

Tanham, George Kilpatrick. *Communist Revolutionary Warfare*. New York: Praeger Publishers, 1962.

Tomlin, B. *Canada's Foreign Policy: Analysis and Trends*. Toronto: Metheun, 1978.

Tornaritis, Criton G. *The Right of Self-Determination with Special Reference to the Republic of Cyprus*. Nicosia: Privately Published, 1973.

Trudeau, Pierre Elliot. *Federalism and the French Canadians*. Toronto: Macmillan Co. of Canada, 1968.

Umozurike, Umozurike Oji. *Self-Determination in International Law*. Hamden, Conn.: Archon Books, 1972.

Wainhouse, David W. *Remnants of Empire: The United Nations and the End of Colonialism*. New York: Council on Foreign Relations, 1964.

Ward, J. M. *Colonial Self-Government*. Toronto: University of Toronto Press, 1976.

Articles:

Abi-Saab, Georges. "Wars of National Liberation and the Laws of War." *Annales d'Etudes Internationales* 3 (1972), pp. 93-117.

Anderson, Carla. "Portuguese Africa: A Brief History of United Nations Involvement." *Denver Journal of International Law and Policy* 4, no. 1 (Spring 1974), pp. 133-51.

Andrews, J. A. "Concept of Statehood and the Acquisition of Territory in the 19th Century." *Law Quarterly Review* 94 (June 1978), pp. 408-27.

Arbour, J. Maurice. "Secession and International Law—Some Economic Problems in Relation to State Succession." *Les Cahiers de Droit.* 19, no. 2 (June 1978), pp. 285-338.

Ashab, Naib. "To Overcome the Crisis of the Palestinian Resistance." *World Marxist Review* 15, no. 5 (1972), pp. 71-78.

Bassiouni, M. Cherif. "The Middle East: The Misunderstood Conflict." *Kansas Law Review* 19 (1971), pp. 373-402.

_____. " 'Self-Determination' and the Palestinians." *Proceedings of the American Society of International Law,* 65th Annual Meeting (April 1971), pp. 31-40.

Bassiouni, M. Cherif, and Fisher, Eugene M. "The Arab-Israeli Conflict—Real and Apparent Issues: An Insight into Its Future from the Lessons of the

Past." *St. John's Law Review* 44, no. 3 (January 1970), pp. 399-465.

Beckett, J. C. "Northern Ireland." *Journal of Contemporary History* 6, no. 1 (1971), pp. 121-34.

Bos, Maarten. "Self-Determination by the Grace of History." *Netherlands International Law Review* 15 (1968), pp. 362-73.

Bowett, Derek W. "Self-Determination and Political Rights in the Developing Countries." *Proceedings of the American Society of International Law*, 60th Annual Meeting (1966), pp. 129-35.

Brown, Philip Marshall. "Self-Determination in Central Europe" *American Journal of International Law* 14, (1920), pp. 235-39.

Carey, Thomas C. "Self-Determination in the Post-Colonial Era: The Case of Quebec." *ASILS International Law Journal* 1, no. 1 (Summer 1977), pp. 47-72.

Chen, Lung-chu, and Reisman, W. Michael. "Who Owns Taiwan? A Search for International Title." *Yale Law Journal* 81, no. 4 (March 1972), pp. 599-671.

Chowdhury, S. R. "Status and Norms of Self-Determination in Contemporary International Law." *Netherlands International Law Review* 24 (1977), pp. 72-91.

Cohen, Johnathan G. "Les Iles Falkland (Malvinas)." *Annuaire Français de droit international* 18 (1972), pp. 235-62.

Connor, Walker. "Nation Building or Nation Destroying?" *World Politics* 24, no. 3 (April 1972), pp. 319-55.

Crawford, James. "The Criteria for Statehood in International Law." *British Yearbook of International Law* 48 (1976-1977), pp. 93-182.

Dawn, C. Ernest. "The Arab-Israeli Confrontation: A Historian's Analysis." *Denver Journal of International Law and Policy* 5, no. 2 (Fall 1975), pp. 373-86.

Dinstein, Yoram. "Collective Human Rights of Peoples and Minorities." *International and Comparative Law Quarterly* 25 (January 1976), pp. 102-20.

_____. "Terrorism and Wars of Liberation Applied to the Arab-Israeli Conflict: An Israeli Perspective." *Israel Yearbook on Human Rights* 3 (1973), pp. 79-92.

Eagleton, Clyde. "Self-Determination in the United Nations." *American Journal of International Law* 47, no. 1 (January 1953), pp. 88-93.

Emerson, Rupert. "Self-Determination." *American Journal of International Law* 65, no. 1 (June 1971), pp. 459-71.

Finger, Seymour Maxwell. "A New Approach to Colonial Problems at the United Nations." *International Organization* 26, no. 1 (Winter 1972), pp. 143-153.

Franck, Thomas M. "The Stealing of the Sahara." *American Journal of International Law* 70, no. 4 (October 1976), pp. 694-721.

Franck, Thomas M., and Hoffman, Paul. "The Right of Self-Determination in Very Small Places." *New York University Journal of International Law and Politics* 8, no. 3 (Winter 1976), pp. 331-86.

Franck, Thomas M., and Rodley, Nigel S. "The Law, the United Nations, and Bangla Desh." *Israel Yearbook on Human Rights* 2, (1972), pp. 142-75.

Friedlander, Robert A. "Proposed Criteria for Testing the Validity of Self-Determination as It Applies to Disaffected Minorities." *Chitty's Law Journal* 25, no. 10 (December 1977), pp. 335-38.

_____. "Self-Determination and the Baltic States: A Legal Analysis." *Globe* (Illinois State Bar Association) 12, no. 3 (November 1974), pp. 3-6.

Garrett, J. "Lessons of Angola: An Eye-Witness Report." *Black Scholar* 7 (June 1976), pp. 2-15.

Glazer, Nathan, and Moynihan, Daniel. "Why Ethnicity?" *Commentary* (October 1974), pp. 33-39.

Green, Leslie C. "Double Standards in the United Nations: The Legalization of Terrorism." Schlochauer, Hans-Jürgen, ed., *Archiv des Volkerrechts* 18, no. 2 (1979).

_____. "Self-Determination and Settlement of the Arab-Israeli Conflict." *Proceedings of the American Society of International Law*, 65th Annual Meeting (April 1971), pp. 40-48.

Gross, Ernest A. "The South West Africa Case: What Happened?" *Foreign Affairs* 45, no. 1 (October 1966), pp. 36-48.

Guggenheim, Malvina H. "Key Provisions of the New United Nations Rules Dealing with Human Rights Petitions." *New York University Journal of International Law and Politics* 6, no. 3 (1973), pp. 427-54.

Gunter, Michael M. "What Happened to the United Nations Ministate Problem?" *American Journal of International Law* 71, no. 1 (January 1977), pp. 110-24.

Hudson, Michael C. "The Palestinian Arab Resistance Movement: Its Significance in the Middle East Crisis." *Middle East Journal* 23, no. 3 (Summer 1969), pp. 291-301.

Ijalaye, D. "Was Biafra at Any Time a State in International Law?" *American Journal of International Law* 65, no. 3 (July 1971), pp. 551-59.

Johnson, C. Don. "Toward Self-Determination—A Reappraisal as Reflected in the Declaration on Friendly Relations." *Georgia Journal of International and Comparative Law* 3, no. 1 (1973), pp. 145-63.

Lauterpacht, Elihu. "Some Concepts of Human Rights." *Howard Law Journal* 11, no. 2 (Spring 1965), pp. 264-74.

Levesque, René. "For An Independent Quebec." *Foreign Affairs* 54, no. 4 (July 1976), pp. 734-44.

McDougal, M.; Lasswell, H.; and Chen, Lung-chu. "The Protection of Respect and Human Rights: Freedom of Choice and World Public Order." *American University Law Review* 24, nos. 4-5 (January 1975), pp. 919-1086.

McWhinney, Edward. "Credentials of State Delegations to the U.N. General

Assembly: A New Approach to Effectuation of Self-Determination for Southern Africa." *Hastings Constitutional Law Quarterly* 3, no. 1 (Winter 1976), pp. 19-35.

_____. "Nationalism and Self-Determination and Contemporary Canadian Federalism." In *Miscellanea W. J. Ganshof van der Meersch,* Vol. 2 (Paris: Librairie Génerale de Droit et de Jurisprudence, 1972), pp. 219-39.

Mallison, W. T. "Legal Problems concerning the Juridical Status and Political Activities of the Zionist Organization: Jewish Agency: A Study of International and United States Law." *William and Mary Law Review* 9, no. 3 (Spring 1968), pp. 556-629.

_____. "The Zionist-Israel Juridical Claims to Constitute 'the Jewish People' Nationality Entity and to Confer Membership in It: Appraisal in Public International Law." *George Washington Law Review* 32, no. 5 (1964), pp. 983-1075.

Mead, Margaret. "The Rights of Primitive Peoples—Papua–New Guinea: A Crucial Instance." *Foreign Affairs* 45, no. 2 (January 1967), pp. 304-18.

Means, Gordon P. "Human Rights and the Rights of Ethnic Groups—A Commentary." *International Studies Notes* 1, no. 2 (Summer 1974), pp. 12-18.

Modeen, Tors. "The International Protection of the National Identity of the Aaland Islands." *Scandinavian Studies in Law* 17, (1973), pp. 177-210.

Moore, John Norton. "The Control of Foreign Intervention in International Affairs." *Virginia Journal of International Law* 9, no. 2 (May 1969), pp. 209-342.

Morgan, E. "Geographic Evaluation of the Ethiopia-Eritrea Conflict." *Journal of Modern African Studies* 15 (December 1977), pp. 667-74.

Mustafa, Zubeida. "The Principle of Self-Determination in International Law." *International Lawyer* 5, no. 3 (July 1971), pp. 479-87.

Nanda, Ved. P. "A Critique of the United Nations Inaction in the Bangladesh Crisis." *Denver Law Journal* 49, no. 1 (1972), pp. 53-67.

Nayar, M. G. Kaladharan. "Self-Determination beyond the Colonial Context: Biafra in Retrospect." *Texas International Law Journal* 10, no. 2 (Spring 1975), pp. 321-45.

Nekhleh, E. A. "Anatomy of Violence: Theoretical Reflections on Palestinian Resistance." *Middle East Journal* 25, no. 2 (Spring 1971), pp. 180-200.

Novogrod, John C. "Internal Strife, Self-Determination, and World Order." *JAG Journal* (December 1968–January 1969), pp. 63-72.

Pinter, Frances. "Changes in the South Tyrol Issue." *Yearbook of World Affairs: 1977* (1977), pp. 64-74.

Pomerance, Michla. "Methods of Self-Determination and the Argument of 'Primitiveness.'" *Canadian Yearbook of International Law: 1974* 12 (1974), pp. 38-66.

_____. "The United States and Self-Determination: Perspectives on the Wilsonian Conception." *American Journal of International Law* 70, no. 1 (January 1976), pp. 1-27.

Richardson, Henry J. III. "Self-Determination, International Law, and the South African Bantustan Policy." *Columbia Journal of Transnational Law* 17, no. 2 (1978), pp. 187-219.

Rosenstock, Robert. "The Declaration of Principles of International Law concerning Friendly Relations: A Survey." *American Journal of International Law* 65, no. 5 (October 1971), pp. 713-35.

Schoenberg, Harris O. "Limits of Self-Determination." *Israel Yearbook on Human Rights* (1976), pp. 91-103.

Schwebel, Stephen M. "Wars of Liberation—As Fought in U.N. Organs." In John Norton Moore, ed., *Law and Civil War in the Modern World* (Baltimore and London: Johns Hopkins University Press, 1974), pp. 446-57.

Schwelb, Egon. "Entry into Force of the International Covenant on Human Rights and the Optional Protocol to the International Covenant on Civil and Political Rights." *American Journal of International Law* 70, no. 4 (July 1976), pp. 511-19.

_____. "The International Convention on the Elimination of All Forms of Racial Discrimination." *International and Comparative Law Quarterly* 15 (October 1966), pp. 996-1068.

Segre, Dan, and Adler, J. H. "The Ecology of Terrorism." *Encounter* 40 (February 1973), pp. 17-24.

Sinha, S. Prakash. "Self-Determination in International Law and Its Applicability to the Baltic Peoples." In Sprudzs, Adolf, and Rusis, Armins, eds., *Res Baltic* (Leiden: A. W. Sijthoff, 1968), pp. 256-85.

Smith, D. "Preparing for Independence." *The Economist* (November 20, 1976), pp. 15-16.

Stern, David. S. "Notes on the History of Puerto Rico's Commonwealth Status." *Revista Jurídica de la Universidad de Puerto Rico* 30, nos. 1-2 (1961), pp. 33-56.

Suzuki, Eisuke. "Self-Determination and World Public Order: Community Response to Territorial Separation." *Virginia Journal of International Law* 16, no. 4 (Summer 1976), pp. 779-862.

Syatauw, J. J. G. "Old and New States: A Misleading Distinction for Future International Law and International Relations." *Indian Journal of International Law* 15 (April–June 1975), pp. 153-72.

Tiewul, S. Azadon. "Relations between the United Nations Organization and the Organization of African Unity in the Settlement of Secessionist Conflicts." *Harvard International Law Journal* 16, no. 2 (Spring 1975), pp. 259-302.

Journal Special Issues:

Brown, William O., ed. "Contemporary Africa: Trends and Issues." *Annals* 298 (March 1955).

Heisler, Martin O., ed. "Ethnic Conflict in the World Today." *Annals* 433 (September 1977).

Strausz Hupe, Robert, ed. "A Special Issue Dedicated to Hana Kohn." *Orbis* 10, no. 4 (Winter 1967).

The Contributors

Yonah Alexander (co-editor) is professor of international studies and director of the Institute for Studies in International Terrorism (State University of New York) and, concurrently, research associate at the Center for Strategic and International Studies (Georgetown University). He is editor-in-chief of *Terrorism: An International Journal*; editor of *International Terrorism: National, Regional, and Global Perspectives*; co-editor of *Terrorism: Interdisciplinary Perspectives, Terrorism: Theory and Practice, Political Terrorism and Business: The Threat and Response, Control of Terrorism: International Documents*, and *Crescent and Star: Arab and Israeli Perspectives on the Middle East Conflict*; and author of *The Role of Communications in the Middle East Conflict: Ideological and Religious Aspects*.

Ray S. Cline is executive director of strategic studies at the Georgetown University Center for Strategic and International Studies (CSIS). He is also adjunct professor of international relations in the School of Foreign Service, Georgetown, and adjunct professor at the Defense Intelligence School. Dr. Cline served as deputy director for intelligence in the Central Intelligence Agency from 1962 to 1966 and Director of the Bureau of Intelligence and Research in the Department of State. Dr. Cline holds a Ph.D. degree from Harvard University. He also studied at Balliol College, Oxford University, as a Henry Prize Fellow and later was a member of the Society of Fellows at Harvard. Dr. Cline is the author of *Washington Command Post* (1951); *Secrets, Spies, and Scholars: A Blueprint of the Essential CIA* (1976); and *World Power Assessment* (1977).

Yoram Dinstein is dean of the Faculty of Law at Tel-Aviv University. He has served as Consul of Israel in New York and Deputy Head of the General Director's Office in the Israeli Ministry of Foreign Affairs. He is the founding editor of the *Israel Yearbook on Human Rights* and author of numerous scholarly articles in the field of international law. His major book is *The Defense of "Obedience to Superior Orders"* (1965) which earned him the Arlosoroff Prize in 1966.

Edgar S. Efrat teaches political science at the University of Victoria. He has also taught at the University of Texas and the University of Washington. Among his publications are *Federations under Stress: The Failure of the Old Order* and *Introduction to Sub-Saharan Africa*.

Seymour Maxwell Finger is professor of political science at the Graduate School and the College of Staten Island, CUNY, and director of CUNY's Ralph Bunche Institute on the United Nations. His service as a career diplomat includes fifteen years at the U.S. Mission to the UN, where he served as ambassador for four years. He is co-editor of *U.S. Policy in International Institutions*.

Robert A. Friedlander (co-editor), professor of law at the Ohio Northern University College of Law, is the author of thirty articles and review essays dealing with domestic and international law and politics and a two-volume study of international terrorism. He is a life member of Delta Tau Kappa (International Social Science Honor Society), a life member of the Academy of Diplomacy and International Affairs (Cologne, West Germany), a member of the Committee on International Terrorism of the World Association of Lawyers, and on the Advisory Board of the *Denver Journal of International Law and Policy*.

Thomas E. Hachey is professor of Anglo-Irish history at Marquette University and a former visiting professor at the Dublin School of Irish Studies. His major publications include: *Voices of Revolution: Rebels and Rhetoric* (1972); *Confidential Dispatches* (1974); and *Britain and Irish Separatism: From the Fenians to the Free State* (1977). His articles have also appeared in more than a half-dozen scholarly journals.

Harold S. Johnson received his Ph.D. in political science from the University of Michigan and is currently professor of political science and director of the Field Experience Program, Justin Morrill College, Michigan State University. His research interests include foreign policy, international relations, and international law. Professor Johnson has published several scholarly articles in journals such as *United Asia* and *World Justice*, and he is the author of *Self-*

Determination within the Community of Nations (1967) and co-author of *International Relations: An Annotated Bibliography* and *International Organization: A Classified Bibliography.* The chapter "EEC-US Relations in the Post-Kissinger Era" will appear in a forthcoming book, *Contemporary Perspectives on EEC Integration.*

Natan Lerner is an associate at the Horowitz Institute for Research of Developing Countries at Tel-Aviv University. A graduate of Buenos Aires University (doctorate in law), Dr. Lerner taught international law at Haifa University and Latin American studies at Tel-Aviv University.

Ilya Levkov is a research associate at the Ralph Bunche Institute on the United Nations, City University of New York. A graduate of Brandeis University (M.A.) and a Ph.D. candidate in political science at CUNY, Mr. Levkov has written on Soviet domestic policies. His current research deals with Soviet relations with the Social Democratic Party of the Federal Republic of Germany during 1959-1966.

Christopher C. Mojekwu was the attorney-general of the former Eastern Region of Nigeria and later the minister of home affairs and local government in the defunct Biafran regime. Educated in England and the United States, Dr. Mojekwu holds an LL.B. degree from the London School of Economics, University of London; LL.M. and S.J.D. from Northwestern University School of Law. He is barrister-at-law of the Honourable Society of Gray's Inn, London, a member of the British and the Nigerian Bars, and an associate member of the American Bar Association. Presently, he is an associate professor of politics at Lake Forest College and a visiting faculty member of the School for New Learning, DePaul University.

John F. Murphy is professor of law at the University of Kansas School of Law, where he served as associate dean from January 1975 to July 1977. He has been in the private practice of law and has been an attorney with the Office of the Legal Adviser of the U.S. Department of State. Co-editor of and contributor to *Legal Aspects of International Terrorism* (1978), he has also published a wide variety of articles on international law and policy.

Ved P. Nanda is professor of law and director of the International Legal Studies Program at the University of Denver College of Law. He serves on the Editorial Board of the *American Journal of Comparative Law,* the Advisory Board of the *Journal of Legal Education,* and the Advisory Council of the U.S. Institute of Human Rights. Winner of the Hyde Prize in International Law, he has published numerous articles on a variety of legal topics, is editor of *Water Needs for the Future,* and is a co-editor of *A Treatise on International Criminal Law.*

Jordan J. Paust is a Fulbright Professor of Law at the University of Salzburg, Austria, on leave from the University of Houston Law School. Professor Paust has written several articles on international terrorism and was a member of the American Society of International Law Working Group on International Terrorism (1975-1977) and Chairman of the A.B.A. Committee on International Law and the Use of Force (1975-1978). He is co-author of *War Crimes Jurisdiction and Due Process: A Case Study of Bangladesh* (1974) and *The Arab Oil Weapon* (1977).

Baljit Singh is professor of political science and assistant dean for academic affairs, College of Social Science, Michigan State University. He obtained his B.A. from Agra University, M.A. from Aligarh University, D.F.A. (Diploma in Foreign Affairs) from Aligarh University, and Ph.D. from the University of Maryland. He is the author of *Indian Foreign Policy: An Analysis* (1976) and co-author of *Theory and Practice of Modern Guerrilla Warfare* (1971). He is currently completing a volume entitled *Politics in India.*

Dr. Gurcharan Singh, a native of Punjab (India), received his Ph.D. from the City University of New York in 1973. He has taught at Brooklyn College and Yeshiva University, New York, and is now adjunct associate professor of Political Science at Hunter College, CUNY, New York. His book, *The Middle East and Indian Diplomacy*, was published in 1975.

Index

Date Due

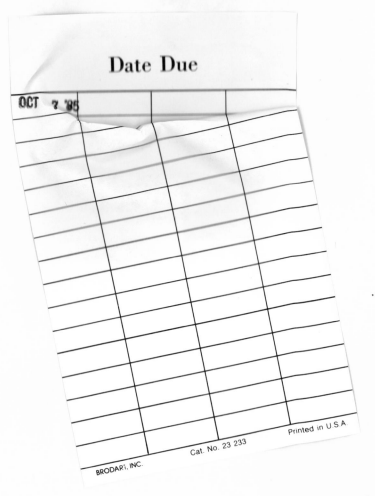

OCT 7 '95

BRODART, INC. Cat. No. 23 233 Printed in U.S.A.